CW01457663

The Lost Pre-Raphaelite
George Wilson
His Life, Work and Associates

For Cynthia

The Lost Pre-Raphaelite

George Wilson

His Life, Work and Associates

Robin J H Fanshawe

Castle Park Publishing

The Lost Pre-Raphaelite – George Wilson

First published 2007
© Robin J H Fanshawe
World copyright reserved
Also available in hardcover

ISBN 978-0-9556626-0-7

The right of Robin J H Fanshawe to be identified as author
of this work has been asserted by him in accordance with
the Copyright, Design and Patents Act 1988

All rights reserved. No part of this publication may be
reproduced, stored in a retrieval system, or transmitted
in any form or by any means, electronic, mechanical,
photocopying, recording or otherwise, without the prior
permission of the author

British Library Cataloguing in Publication Data:
A catalogue record for this book is available from the
British Library

Published by Castle Park Publishing

www.fanshawe.org.uk/castlepark

E-mail: castlepark@fanshawe.org.uk

Cover illustration:

George Wilson (1848-1890)
Asia ca. 1881-1884
Oil on canvas, 37½ in x 29¼ in (950 mm x 745 mm)
Private collection

Title page illustration:

George Wilson (1848-1890)
*Title unknown (Study of a female figure in a cloak
and hood)*; date unknown
Red chalk, size unknown
Whereabouts unknown

Back cover illustration:

George Wilson (1848-1890)
The Fall of the Leaf ca. 1878-1882
Watercolour, 9¾ in x 13½ in (247 mm x 343 mm)
Private collection

CONTENTS

FOREWORD

The Scottish perspective

The poet is a magician – his vocation to incessantly evoke dreams and do his work so well, because of natural gifts and acquired skill, that his dreams shall have a potency to defeat the actual at every point....[1]

These words, written by the poet and artist J.B. Yeats to his famous son W.B. Yeats, apply equally to the work of his close friend George Wilson, who in his paintings attempted to capture a similar dreamland: a poetic vision that would cast a spell upon his viewers. I am delighted that this unsung hero of Scottish art has been celebrated in this excellent book, which is the first attempt to cover this remarkable artist's entire career and output.

George Wilson was closely associated with the North-East of Scotland. The gentle, rolling countryside of his native Banffshire provided much of the inspiration for his landscape paintings. Elegiac, contemplative and delicate, his art epitomised the *fin de siècle*, when artists rejected the cold realities of the industrial world and turned instead to the writings of Oscar Wilde and Sigmund Freud for inspiration when creating dreamlike paintings of imagined scenes. Equally, when he painted real landscape, Wilson turned these views into delicate visions that echoed the poetry and writings of the day.

Over one hundred years later these images of this bygone era capture the mood of the time; creating an unreal canvas of an impossibly romantic world, its strange beauty now heightened by our knowledge of the horror of the First World War that was - unbeknown to all those present at the time – soon to bring to an abrupt end this life of dreamy isolation.

Jennifer Melville
Keeper of Fine Art
Aberdeen Art Gallery & Museums

The wider perspective

George Wilson occupies a unique position within the history of British art. Born in 1848 at the genesis of the young Pre-Raphaelite Brotherhood, and living through the birth of an English school of Impressionism, his work bears witness to these two significant moments in the art of the British Isles. Both his subject paintings and landscapes reflect a fascinating combination of close observation and ethereal absorption of the world in which he lived.

Residing and working in London in the 1870s Wilson was propitiously placed to associate with and observe the works of such disparate personalities as Dante Gabriel Rossetti, James McNeil Whistler and the French expatriates Camille Pissarro and Claude Monet. Wilson's own work suggests his open reception to all of these diverse influences. In subjects such as *The Spring Witch* (no. 14) Wilson presents in microscopic detail the last seedpods of Fall making way for the early flowering shrubs of Spring as a backdrop to a dream-like vision of Persephone emerging from the underworld. A similar synthesis of reality and fantasy is presented in landscapes such as *The Fall of the Leaf* (no. 18) in which Ruskinian detail and Pre-Raphaelite color are fused to create a poetic, fairytale-like woodland image.

Wilson's present day anonymity is largely based on the limited surviving documentation of his work and life. His own self-effacing character as well as what is believed to have been the destruction of a significant portion of his work make any assessment a difficult task at best.

In this volume, Robin Fanshawe has painstakingly pieced together the fragments of Wilson's life and work to recreate a thoughtful and astute chronology of his biography and style. This careful scholarship as well as the numerous color illustrations of many works which have not been seen in public since the artist's death, will go far towards re-situating George Wilson within the canon of 19th century British cultural studies.

Margaretta S. Frederick
Curator, Bancroft Collection
Delaware Art Museum

PREFACE AND ACKNOWLEDGEMENTS

Preface

In his early diary memoir of 1914, entitled Reveries over Childhood and Youth, W.B. Yeats wrote about his father John Butler Yeats and the circle of painter friends that he came into contact with during J.B. Yeats's student and subsequent days in London. In that short work, he recalled the landscapes of one of those friends, the Scot George Wilson, as having been painted 'with phlegm and melancholy, the romantic movement drawing to its latest phase.'[2]

Yeats was hardly likely to be intimating that he thought that Wilson was representative of the dying phase of *the* Romantic Movement and that is not, in fact, what he said. Indeed, romantic painting lasted long after Wilson's death in 1890 and well into the 20th century. But just as Romanticism much influenced the work of the better known names of the second generation of Pre-Raphaelites led by Edward Burne-Jones from around 1858, so it also certainly influenced Wilson and, to start with at least, his other student friends from 1868. Rather more so, of course, Romanticism almost entirely dominated the work of the even later (and also rather more 'commercial' – and, thereby, better-known and so more famous) painters who evolved from that influence, such as Waterhouse, Gotch and Dicksee, as well as the neo-classical and highly decorative Victorian painters led by Leighton, Poynter and Alma-Tadema.

But although Wilson and Waterhouse (for instance) were virtual contemporaries by age, Wilson adhered rather more closely to the Burne-Jones school, which, despite producing work that was not often recognisable in relation to the original Pre-Raphaelite art of 1848, remained closely aligned both to the Aesthetic Movement and to Symbolism. In actual fact, Wilson's few remaining larger figurative works seem to owe a greater allegiance to the even earlier, and more emotionally expressive, symbolic realism of William Holman Hunt. Had Wilson lived as long as Waterhouse, then undoubtedly his art would also have developed into new realms. Certainly, his later watercolour landscapes show a distinct developmental trend – not towards classicism, however, but towards a degree of almost impressionistic influence of light and colour.

This book is not the first attempt – or rather suggestion (for that is all the previous attempt ever turned out to be) – to try to get the work of Wilson and his friends recognised, since W.B. Yeats wrote on November 21st 1912 to his father John Butler Yeats, who had been one of Wilson's earliest student colleagues, to try to persuade him to write his autobiography, saying:

> *...Later on, your memories of Potter and Nettleship and Wilson would have real historical importance. ... I will get the publisher to illustrate the book. There are your own pictures to choose from ... and the pictures from the Tate Gallery by Potter and at Aberdeen by Wilson, and Mrs Nettleship has still those early designs of Nettleship's and would probably be glad to have them published and him praised.*[3]

This might seem to be a somewhat patronising approach from son to father, but W.B. appears from his correspondence at that time to have been keen to elevate the standing of his father and friends through what he announced at the outset of the letter to be 'a great project'. However, others have analysed that relationship to a far deeper level than is of prime importance here. Nevertheless, what W.B. Yeats had clearly, and maybe rather surprisingly, omitted to recall when he wrote this, was the very considerable collection of works by each of these artists that had been amassed by his father's (and his own) long-standing friend, the Irish dramatist Dr John Todhunter. Indeed, Dr Todhunter had, well before 1912, helped to organise two retrospective exhibitions of Wilson's work alone.

In 1989, the Barbican Art Gallery in London staged a very successful exhibition with the seemingly impossibly broad title: *The Last Romantics – The Romantic Tradition in British Art – Burne-Jones to Stanley Spencer*. John Christian, in his introduction to the published catalogue of the exhibition,[4] tells us that the title was taken from Yeats's poem *Coole Park and Ballylee, 1931*. This poem, published in *The Winding Stair*[5] many years after *Reveries over Childhood and Youth* was written, shows an enduring theme which would most certainly have appealed to George Wilson's own artistic influences through the romantic poets – particularly since he had frequently been in the company of the young William and other Yeats children during his regular visits to their father's house in London. It is no great coincidence then that these few brief lines should have been in mind to include here as well:

> *We were the last romantics – chose for*
> *theme Traditional sanctity and loveliness;*
> *Whatever's written in what poets name...*

It has been suggested that it is surprising that no paintings by George Wilson were displayed at the Barbican exhibition. Quite how any more pictures could possibly have been fitted into that expansive exhibition is another matter, but in fact it is not at all surprising that Wilson was not even considered: Apart from a small exhibition of around 20 works and sketch items staged by the Aberdeen Art Gallery in 1990 to commemorate the 100th anniversary of Wilson's death, until very recently no pictures by Wilson had appeared in any publicly staged exhibition since 1903. Indeed, apart from a very small number of pictures in the collection of the Aberdeen Art Gallery, there presently appear to be only two paintings in the possession of other public collections – one small watercolour landscape in The National Gallery of Scotland in Edinburgh (which in fact was also exhibited immediately following its bequest), and one larger figurative oil painting in the excellent Bancroft Pre-Raphaelite collection of the Delaware Art Museum, in Wilmington, USA. Additionally though, there are two drawings in each of the collections of the Victoria and Albert Museum and the British Museum.

The reason for this vacuum is due to many factors. Certainly, the quality of Wilson's work, and the place it deserves to hold within the art of the late Victorians, should only endorse consideration for its inclusion in appropriate exhibitions and collections. The real reasons, therefore, principally relate back to Wilson's very short life; his utter indifference towards exhibiting or attempting to sell his work during that short lifetime, and the unfortunate disappearance over the years of the major proportion of his works – which remained largely scattered amongst his family and various close friends, and just a few enthusiastic patrons.

In respect of his work ethos then, Wilson would have fitted in well with the remark that the French 'realist' novelist, Gustave Flaubert, wrote on the subject of artists and their art in a letter to his friend the romantic writer George Sand. In that letter (written in December 1875, just as Wilson was setting out in the world following his art student days), he made the now famous statement that *L'homme n'est rien, l'œuvre tout* ('The man is nothing; his work is everything'). Although during his lifetime Wilson remained best known as a person only to quite a small circle of close friends and patrons, the outcome of his work meant everything to him. And indeed, it was John Todhunter, one of his closest friends and benefactors, who continued this encouragement throughout Wilson's life-long illness, right up to his early death in 1890. Todhunter formed a significant collection of Wilson's works, and it was he who organised both retrospective exhibitions of his work – initially in Aberdeen in 1893, followed 10 years later by the last important exhibition of his paintings at the John Baillie Gallery in 1903. This latter exhibition was designed to represent the first of a proposed series at Baillie's that would focus on the work of 'Neglected Artists'.

Those who have read Percy Bate's slightly curious account of Wilson's work in his immediately post-contemporary book *The English Pre-Raphaelite Painters, Their Associates and Successors* [6] may well have shared Bate's initial comment that exception might be taken at the inclusion of Wilson in an account about the Pre-Raphaelite painters. They might also have wondered why he was included in the first place – and indeed, what has happened to his work since. However, Bate is clear in explaining his rationale, and why Wilson was included is not so difficult to understand if one takes the title of the book at face value: George Wilson was without doubt a strict follower of Pre-Raphaelite values. But, it is in order to try to address – and maybe redress – some of these questions that this present book has been compiled. Whether this aim succeeds, and whether George Wilson manages to become reinstated within the realms of those later followers of the Pre-Raphaelite movement, will remain to be seen. If only a little attention can be brought to this artist's sometimes quite beautiful work, then generations to come may hopefully, and perhaps with expert help where appropriate, rediscover some of his 'lost' works from time to time.

In parallel with the principal attention paid to Wilson's life and work, some attempt has been made to highlight the relationship and relevant importance of those who worked with and around him – in particular, John Trivett Nettleship and John Butler Yeats. Little at all has ever been written about the former, but inevitably much more has been recorded about the latter, particularly in relation to the wider literary and artistic interests of his children.

George Wilson certainly deserves some recognition. At times his work has a unique charm, and one can easily recognise the very different approach that he adopted towards his watercolour paintings – wooded landscapes in the main – which seem almost to have flowed from his brushes, and his larger symbolic oil paintings, which on occasions quite evidently did not! At times these oils are laboured and inconclusive and are often over-worked through Wilson's own enduring self-critical dissatisfaction with the results. Indeed, like many artists before and after him, he is recorded as having more than once destroyed a canvas when this continued to disappoint him.

But at their best his pictures can be quite exquisite. He often employed really very bold colouring, with several colours – particularly vivid oranges, greens and blues – standing out almost as a 'trademark' of his depiction of woodland, leaves, drapery, sky or water. Wilson's autumn leaves would crunch if you touched them; his moss would simply ooze water if squeezed! And if this short biography of all that is presently known about Wilson's life can help to elevate an interest in his work, and at the same time recognise the association with his friends and colleagues within their 1869 'Brotherhood', then it will be a minor contribution towards reinstating a small and somewhat neglected group of very good, if never quite very great, Victorian artists.

It is probably at this point that the author's personal interest in George Wilson (as his great-great-nephew) should be admitted, and this of course is why this book is not a more generic critique of the work of the wider group who existed around Wilson at the time. Its purpose is in fact deliberately to veer towards the life of Wilson, more so than the others in his group, and this is more than partially intentional in seeking to demonstrate the extent to which George Wilson (unlike one or two others in the group) was entirely disinterested in personal fame and therefore didn't profess or record anywhere his involvement or association with the 'good and the great' of the time.

To the same extent, this philosophy extended to the family successors of Wilson and his colleagues who also painted. Of these, J.B. Yeats's younger son and namesake, Jack B. Yeats is by far the most renowned, with J.T. Nettleship's daughter, Ida, only so acknowledged (most unjustly) by association through her husband, Augustus John. But Wilson's own niece, Rachel Cassels Brown became a most accomplished artist and illustrator in her own right, although her work is now largely unrecognised. Unfortunately, her career also suffered a premature closure with macular degeneration of her eyesight at an early age. She worked briefly with Frances Macdonald MacNair and her sister Margaret Macdonald Mackintosh of Glasgow Group renown whilst in Liverpool in the early 1900s, but like her uncle before her, her professional career was cut short and she is now virtually unknown.

A number of Wilson's, and his niece's, pictures have always hung on the walls of the homes of a constantly diminishing number of their family's descendants. Regrettably, over the generations, there seems to have been a rather carefree attitude towards what were frequently referred to somewhat blasély within the Wilson family as 'Uncle Dodie's* pictures', and rather than ensuring that they passed down to subsequent family members, it would appear that they were as often as not disposed of or dispersed in other ways. One problem that exacerbated this was that the overall number of descendents was diminishing rapidly, but it was they who had to accommodate the correspondingly increasing number of bequeathed pictures as each previous generation diminished!

Of George Wilson's twelve brothers and sisters, only four married and just two of those produced any offspring. All but one member of the few branches of this line of the Wilson family that are still extant therefore are descended from George's eldest brother, John, to whom he was very closely attached, and whom he visited at Castle Park in Huntly, Aberdeenshire, every year throughout his adult life – and indeed, where he eventually died in 1890.

The author's earliest recollection as a small boy, of a Wilson picture, was of one of only two that he exhibited at the Royal Academy – although that fact was not then apparent. This picture, in its original dark oak frame with gilt sub-frame, was the chalk *Study of a Head* (RA No. 296 of 1877). This clever, enigmatic, drawing of a man's head used to hang at that time at the end of a long dark corridor, where he appeared to scrutinise everyone who approached. It was eventually discovered that there were other Wilson watercolours within the family, but by that time very few still graced the walls since most, with damaged frames or broken glass, had long since been relegated to the attic. Later investigation at the outset of this work exposed a very similar situation within the few other remaining branches of the family. Speed of action, therefore, became of the essence in order to save and record what remained.

There were a number of particular challenges in putting together this all too inadequate account of Wilson's life. One significant factor that has no doubt affected the recognition of his work by later generations of the family, and by those who have not studied it, is that (so far as is presently experienced) Wilson never, *ever*, signed or dated or titled the front of his pictures in any way. His name is only very occasionally recorded on labels on the back of a few pictures that still possess their original frames – and where this is in his own hand, these few paintings do effectively bear a signature, since his signed name was typically (of the time) never more than an extension of his everyday written hand.

However, probably the most important single task in compiling this book was actually to try to trace the present whereabouts of as many as possible of his paintings and drawings – including those still remaining within the family – and to relate these

---

* 'Dodie' is a common Scottish nickname for George

to exhibition lists and other recorded evidence of Wilson's work. The aim has been to compile a largely illustrated *catalogue raisonné*, although in Wilson's case the dearth of both information and evidence available produces a list that remains quite small with only around 150 titles. Nevertheless, a catalogue has been compiled, including illustrations of several 'lost' works, so hopefully with time, this might initiate further discoveries of new or lost works to add to the list.

To achieve the aim of a first list, all the paintings needed to be identified and cross-referenced to the one hundred or so works that were recorded (but were not always all the same) in the two exhibitions that followed his death – the first at the Aberdeen Art Gallery in 1893, and the second 10 years later in 1903 at the Baillie Gallery in London. In respect of the larger oil paintings – only one of which remains within the Wilson family – this proved to be a fascinating area of research, from which just one or two important further results were uncovered. Similarly, some sad discoveries indicating the probable permanent demise of numerous significant paintings have also been noted.

Not only was there immense difficulty in trying to track down the missing Wilson pictures, but also the unearthing of any documentary evidence relating to his short life was an extremely rare event. To a large extent, it turned into quite a detective saga – with occasional small leads producing others, but with many doors closing in most blunt and thankless ways. I can therefore now empathise fully with the person who once said that: 'Research is like a shrub – occasionally watered, sap rises to the tip of the branches – produces new shoots and occasionally blooms, but ultimately frequently produces dead ends – so returns back down the branches to seek a new route next time'.

Regardless of this, it has been a fascinating and rewarding process. But more importantly, there has been one particular revelation that turned out to be quite surprising. Everything that I had heard and read about George Wilson as I started out, led me to anticipate that I would find only a shallow personality who lacked ambition; who avoided all public contact and recognition; who was insular, nomadic and insecure in his conviction of his ability as an artist, but most of all, who was no more than mildly peripheral to the art of his age.

Undoubtedly, some of this holds true – but only ever to some extent; otherwise, there would have been little truth in the one contemporary account of his life and work (written by his lifelong friend and patron, Dr John Todhunter), which has come to form the crux of virtually everything that has been written thereafter. And while Todhunter's somewhat eulogistic account pays strong tribute to the beauty and poetry of Wilson's painting, it also plays heavily on his retiring nature, his outright disinterest in becoming involved in the rigmarole of self-promotion towards artistic success – and, unfortunately, on his constant debilitating ill-health.

What is missing in this and the subsequently perpetuated stereotyping of certain obvious characteristics that were undoubtedly significant to Wilson's persona, is the account of an evidently sensitive and highly intelligent, much-travelled and well-versed person, who appears to have been made most welcome wherever he landed. It is hoped that by the end of this account, some of the greater depths and attributes of the character, as well as his work, will have become more apparent and will be perpetuated.

Acknowledgements

Although it has indeed been a rewarding experience, somewhat inevitably, it has not always been an entirely successful one. This means that I have undoubtedly badgered many people for sometimes seemingly quite trivial detail in order to squeeze the very last ounce of information out of a source. I am greatly indebted to all those who have suffered from this attention. In particular, I am most grateful to Professor William M. Murphy, author of *Prodigal Father, The Life of John Butler Yeats (1839–1922)* [7] amongst other erudite works, who showed me the greatest of courtesy and patience over many years. Having been assailed with repetitive questions when I could never quite accept that he had already told me all he knew of Wilson from his own extensive Yeats researches and sources, he still never failed to give me sound and valuable advice. Professor Murphy's generous permission to allow me to utilise, and to quote freely from, the product of his own researches as published in *Prodigal Father* has been a most valuable – or rather, essential – contribution to my own efforts.

I have received nothing but the kindest consideration from everyone whom I have had the privilege to consult. At times, I was offered even greater assistance than I could accept. Regrettably, this was always due either to time or economic constraints. Had it been practicable, within a heavy working life far removed from this project, to visit New York, I could have accessed copies of both J.B Yeats's original manuscripts of his unpublished *Memoirs* and letters, and William Murphy's transcriptions of those documents. The former reside in the Department of Special Collections of the State University of New York at Stony Brook, where Kristen J. Nyitray, the Head of Department and all the staff were exceedingly patient with me. Similarly tolerant was Ellen H. Fladger, Head of the Special Collections department in the Schaffer Library at Union College, Schenectady, where the transcriptions lie.

In the end, and having gleaned some fascinating allied information from these two sources, I concluded that the minute extra detail that I might (or might not) have discovered beyond William Murphy's published disclosures, by going back to all of the original documents, would have to submit to the law of diminishing returns, and perhaps wait for another time.

Acknowledgements

Although it might suggest a degree of belittlement towards the broader help that I have received from so many, this really is not so, but there are one or two others whom I do have to single out for particular thanks – because, without them I quite simply would not have been able to pursue my trail. The following are in no particular order of precedence:

I suppose my few Wilson cousins – those remaining descendants of George Wilson's family line – might have something of a vested interest in helping me with this work! Nevertheless, those whom I have badgered have tolerated well my persistence of enquiry and have allowed me free access to their paintings and their own observations. I must thank in particular Carolyn Botterill and Frances Wilson; and Alan Victor, whose photographic support and sound comment helped me no end. Also Duine Campbell to whom I am most grateful for his detailed family contributions including the transcription of Anna Wilson's letters, as well as for his carefully considered comment and proof reading. There are others who know who they are and I will preserve their anonymity. I particularly wish to remember those last few members of the Wilson family, regrettably now all passed on, from the generation whose own parents knew George Wilson personally as a much loved uncle. These include David Cassels Brown, Jane Macfie, Nancy Morris, Peg Wilson and Esmé Drury, all of whom passed on to me anecdotal family snippets that are now hidden away within this text

Then equally importantly, I must acknowledge the help of the present day family descendants of those other friends and colleagues who were most important to George Wilson and so equally to the compilation of this book. In particular, Mark Bertram, who has consistently delivered me valuable information about his great-grandfather, Halsey Ricardo, as did Dr. Camilla Bosanquet, and the late Dr. Colin Bertram. The late Mrs Joan Lambe put up with my constant enquiries about her grandfather, Dr. John Todhunter – in addition to my having been granted access to the valuable archives of Todhunter, Nettleship and Ellis material in the Library of Reading University, where Michael Bott, Keeper of Archives and Manuscripts, and Brian Ryder also, went far beyond the call of duty to help me out with my research.

I should also mention John Scott in relation to the descent from Russell Scott; and Mark Willcox Jr., great-nephew of Ralph Radcliffe Whitehead, who gave me the valuable leads to the Byrdcliffe manuscript collection at the Winterthur Library, and the Delaware Art Museum, to which he had bequeathed Wilson's major allegorical oil painting *The Spring Witch*. In the Whitehead area of research, I had some delightfully enthusiastic correspondence with Nancy E. Green, Senior Curator of Prints, Drawings, and Photographs at the Herbert F. Johnson Museum of Art, Cornell University, who was in turn researching the Whiteheads and the Bydcliffe Art Colony archives. As stated, these archives lie predominantly in the Winterthur Museum and Library, Delaware, where I received immediate and most helpful assistance with my queries from Jeanne Solensky, Librarian of the Downs Collection of Manuscripts and Printed Ephemera.

In relation to John Trivett Nettleship, his great-granddaughter Mrs Natalie Protopapa assisted me all she could via her records of the Nettleship family – now lodged with the Northamptonshire Records Office, where again I received the greatest assistance from

Crispin Powell and all of their staff. This comparatively recent access provided a new and broader view of the relationship between Wilson and Nettleship, and at the same time brought this relationship into much clearer and closer focus.

From public galleries, libraries and records offices, again I received nothing but the greatest courtesy and help. Dr. Jennifer Melville, Keeper of Fine Art at Aberdeen Art Gallery, where three watercolour drawings by Wilson reside, has always professed and shown a real interest in helping to investigate and promote her local 'unsung' artist. This has been a continual great source of motivation on the numerous occasions when progress became more than a little difficult over the years. Ultimately, Dr Melville kindly agreed to contribute to the foreword to this book from the Scottish perspective, whilst Emily Thomson, her Assistant Keeper of Fine Art made life very easy in relation to all available information from Aberdeen.

Similarly, and although she will be quite oblivious of the fact, Dr. Hilary Pyle, recently retired Yeats Curator at the National Gallery of Ireland, became something of a mentor to me via the wonderful and exemplary work she has produced over the years relating to the Yeats family dynasty – and in particular through her benchmark publication: *Yeats, Portrait of an Artistic Family.*[8] Subsequently, Dr Róisín Kennedy, the current Yeats Curator, and Marie McFeely in the picture Library of the National Gallery of Ireland have continued that valuable assistance.

More recently, I have received greatest encouragement from Dr. Margaretta Frederick, Curator of the excellent Bancroft Collection of Pre-Raphaelite paintings at The Delaware Art Museum in Wilmington, Delaware, where *The Spring Witch*, the only sizeable oil painting by George Wilson that is known to rest in a public collection can be seen on display. Again, Dr Frederick's unerring encouragement during the final difficult stages towards completion of the manuscript, and ultimately her generous reading of this; her astutely constructive criticism, and the consequent significant improvement of the final text were all crucial to the outcome. I am further grateful to Dr. Frederick for also agreeing to write a contribution to the foreword to this book – in her case from the wider perspective.

The only other paintings at all in public collections (apart from the drawings in the British Museum and Victoria and Albert Museum collections) are the previously mentioned paintings in the Aberdeen Art Gallery and the fine watercolour entitled *A Fallen Beech* that resides in the National Gallery of Scotland in Edinburgh. Here again, I was afforded all the attention I needed by Valerie Hunter, Curator of Prints and Drawings and other helpful members of the gallery's staff.

I should thank Dr Emma Chambers, the Curator of the University College London (Slade) Art Collections and Helen Robinson and other helpful members of staff at the UCL Art Collections and Records Offices for their immediate response to my frequent enquiries. At the Williamson Art Gallery in Birkenhead, where just a few of Rachel Cassels Brown's works lie, Colin Simpson, the Principal Museums Officer, afforded me great courtesy. Similarly, Jennifer Reeves at the National Art Library of The Victoria and Albert Museum and Eva White in the Department of Prints and Drawings, could not have been more constructively helpful; as were Mike Craig, Curator of the George Washington Wilson photographic archive at Aberdeen University, and Peggy Kennedy, Manager of the Records

Acknowledgements

Management & Archives at the Australia and New Zealand Banking Group Limited.

Elsewhere, the help of various departmental staff members was never lacking from The Royal Academy of Arts Research Department; The National Gallery Archives and Library; The British Museum Department of Prints and Drawings; the Walker Art Gallery, Liverpool; Liverpool School of Art and Design, Liverpool John Moores University; The Ashmolean Museum, Oxford; the Alfred East Gallery in Kettering; the Birmingham Institute of Art and Design at the University of Central England; the Whitworth Art Gallery at the University of Manchester, and The Witt Library. Disappointingly, although most willing and keen to help, the Director of the Heatherley's School of Fine Art was unable to give me the background information that they would genuinely have wished to provide, as their early records are believed to have been sold commercially many years ago, and are understood now to be untraceable.

The extent of the general and greatly enthusiastic help that I received from both personal and more distant acquaintances when approached is demonstrated by the immediacy with which such assistance was given to me when requested. Locally, Norman Shepherd provided me with the optical enhancement of very old photographs, and at a distance, Bernie Driver of the Kettering and District Photographic Society generously photographed items when I was unable to access them myself.

In a similar but more amusing vein, Robert Croucher, Editor of the *K'nocker*, the village magazine of Portknockie on the Moray coast of Banffshire, epitomised the extent of the broader altruistic support I received when he 'grilled' the older local inhabitants in the area for information on my behalf. Between them they identified certain views painted by George Wilson along that coastline, and debated at length how George Wilson could possibly have accessed the seaward side of *The Whale's Mouth* (q.v.) to paint that fascinating rock formation – and indeed, came up with the probable answer.

Also in Banffshire, it was a privilege and an experience to spend some generous time with Bill and Mabel Gauld, who have farmed the ancient Wilson farmstead of Tochieneal for so many years themselves, and who still seemed to know as much about the Wilson family as anyone does locally – even after well over 100 years since they departed the area. Bill; always fascinating to talk to, but equally impossible for a demi-Sassenach to comprehend, and Mabel; mercifully there to interpret and to respond to the inevitable subsequent enquiries in correspondence.

Thankfully, and because of the considerable length of time it has taken to complete this work (partially due to having been continually inconvenienced by a full 'working' life!), many of those who had to put up with my probing – as well as those whom I may have failed to mention through my own forgetfulness (but certainly through no intention of discourtesy) – will hopefully have forgotten about it themselves, so will not be too offended. Sadly though, and again because of the time it has taken to complete the book, several of those who assisted me at one time or another have since passed away, so will not even be aware of its completion or have the tiny reward of my most grateful thanks for their contributions.

Over the many years of researching this subject, there have inevitably been one or two moments that could be described as 'defining'; but there is one that will always stand out as being especially memorable. After a number of years of false trails in the search for any evidence whatsoever that might identify the whereabouts of one or two of Wilson's larger oil paintings, a long-shot approach was made to the Managing Director of Ricardo plc. It had been discovered that this company was descended and developed from the engineering business founded by Sir Harry Ricardo, the son of Victorian architect Halsey Ricardo, who was in turn one of George Wilson's good friends and patrons. Halsey Ricardo had bought several of Wilson's paintings, including one considered to be amongst his finest, entitled *Asia*, which was reported in the press following Ricardo's death to have been bequeathed by him to the National Gallery in London. However, the painting was apparently either not accepted by the gallery or the offer was withdrawn, as their archives hold no record even of discussing the matter; and so apparently the painting had in consequence 'disappeared' from any public arena.

Luckily, the Ricardo Company had still been identifiable through retaining the family name and was also still very much in existence, although the Managing Director had no knowledge of the painting or its whereabouts. He could, however, offer leads to two local descendents of their founder, and these bore fruit when that defining moment arrived with an unexpected telephone call. That call came from the late Dr Colin Bertram, who announced that he was the husband of one of Halsey Ricardo's grand-daughters, and added something along the lines of, 'I have received your letter about *Asia*. You will be pleased to know that your search is at an end, as she is looking down on me from the wall as I speak to you. When would you like to visit her?' This was one of those small, but inspiring moments that made the whole process, which had been flagging badly at the time, immediately worthwhile once more. It led to the identification of one further large 'missing' oil and other unknown pictures still extant within that descent, and eventually to the pursuit of the American connection and discovery of the hitherto 'unknown' painting of *The Spring Witch* within the collection of the Delaware Art Museum.

Finally, as a purely frivolous observation, I would like to thank publicly whoever the clever person was who invented the Internet and email! Without the benefit of those extraordinary tools, and the splendid speedy response that email seems to elicit from the vast majority who use it, I doubt whether I would ever have completed this task in one lifetime. It also makes me realise precisely how proficient were those historians and researchers who have gone before me without the benefit of any such aid!

* * *

Last to be mentioned here, but of course by no means least, are those who have had the greatest burden to tolerate throughout the extended length of time it has taken to bring this manuscript together. These are my wife, Cynthia, and my two children, Nikki and Tom – who, although the latter were indeed children when it all started, have long since fled to lead their own lives. It is for Cynthia's unyielding and staunch tolerance that I can dedicate this book to no-one else; from being dragged around the Wilson family gravestones in the churchyard of the ever-so-beautiful (but oh-so-freezing!) village of Fordyce in Banffshire, through to sharing my joy at the regrettably all too infrequent successful artwork discoveries, and finally to critiquing so practically what I have written.

RJHF
Sussex, 2007

CHAPTER ONE

An age of 'brotherhoods'

To all intents and purposes in terms of history of art, the expression 'Brotherhood' might primarily only be recognised in respect of that original group of seven young colleagues who adopted it for the first time in September 1848. That group founded through their 'Pre-Raphaelite Brotherhood' – the 'P.R.B.' – an ethos and consequent movement in art that would secure its advocates and, equally inevitably, its detractors, for generations and no doubt, centuries to come.

There were, however, subsequent small groups who developed from that ethos and movement, who were akin to, or empathetic towards, the principles of the original P.R.B. to a greater or lesser degree. Occasionally these groups even adopted the same collective term, thus rendering 'brotherhood' an almost generic expression. George Wilson and his colleagues became gelled into one such group that had its vision in its earliest days quite closely aligned to that of the original P.R.B. – although there was no apparent deliberate association beyond the name. Nevertheless, a brief résumé of the evolution of the movement and ethos that was to influence George Wilson, in particular, so profoundly throughout his life, is reasonable here.

When in 1848 the original Pre-Raphaelite Brotherhood had first banded loosely together in John Millais' family home at 83 Gower Street in London, their enduring ethos was also 'founded' through sharing the same profound ideals. Of the seven founder members of the P.R.B., only three really remain today as household names to the wider public – those of John Everett Millais (1829-1896), Dante Gabriel Rossetti (1828-1882), and William Holman Hunt (1827-1910). The other members are generally remembered now by a far smaller sector of the public.

The group members were profoundly disaffected with the Royal Academy and its Drawing Schools, with its long and tedious traditional methods of tuition, and were rebellious towards its institutionalism. This is more than a little paradoxical in view of the fact that they had not only first met as students at the RA, but had also had many of their earlier imaginative paintings hung on the Academy's walls. They were intensely influenced by the religious fervour and integrity of the Italian painters who worked before the period dominated by what John Ruskin (1819-1900] referred to rather bluntly in *Modern Painters III* as 'the clear and tasteless poison of the art of Raphael'. [9]

Not only did the P.R.B.'s techniques go radically against traditional teaching and methodology, but also their subject matter was equally radical in the way in which this was portrayed in a thoroughly non-grandiose style, to display scenes as everyday elements of everyday life. The minutiae of pedantic detail, built up laboriously over long periods of time, the avoidance of centrally lit subjects, and an adherence to working the whole picture through from nature alone, challenged everything that the art establishment stood for.

Their frequent interpretation of texts from Tennyson and Keats and other contemporary and Romantic poets established their rebellion against the industrialisation and commercialisation of the present-day world they lived in. They had rejected the dogma of traditional teaching and concentrated on simplicity and true-to-life realism. But it was primarily the poetic and eclectic facets that developed into the second phase of the movement, and it is this phase with which Pre-Raphaelitism is probably more commonly now associated by the broader public.

In 1853, five years after the formation of the P.R.B. and a year after it had effectively dissolved, William Morris (1834-1896), the socialist visionary and designer, went up to Exeter College, Oxford. In Oxford, Morris was to meet with new friends, and in particular the young Edward Burne-Jones (1833-1898), who was the son of an impoverished Birmingham picture framer – much in contrast to Morris's wealthy upbringing.

The medieval stone surroundings, all 'wrought by hand' within that beautiful and ancient city, would serve to focus Morris's early vision towards a socialist society opposed to the materialism of the Victorian age. That vision would be achieved by returning to the principle of achievement of man through his most human of qualities – his work. This was the view of Thomas Carlyle (1795–1881), who, through the power and imagination of his writings, convinced Morris and others of the social anguish that had been inflicted upon the poor. He, and they, saw a culture of exploitation that was epitomised by that much-heralded 'monster' that they all so hated for what it portrayed – the Great Exhibition of 1851.

Morris was joined by a number of determined friends, many from Birmingham including Edward Burne-Jones, who decided to set up a new 'brotherhood' – a mock monastic order, as they once put it, for a 'Crusade and Holy Warfare against the age and the heartless coldness of the times'. At this stage, Burne-Jones and Morris were both destined for the Church, and engrossed themselves in High Church theology. Morris also spent an extensive amount of time in the Bodleian Library, where he became entranced by the beauty of medieval illustrated manuscripts that were so much to influence his work – as well as to inspire his own magnificent collection of immensely valuable manuscripts in the library of Kelmscott House.

It was at Oxford that Morris and Burne-Jones first read of the Pre-Raphaelite movement, and first heard of the name that was to so influence their lives – that of Dante Gabriel Rossetti – through the text of Ruskin's *Edinburgh Lectures*. Of course, although Ruskin himself stood somewhat imperially outside the original Pre-Raphaelite group of brethren, his views on art – where he saw the art of the Middle Ages as the epitome of expression of man's delight in his labour – fully supported and promoted the ethos of the Pre-Raphaelite movement.

However, this was not, of course, the only viewpoint, and when the art establishment in particular fought back against what it considered to be the philistine approach of the Pre-Raphaelites, it was in his vehement advocacy of their principles that Ruskin's distinction as an art critic flourished. He had begun his life-long battle with his defence of Turner (1775-1851), and he came to view the Pre-Raphaelites' work as a continuance of that battle.

Thus, the influence of John Ruskin upon the later group was also, of course, paramount. His passionately argued piece, *The Nature of Gothic*,[10] against what he perceived to be the appalling consequences of Victorian industrialisation, was to strike a particular chord with Morris. The perceived vulgarity of machine-made 'advancements' that were replacing the ancient-founded and naturally developed skills of man was equally abhorrent to both – as was the division of labour and the unemployment created by the great new machines of the age. Thus, the most radical and influential movement in Victorian art and vision came together as an on-going philosophy, demonstrated through the various media of art and architecture, ceramics, tapestry and other decorative arts, and through literature and poetry.

So when Burne-Jones went to London and sought the tutelage of Rossetti to 'learn painting', and Morris decided to article himself to the Gothic Revivalist architect, George Street*, the second phase of Pre-Raphaelitism, encompassing its broader relationship to Arts and Crafts, was secured. Both the pupil, Burne-Jones, and Rossetti, his teacher, regarded painting to be the creation of beautiful objects, and like his tutor, Burne-Jones was determined to be a poetic painter. Throughout his career, he made little attempt to depict the natural world, but preferred instead to paint what he defined in his frequently-quoted and memorable remark in a letter to a friend as 'a beautiful romantic dream of something that never was, never will be...'.

Morris, meanwhile, spent most of his weekends with Rossetti and Burne-Jones, and so the links were cemented. Despite the inevitable bohemianism that their new relationships generated, and despite also the tangled web of personal relationships that were later to emerge, there was an enduring attraction about the fundamental principles of the Pre-Raphaelite movement that sublimely influenced its many followers over the next forty or so years.

So although George Wilson, a whole generation later, was never in any way a leader within his own small group – indeed he was very much the opposite – that group certainly

---

* If William Rossetti's opinion expressed in his Diary entry for 6 December 1866 is to be accepted, then George Street might seem to have been a surprising choice of master for Morris, who is considered to be a founding father of British Socialism. In Rossetti's entry for that date, he intimated that Street '...seems to be (as I should have surmised) a strong Tory...'! (Rossetti, William M., Rossetti Papers 1862 to 1870, Sands & Co, London, 1903)

started out by being heavily influenced by the Pre-Raphaelite philosophy and the members were seldom far away from that revered circle of the original and immediately succeeding Pre-Raphaelites.

It sometimes seems to be almost intrinsic in circles and movements in art for individuals with both similar and opposing ideas and ideals to form into tight – or loose – groups for interest, debate and self-criticism; and indeed, this has happened frequently over the centuries, both in England and more particularly on the Continent. Former members of many such cliques now number among the greatest recognised artists of all time, whilst many of their colleagues subsequently faded and are now known only occasionally to scholars.

And so it transpired with George Wilson's group; for, although John Butler Yeats is occasionally recognised – possibly largely by association through his children (although sometimes, rather less fortunately, in confusion with his son Jack B. Yeats) – none of the others from that small group of artists who are the focus of this book ever became really *great* in terms of recognition, either then or subsequently. In 1869, and just 21 years after the founding of the original P.R.B., this later group, who all first met whilst attending the highly-respected art school of Thomas Heatherley* at 79, Newman Street, off Oxford Street in London, decided to form – or rather, drifted into yet another 'Brotherhood'.

In fact, there was nothing that *actually* connected this latest 1869 Brotherhood in any direct way with the original P.R.B. – and the later group never claimed that there was. In fact, they only used the term 'brotherhood' as descriptive of their association and not a formal title, and certainly none of them adopted the P.R. initials for their work – as did the members of the original P.R.B. before them. Although chronologically they were a generation apart, there were, nevertheless, many similarities of interest and vision between the members of the two groups.

The original Pre-Raphaelite Brotherhood, the 'P.R.B.', had effectively dissolved within four years of semi-formal existence, and in similar fashion, the later group of artists had also largely dispersed and gone their own ways within the same number of years. As individuals, they kept in touch with each other for the majority of their lives, but by the mid 1870s each was effectively pursuing his own very different destiny.

Certainly, in their early student days, this later 'brethren' were all significantly influenced by the work of the Pre-Raphaelites and their immediate followers. They had all

---

* Heatherley's School of Fine Art is of course still very much in existence. Now located in Chelsea, the school specialises in portraiture, sculpture and figurative work. It remains the oldest established independent school of art in London, having been started originally by James Leigh in Maddox Street in 1845, and subsequently bought by Thomas Heatherley and moved to Newman Street in the 1860s. As with most art schools at the time, it was largely a preparatory school for entry into the Royal Academy Schools. However, it was extremely popular and even then quite avant-garde in allowing women to attend life classes! The list of famous pupils to have attended the school is almost endless, and Thomas Heatherley seems to have been highly respected and held in great affection by all of them.

rejected what they saw as the straightjacket of traditional teaching at the Royal Academy schools. And, to a greater or lesser extent, each initially embraced the fundamental principles of the Pre-Raphaelitism of 20 years earlier, which had been so strongly advocated by Ruskin through the 1850s in his series of *Modern Painters*. Ruskin had declared in his *Edinburgh Lectures* that,

> *Pre-Raphaelitism has but one principle, that of absolute, uncompromising truth in all that it does, obtained by working everything, down to the most minute detail, from nature, and from nature only.*[++] *Every Pre-Raphaelite landscape background is painted to the last touch, in the open air, from the thing itself. Every Pre-Raphaelite figure, however studied in expression, is a true portrait of some living person. Every minute accessory is painted in the same manner.*

> And he added a footnote,[++] *Or, where imagination is necessarily trusted to, by always endeavouring to conceive a fact as it really was likely to have happened, rather than as it most prettily might have happened.*[11]

Only one of the 1869 group, the Scottish-born artist George Wilson, stuck emphatically to those principles throughout the whole of his short life and this, it would seem, earned him his place in Percy Bate's immediately post-contemporary account, *The English Pre-Raphaelite Painters, Their Associates and Successors*. In this benchmark volume, Bate included a chapter entitled *The Romantic Influence*, in which he described the work of three artists: Frederick Sandys (1829–1904), Simeon Solomon (1840-1905] and George Wilson (1848-1890). Bate may, in fact, have retained a further interest in Wilson during the last few years of his own life, when he took up the curatorship of the Aberdeen Art Gallery and Museum, in which town there was still at that time much parochial interest in their home-grown artist. However, it is not presently known whether the small group of Wilson's paintings that were given to the gallery by the family had been donated before the time of Bate's death in 1913.

The other principle enduring members of this later 'Brotherhood' were John Butler Yeats (1839–1922), John Trivett Nettleship (1841–1902), and Edwin John Ellis (1848–1916). As with the P.R.B., there were other occasional members – mainly in the earlier days. Apart from their painting, they were all passionate about the romantic poets, in particular Shelley and Keats, and the works of Robert Browning – and of course, William Blake was a principle mentor. This influenced their conversation and the debate that revolved around their meetings and their work to the extent that poetry, romanticism and painting were inextricably intertwined during those early years. Furthermore, it was undoubtedly partly from listening to J.B. Yeats's almost ceaseless debates with his friends, that the young W.B. Yeats, aged just seven years in 1872 at the height of the group's art student years, had the seeds sown for his future.

Similarities of philosophy and intent apart, there is now very little left to compare the two sets of 'brethren'. None of the 1869 group aspired to the very great heights of fame and popularity that were reached by the original and far better known P.R.B. members and their immediate followers – both within their lifetimes and again in their present-day popular revival. Not one member of the later group is now widely recognised either as an artist of particular influence – or indeed, recognised at all by much of the world. Yet, a small number of their works appear within the collections of one or two important galleries, and all of them, at times, produced some very fine work indeed

As already noted, the main focus of this particular book is the elusive and enigmatic figure of George Wilson. This is primarily because, although there is probably less recorded about his life and work than any of the others within his later Brotherhood, Wilson was the only member to remain entirely faithful to his early principles. However, because of his very short life, perpetually dogged by debilitating ill health, he never progressed his work to expand the undoubted hidden resources that he possessed. Although maturing in confidence considerably towards the end, his life's work remained unfulfilled, and this was also reflected broadly within many of his larger individual oil paintings – with which he was never entirely happy.

George Wilson; detail from a formal family group photograph, undated, but estimated to be ca. 1875 when Wilson would have been 27 years old and just as he was making his way in the world as a professional artist. This picture of Wilson in such formal attire somewhat belies the image that is more generally portrayed of the nomad who lived from hand to mouth on a daily basis, with no interest in finery, fame or fortune.

In respect of the work of Wilson's colleagues, there are varying amounts of information available. Certainly, the life of John Butler Yeats has been chronicled in exacting detail by William M. Murphy in his book *Prodigal Father, The Life of John Butler Yeats (1839–1922)* [12] as well as by a number of other academics. *Prodigal Father*, and its own reference sources, has been a most important source of additional information about that particular period of Wilson's life that revolved around the Brotherhood.

If it had been suggested to Wilson during his life that he was 'an intriguing figure', he would probably have been frankly incredulous. He would quite simply not have understood how anyone might even begin to think this of him. And, of course, outwardly, he was exactly the opposite. The evidence of his peers indicates a man of total transparency; a man who was clearly loved and admired by all who had the good fortune to know him; a man who displayed his loyalty to his friends quite naturally and unquestioningly, and who sought no reward for anything that he did.

However, it is not his reported persona that gives rise to the enigma, but rather the unanswered (and to him, completely irrelevant) question as to what it was that he was aiming to achieve. He had a very clear and unswerving attitude towards his chosen profession, yet a totally self-effacing opinion of his work. Certainly, John Todhunter, the Irish playwright and Wilson's life-long friend and patron, was quite emphatic that he painted solely because he loved what he was doing. He was completely disinterested in exhibiting his pictures and consequently, he seldom managed to complete pictures in time for exhibitions, nor did he often try to sell them – unless badgered to do so by his small band of admirers and friends. As will be remarked with regularity throughout this book, he also never even bothered to sign them.

The reason for this latter characteristic is unknown, but it is most likely from what is known of his persona that he quite simply did not feel that either the 'stature' of his name or the importance of his individual works merited these being formally signed off for posterity. Other colleagues around him at that time, and many subsequent admirers of his work since, would demur at this opinion – but either way, it certainly makes identification that much more difficult for anyone without reasonable experience of his work. Nonetheless, and conversely for those fortunate enough to have experienced much of his work, such a formal signature is largely superfluous, as Wilson's technique is of course a clear signature in itself.

Towards what turned out to be the quite sudden end to George Wilson's life, John Todhunter had been trying to persuade Wilson to allow him to mount an exhibition and sale of his work. But, even as he lay dying during the early months of 1890 in his brother's house of Castle Park in Huntly, Aberdeenshire, he could not countenance anyone 'paying good money' for his pictures. Yet at last, he agreed to allow Todhunter to proceed with his plan, if only because Wilson saw it as an opportunity to repay some cash to his brother and sister-in-law in return for their caring for him for so long during his final illness. However, in the event, and as an inevitable result of Wilson's sudden death, this was prevented from happening until some three years later.

George Wilson painted in both watercolour and in oils; occasionally in tempera and gouache, and he has also left some highly accomplished chalk studies and drawings. Apart from the telltale traits of his very individual style – as so often, a clear signature in itself – it would appear that he adopted two very different approaches towards the two principal media he employed. And, one is tempted to surmise, this was probably for two entirely different reasons.

In the first place, there is no doubt whatsoever that Wilson was at his most fluent, relaxed and – one might well believe – at his happiest when painting his smaller watercolours among his beloved rivers, wooded hills and forests of Scotland and the south of England, and in the mountains of northern Italy. These intensely personal pictures represent the significant majority of the very small number of his paintings that are presently recorded as still existing.

Conversely, his larger oil paintings – mainly of allegorical figurative subjects depicting classical subjects or romantic verse – appear, almost always, to be the product of an over-exertion towards achieving perfection through frequent re-working and change. Although his compositions are always innovative and original, this over-working renders them somewhat stilted at times, and it may simply be that these paintings were produced almost entirely as exhibition or commissioned pieces, hence Wilson's unremitting attention to detail. Nevertheless, from the small amount of correspondence he left, it is evident [q.v.] that he certainly still gained considerable pleasure from the painting of these works as well.

Regrettably, very many more works, including many of his finest recorded paintings are now missing. These include, it would appear, those that were referred to by W.B. Yeats as belonging to his two sisters when he wrote...

> *There is a public gallery of Wilson's work in his native Aberdeen and my sisters have a number of his landscapes – wood-scenes for the most part – painted with phlegm and melancholy, the romantic movement drawing to its latest phase.* [13]

With this reference in mind, there still are, indeed, a few pictures in Aberdeen Art Gallery; but all attempts at identifying the whereabouts of the pictures that belonged to the Yeats sisters, Lily (Susan Mary) and Lolly (Elizabeth Corbett), suggest that they have not survived within the Yeats family.

It does not appear to be recorded how W.B. Yeats's sisters came to possess some of Wilson's pictures, but it is most probable that they simply passed into the girls' hands when their father finally emigrated to America in December 1907, leaving behind most of the personal belongings of his past. As to Yeats's likely acquisition of the works: well, Wilson loved children, and of course knew all the Yeats boys and girls from his frequent visits to their house in Fitzroy Road, Regent's Park. He would undoubtedly have given to his friend any painting in which he expressed interest, simply in return for 'such faint praise' – to use Todhunter's words. It is most unlikely that Wilson would have accepted much, if any, payment for them, and in any case, it is even less likely that Yeats could have afforded to pay anything at all. It would therefore be very easy to believe that these paintings simply fell off the end of the conveyor belt that was J.B. Yeats's singularly undirected life, being no more than trappings of his past as Yeats himself moved inexorably on, living – as always – only for the present.

CHAPTER TWO

From Banffshire to London

George Wilson was born on 18th November 1848*, at Tochieneal in the hamlet of Lintmill, just south of the pretty Royal Borough of Cullen on the Moray coast of Banffshire in north-east Scotland. His father, John Wilson, was the fourth in a line of Wilson Factors† to the Earls of Findlater and Seafield, for whom he managed the vast Cullen district estates that formed the major part of the tens of thousands of acres of Estate land in the region. John Wilson's uncle Alexander, and

---

* As with so many facts concerning George Wilson's life, we immediately meet a conundrum. In the Register of Baptisms for the Parish of Cullen dated 29th December 1848, Wilson's birthdate was recorded as being '18th inst.' – i.e. 18th December 1848. However, throughout any writings about his life, he has always been referred to as having been born on 18th November 1848. These records include the history of the Wilson family, as well as a contemporary hand-written page entitled 'Family Register' (possibly extracted from a family Bible, or similar) which lists his parents and all their children, along with their birthdates. Almost without exception, all subsequent writings about George Wilson have been based upon John Todhunter's article about his life published in *The English Illustrated Magazine* of 1891, which also quoted November as his month of birth.

It is probable that such a close friend as Todhunter knew Wilson's birthday in any case, but this information is certainly confirmed by one particular letter from George's brother, John, to Todhunter after George's death, in which he gives a 'thumbnail sketch' of Wilson's life and clearly states November as the month of his birth. It is almost inconceivable that such an error could have been perpetuated by both George's father and his brother, so it has to be deemed most likely that the Register of Baptisms is wrong and should have stated 'ult' rather than 'inst'.

There are just two minor counter-arguments to such a conclusion: Firstly, it would have been quite unusual in those times of high infant mortality for a strong Scottish Presbyterian family to put off a baptism for six weeks. And secondly, the record of the baptism was witnessed by two of George's uncles – one a solicitor, and the other a doctor, neither of whom would have been likely to permit such an error – had they noticed it, of course!

In the interests of continuity, the November date is recognised throughout this book.

† Land agent, steward and estate manager

two of this Alexander's own uncles (confusingly also called John and Alexander) had held this post before him, so that it had become an almost hereditary one within the Wilson family over several generations.

In 1801, the younger Alexander Wilson took a tack* on the ancient Grant family farmstead of Tochieneal on the edge of Lintmill, and moved into the estate house, an already imposing

George Wilson's birthplace, Tochieneal, near Cullen, Banffshire. Photograph by Rachel Cassels Brown (née Wilson), ca 1935.

three-storey building curiously called Tochieneal 'Cottage', which he promptly further extended considerably.

By all accounts from within the Wilson family archives, very many of the Wilsons over the generations had acquitted themselves exceptionally in the region, from farming skills and cattle breeding through to their country sporting abilities, as well as in their business acumen. This Alexander, though, was an extraordinary man – only to be outshone eventually by the subsequent efforts of his nephew John (the artist George Wilson's father).

The Wilson family history, *The Wilsons; a Banffshire Family of Factors,*[14] by Andrew Cassels Brown is full of interesting anecdotes, which, if nothing else, serve to identify family traits that evidently descended through subsequent generations. Apart from their personal accomplishments within the community, they also developed very considerably the amenities within the Findlater and Seafield estates by capitalising on every natural opportunity that arose.

George Wilson's father, John, was born in 1802. He entered his uncle Alexander's 'Factory' in 1818 and took over the Factorship upon his uncle's death in 1839. There were many examples of the diverse opportunism shown by both Factors: In 1820, Alexander had manipulated the course of a passing burn to provide the water for the new Tochieneal Distillery, which he built to manufacture a pure malt whisky, on the opposite side of the road to the old Tochieneal farmstead outside Lintmill. Then in 1841, his nephew John had recognised the existence of an underlying

---

* 'Tack' is a largely archaic Scottish term broadly equivalent to a modern formal lease.

stratum of clay that proved ideal for the manufacture of land drainage pipes, bricks and tiles. The kilns that John built contributed in no mean way to the considerable improvement in the quality of a widespread area of land in that previously barren region of Scotland.

Another of John's major undertakings was the planting of over 31 million young trees of both soft and hardwood, covering over 8,000 acres of land. Much of this timber was cut down half a century later for use during the First World War when much of the softwood found its way to northern France to be used to shore up the trenches.

The death of George's father, John, in 1852 at the early age of 50 years, introduced a circumstance that certainly influenced the future of the young four-year-old George. John had a younger brother who had never married – a third Alexander – who moved quickly into Tochieneal House, and also, with the agreement of the Earl of Seafield (by 1811 the Findlater title had died out), he managed the Factorship in preparation for his brother's eldest son, confusingly yet again another John, to take over in due course.

This, in fact, was destined never to come about, but in the meantime, 'Uncle Sandy' as Alexander was known to almost everyone in the north-east of Scotland, became much of a father figure, particularly to the youngsters within his late brother's extensive family of 13 children. He evidently passed on a great deal of his fun-loving nature, his devotion to children, and his love of the countryside, to George in particular. And so it was these traits, rather than the business acumen shown by so many of the Wilsons, that were to mould George's own values in life.

The purpose of this background information concerning the earlier Wilson generations that led up to the birth of George Wilson is intended to give some 'colour', and maybe introduce to what follows a bit more of an understanding of what influenced the inherent nature of the artist.

For instance, it will be deduced that Wilson's family were certainly by no means impoverished. Indeed, they were quite considerable farmers in their own right. They were held in very high esteem not only by their masters, the Earls of Findlater and Seafield, but also by the Estate's, and their own, numerous tenants. So strong, indeed, was this regard that the family is still remembered among the tenants' descendants over a hundred years after George Wilson's eldest brother John left the area to become instead Factor to the Duke of Richmond and Gordon's estates in Huntly, Aberdeenshire.

The Wilsons eventually left Tochieneal in 1871, but only after a change in succession within the Seafield line that had caused a breakdown in their long-standing and mutually respected relationship. One of the final straws was the singularly unreasonable objection by the new Countess to the location of a distillery on their lands – backed up by a sudden doubling of the rent! In canny anticipation of this, 'Uncle Sandy' Wilson had in fact, the year before, already started building a new and much larger malt whisky distillery, to be called Inchgower (as it still is today), no more than seven miles to the west, just outside the pretty fishing port of Buckie.

Inchgower remained in the Wilson family hands until 1936 when, during the Depression, the distillery stocks of 120,000 gallons of maturing pure malt whisky were sold off, while the distillery itself was also sold for its water rights (in theory) to Buckie District Council, who promptly sold it on to distillers Arthur Bell & Co – in whose hands it still remains today.

One consequence of his family's comparative prosperity was that George Wilson was afforded a very good education from an early age, and, despite making very few if any demands upon his family throughout his life, he always had the valuable comfort of knowing that he would never have to worry if the worst came to the worst. He also had the benefit of numerous relatives' houses in which to stay when he returned home – as he did, regularly each year – to his beloved Aberdeen and Banffshire.

There is an interesting Moray region news cutting dated Saturday, 8th July 1882,[15] which indicates the extent to which George Wilson had already by then become recognised locally for the quality of his artistic depiction of local scenes. There is an evident local parochialism displayed in this article – which recounts the events surrounding the neighbourhood annual Games held on the Letterfourie Estate of Sir Robert Gordon – immediate neighbour to George Wilson's brother James, who was by then running the Inchgower distillery – and with whom George frequently stayed in order to paint in the area. The article states:

> *Due largely to the encouragement of Sir Robert, and his amiable sister, Miss Gordon, the annual Drybridge gathering was held this afternoon, amongst the rich foliage green of the valley that skirts Letterfourie woods, from the Hamlet of Drybridge, Buckie, towards Linnhouse. Beautiful scenery all over Sir Robert's old policies*, and better than can be described. Mr Wilson, brother of the respected proprietor of the Inchgower Distillery, is deemed the only painter who has succeeded in conveying to canvas, anything like it's [sic] natural beauty.*

This was a typical accolade in relation to his landscape painting, which was to be repeated throughout Wilson's far-too-short career.

George Wilson was the seventh son and third youngest child within a family of 13 children. He was educated first at the local school in Cullen, then at the highly renowned Gymnasium, Old Aberdeen, under its doyen, Dr Anderson. Although there was no previous history of serious painting in the family before him, it seems that from an early age he showed a desire not simply to paint, but to make painting his life. Thus, in 1865, while still aged 16, he enrolled at Edinburgh University to study Arts. He had just turned 17 when the university year started and he is recorded as having spent the next three years studying there – although there is no record existing to confirm his date of graduation from the university.[16]

Following his time at Edinburgh, and having by then crystallised his aim in life, in the late summer of 1868, at the age of 19, he went to London and entered Thomas Heatherley's School of Fine Art, then situated at 79, Newman Street – an area of London that was to become a focal part of his life over many years. It is not known where he discovered the contact for Heatherley's, but possibly it was directly through advice from

---

* 'Policies' is a Scottish term for the grounds that are attached to a large country house, equating broadly to 'estate'.

Edinburgh University. Whatever the stimulation for the choice, for a multitude of reasons, he could not have entered a more appropriate school.

It was through his time at Heatherley's, and his relationship with the group of friends that he met there, that his outlook and his raison d'être throughout his short life would become moulded. Indeed, it is only through his early association with those friends – and the fact that they 'adopted' this quiet and unassuming young Scot into their fold – that we have much at all in the way of an account of his life. Indeed, one of his friends in particular, John Butler Yeats, had just three years earlier, on 13th June 1865, become father of the son who would turn out to be one of the greatest names in Irish literature, William Butler Yeats. Without the correspondence, writings and archives of the Yeats family from that era, much of the earlier insight into Wilson's life as an art student, and his post-student life, would have been missing – and with it much of the insight into those informative days.

It must have been a fascinating, perhaps even quite daunting, period in which to be contemplating entering the creative world or art. The Pre-Raphaelite movement, one way or another, still much influenced the artistic world, although the original P.R.B. – the Pre-Raphaelite Brotherhood – had dissolved as an active group some 16 years earlier. Indeed, George Wilson had only been born just three months after the P.R.B. was first founded in the Millais family's house in Gower Street, London.

There were, though, many other influential movements that had either selectively diluted, or redefined to their own ends, the earlier P.R.B. influence that had once rocked – or at least aimed to rock – the established art circles half a generation earlier. At the same time, there was a continuing strong second phase of Pre-Raphaelitism that had commenced towards the end of the 1850s, largely through the influence of Rossetti. Then finally, there was the even wider gamut of followers of Pre-Raphaelitism headed by artists such as Edward Burne-Jones and John Waterhouse (1849-1917).

When Wilson arrived at Heatherley's, he found an established group of young artist friends who had taken their places a year or more before him, and who were already developing a clique based on the mutual interests of debate and poetry – as well as their art. Although he was between five and ten years younger than all but one of them, they seem to have responded quickly to the appealing personality of the new arrival.

The 'Brotherhood', as some of the closer friends within the older group had started to refer to themselves in conversation, consisted originally of John Butler Yeats, John Trivett Nettleship, Edwin John Ellis and Sydney Prior Hall (1842–1922). Hall left very early on and was immediately replaced by the rather younger George Wilson.

The other painter friends who intermingled with the group at the time, but who were never so closely involved, included Samuel Butler (1835–1902); Thomas William Gale Butler (exhib. 1874); Frank Potter (1845–1887), and Robert Catterson Smith (1853-1938).

Of the latter group, the oldest, who was eventually to become quite renowned as a writer, although rather less so as a painter, was Samuel Butler. He had the perceived privilege of being educated at the English public school of Shrewsbury and at Cambridge, and was a wealthy man in his own right. He was destined to join the church, but refused ordination on the grounds of religious doubt. Although he always wanted to devote his life to painting, music and writing, after the falling-out with his father over his planned ordination, he initially went to New Zealand to be as far away from his father's influence as possible. There, somewhat obliquely, he became a successful sheep farmer.

Samuel Butler returned from New Zealand in 1864, and enrolled initially at Cary's Art School prior to Heatherley's, then eventually at the South Kensington Art Schools. He was consequently somewhat older than most of his peers at Heatherley's and tended to sit rather critically outside the group. According to J.B. Yeats, for a while there was a close bond between Samuel Butler and George Wilson, although the latter was 13 years Butler's junior. But Yeats added 'I fancy the shy Scot kept away from the Iconoclast--'. [17] He was probably right; since it is unlikely that Wilson's strong traditional Presbyterianism would have permitted him even to consider debating Butler's radical doubts about the Resurrection.*

Now best known for his satirical novels attacking Victorian life, such as *Erewhon* (1872) and *The Way of All Flesh* (begun in 1874, but published posthumously in 1903), he did also exhibit a dozen or so of his paintings at the Royal Academy between 1869 and 1876. Of these, undoubtedly the best-known is *Mr Heatherley's Holiday: An Incident in Studio Life* (Tate Gallery, London, 1874). Although this time Butler had created the work in paint, it was yet another merciless satirical critique. The painting depicts the Antiques Room at the eminent art teacher's studio, portrayed as being crammed full of inanimate objects, amongst which a gloomy-looking Heatherley is tinkering to repair a skeleton.

Butler's point was that even during a holiday, Heatherley would never leave his school, but used the time for such mundane tasks as this. Once when he had to go out of town on business and did not return till the following day, one of the students asked him how he had got on, saying that no doubt he had enjoyed the change and that he must have found it refreshing to sleep for once out of London. 'No,' said Heatherley, 'I did not like it. Country air has no body.' [18] Nevertheless, and although the painting portrays a rather depressing impression of the reputable old teacher's personal lifestyle, it also very much belies the remarkable number of fine artists to have emerged from the school over the preceding years. These included Millais, Rossetti, Burne-Jones and Frederic, Lord Leighton (1830-1896) – and, of course, Sir Edward John Poynter Bt. PRA (1836-1919), who would shortly become the first Slade Professor of Fine Art when the Slade school opened its doors in October 1871.

Of Thomas Butler, little is known. He exhibited *The Sonnet* at the RA in 1874 (whereabouts no longer known), and is referred to in Henry Festing Jones's edited *Notebooks of Samuel Butler*, first published in 1912. In this book, there is included

---

* Samuel Butler had written his pamphlet *The Evidence for the Resurrection of Jesus Christ... Critically Examined* in 1865, in which he offered the conclusion that Christ had merely fallen unconscious and had not died upon the cross. Butler was about to provide a further ironical setting for this matter, a year or so later in 1873, in his publication *The Fair Haven*.

a letter from Samuel Butler to his colleague Thomas Butler on the subject of human reproduction, dated February 18th 1876, which commences *My Dear Namesake...*! Butler also quotes Heatherley in *Notebooks*: 'Any man, as old Heatherley used to say, will go on improving as long as he is bona fide dissatisfied with his work.' [19] This was a maxim with which J.B. Yeats, and Wilson probably more so, evidently found it quite easy to comply.

Frank Potter went on from Heatherley's to the Royal Academy schools, but it is not known if he departed again quite as quickly as so many of his friends. He became a member of the Royal Society of British Artists (RBA) in 1877, but his work never gained the recognition it deserved within his lifetime. He exhibited regularly in London, including the RA, and at a memorial exhibition at the RBA in Sussex Street in 1887, Samuel Butler was the buyer of many of his paintings. *Little Dormouse* is possibly his best known work and, according to W.B. Yeats, this hung for a while in the Yeats household. This, along with *Girl Resting at a Piano* and six other works of children and young women mainly in listless poses, now all reside in the Tate Gallery, London.

The model in the somewhat 'Whistleresque' *Girl Resting at a Piano* is in fact Potter's fiancée, Ellen (Nelly) Whelan, who also sat occasionally to J.B. Yeats (and presumably to others as well) around 1870 – including for the chalk study and the gouache painting *Pippa Passes* q.v.[20] (both in the National Gallery of Ireland).

Robert Catterson Smith had a more enduring relationship with several of the group, and also with one of their staunchest supporters and patrons – Dr John Todhunter, the Irish playwright. Catterson Smith greatly admired George Wilson's watercolour work in particular, as he himself also painted woodland landscapes. Born in Dublin into an artistic family on 24th February 1853, he was the son of the renowned Irish portrait painter, Stephen Catterson Smith Snr (1806-1872) and Anne Wyke, a miniaturist; while Stephen Jnr (1849–1912) – also a portrait painter – was his brother. Little is known about Robert Catterson Smith's early life except from his brief correspondence, but he exhibited quite frequently at the RA and the RBA between 1880 and 1890.

There was an interesting anomaly in the relationship between the various members of the Catterson Smith family and J.B. Yeats, the principle Irish member of the Heatherley group. Although Robert always remained a good friend to all of the group, his father and his brother, in particular, became loathed personal antagonists towards Yeats when he returned to Dublin during the early 1900s – for no very obvious reason. Stephen (the elder) had been President of the Royal Hibernian Academy and while his son, also Stephen, aspired similarly to this high office, the machinations of the family around various affairs of the art world in Dublin appear to have been well known by most of Dublin society.[21] It was perhaps prudent of Robert to have remained well out of the way in England.

Towards the end of the century, Robert Catterson Smith taught at Central School of Arts and Crafts in London and became associated with William Morris and the Kelmscott Press, where in 1896 he played a critical rôle in the production of that press's greatest triumph, the *Kelmscott Chaucer*. His essential part is often overlooked in that he had to interpret and produce black and white illustrations from the pencil designs by

Edward Burne-Jones, so that these could be transferred to wood blocks for engraving. His interpretation was therefore critical to the success of the result.

By then firmly entrenched in the Arts and Crafts ethos, Catterson Smith headed for the Birmingham School of Art, firstly to become Head of the Vittoria Street branch school for jewellery and silversmiths, but then in 1903 to become overall Head of the School of Art – a post that he was to hold for 17 years.

Birmingham and its surrounds had become accepted by the mid 1800s as a centre for Pre-Raphaelite interest, and the Ruskinian philosophy prospered largely through the active support of wealthy industrialists who were equally influential philanthropists. Likewise, the Arts and Crafts movement flourished in the early 1900s and the Birmingham School of Art under Robert Catterson Smith was a central instrumental force in what loosely became known as the 'Birmingham School'. In 1902, he had co-founded The Craftsman's Club, which had the objective of establishing a high standard of craftsmanship in Birmingham. Only men could be members and they had to be established practicing artists or craftsman with the right credentials and who strictly pursued the Arts and Crafts ethos.

Over the following years, however, Catterson Smith moved towards the development of a system of teaching that advocated the use of mind, memory and visualisation by his students. They were encouraged to draw from memory with their eyes shut, after having been allowed to view lantern-slides for just a few moments. It was not a new technique, and had interesting connotations that harked back to the on-going rumbling undercurrents against the prescribed teachings of the Royal Academy Schools. While Catterson Smith developed the 'shut-eye' idea further, it was one of his students, Marion Richardson (1892-1946), who, with the active support of Roger Fry (1866-1934), the post-impressionist painter and critic, took her pioneering 'child-centred approach' to art education not only into her own teaching, but eventually came to influence many others all around the world.

Robert Catterson Smith held the Headship of the Birmingham School of Art until his retirement in 1920, when he moved to Twickenham. He eventually died there in 1938 at the age of 85 years.[22]

CHAPTER THREE

The Heatherley 'Brotherhood' – 1869

The first days of the new 'Brotherhood' were as an informal association, of which Sydney Hall was one of the four original members. But Hall only remained until the end of 1869, by which time he had found regular work as an illustrator, and so George Wilson was quickly asked to fill the slot.[23] Hall's departure was probably providential in more than one way, as it is likely that there would have been some heady clashes later on, since he found J.T. Nettleship particularly difficult. Nettleship did indeed seem to be the most secure and confident member of the group, but Yeats always felt that their relationship was far from secure or easy. He felt that Ellis showed gentlemanly aspirations of *noblesse oblige* and that although Wilson was outwardly very reserved, there was also a strangely sensitive pride hidden behind that reserve. But in Nettleship's case it was a simple pride in himself and everything he did. Yeats felt that he had a lofty conception of himself, plus an exaggerated sense of his own identity. He always looked calm and serious and he seldom laughed. Yet even when he did ever laugh, then his eyes failed to laugh with him. It is not surprising then that Burne-Jones should have christened him as 'His Nettleship'.[24]

In the same vein, Hall had on one occasion asked Yeats what sort of a man was Lewis Nettleship (Richard Lewis), an Oxford Don and one of J.T. Nettleship's brothers; but before Yeats could reply, Hall cut him short by further demanding if the brother was, 'as near a relation to God Almighty as Jack Nettleship?'[25] Sydney Hall went on to become a renowned portrait painter, whose commissions included the Royal Family, and who on one occasion accompanied the Prince of Wales on his visit to India.

J.B. Yeats wrote in his manuscript *Memoirs* (in October 1918) that although the enduring four of the Brotherhood sat together at art school and gathered together every Saturday evening at his house, it was entirely wrong to think that they ever attempted to paint alike or talk alike. Each was jealous of his individuality and they cherished a sort of mutual aloofness, only they considered that they and they alone knew of the close connection between art and life. He added that three of the four of them had come out of their respective constricting backgrounds – or 'prisons' as Yeats called them –

'Wilson from Scotch Presbyterianism, Yeats from the teaching of J.S. Mill, and Ellis from conventional society.' [26]

Of the eventual four core members of the Brotherhood, John Butler Yeats was the oldest. He came from an established Irish family from the village of Drumcliff in County Sligo, Ireland, although he was born on March 16th 1839 in the parish of Tullylish in County Down, where his father, the Reverend William Butler Yeats, was Rector of the Church of Ireland. After a relaxed early village schooling, he was sent off to boarding school with his two younger brothers; first within a strict puritanical régime near Liverpool, and later to the Atholl Academy, 'ruled by the rod' by a Scottish Calvinist schoolmaster on the Isle of Man. It was here that he first met two brothers by the name of Pollexfen, who also came from his own family's native Sligo.[27]

He entered Trinity College, Dublin, in November 1857, from where he graduated without distinction in spring 1862. He determined to become a barrister and so enrolled at King's Inns to begin his studies. In September of that year, he decided to visit his old Pollexfen school friends in Sligo, where he met and immediately became enchanted by their sister, Susan. Within a fortnight, they had become engaged, and she eventually became his wife twelve months later. [28] Within three years, on June 13th 1865 – a date destined to have a momentous impact on Anglo-Irish literature – Susan Pollexfen Yeats gave birth to her first child, a son to be christened William Butler Yeats.

In January 1866, J.B. Yeats was admitted to the bar; however, he never took to court life. Within a year, and after getting into trouble for drawing satirical sketches in the courtrooms, he had taken the decision that was to change his and his family's lives forever.

At Trinity College, Yeats had met many friends with whom he remained close. Throughout his studies, he had always found debate and intellectual conversation far more attractive than the work in hand. He also took much greater interest in his sketchbook than in his law-books.[29] In particular, he became close friends with the two Dowden brothers, John and Edward, and also with John Todhunter. Within this group, he found the inspiration for the conversation and discussion for which he continually yearned.

John Todhunter was almost the same age as Yeats, having been born on 30th December 1839, the son of a Quaker family; but he arrived at Trinity College four years after Yeats, having first tried a business career in Dublin. He had subsequently decided upon a career in medicine and entered the Medical School at Trinity College, where he gained his Batchelor of Medicine in 1867 and received his Doctorate in 1871. However, in the intervening years, he had developed a love of opera and verse, and for three successive years between 1864 and 1866 he won the Vice-Chancellor's prize for English verse. In 1870, and even before he had completed his medical training, he took up the post of Professor of English Literature at Alexandra College, Dublin, although after four years he had resigned the post to travel in Europe. During this period and whilst he always longed to be a writer or artist, he took up post-graduate medicine in order to earn a living.

Of the two Dowden brothers, John was committed to the church, eventually becoming Bishop of Edinburgh, where he died in 1910. The rather less clerical Edward Dowden was the much closer friend to Yeats throughout his life. His destiny was to follow a literary career, as critic, poet and professor – at one time holding two chairs simultaneously at Trinity College, Dublin. Edward Dowden died in 1913.

It was Todhunter and Edward Dowden who persuaded Yeats to send some of his sketches to Tom Hood, editor of *Fun* magazine in London. Hood responded positively and accepted some of his drawings for the magazine. In March 1867, and in the face of quite understandably open hostility from his wife and her family, J.B. Yeats took the enormous decision to give up his legal work, and departed alone for London, where he enrolled at Heatherley's Art School to 'learn his trade'. He took a six year lease on a house at 23, Fitzroy Road in north London*, where his wife Susan, pregnant once again and accompanied by her (by then) two children, very reluctantly joined him in July of that year.[30]

Yeats at this time had a small but invaluable income from inherited rental property back in Ireland. Unfortunately, because he enjoyed his attendance at Heatherley's so much, he failed to attempt to augment this modest income by continuing his wood-block illustration work for Tom Hood. However, the indecision that was to plague him for the whole of his life was also already beginning to show, as he had begun questioning if art was his real strength and so had started to write autobiographical fiction – which he stated he would also illustrate.

More than once, contemporary account has related a tale that well illustrates Yeats's indecision as to when a painting might indeed be deemed finished. This anecdote tells of a time when he, along with a number of other landscape-painters, used to stay at Burnham Beeches with an elderly couple by the name of Mr. and Mrs. Earle. Yeats is described as having started in the spring of 1876 to paint a pond nearby the Slough to Farnham road. He carried on painting it all through the year, and every time the season changed, then so did the picture need to be changed as well. He eventually gave it up as unfinished once he had painted in the winter snow covering. He just could not be satisfied that he had the painting right.[31]

The first two new friends in whom Yeats took a close interest at Heatherley's were John Trivett Nettleship and Edwin John Ellis, and both were to remain a fascination to him for the rest of his life. Although contact with Nettleship fragmented somewhat after their Heatherley days, Ellis – much more an aspiring poet and a critic than a committed artist – was eventually to transfer his allegiance towards the late 1880's by becoming a closer associate to J.B. Yeats's son William Butler Yeats. Apart from his evident preference for the literary side of life, the fact that J.B. Yeats was ten years older than Ellis, who was thereby only 15 years older than William, might have contributed to this migration of interest.

---

*   Although the Fitzroy Road address was the Yeats family's first home in London, it was by no means the most significant as far as the young W.B. Yeats was concerned. However, it is this house which today carries the official blue historic plaque denoting it to have been his home in London.

Because of this latter association, a lot more has been recorded about Ellis than perhaps his achievements or qualities warranted; but nevertheless, the available information is very largely related to his literary rather than his artistic career. Ellis came from a well-to-do family, and was the son of Dr Alexander John Ellis, an affable and erudite phonetician and mathematician who held a long association with Isaac Pitman, the inventor of stenography and shorthand. However, it seems that Edwin Ellis was driven more by the desire for recognition and financial reward than he was by artistic merit through achievement. In enduring terms, he unfortunately seems largely to have failed in both. During the 1890s he published several collections of poetry and occasionally reviewed art exhibitions for *The Studio*. Certainly, Ellis was well respected by W.B. Yeats as a poet and intellectual commentator, and he received continuing support from Yeats for his poetic works well into the new century, when Yeats included one of Ellis's poems in the 1936 edition of the *Oxford Book of English Verse*.

Ellis's main obsession was with Blake, and although (as with Nettleship) this also influenced his early drawing, arguably his best known and most substantial production was a literary one entitled *The Works of William Blake, Poetic, Symbolic and Critical*.[32] This accomplishment was a three-volume edition of the works of Blake with commentary, which he published together with Yeats in 1893 after four years of extensive and original research. Later, in 1907, he published one further work on Blake, entitled *The Real Blake: A Portrait Biography*,[33] and during the early 1900s he produced a number of other miscellaneous minor works.

J.B. Yeats observed in his manuscript *Memoirs* that he was continuously bemused as to why Ellis did not fulfil his promised brilliant potential. He presumed that it was because he lacked both ambition and application. Ellis not only loved the English poets, but was enamoured with Dante whom he read constantly. He left Yeats in awe of his ability to translate Dante's original Italian into what seemed to Yeats to be brilliant English verse. However, he seemed to be stuck between his two worlds: he neglected his work in art school in order to read and study literature, but then neglected literature so that he might work in the art school.[34]

This succinct observation by Yeats went on to attribute Ellis's failure to succeed to this divided dedication. He suggested that when he painted and found that his work did not please his friends or, indeed, his own judgement, then he simply lost interest. It seems that this view of Ellis as a very clever fellow, yet foolish in his studies was shared by many of his fellow-students. However, Ellis did continue to paint, at least into the late 1880's when he exhibited *A Dance* (present whereabouts not known) at the Royal Academy in 1888. He also travelled widely through Europe, and visited Egypt on at least two occasions – in October 1876, and again in February 1880. This latter interest in Egypt may well have been inspired by the general Victorian enthusiasm of the time towards *Orientalism*. Certainly, there are a significant number of pencil sketches of Egyptian figures and scenes dating from this period within the Ellis archive of the Special Collections at Reading University Library.

J.B. Yeats's son, William commented further on Ellis's persona somewhat later in *The Trembling of the Veil* with the comment that:

The mind is known to attain, in certain conditions of trance, a quickness so extraordinary that we are compelled at times to imagine a condition of unendurable intellectual intensity, from which we are saved by the merciful stupidity of the body; & the mind of Edwin Ellis was constantly upon the edge of trance[35]

Tracing painted or drawn works by Ellis today has proved to be more than a little difficult. The Special Collections at Reading University Library hold an archive on Ellis that mainly contains literary correspondence and Blake-related manuscripts recovered from Germany after he died; but there is also a portfolio of generally quite early drawings and just one or two watercolour and oil sketches. There is one drawing reproduced here that is clearly influenced by Blake (and even, perhaps, by Nettleship's early work) and, although it bears no title, it appears to display significant elements of quite erotic symbolism. The drawing is signed and dated 1872, which means that it must have been drawn shortly after Ellis's return from Italy following the death of his first young wife.

Subject unknown. A Blake-inspired pencil drawing by Edwin John Ellis, signed and dated 1872. 10 in x 7 in (255 mm x 178 mm). Reading University Library.

Although Ellis's return coincided precisely with his earlier colleagues' entry into the Slade, Ellis is not recorded as having entered that school himself, and it is not known if he continued studying, or where he was living at this time. Nevertheless, the quality of the second pencil line drawing reproduced here shows Ellis to have been a rather more accomplished draughtsman than J.B. Yeats had implied. Indeed, amongst the Reading drawings, there are a number of sketches that indicate that Ellis's tendency was towards a clear and skilful use of the single line to depict what he wanted. This is a very different approach to the teaching of Poynter, for instance, and somewhat more akin to the illustrative style of his contemporary, at least by age, Kate Greenaway (1846-1901).

Unfortunately, the Reading portfolio chiefly only contains a quantity of pen or pencil figure sketches in Egyptian or classical attire, and an apparent high propensity that Ellis seems to have displayed for drawing cherubs and cupids! There is only a very small number of watercolour sketches – all of which display some naïvety – plus two insignificant oil works of no real value in helping to identify Ellis's modus operandi or oeuvre. What happened to his one and only submission to the RA in 1888 is not known.

In painting terms today, there is unfortunately a continual tendency to confuse Edwin John Ellis with his namesake, Edwin Ellis of Nottingham (1841-1895) – who was a far more prolific, and very different artist renowned for his shoreland and fishing seascapes. Edwin John also had a brother, Tristram J. Ellis, who is somewhat better recognised today. Having started out as an engineer

Subject unknown. Pencil drawing on lightweight paper by Edwin John Ellis. 7 in x 4½ in (178 mm x 114 mm), uneven. Reading University Library.

in London, Tristram Ellis went to study under Léon Bonnat (1833-1922), in Paris, and then travelled widely before eventually returning to paint and exhibit regularly in London. Undoubtedly well known to the Heatherley group, he was however never closely associated with them, although he did at one time share a studio with Yeats in the late 1870's. Yeats, however, thoroughly disapproved of Tristram Ellis's abandonment of 'serious painting' for the allure of easy sales through exhibiting what the Royal Academy wanted to show – which indeed he did, and with no mean success, for many years.[36]

With reference to those early Heatherley days, Yeats intimated (somewhat curiously in view of Ellis's own passion for Blake) that whereas Nettleship was so strongly influenced by Blake, Edwin Ellis would be 'enchanted' to discover in any model of his own perhaps just some of the elements of a Rossetti model – whether with the renowned red hair, cupid-bow lips or the columnar throat. There also followed the first intimation by Yeats of his own ultimate destiny in (eventual) painting success, in that he aimed to keep as close as possible to 'accurate portraiture' – avoiding *imaginative influences*. He further felt that Wilson was of the same way of thinking in that he was the only one of their group able to put aside any thought of a model's face or personality, so as to devote his whole attention

to the modelling of the figure. In retrospect, Yeats felt sure that Wilson was indeed right and that purely as a student, he was clearly the best among them. He said he believed (somewhat eulogistically) that had Wilson lived rather longer then they would all have fallen in line with what he was aiming to achieve and would have recognised him as being the 'master'.[37]

Although 10 years his junior, Edwin Ellis quickly became attached to Yeats, and began to exert an influence on his life. Ellis was living at that time with his parents in Argyll Road, Kensington, but he started to become an ever more frequent visitor to Fitzroy Road, where they conducted long and profound discussions about art and poetry. This annoyed Susan Yeats immensely. She did not like Ellis one bit – and he was evidently remarkably rude to her, usually totally ignoring her whilst he talked directly to her husband, often till so late at night that he would have to stay at the Yeats household overnight.[38]

However, in 1870, some relief arrived when Ellis suddenly left for Italy to become married. He only stayed away about a couple of years however, since his wife died equally suddenly and he returned home once again.[39] Ellis did marry again later, but, as with John Todhunter, his second wife – a German lady – appears to have been made of much sterner and more possessive stuff, so, and again like Todhunter, it was partly to escape this domineering environment that Ellis willingly became engrossed with the young, and very talkative, W.B. Yeats. He found his old friend's son to have many interests after his own heart, and very shortly they were to become engrossed in the study of Blake's mystical poetry.

The latter years of Ellis's life are not very clear, but he had moved to Germany before the First World War, where he lived with his second wife in her birthplace of Seeheim, and where he died in November 1916, during the height of the Great War. At his interment, a brief but rather over-eulogistic obituary address was given by his friend, the art deco influenced artist and sculptor, Dr Daniel Greiner (1872-1943). The address was evidently politically motivated by the fury of the war and painted Ellis as having somewhat anti-British views and that 'he did not belong to the England that now wages this terrible war against us'! Greiner also appeared to be somewhat curiously informed in continuing that Ellis 'belonged to the old England of Carlyle, that made pilgrimages to Germany as the land of Goethe and Schiller, whom he himself particularly loved.[40] So no mention of Blake or Yeats; and one wonders also perhaps what Yeats himself might have made of the anti-British political innuendos of the address at such a time, having just published his own poem *Easter, 1916*!

Of all his Heatherley colleagues, though, it was J.T. Nettleship who appears to have fascinated J.B. Yeats the most. Although it seems from his early comments that he did not at first take to Nettleship's haughty bearing, he very soon came to admire his work. Indeed, he referred to Nettleship more than once as 'a genius'. He considered that one of his early designs of 1868, the now believed lost work called *God Creating Evil*, was the grandest and most profound concept that he had ever seen. And he was not alone in this praise, as Rossetti had similarly admired the design.[41]

But, as he admitted in his unpublished *Memoirs*, Yeats found that his relations with Nettleship were always 'uneasy and precarious'. To illustrate this, he recorded one most unfortunate incident that had occurred a year or so later, and which he feared neither he nor Nettleship would ever forget – although undoubtedly Nettleship most certainly would have done so: Yeats was always short of money, and Wilson and Ellis had proposed a visit to the opera that evening, but Yeats of course had no money. However, only a few days beforehand, he had made Nettleship a loan of £5 (a significant sum to the young artists at that time) and so he decided to ask for it back – walking especially around to Nettleship's lodging for the purpose. Nettleship was immediately delighted to see them, they having gone some distance out of their way to visit – until Yeats made his request, whereupon Nettleship went straightaway to fetch the money; but all his pleasure at their meeting was immediately destroyed – as was that of Yeats, particularly since he had in any case very little interest in opera.[42]

* * *

So, to return to the evolving relationships within this Heatherley group; it was into this circle of developing friendships, yet with widely differing personalities, that the new fourth member, the 19-year old George Wilson, inadvertently dropped in the late summer of 1868. He had left Edinburgh University in July of that year, and after briefly returning home to Cullen, he somewhat bravely uprooted himself permanently from his close-knit family ties and migrated to London to further his artistic career.

It is not recorded where Wilson stayed when he first arrived in London, but his close first cousin, Jessie Scott (née Thurburn) had recently married and was at the time living, rather conveniently, at No. 1, The Chestnuts, Branch Hill, near Hampstead Heath, an area that was popular with many of the artistic community at that time. It would have been an opportunity unlikely to have been missed, and an obvious secure base from which the young highland Scot could start out on what must have been, to begin with at least, a bewilderingly alien life in London.

Jessie Thurburn had married Russell Scott, the elder brother of C.P. Scott, the much-acclaimed proprietor of the Manchester Guardian.[43] George Wilson and Russell Scott remained good friends throughout his life and, at the request of the Wilson family, the latter acted as George's *de facto* executor to his affairs (he left no will or instructions) after he died.

Upon arrival in London, Wilson immediately entered Thomas Heatherley's Art School and had been there, working quietly for the best part of a year before he was also befriended, in 1869, by Edwin Ellis. Ellis invited him for coffee at his family home in Argyll Road, and Wilson is reported to have been moved by Ellis's poetry.[44] Ellis had been born in 1848, the same year as Wilson, and so was the only one of the group clearly of his own age. Thus, when Sydney Hall found regular work as an illustrator and left the group, at Ellis's suggestion, George Wilson fitted naturally into his place.

In stark contrast to Ellis's father, Alexander, who is described as having been of a thoughtful, sociable, and affable disposition, and who was entirely modest about his considerable erudition, his son, Edwin, appears to have been of a very brash nature – despite evidently having an effervescent intellect, which endeared him greatly to Yeats.

And, initially at least, it was only Yeats's great enthusiasm for him that persuaded his other friends to put up with his obnoxiousness.

Yet, Ellis seems to have taken somehow to Wilson – who could not have been more different in character. Perhaps it was a question of 'opposites attract', however, Wilson was also becoming more and more entranced by the poetry of Blake and the other poets who so influenced his new friends, and so he was probably an appealingly attentive listener. There was an interesting admix of characters within the group: There was a literary or poetic artist from each age group present in Nettleship and Ellis, and also a dedicated artist (albeit both dramatically influenced by poetry) from each age group in Yeats and Wilson.

With reference to what Yeats referred to as 'our intellectual equipment', he commented that whilst Nettleship had a complete and detailed knowledge of Browning, and Ellis had a very extensive but quite inaccurate knowledge of many poets, he himself only 'knew thoroughly the writings of J.S. Mill'. And he added, 'and what did Wilson know?' then went on to relate an anecdote told him directly by Wilson concerning his student days at Edinburgh University. Accounts from George Wilson's life are few and far between, but this particular one was handed down as an entertaining family anecdote – presumably having amused Wilson enough to have related it to some of his closer family. It was also repeated by John Todhunter when he wrote his account of Wilson's life and work in *The English Illustrated Magazine* of August 1891, following his death: [45]

Apparently, while George Wilson had been lodging in Edinburgh when studying Fine Art at the University, he somewhat puzzled and (in Todhunter's words) 'scandalised' his landlady because she simply could not understand this quiet young gentleman. Although he was always reading his Bible, yet he seemed also to be addicted to drawing pictures of naked men and women, which, to her horror, stared her in the face from all around the room, whenever she came in. And as Yeats added in answer to his own earlier question, 'He knew not only the Bible, being a constant student of Shelley;' and then, 'Notwithstanding his interest in drawing naked women ... None of us, not even his intimate friend Nettleship, was able to discover a peticote [sic] in his lonely life, for lonely it was, and spare and ascetic.'[46] However, it has become apparent that Wilson formed at least one very loyal, albeit that we don't know quite how close, female relationship with the model who was to sit to him for many years hence.

Yeats's reference to Wilson's 'intimate friend Nettleship' was written much later on in his unpublished 1918 *Memoirs*, but still refers to their early student and immediately subsequent days. It is interesting that this close bond was recognised at such an early date, and it shows that Wilson (the quietest and most reserved of the lot) had somehow broken through the legendary Nettleship aura. It also endorses W.B. Yeats's comment not long afterwards that he had actually found Nettleship to be proud and shy.

Wilson was indeed normally quiet and reserved, but when he did interject a comment, his remarks always carried the same succinct and sound sense that had held his forebears in Scotland in such good stead before him. Indeed, after a dinner held by Yeats in John Dowden's honour, and at which a couple of guests apparently didn't match up to Ellis's grandiose intellectual requirements, Ellis suggested that perhaps George Wilson should be substituted another time! [47]

Of the four painters who persisted within their group until it quietly dispersed, entirely without ceremony, between 1871 and 1872 (and after no longer a period than the original Pre-Raphaelite Brotherhood had, 21 years earlier), George Wilson appeared, understandably, to be the least self-assured. After all, he had, only a couple of years earlier at the age of just 19, migrated south from the still relatively obscure and somewhat wild and bleak farming region of Banffshire in northern Scotland to the already overcrowded hubbub of Victorian London.

Writing again for his 1918 *Memoirs*, J.B. Yeats reported that Ellis had once said (somewhat misguidedly, in the event) that Wilson would have to live to a great age, since he was completely 'indifferent to quick returns'. He added that he was a true artist – ambitious to the extent that he was continuously in pursuit of what he described as 'the ultimate picture'.[48] This reference to Wilson's perpetual dissatisfaction with the potentially finished picture identified a trait that he shared equally with Yeats – yet Wilson went further than that in his apparent total (and possibly naïve) lack of interest in any form of reward at all, whether through accolade or sales. Interestingly, Yeats also remarks in the same context that he 'never saw Wilson to be ill or tired as he worked along acquiring a technique of infinite subtlety' – which bears out Russell Scott's statement in a letter to Todhunter dated 22nd December 1890, several months after his friend's death, that he believed that Wilson managed successfully to hide the extent of his serious debility from all but those who persisted in taking an intimate interest.[49]

Yeats's recollection of the earlier facts is frequently variable. He continues his record that he remembers Wilson reading Shelley constantly, because of his admiration for what Yeats suggests is 'the Shelley Landscape' – and here he is partially correct, since interpretation of Shelley was a theme that Wilson returned to repeatedly. He described Wilson as having 'large beautiful eyes and his fingers were long and prehensile'. He found it a pleasure to watch Wilson at work on a picture, analysing and transcribing all the subtleties and intricacies in the model or subject before him every step of the way. However, he also added that this 'poor fellow' whom Ellis had said should live to a great age, and indeed dearly hoped for it himself, died when he was 'a little over 30'. Wilson was of course 41 when he died, but Yeats did share the generally accepted view that if he had lived to become 'an old artist', as they had all hoped, there was no doubt that he would have achieved 'an immense reputation'.[50]

It is not recorded which one of the Heatherley group first proposed adopting the name of the *Brotherhood*, but there is good reason to surmise that it was probably Nettleship – as it was not the first small clique with an inclusive name of which he had been a member. The friendship that Nettleship had formed rather earlier in 1866 with the two young poets, Arthur O'Shaughnessy and John Payne, they had jointly denominated as 'The Triumvirate'.[51] Regardless of who proposed the name of *Brotherhood*, it appears, ironically, that they all in fact believed that it was actually misleading. When Edward Dowden assumed that the group must have some fixed principles, it was Ellis who corrected him, pointing out that it was personal friendship and not dogma that bound them together:

The Brotherhood is really only a handful of men here in London, who hold opposite opinions, take each his solitary path in art, delight in the power and anxiously try to help on the progress of one another and are in a perpetual state of artistic civil war.[52]

Similarly, Yeats wrote to John Todhunter in November 1869 to contend that he was 'greatly in error' in describing them as a 'clique', adding that they all differed greatly from each other; that they were very universal in their enjoyment of pictures, of which every style was acceptable to them.[53]

Whilst Ellis mixed immature boorish behaviour and bad manners with an irrepressible vitality and great intellect, it was J.T. Nettleship who exerted an overall air of natural leadership within the group. Although two years younger than Yeats, he was much worldlier, with a forceful personality and great self-confidence: Yeats referred again in his *Memoirs* to Nettleship as having been their 'inspiration', largely because his nature revealed a level of fearlessness in the pursuit of his ideals and a worldliness that was beyond them all.[54] From around 1868 until 1874, he also had his own studio at 22, Newman Street, close to the art school at Heatherley's – something that Yeats and Ellis both longed for, and indeed eventually emulated in October 1869, when they also took a studio together at number 74, Newman Street. However, as usual, there was a lot more talking done than constructive painting and rather inevitably the two couldn't afford to keep up with the rent beyond nine months and had to give up the studio in June of the following year.[55] [56]

CHAPTER FOUR

J.B. Yeats and the Todhunter influence

John Todhunter, who was to become such an encouragement to Yeats over the years – but yet an even more devoted friend to George Wilson – had been pursuing his medical studies and literary interests in Dublin. However, his heart was not in medicine and he was keen to be in London himself, among what he perceived to be the hub of the literaryworld.

On one of his trips back home to Sligo to look after his family affairs, Yeats had called on Todhunter in Dublin to try to persuade him to move to London. Later that year, on his way to Vienna on a medical trip, Todhunter decided to call in to see Yeats in Fitzroy Road, where he also met Nettleship for the first time – and whose studio he visited on the following day. He also met Ellis whom, after some severe early reservations when he told Edward Dowden that he found Ellis's manners to be 'disgusting',[57] he eventually grew to like, if only for his lively intellect.

It was John Todhunter who gave Yeats his first serious commission, for the sum of ten pounds, in March 1869. The commission was to make a

John Butler Yeats from a photograph ca. 1875, as published in *Prodigal Father* (Murphy), p103 (see acknowledgements), from the collection of the late Michael Yeats.

watercolour drawing of *Pippa*, the character from Browning's poem, *Pippa Passes*, published in 1841 and set in the 14th Century in his beloved Asolo in northern Italy. Yeats decided to paint it in gouache on paper and, although he started work on the picture immediately and with great enthusiasm – but also, most importantly, with a five pounds deposit in his pocket to help him on the way – the commission was dogged with what had already become his stereotypical indecision and discontent with the results of his efforts.

'Pippa Passes' John Butler Yeats, 1870-72. Gouache on paper.
19 in x 13½ in (480 mm x 340 mm). National Gallery of Ireland.

Indeed, it seems to have taken the further payment of the remaining five pounds in mid 1870, and a great deal more correspondence on the subject, plus much reworking of the design, before *Pippa* was eventually deemed finished. Or at least it was sufficiently finished it seems to be hung one year later, in January 1871, in the Dudley Gallery's seventh winter exhibition of watercolour drawings. The added 'incentive' of a (possibly?) inadvertent comment to Edward Dowden (which was of course bound to get back to Todhunter) that it had already cost Yeats somewhat more to paint the picture than the £10 commission, may have helped to stimulate the early final payment.

However, although now exhibited, Yeats was still dissatisfied with the result and he retrieved the painting immediately after the exhibition and worked on it for a further year.

John Todhunter did not receive the finished work until April 1872.[58] Although evidently painted in a style that followed his early Pre-Raphaelite influenced training, *Pippa* seems somehow also to retain an element of the illustrative work that Yeats had commenced for Tom Hood when first he arrived in London.

In addition to negotiating continuous extensions in time throughout 1870 for his own commissioned painting, in June Yeats was also endeavouring to engineer a commission for Nettleship to undertake a work for Todhunter as well. It seems that Yeats was taking Nettleship's part as 'agent' (seemingly, with no little protective zeal!) whilst the latter was working studiously, *en plein air,* in parkland at Sevenoaks and later on in November on Dartmoor, following his acceptance by the Royal Academy Schools. Todhunter appears to have been angling to acquire a painting that Nettleship had proposed, entitled *Psyche* (now presumed lost), but Yeats made it quite clear that Nettleship intended this to be a 'significant' work in his career, so he couldn't possibly recommend him selling it for just the £5 offered![59]

There is a trend showing here in Todhunter's negotiations that may be entirely innocent, but which repeats itself on occasions and so has to be considered open to question. Although he was extremely philanthropic and generous in his support for certain artists, Todhunter obviously didn't like to miss an opportunity. This was made quite clear when he worked so hard effectively to 'manage' an exhibition of George Wilson's work during the last months of his life, and to engineer sales on Wilson's behalf.[60] George Wilson's brother, John, also had to make it clear to Todhunter that their mother was most unwilling to allow Todhunter to sell (or buy) the remaining works in Wilson's studio after he died.[61]

Nevertheless, by November back in 1870, Todhunter had moved into direct negotiation with Nettleship and appears to have agreed to purchase one work for the original £5 offered, plus the *Psyche* as well for a negotiable sum around its cost plus £10. Nettleship wrote to him from Ashburton, on the edge of Dartmoor, to thank him for the £5 in advance:

> ... - *First to despatch business, I will get the picture done for this £5 as soon as I can : you understand that at this moment and for the remaining months until March I must needs works [sic] at the Academy picture I have here. – As to the Psyche, I will paint it for £15, <u>or</u> : should it cost me more than £5 then £10 and whatever it costs. For <u>you</u> I will certainly do it for £15 and take the risk. Only please, as you are so very kind in interesting yourself for me, don't quote this, or the £5 picture, as usual prices : as I ought to ask a higher rate now, for animal pictures at least. You notice how mercenary I am becoming. Now damn business and let's get to pleasure. ...*

The 'pleasure' doesn't in fact appear to be very evident, as Nettleship then goes on to describe the difficulties he is having in getting a local builder to construct a timber shelter to house himself plus an enormous seven feet by five feet canvas for his 'Academy painting'. The builder failed to turn up during several initial fine weather days, and then proceeded to try to carry out the work 'in a tempest of wind and rain.'[62]

Yeats's *Pippa* is thought to have been the first painting that Todhunter had acquired from him, although over the years he was to become an occasional but faithful patron and collector of the works of both Yeats and Nettleship – though more particularly, and even more regularly, those of George Wilson. At the same time, he also purchased works from some other now rather better recognised artists of the period. One such known work that he purchased from Frederick Sandys was one of his many versions of the drawing entitled *Proud Maisie* (or *Maissie,* as spelt in Todhunter's version),[63] each modelled on the beautiful actress, Mary Jones, who was Sandys' model, mistress and mother of several of his children. Out of well over 100 paintings and drawings that were exhibited variously at the two retrospective exhibitions of George Wilson's work in 1893 and 1903, at least 20 were, over that period, in the ownership of John Todhunter, but it seems most unlikely that these represented the whole of his Wilson collection.

Regrettably though, it has been intimated from a number of separate sources (although the original source of the report may well be one and the same) that, tragically, Todhunter's whole extensive art collection may well have perished in a fire after his death. The collection must have been quite considerable by that time; however, there is no concrete evidence as to where or when the purported fire took place.

Todhunter's popular first wife, Katherine Gresley (née Ball), died in childbirth in March 1871, within the first year of their marriage, and he was left widowed with a baby son, Arthur Henry – who sadly also died just three years later in 1874. Todhunter was married again in 1879 to Dora Louisa (née Digby), and they moved into Bedford Park,

Dr. John Todhunter, from a photograph ca. 1893, as published in *Prodigal Father* (Murphy), p165 (see acknowledgements), from the collection of the late Mrs Joan Lambe.

the Arts and Crafts designed Mecca for artists and writers in London at that time, and where he built himself a house that he named 'Orchardcroft', after the road in which it stood, called The Orchard.

Unfortunately, his second wife – although she was said by those who met her to be a person who could match Todhunter's intelligence in every way – was an aggressive woman of highly assertive opinions, who made a strong and not always pleasant impression upon everyone she met. So much was this so that people started pointedly to avoid her, and along with her, regrettably, they ended up avoiding Todhunter as well.[64] It was in recollection of this period of Todhunter's life that W.B. Yeats referred to him (somewhat in contradiction to his own earlier literary relationship with him) as,

> ...a well-off man who had bought my father's pictures while my father was still Pre- Raphaelite. Once a Dublin doctor he was a poet and a writer of poetical plays: a tall, sallow, lank, melancholy man, a good scholar and a good intellect; and with him my father carried on a warm exasperated friendship, fed I think by old memories and wasted by quarrels over matters of opinion.[65]

The second Mrs Todhunter bore him three children. The eldest daughter, Edith, was followed by their only son, John, and then a second daughter, Margery . After the senior John Todhunter died in 1916, his wife stayed on at 'Orchardcroft' until around 1930, when the house was sold and she went to live with her youngest daughter, Margery, until Dora also died in 1935. The furniture from 'Orchardcroft' is reported via family account to have been stored in one of the familiar Army and Navy Stores repositories in London, and the submission from the family is that it could have been in a fire caused during the Second World War Blitz of London that all the furniture perished, including Todhunter's fine collection of pictures.[66] However – and it is only in a slender hope of possible reprieve – that event would have been nearly ten years after the furniture was first stored.

In some small support for this slender hope, it is of considerable relief that, through whatever possibly fortuitous quirk of fate, one painting from the collection, *Pippa Passes*, does indeed still exist and now resides safely in the National Gallery of Ireland in Dublin. It is not known how or when the painting may have passed out of Todhunter's collection, but since it remains one of only very few pictures from J.B. Yeats's early Pre-Raphaelite-influenced period, the fact that it has survived at all can only be deemed as extremely fortunate. In 1943, a Mr A.C. Hunt from Cheshire acquired the painting 'for quite a nominal sum' in a country village near Shrewsbury. In 1952, he offered it on loan to the Cheltenham Art Gallery, but 'after an agreeable talk with the Curator', the latter declined the offer and recommended that it should go to the National Gallery of Ireland. Mr Hunt eventually followed through this sound recommendation in October 1962.[67] This small painting, which measures just 19 in x 13½ in, was originally laid onto a wooden panel, from which it was removed in 1972.

Many pencil and chalk sketches, but very few paintings from Yeats's early days appear to have survived, and Hilary Pyle, in her book, Yeats, Portrait of an Artistic Family reproduces just two 'non-portrait' paintings from within the collection of The National Gallery of Ireland. These works are Pippa Passes and an un-named woodland landscape, again in gouache, dating from 1871 and believed to have been commissioned by Edward Dowding. With reference to this landscape, Hilary Pyle gives an interesting and perhaps somewhat surprising quote when recording that J.B. Yeats '...was justly admired for his portraits, but that he told his daughter years later, "I have always wished to be a landscape painter".' In respect of his early style, and whereas Nettleship's early work was heavily influenced by Blake, Hilary Pyle suggests that in Yeats's case

Study for 'Pippa Passes' by John Butler Yeats. 1870. Black chalk on cream paper 15 in x 13¾ in (380 mm x 350 mm), uneven. National Gallery of Ireland.

he 'never aimed for such heights of colour and sensuousness as Rossetti. His style at the time was more in the region of Watts's (George Frederic Watts, 1817-1904) best work, but with a puritan quality that gave it an air of individuality.' [68]

This latter statement is fully endorsed by the existence within the collection of the National Gallery of Ireland of the additional black chalk study for *Pippa*. Dr Pyle further suggests that the girl's flung-back head could show an influence of Rossetti's *Beata Beatrix* (of which Rossetti made six commercial copies in various media as well as the original now in the Tate Gallery, London) – which Yeats undoubtedly would have seen.[69] Interestingly, a further slight similarity of pose is also taken up by George Wilson in his somewhat later allegorical oil painting of *Asia* from Shelley's *Prometheus Unbound* – although, like Yeats's finished gouache of *Pippa*, the overall posture of *Asia* bears little relationship to Rossetti's composition.

Elsewhere, perhaps Wilson's *Asia* does bear more of a likeness in demeanour to that in the oil painting by Annie Swynnerton (1844-1933), entitled *Sense of Sight* (Walker Gallery, Liverpool), although this was painted many years later than *Asia,* in 1895.

Detail from Asia by George Wilson, ca. 1881-1884. Oil on canvas. Private collection

After his earlier two decades of theatrical successes and latterly his cooperation with W.B. Yeats towards 1890, and despite living almost next door to the Yeats family during their own latter years in Bedford Park, Todhunter maintained only somewhat sporadic contact with J.B. Yeats and his son W.B. Thereby inevitably he also had no more than limited contact with Edwin Ellis as well into the first few years of the new century. This was undoubtedly due in part to the irascible nature of the second Mrs Todhunter, but equally as well, the somewhat similar nature of the second Mrs Ellis. Furthermore, as Todhunter's plays diminished in popularity and largely failed to attract any acclaim during the 1890's, and as he personally developed a growing degree of senility towards the end of his life, he simply retreated into his very comfortably endowed home away from public life. He died there on 25th October, 1916 and was cremated at Golders Green.

Nevertheless, it is pleasing to know that in the next generation, J.B. Yeats's daughters, Lily and Lolly, did keep in touch with Todhunter's daughter, Margery. Enclosed within a pleasant letter that she received from Lily, dated 10th July 1939 and following shortly after her brother W.B.'s death, was a pencil sketch of John Todhunter entitled *Dr Todhunter as a Calumet*. [70]

Signed by J.B. Yeats and dated Feb. 4th 1901, the sketch was little more than a 'doodle' that was so typical of the hundreds of such spontaneous drawings that J.B. Yeats produced almost incessantly throughout his life. This little sketch had evidently been made very quickly during one of the

Dr Todhunter as a Calumet. Pencil sketch by John Butler Yeats, dated Feb. 4th 1901. Reading University Library. (Note: The term *'calumet'* may refer to a North American Indian peace-pipe – presumably adopted as the name for their conversation club in order to reflect upon the expected nature of their debating!) The drawing shows Todhunter looking somewhat more aged and drawn than in the previous photograph of ten years earlier.

conversation evenings of the informal 'Calumet Club', which met in alternating members' homes in Bedford Park on every other Sunday evening, starting at 9.00 or 10.00 p.m. and lasting through into the early hours of the following morning.

In contrast to Todhunter's early interest in J.T. Nettleship's more visionary and Blake-inspired work, his subsequent melodramatic animal paintings did not appeal to

Todhunter one little bit once Nettleship was deemed no longer 'still Pre-Raphaelite'. Thus, he never remained quite so close to Nettleship during the latter years of his life. However, Todhunter's very good friendship and interest in George Wilson endured for the whole of Wilson's short life – and indeed, for very many years afterwards – and he had some particularly touching correspondence with Wilson during the last months of his final illness in Scotland.

It would be wonderful to believe that perhaps many more of Todhunter's collection – including those numerous important works by George Wilson that are understood to have been lost – might, like *Pippa Passes*, have passed out of his collection before the alleged fire that is purported to have destroyed them. However, at this point in time, that possibility can only remain wishful thinking.

CHAPTER FIVE

J.T. Nettleship; his family and friends

John Trivett Nettleship was born in Kettering, Northamptonshire, on 11th February 1841, the second son of a local solicitor and within a family of six boys and one girl. The youngest son died when only 15 and the daughter after just two weeks, but all the remaining boys went on to achieve considerable academic and professional acclaim.

J.T. Nettleship was educated as a chorister at New College, Oxford and the Cathedral School, Durham, before being articled initially into his father's firm of solicitors and afterwards in London for a short while. After a very short period in practice as a solicitor, he decided on a career in art – at which he had been proficient since childhood. So in 1861, at the age of 20, he entered Heatherley's School of Fine Art in Newman Street, Off Oxford Street in London. George Wilson was only 13 at the time and still at school in Aberdeen. Nettleship was therefore destined to spend the next nine years or so studying at Heatherley's, and seven years even before Wilson caught up with him. In contrast, Wilson's own total time spent at all three of the various art schools he attended was just five years between 1868 and 1873.

John Trivett Nettleship, ca. 1868, aged about 27 years. This photograph by Elliott and Fry, as published in Thomas Wright's *The Life of John Payne*, displays much of the oft-quoted self-assured aloof bearing of the young Nettleship, which is completely lacking in the later photograph (q.v.) of a very kindly looking elderly gentleman.

Nettleship's early designs display a virility that reflected his own enthusiasm for physical exercise. He was a keen sportsman who once took lessons in boxing from a famous prize-fighter and was known more than once to have walked from London to Brighton in a day. On one occasion, he accompanied his friend, Sir Henry Cotton, on an Alpine mountaineering expedition for which they trained together bare-footed around Regent's Park.[71] On another occasion, when similarly training alone, but equally bare-footed, he was apprehended by a policeman under suspicion of being a potential burglar. It took a half-crown bribe (about £10 today [72]), but more importantly, a promise to put on his boots in case he met another policeman, before he was allowed to continue on his way![73] To some extent, it was this interest in physical prowess and the necessary survival of the fittest in animals in the wild that drew him towards his lifetime's work as an animal painter

However, Nettleship also considered himself a serious essayist and critic, and he did gain some immediate kudos at Heatherley's when, in 1868 at the age of 27, he published a volume of *Essays on Robert Browning's poetry*.[74] This publication was well received by both public and, perhaps more importantly, his subject Robert Browning, to the extent that it served to commence his life-long friendship with the poet, culminating in his 1895 publication entitled *Robert Browning: Essays and thoughts*.[75]

During his early period within the Heatherley 'Brotherhood', Nettleship's black and white drawings owed much to the influence of William Blake, and it is rather to be regretted that he did not continue to pursue these powerful and imaginative designs to their conclusions. Instead, he headed in an almost diametrically opposed direction, towards the ever grander and more dramatic paintings, frequently of the larger wild cats or bears, but for which he found sales even more difficult to come by. In his later years, Nettleship

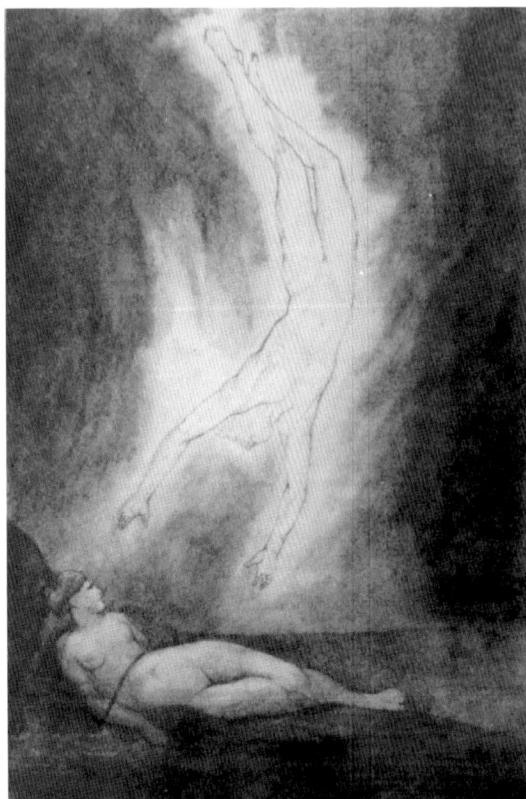

Subject Unknown. A typical early black and white pencil and chalk sketch by J.T. Nettleship (from an autotype published to illustrate Alice Cholmondeley's *Emblems* in 1875.) Original sketch pad used was typically 14 in x 9⅞ in (355 mm x 255 mm). This sketch, depicting a mythical scene, shows the strong early influence of Blake. Reading University Library.

took to drawing in the medium of pastel; working on similar subjects but to a rather smaller scale, and these did indeed achieve a somewhat readier market.

Disappointment that Nettleship had abandoned his Blake inspired designs was almost unanimous, although the artist himself was perfectly content with the move – perhaps even inspired originally by Blake's own splendid drawing of *The Tyger* in his well-loved poem of that name, but better known to all children by its first line, *Tyger Tyger, burning bright...*, in *Songs of Innocence and Experience* (1794).[76] But Robert Catterson Smith found fault in Nettleship's earlier Blake-orientated enthusiasm when, on one occasion after he had been looking through a book of Blake's designs in the British Museum, he went so far as to accuse Nettleship of plagiarism. In a letter to John Todhunter in 1874, he wrote:

> *I was sorry to see on looking through those designs that Nettleship copied one of them into a design of his of the souls of flowers blending together. There is a very beautiful little one of that sort in Blake's designs of a male and female blossom. Now this discovery has done him an injury in my mind, it is not a pure thing to do – and it is one of the designs by which I judged him of an intense poetic nature. He should love these things too much to steal and honour Blake too much to lower him to himself. I don't think either that it shows a proper appreciation of any work to copy it. ...*

But without both the original Blake design and Nettleship's supposed 'copy' to compare it to – or indeed, any opportunity for Nettleship to explain his work – it is impossible to tell whether Catterson Smith was justified or not in his indignation. It may have been that Catterson Smith was trying to justify himself in this letter, which was largely given over to his own perceived inadequacies both in painting and in the art of conversation. In this latter respect he had commenced the letter by saying that, 'The conversation of a man of [Yeats's] education always makes me feel helplessly ignorant in some ways ...', and, 'The night I was at Dowden's with you I was made miserable by my own ignorance.'[77]

Throughout his life, Nettleship also undertook occasional book illustration – notably in 1870, for his friend A.W.E. O'Shaughnessy's *An Epic of Women* and in 1875 for Mrs Alice Cholmondeley's *Emblems*. A decade later, in 1885, he illustrated *Natural History Sketches among the Carnivora: Wild and Domesticated* by A Nichols, and a further decade on in 1895, *Ice-bound on Kolguev* by Aubin B.R. Trevor Battye. Finally, in 1898, he wrote *George Morland and the Evolution from Him of Some Later Painters*.[78]

But his main focus became his melodramatic animal paintings – for which he had become well renowned, and in October 1880 this resulted in an invitation to India to paint an equestrian portrait and a cheetah hunt for the Gaekwar of Baroda. The latter painting, entitled *The Last Leap but One* was exhibited at the RA in 1881 (whereabouts no longer known).

But the trip served an important secondary purpose as an adjunct to being purely a new and exciting experience, as it proved to be an opportunity for Nettleship to view some of his favourite wild animals in their natural habitat, well beyond the restrictive and comparatively demeaning cages of the London Zoo. Many of Nettleship's animal and wildlife paintings were published in popular magazines and reproduced as prints – such as the chromo-lithograph study of a lion, reproduced hee.

'Stealthy Fate', published as a chromo-lithograph in the 1895 Annual of the Boys Own Paper, from an original oil painting by J.T. Nettleship, exhibited at the New Gallery in 1894 (whereabouts no longer known).

Entitled *Stealthy Fate*, it was published in the 1895 Annual of the Boys Own Paper,[79] from the original painting exhibited at the New Gallery in 1894. Over the years, both Nettleship and also Sir Frank Brangwyn (1867-1956) regularly contributed paintings for publication in issues of Boys Own Paper. But elsewhere he created such a specialism for painting animals that he was also occasionally commissioned to paint the animals or birds in other people's pictures – such as the pigeons in the large and often reproduced 1884 painting by Henry Holiday (1839-1927) of *Dante and Beatrice* (Walker Art Gallery, Liverpool). Perhaps the only other contemporary of his era who came near to Nettleship's competency in portraying wild animals *as* wild animals was J.M. Swan, RA (1847-1910).

In furtherance of his insistence upon such proper portrayal, Nettleship is quoted as having claimed that it should have been he, and not Landseer (Sir Edwin, 1802-1873), who designed the lions at the foot of Nelson's Column in Trafalgar Square. In fact, these sculptures had originally been commissioned as early as 1845, initially from the Northumbrian sculptor John Graham Lough (1798–1876), but then subsequently from Edwin Landseer. However, Landseer was extremely dilatory in his commission and, inciting much public criticism in the process, it took him over 20 years until 1868 to complete the final castings. Writing nearly 20 years later in 1886, Nettleship was still criticising Landseer's lions:

> *The Trafalgar Square lions must be quietly damned, because, pretending to be done from nature, they absolutely miss the true sculptural quality which distinguishes the leonine pose, and because a lion couched like that has not a concave back like a greyhound, but a convex back, greatly ennobled in line from the line of a cat's back in the same position.*

Thomas Wright, who in 1919 wrote his biography *The Life of John Payne* about Nettleship's early 'Triumvirate' friend and poet from the mid 1860s, remarked that although Payne and Nettleship had drifted apart long before the latter died, he was still considered to be:

> *...a true man of genius, who had obtained far less recognition than he deserved. He differed from the school of Landseer as light differs from darkness. He painted animals as they were. His tigers were lithe, sly and savage – with teeth, oh what teeth! His lions ... were not noble domestic animals such as one sees in Trafalgar Square or on the obverse of a shilling. They are bloody-minded brutes with eyes – oh what eyes!* [80]

In a footnote to the page, Wright records that in April 1918, he saw a number of Nettleship's animals at 28, Wigmore Street[*], when he 'had tea among them'! Presumably, this would have been while he was researching for the book, which includes Nettleship's widow in the list of acknowledgements. His description of Nettleship's lions and tigers with their *oh what teeth* and *oh what eyes* harks back again to the allusion that there might indeed have been an element of Blake's influence in this work!

John Payne had, like Nettleship, spent some time training as a solicitor in London, and this is possibly how they first met. They soon formed their inseparable friendship with another poet, Arthur O'Shaughnessy, who was the assistant librarian of Zoology at the British Museum, and for whom Nettleship produced his Blake-like fantastic illustrations for two publications of his works – although his drawings for the second were rejected by the ridiculously 'over-respectable' publisher due to the lack of drapery on the figures! [81]

By 1868, Payne had become acquainted with many of the better-known artists of the day, including Ford Madox Brown (1821-1893), Edward Burne-Jones, William Bell Scott (1811-1890) and Simeon Solomon, and it was in the Madox Browns' huge house at

---

[*] Wright may have meant No 58, which was the address generally used by the Nettleships. However, the Nettleship family seems to have owned or leased a significant number of properties in Wigmore Street at one time or another. J.T. Nettleship was living at No. 58 from 1889 until he died in 1902, but wrote to Halsey Ricardo in 1891 from No 60. In the early 1900s there are also a number of references in relation to his widow and various sub-leases concerning Nos 28, 30, 32 and 34 – possibly relating to her dressmaking business.

37 Fitzroy Square where the aspiring poets met the three Rossettis – Dante Gabriel, his brother William, and their sister Christina. This led to direct invitations to the houses of the Rossetti brothers, as well as to a string of correspondence over the years;[82] and while the connection undoubtedly did much for the reputations of the two poets, unfortunately the efforts of Nettleship, the artist, gleaned far less reward and he appears to have made little progress beyond his much acclaimed *God Creating Evil* and a couple of other works:-- *Prostituted Genius returning to her First Love for the Truth* and *Jacob and the Angel*. Where any of these works now reside is not known.

Thus, by as early as 1870, Nettleship had commenced painting the melodramatic animal paintings that D.G. Rossetti later referred to as his 'pot-boilers'. W.B. Yeats said that he always hated Nettleship's big lion pictures, but that it was actually Nettleship himself who had recalled that it was Rossetti who first used the 'pot-boiler' expression. But Nettleship went on to plead, waving his arms at the canvases, 'but they are all – all, symbols'. Yeats said he wanted him to 'design gods and angels and lost spirits once more', but he always alluded that nobody would be pleased with such subjects any more. 'Everybody should have a raison d'être.' was one of his phrases, adding, 'Mrs ——'s articles are not good but they are her *raison d'être.'* Yeats also remarked in passing that, somewhat in contrast to the earlier impression conveyed by his father and others about Nettleship's arrogance and self-assuredness, he actually found him to be 'very proud and shy'.[83]

No doubt Nettleship would have seen some irony in Rossetti's 'pot-boiler' remark, since at least he was getting on with painting his animals, whereas Rossetti's own propensity at that time was merely for collecting them – rather too avidly! He possessed – but unfortunately housed none-too-securely – a range of weird and wonderful pet animals within his house and gardens in Cheyne Walk. These included a racoon; a pair of armadillos; a couple of kangaroos; a peacock; some fallow deer, and a parrot! Most were inveterate escapologists, much to the consternation of his Chelsea neighbours, whilst the rest either ate or destroyed each other; and many had to be returned to the importer following far too numerous complaints about their appalling behaviour in the neighbourhood.[84]

In fact, Rossetti took much interest in Nettleship at this time for both his literary works in relation to Browning as well as his early Blake-inspired sketches. Henry Treffry Dunn, Rossetti's studio and house assistant at 16, Cheyne Walk, and whom Rossetti referred to as 'the best of fellows and my guardian angel',[85] noted in his edited *Recollections of Dante Gabriel Rossetti, or, Cheyne Walk Life* that 'F.T. [sic] Nettleship would sometimes bring his sketches of conceived but hardly half worked out wondrous ideas, those of a Blake-like kind that amazed and delighted him [Rossetti] with their audacity of treatment.' Dunn goes on to record that the occasional various stories that he passed on to Rossetti 'about F.T.N. [sic] and his peculiarities amused and excited his curiosity vastly.'

However, William Rossetti, in his Diary entry for 18th December 1868, was rather less enthusiastic about Nettleship's efforts of that time. Despite recognising his 'obvious force of ideas,' he recorded that, 'his executive unadaptabilities are glaring, and I should fear hardly conquerable – at any rate, for pecuniary success.' But curiously, he went on to note that Nettleship was already showing a particularly good feeling for the study of animals. And indeed, at the same time, D.G. Rossetti himself acquired a number of Nettleship's animal studies.

William Rossetti was quite close to the mark in his observations at this stage of Nettleship's career; however, by the time he had published these remarks in his 1903 *Rossetti Papers 1863 – 1870*, he had added a footnote with reference to Nettleship's eventual direction in animal painting, to the effect that 'having settled down into this different class of pictorial subjects, [he had] coped with and fairly surmounted his difficulties.' William Rossetti also claimed that it was from this first meeting, that also included Ford Madox Brown and William Bell Scott, that they suggested that Nettleship should 'illustrate some congenial book',[86] which of course he also went on to do.

Unfortunately, very little at all has been directly recorded and published about the life and work of J.T. Nettleship, and the subject certainly deserves more dedicated research. Neither has it been possible to locate the present whereabouts of many of Nettleship's paintings. His work very occasionally appears at auction, but the only small group of works (or so it is believed) that can be traced within a public gallery is held by the Alfred East Gallery in the Nettleship family's home town of Kettering in Northamptonshire. This small group amounts to just six canvases, four of which are of animal subjects, entitled respectively: *Touch me if you dare; Two Lions at a Pool; Ruminating,* and *A Travelling Bear.* The first two are paintings of lions and the second two are both paintings of bears.

However, it is the remaining two paintings that are of greatest interest, as, even though these appear to be neither signed nor dated, both would seem to be rare examples of the artist's very much earlier style.

The first painting, entitled *Reclining Nude in a Glade*, is a figurative composition which certainly seems to be representative of Nettleship's earliest Blake-influenced work – most specifically in so far as the painting of the nude figure is concerned. The second painting is a landscape entitled *The Moors,* and this is in fact remarkably reminiscent of George Wilson's own landscapes, with

Reclining Nude in a Glade, John Trivett Nettleship, 14 in x 18½ in (350 mm x 470 mm). Oil on canvas. Date unknown, but possibly ca. 1870. Reproduced by permission of The Alfred East Art Gallery, Kettering, UK.

The Moors, John Trivett Nettleship, 20 in x 30 in (510 mm x 760 mm). Oil on canvas. Date unknown, but possibly painted on Dartmoor in November 1870. Reproduced by permission of The Alfred East Art Gallery, Kettering, UK.

a great deal of detail in the foreground. This attention to the foreground foliage became far less important in Nettleship's later animal paintings, where the animal's poise and 'intent' became everything.

Unfortunately, for some reason, both paintings are now extremely dark,* and it is impossible to reproduce adequately (or indeed to be entirely sure of) their true original colours. Nevertheless, these two works are both reproduced here in the absence of alternative examples from the period.

Although there are no dates attached to either painting, it is conceivable that *The Moors* is one of the paintings that Nettleship was working on whilst on his trip to Dartmoor in November 1870. That excursion was referred to in correspondence between several of their group of friends, at the time when Nettleship had just been accepted into the Royal Academy Schools. He wrote to John Todhunter that he was painting an enormous 7 ft by 5 ft canvas, which he referred to as his 'Academy picture', *en plein air* and with great seriousness and not a little hardship through the inclement weather on the moors. Unfortunately, this truly Pre-Raphaelite approach was not to last long![87]

Although an in-depth search has not been possible, apart from these six paintings in Kettering, the only other public gallery that appears to hold items by Nettleship is the Ashmolean Museum in Oxford. In the Ashmolean, there are two small works in watercolour – one is a *Study of a Tiger* (120 mm x 215 mm) and the other, a *Study of a Capercaillie* with a brown wash *Study of a Seated Lion* verso (124 mm x 181 mm). The provenance of these two works shows that they were originally among those owned by D.G. Rossetti, and the latter may indeed have been the sketch that Todhunter 'found fault with' when visiting Nettleship's studio in 1869 to view *God Creating Evil*.[88]

---

* The Alfred East Gallery suspects that the darkness may have been caused by Nettleship's possible use of bitumen as a brown pigment, or mixed within the pigments, which has subsequently darkened with time.

* * *

Not only did John Nettleship maintain close contact and a firm friendship with George Wilson over the years, but he evidently also introduced him to his family, including his four brothers. All of these brothers held high academic or professional posts, and some of them also bought paintings from Wilson – in particular, Edward (Ned), who was a renowned London ophthalmic surgeon and who also became a particularly good friend to Wilson. It is interesting to note that, apart from one small gouache portrait by Wilson of his niece, Rachel, aged about two years (q.v.), there are just two other recorded portraits that are known about from exhibition lists, and both of these were owned by members of the Nettleship family. One was an unnamed (and described as unfinished) portrait painted in oil on canvas and loaned to the Baillie exhibition of 1903 by Mrs J.T. Nettleship, whilst the other was a chalk drawing entitled *The Late Mrs H.J. Nettleship*, loaned on the same occasion by Mrs E. Nettleship*. H.J. Nettleship was the brothers' father, and his widow did not die until 1898 – some eight years after George Wilson. However, the poor woman experienced much tragedy within her own family during her last years before she died.

From correspondence written both before and after Wilson's death, it is evident that many members of the family held Wilson in high regard. Of John and Edward Nettleship's three other surviving brothers, Richard Lewis was a Fellow and Tutor at Balliol College, Oxford, who also appears to have known Wilson quite well. Less close perhaps were Henry, the eldest brother, who was Corpus Professor of Latin at Oxford, and James (Jim), who was a Harrow schoolteacher. Finally, there was also the youngest brother, Horace, who died at the age of 15, and one daughter as well who died when just two weeks old.[89]

In respect of the tragic events that occurred during the last few years of their mother's life, it is relevant to record that both Richard and Henry had also died within two years of George Wilson. Richard fell in a climbing accident on Mont Blanc in 1892 and Henry died from typhoid fever just one year later. Then, following on from Henry's death in 1893, his only son, Henry Melvill Nettleship (known as Melvill) also died just three years later in March 1896 at the age of only 21 years, and while in his second year as a student at the Slade. Melvill Nettleship's first cousin Ida (q.v.), J.T. Nettleship's daughter, was attending the Slade at the same time, yet it is curious that there is no obvious reference to this direct connection in any of the considerable subsequent writings about the lives of Ida and Augustus John (1878-1961) – whose relationship of course commenced at almost exactly the same time, immediately outside of the Slade classes.

---

* It is curious to note that while contributions were made to the 1893 Aberdeen exhibition of Wilson's work by 'E. Nettleship Esq.', in the 1903 London exhibition, loans were made 'from the collection of Mrs E Nettleship', and '...Mrs J Nettleship'. Although J.T. Nettleship had indeed died in 1902, Edward was still very much alive and well at the date of the second exhibition, and indeed, he did not die until ten years later in 1913.

With the death of Melvill Nettleship, in the March of 1896, the male line of the Nettleship family died out. But in memory of her son, his late father's widow, Matilda, founded the Melvill Nettleship Prize at the Slade; [90] and this highly coveted of Slade prizes is still awarded today for Figure Composition, on the personal recommendation of the Slade Professor of Fine Art. It is a further coincidence and curiosity that although one of the earliest recipients of this prize was Ida Nettleship's close friend, Gwen John (1876-1939), the sister of her eventual husband Augustus John, again there is scarcely any mention of the connection.

It may well have been through the Nettleship brothers that George Wilson first met two other friends and patrons – the philanthropist Ralph Radcliffe Whitehead (1854-1929) and the architect Halsey Ricardo (1854-1928) – although recent documentary evidence points to quite an early relationship with both. It may simply, therefore, have been a case of all these contacts emerging over the period of developing connections following the friends' departure from their art schools – and the small amount of public exhibiting that each had commenced by that time.

Halsey Ricardo. This spontaneous small sketch (6½ in x 4½ in overall) shows a fine likeness of Ricardo at the age of 27. It is inscribed and dated verso (in the hand of Ricardo's wife, Kate): *'Halsey Ricardo, March 1882. Drawn by G. Wilson'*. It will be noted that the scrap of paper on which the sketch is drawn has been put to maximum use by the frugal Scot with a faint impulsive study of girl at right angles across the top of the page! Private collection.

Although Ricardo was 13 years junior to John Nettleship, he and his wife were certainly very friendly with both John and Edward Nettleship; and R.L. Nettleship referred to Wilson after his death with great affection in correspondence to Whitehead. Furthermore, we know that Whitehead disposed of at least one of his larger symbolist oil paintings by Wilson (*The Rape of Proserpine*) to Ricardo around the time that Whitehead emigrated to America in 1901.

It was also almost certainly through Edward Nettleship that George Wilson was introduced to Sir Thomas Barlow, Bt., the famous oculist and physician to Queen Victoria (and later to King Edward VII and King George V). Barlow (then simply 'Dr') is recorded as having loaned one painting *The Old Castle of Huntly* to the 1893 retrospective Wilson exhibition in Aberdeen (see appendices*), but there is a much more appealing record of another Wilson watercolour that he also once owned – and which now resides happily in Edinburgh within the collections of the National Gallery of Scotland. The painting in question is a particularly fine woodland watercolour, entitled (now) *A Fallen Beech*, which was bequeathed to the gallery in April 1976 within the wonderful private collection of 56 English watercolours and drawings from the estate of Sir Thomas's daughter, Miss Helen A.D. Barlow.[91]

However, there is a curious anomaly attached to the provenance of this painting: There is a photograph of the very same watercolour (numbered 10[a.]) within a set of 12 phototypes produced by George Washington Wilson to commemorate the 1893 exhibition. In that publication, and also in the exhibition catalogue (the same catalogue that records Dr Barlow's loan of the Huntly Castle painting), this painting is entitled simply *Trees* and is recorded then as being in the possession of, and loaned by, a Dr Anderson of London. In view of the later recorded Barlow Bequest provenance, which ties-in completely with separately recorded evidence of Nettleship's excessive drinking following a riding accident, the Aberdeen exhibition information may simply have been in error. The catalogue certainly contains other errors – as does the later 1903 John Baillie London exhibition catalogue, in which, incidentally, no Barlow or Anderson loans are recorded – nor any reference to either *A Fallen Beech* or *Trees*. Another alternative possible explanation for the anomaly might be that the painting did indeed change hands twice from Barlow to Anderson and back again, between its original gift from Wilson to Barlow in the early to mid 1880s and the development of the Barlow collection – but this explanation would seem somewhat convoluted.

In the late 1860's, J.T. Nettleship's father-in-law, the renowned otologist, James Hinton, travelled to Germany with a Dr James Anderson to study developments in aural practice.[92] There is just a possibility that this could be the same Dr Anderson, through the Nettleship connection. And the correlation may not stop there, as Edward Nettleship was also a close acquaintance of Sir Thomas Barlow, who gave a eulogistic speech about him following his death in 1913. It is entirely conceivable then, that within the hierarchy of specialist medicine at the time, the Dr Anderson referred to in each instance is one and the same.

Within the documentation at the National Gallery of Scotland that accompanied the Barlow Bequest is a list of all the paintings and the rooms in which they originally hung in No. 10, Wimpole Street, London. Additionally, there is the following delightful anecdote relating to the Wilson picture:

---

* All references to the various 1893 and 1903 retrospective exhibition loans may be cross-referred via the relevant appendices that follow the main text

George Wilson was an Aberdeen artist. A portfolio of his drawings* accompanies this collection. He was a great friend of John Nettleship the animal artist, a patient of Sir Thomas Barlow's who suffered from alcoholism. Wilson took Nettleship away on a painting tour and never left him for six months at the end of which Nettleship was permanently cured. This picture was a gift to Sir Thomas from Wilson.[93]

This reference to Nettleship's drinking problems is reiterated at intervals throughout contemporary comment. W.B. Yeats narrated in *The Trembling of the Veil* how, as a young man in the late 1880's, he had been berated by his father for being far too talkative at a dinner party held at Nettleship's the previous night, and how his father's anger had thrown him into a deep depression. J.B. Yeats had accused his son of talking for effect, which he made clear was completely unnecessary in good conversation. Rhetoric and emphasis were traits that J.B. Yeats had always hated and that distaste had worn off onto his son too, but he was evidently unhappy at having fallen into the trap in front of his father.

W.B. Yeats had therefore immediately called round the following day to see Nettleship in order to apologise, only to find his apology was apparently quite unnecessary, and that Nettleship in fact admired his volubility because he himself had become so much quieter as he got older. When Yeats called in, he had found Nettleship continually sipping cocoa from an enormous cup, not caring how cold it became. In support of the Barlow reference to Wilson's dedication towards curing Nettleship's drinking, Yeats described how some years earlier Nettleship had been thrown from his horse while out hunting and had broken his arm. Unfortunately, it had been badly set and this left him in great pain for a long time. He had found that a dram of whisky would always stop the pain, but soon a drop developed into a lot and he became an alcoholic. Yeats reported that he had 'signed away his liberty for several months', following which he was fully cured – although he found that he needed to have a cup of some liquid to hand to sip continuously.[94]

On another occasion, Nettleship had asked W.B. Yeats whether Edwin Ellis had ever said anything to him about the effects that drinking might have had upon his 'genius'. Although Yeats had tactfully replied 'no', Ellis had in fact only a few days beforehand used the very words that Nettleship had 'drunk his genius away'.[95]

It seems from these various references that J.B. Yeats's comments from his student days that Nettleship had at least an element of 'genius' was (to some extent at least) shared by others at that time – including Nettleship himself, apparently! Yeats's son,

---

*   Alas, this portfolio did not accompany the bequest to Edinburgh. Despite best attempts to try to track its possible ultimate destiny following the death of Miss Helen Barlow, unfortunately its whereabouts is now no longer known. Sir Thomas's three children all inherited his love for the collection and medium of watercolour, but it was Helen who added considerably to the collection herself. Her father was born in 1845 and she died in 1975 – so between them their lives spanned 130 years, he alone living to be almost 100!

W.B., recounted that he had learned to admire Nettleship from his early childhood, and that his father had always said that 'George Wilson was our born painter, but Nettleship our genius.' And even though the younger Yeats could not bring himself to like Nettleship's later animal paintings, his admiration for the painter, based upon his father's earlier assertions during his childhood, had remained deeply entrenched within him and he even occasionally tried to persuade Nettleship to pursue his earlier Blake-influenced designs once again.[96]

Although all of the Brotherhood admired Blake as a founding father, it was Nettleship (and to a lesser extent, Ellis) who, in the early days, showed a very strong influence of Blake in his black and white designs. However, it would seem that he quite quickly lost his confidence to paint with such fervour and very soon, he had moved on from those grass roots to become the melodramatic 'animal painter' for which he was later so much better known. These supposedly more saleable pictures became his 'pot-boilers', as Rossetti called them; however, Nettleship himself was still perfectly content with his work. He studied long and hard in the Zoological Gardens in Regent's Park, where he at least perpetuated the Pre-Raphaelite ethos of sketching and painting from life. Indeed, he almost certainly did know a great deal more about the anatomy of lions than did Landseer! – and was eventually even elected to membership of the Zoological Society in 1890.

CHAPTER SIX

Recognitions gained – opportunities lost

During the early 1870s, the work of the various members of the Heatherley Brotherhood did attract the attention of a number of the important artists of the day. Rossetti (who had himself been through Thomas Heatherley's Art School many years earlier) had seen Nettleship's design for *God creating Evil* and had greatly admired it. This painting, often deemed to have been Nettleship's early *pièce de résistance*, is now believed lost, possibly within the Todhunter collection – although, curiously, it is not at all clear that he really liked the painting. He described it to Edward Dowden as 'a truly awful face, like a rock, its wrinkles deep cut fissures, the eyes glaring with darkness and without pupils, the lips sucked in and pressed together with supreme volition, the chin massive and stern.'[97] Again, W.B. Yeats leaves us with another brief and somewhat lurid description of the work as, 'the death-like head with a woman and a tiger coming from the forehead'![98]

On 2nd May 1870 – the day the Royal Academy summer exhibition opened – J.B. Yeats wrote to John Todhunter:

> *Nettleship has had a letter from Rossetti with some <u>forcible</u> expressions about the hangers at the Academy. Fance <u>Hook Sant</u>* and <u>Chas Landseer</u>. Fancy such men given so much power. ... Rosetti [sic] sent Nettleship his book. You saw the advertisement of O'Shaughnessy's book of poems "with designs from the pencil of Mr. Nettleship".*[99]

---

* The reference to 'Fance Hook Sant' is not immediately understood. However, the eminent portrait painter James Sant (1820-1916) had been elected RA in 1869, and was shortly to be appointed Painter-in-Ordinary to Queen Victoria in 1872 – for which he was created CVO. His idealised style when painting children and young women was far removed from the minute accuracy being pursued by the Pre-Raphaelites, and so this may have been a somehow derogatory reference to him by Yeats. Nevertheless, he outlived them all considerably in years alone, dying aged 97 and exhibiting at the RA for the final time only the year before he died.

Evidently, Rossetti held a similar opinion as to Landseer's qualifications for the hanging committee at the RA as did Nettleship in relation to his sculpture of the Trafalgar Square lions! But when Rossetti saw J.B. Yeats's *Pippa Passes* in the Dudley Gallery in January 1871, he was so impressed* that he sent his brother William to invite Yeats to visit him. Despite a further repeated invitation, Yeats never did accept, nor did he of course make the visit – which, had he done so, could only have benefited him considerably at the time.[100]

In a similar vein, but somewhat later in 1878, Robert Browning had heard about Yeats's interpretation of *Pippa* from his dramatic poem and had visited John Todhunter to view this and another picture of Yeats's that he possessed called *In a Gondola* (now supposed lost within the Todhunter collection) – presumably again interpreting Browning's poem of that name. Browning was very impressed and immediately called round to see Yeats personally to congratulate him. Unfortunately and rather inevitably, Yeats was again not at home and the note left by Browning inviting him to call and see him was, equally inevitably, ignored – or, rather more likely in fact, continually postponed.[101]

Elsewhere, Yeats and Nettleship, who by their ages alone straddled both the earlier Pre-Raphaelite movement and the younger friends within their own group, had passing or better acquaintances with several established painters, all of whom, if Yeats had bothered to cultivate the contact, would have benefited him enormously. George Watts is known to have visited Yeats's studio, and one painter whom Yeats did actually bother to visit, as early as 1868, was Frederick Sandys, whose own work had been purchased by Todhunter. Sandys warmly praised some of Yeats's sketches and offered to be of any service he could be to him, inviting him to return to visit his studio whenever he liked.[102] This was only shortly after Yeats first settled in 23, Fitzroy Road in north London in 1868, where he discovered that Ford Madox Brown was a near neighbour. Madox Brown was, at almost exactly this same time, becoming acquainted with Nettleship via the Rossettis. He also had a precocious son called Oliver, who became infatuated by Yeats's sister-in-law, Isabella Pollexfen – despite her being six years his senior. Yet, even so, none of these openings was ever permitted either the time or the opportunity to develop into the useful contact it undoubtedly would have been.[103]

And a similar theme was to run throughout all of Yeats's time in London. Some 20 years later, W.B. Yeats became a regular visitor to the William Morris household at Kelmscott House, where his sister Lily Yeats worked – or rather slaved – as an embroideress for Morris's daughter May for five and a half years. However, J.B. Yeats himself thought that Morris had 'no philosophy'; and that he 'solved all questions of conduct by the immediate intuition of an optimistic disposition, or of explosive temper'

---

* Rossetti's wife, Elizabeth Siddal (1829-1862), who had died so tragically young at the age of only 33, had drawn a pencil illustration to Pippa Passes in 1854 (Ashmolean Museum, Oxford) and the memory of this may have stimulated Rossetti's interest in Yeats's interpretation.

– a temper for which Morris was justly renowned. J.B. Yeats decided to leave him well alone! [104]

Although there was obviously an important link between Edward Burne-Jones and Morris, as well as with Robert Catterson Smith from the old Heatherley group, there is no particular cross-reference to Yeats. However, Burne-Jones did evidently know Nettleship well enough to have referred to him somewhat scathingly as 'His Nettleship'. Similarly, J.B. Yeats in his unpublished *Memoirs* recalls that Simeon Solomon had laughed at the four Nettleship brothers because he thought that they were all so very serious.[105] But then, since the early 1870s commenced the period when Solomon was twice arrested for indecency and his descent into alcoholic decline accelerated, the conservative society of the Nettleships was unlikely to be very impressed.

It is evident then from these few references alone that the lives of the friends within the 1869 Brotherhood revolved closely around – if never entirely within – the circles of the already influential painters and writers of the day. Unfortunately, the dearth of information relating to George Wilson and the nature of his persona make it impossible to ascertain exactly how his peers or mentors viewed his work. But by association alone, the painters' world around him must have been well aware of this somewhat solitary and nomadic friend to all, since he was close to at least one participant in each of the relationships discussed above. But in any case, he had a good small but close personal following, and some eulogistic accounts followed his untimely death in 1890.

George Wilson has often been described generically, and not entirely accurately, as a follower of Burne-Jones. There is really only very little, if anything at all, of a passing awareness of Burne-Jones in his larger symbolist oil paintings, although possibly a trifle more so in some of his smaller figurative works in watercolour or tempera; but that really is all. In some ways, Wilson's affiliation might appear to have been more closely aligned to the much earlier 'symbolic realism' of Holman Hunt, whose figures always seem to carry so much more of an expressive countenance than the later, often resoundingly beautiful, models of Rossetti and Burne-Jones. Not only were Hunt's figures often full of clear and relevant emotion, but in parallel he also painted a significant number of landscapes in a manner that no doubt much pleased Wilson. What is far more visibly evident, though, is the major influence that resulted from Wilson's tuition under Poynter, and this can be clearly seen in his work, and particularly in his chalk and pencil studies. This influence is scarcely surprising since Poynter was the last formal tutor under whom he studied at the Slade, before making his own way in the world.

There is no doubt from the few remaining examples of Wilson's more finished pencil and chalk works, that he was an extremely accomplished draughtsman in those media. His first picture to be hung in the RA in 1877, the chalk drawing *Study of a Head,* as well as the various studies now in the V&A, the British Museum, and in private collections, are of the very highest quality, and continually demonstrate Poynter's influence. To this end, where the drawings were evidently intended to lead towards finished works, they are even quite formal and classical, whereas Yeats's sketches, by contrast, although they seldom fail to delight, do so through their great fluidity and freedom.

Elsewhere, as previously alluded to, there is something of a passing similitude to Wilson's work in one particular work by Annie Swynnerton, who was certainly Wilson's contemporary by age, if not necessarily by acquaintance. Swynnerton was influenced by G. F. Watts and the French impressionists. She studied initially in Manchester and, although she exhibited at the RA, Grosvenor and New Galleries from 1879, she lived mainly in Rome from her marriage in 1883 until her husband died in 1910.

The angel in Swynnerton's *The Sense of Sight* (Walker Art Gallery, Liverpool), painted in 1895, bears an interesting similarity of pose, demeanour and colour to Wilson's *Asia* (q.v.), painted around 12 years or so earlier. Although *Asia* is a somewhat softer and more evocative subject, both figures share the same up-turned 'visionary' face (although for somewhat different reasons) with wide, focused eyes, and curled hands and fingers – which even share some of the same technical difficulties that Wilson often encountered – plus some distinctly similar elements of colouring.

However, in Swynnerton's painting, the subject figure is everything. There is no foreground, and the background is bleak and simple; whereas the very detailed treatment of both the foreground and background in *Asia* is integral to the whole allegory of the painting, shouting out its very strong Renaissance and Pre-Raphaelite influences. There is of course no suggestion that *The Sense of Sight* was directly influenced by *Asia*, and the similitude is most likely to be of an entirely coincidental nature. Nor indeed is there any indication that Wilson ever even met Annie Swynnerton or that she knew of his work, although it is not implausible that they could have met during his regular painting trips to Italy.

Another painter of not totally dissimilar figurative designs, and whom Wilson probably could well have known,[*] was Evelyn de Morgan (née Pickering, 1855-1919) who was to marry William de Morgan (1839-1917) later in 1887. Although in this case, Wilson was some seven years older than de Morgan, both of them had studied at the same time at the Slade under Edward Poynter for a short period in 1873, and both spent at least some of the subsequent three years furthering their education in Italy. De Morgan spent the time as pupil to her uncle, John Roddam Spencer Stanhope (1829-1908), but we do not know Wilson's precise movements at the time – except that his brother John recorded that he had spent two years in Rome.[106] Nevertheless, both Wilson and de Morgan did share a great admiration for, and were consequently influenced by, the work of Botticelli (Sandro, 1445 – 1510); although in de Morgan's case, the aesthetic influence of Burne-Jones is somewhat more evident – and the results of her larger figurative oils are generally considerably more 'decorative' and

---

[*]   The suggestion that Wilson might only *probably* have known a young woman who was studying at the Slade at the same time as him is partly down to the careful segregation of the sexes that existed in the school at that time. The only class that they shared was in the Antique Rooms, and even Poynter himself could not be seen in the women's Life Class at the same time as his students when a female nude was sitting. The students would be required to troop out of the room, while the master appended his comments in writing to the edges of their works.

therefore probably considered to be rather more successful than are Wilson's. De Morgan's oeuvre is certainly far more prolific – if only because her working life was considerably longer than Wilson's.

Although Wilson never sought out commissions or sales, he was patronised by some of the less flamboyant collectors of the day. Whilst it was most probably through the Nettleship family connections that he met two of these, Ralph Radcliffe Whitehead and Halsey Ricardo, it could just as easily have been through the Yeatses and William Morris, or indeed his colleague William de Morgan. De Morgan, of course, worked directly with Morris, producing his ceramic tile designs from the Sands End Pottery in Fulham, that he had originally started up in 1870. It was later in 1888 at Sands End that he established William de Morgan & Co. in partnership with Ricardo, the architect, thereby providing de Morgan with a regular route via Ricardo's house designs for the placement of his tiles and other wares in situ.[*]

The significant point of relevance here is that the art world at that time in London was not enormous, and those of a 'like mind' tended to move in and out of the same circles. So it is almost inconceivable that they would not know, from the exhibitions and the gossip surrounding them, what each other was up to – even if some, like J.B. Yeats, were rather less responsive to the friendly approaches of others.

One of Wilson's most enthusiastic patrons was Ralph Radcliffe Whitehead. Born in the same year as Ricardo in 1854, he came from a rich textile milling family from Saddleworth in West Yorkshire, whose successful business manufactured the felt used in pianos. He was educated at Harrow and at Balliol, Oxford, where he studied under Ruskin and which was where he met two of the Nettleship brothers. One of Halsey Ricardo's daughters, Esther, remembered him almost too candidly in a letter to her niece, Kate, as 'a wealthy dilettante much given to projects for the betterment of mankind via the art world.' She went on to describe him as 'an excellent and charming man … but he suffered from too much money and too many ill-judged enthusiasms.'[107] All in all, a splendid epitaph!

Whitehead travelled extensively in Europe, and was married firstly in Austria or Germany. He later divorced his first wife (apparently with some difficulty)[108] and married secondly in 1892, Jane Byrd McCall from Philadelphia, an American socialite doing the European tour. Jane McCall had taken instruction in drawing from Ruskin; had then studied art at the Académie Julian in Paris, and was 'presented' to Queen Victoria in 1886! Whitehead was passionate about everything that Ruskin and subsequently William Morris had promulgated and which had developed into the Arts and Crafts movement in England, and Jane McCall was equally enthusiastic about her husband's utopian vision to develop an Arts and Crafts colony of their own in America.

---

[*]   In 1906, Halsey Ricardo designed one of the classical architectural gems of the period for Lord Debenham – the brilliant Peacock House in Kensington, London. This house contains the largest collection in the world of de Morgan tiles still in situ, and depicts peacocks everywhere: on tiles; on mosaics; on paintings, and in stonework.

By the early 1870's Morris and Co. were exporting to America, and throughout the following years the Arts and Crafts movement as a whole took off and developed its own enthusiastic style in the United States. On the back of this, Jane took Whitehead back to America and they searched for a suitable site on which they could progress their vision. In 1902 they located and bought seven farms covering 1500 acres on Mount Guardian, just outside the hamlet of Woodstock in the Catskill Mountains of New York State, and it was there that they founded the Byrdcliffe Arts Colony (so styled out of an amalgamation of their respective middle names of 'Byrd' and 'Radcliffe').

The Colony is still operated today by The Woodstock Guild of Craftsmen, although the village of Woodstock itself has, for many people worldwide, inherited a possibly somewhat less enviable reputation (in the eyes of some people, that is). In 1969, the village had been proposed as the original site (although Woodstock was never actually utilised in the end) that gave its name to the legendary rock music and protest festival – which was reputed, somewhat doubtfully in truth, to have been attended by half a million people.

Ralph Whitehead became a very good patron and friend to George Wilson, but he is known to have disposed of probably almost all of his paintings before he finally emigrated to America. However, there is one picture that Whitehead did not part with, and which is presently believed to be the only large symbolist oil painting by Wilson that currently resides in a major public gallery. This picture, entitled *The Spring Witch*, was part donated by Whitehead's descendants to the Delaware Art Museum in Wilmington – which in its Bancroft Collection contains arguably the finest collection of Pre-Raphaelite paintings outside the UK. In addition to the donation of *The Spring Witch*, at the same time in 1991 the family lodged in the Winterthur Museum and Library in Delaware, USA, a considerable quantity of Whitehead family correspondence, photographs and documentation, particularly relating to the Byrdcliffe Colony archives.[109]

CHAPTER SEVEN

Continuing study

Reverting to the continuing evolution of the Brotherhood at Heatherley's, from late 1869 to early 1870, they settled – or rather, they intended to settle – into a serious and hard-working group of like-minded, though thoroughly different, characters during the day. They were likewise happy to become an equally hard-talking group during the evenings and nights, when they would discuss poetry and art at great length. Unfortunately, though, and with Yeats and Ellis in particular, the daytime and evening objectives became intrinsically blurred, so that there tended to be much more talk at all times about subjects such as their mentor Blake, and of poetry in general, than ever there was practical painting pursued.

The result was that when, in autumn 1869, Yeats and Ellis took their own long coveted studio at 74, Newman Street, opposite Nettleship's and close to Heatherley's Art School at No 79, the studio quickly proved to be an expensive luxury and had to be given up again within the year. Nevertheless, although Yeats somewhat inevitably failed to generate any income from use of the studio, it did give him his first opportunity to concentrate on his drawing and painting technique. He often worked alone for long hours direct from models, concentrating hard to develop many of the techniques (and habits) that would stay with him for life. It was also at this time that he received his commission from Todhunter for *Pippa Passes* and, while he evidently didn't work much on the composition from the studio, at least it might be said to have assisted somewhere in the design.[110]

By the summer of 1871, Yeats's wife Susan was pregnant with her fifth child, and third son, eventually to be christened John Butler Yeats after his father, although this was very quickly shortened to Jack.[111] Jack B. Yeats, as with his elder brother W.B., was to grow up to achieve far greater renown within contemporary society than ever his father managed – in Jack's case as a fine post-impressionist artist. With only his nominal income from lands in Ireland to support him, the size of his growing family must have been an impossible burden on J.B. Yeats senior – and very much more so on his long-suffering and fretful wife, Susan.

On August 2nd 1870, J.B. Yeats wrote to John Todhunter to give him an update about his *Pippa* commission. In that letter, he mentioned that J.T. Nettleship had been admitted to the Royal Academy as a probationer*...

> *...which has much delighted every one – he is recruiting himself at Sevenoaks, drawing trees all by himself in the park & spending half the night wandering about under the trees – in fact he sleeps a good deal in the park.*[112]

The scheme of 'probationer' at the Royal Academy Schools was introduced in 1814, and gave a potential student three months provisional access to the facilities of the Royal Academy. It had always been understood that concerted drawing from classical sculpture was an important part of traditional art training. For many potential students, the probationary route would have been the only way they would have been able to access such resources that were needed to prove themselves capable of taking a full time place at the Schools. It was against this very culture of traditional dogma that the Pre-Raphaelite Brethren had rebelled some 20 years earlier – and, it seems, little had changed to enthuse the latest recruits.

The RA records show that in George Wilson's case, Thomas Heatherley thought highly enough of his potential that he recommended him personally to the RA, and so Wilson was also admitted as a probationer one year later than Nettleship on 17th July 1871, giving as his address at that time No. 3, Well Road in Hampstead.† Finally, the archives show that J.B. Yeats enrolled at the Royal Academy Schools at the stated age of 32 and so this must have been at approximately the same time as Wilson – i.e. unless this age was a wide approximation, he must have entered sometime after 16th March 1871, which was when he would have reached his 32nd birthday.

Although the RA has no further record of any of these three students' attendance or continued learning at the Schools, it may be presumed that Wilson and Yeats both managed to survive the rigours of the school's academic approach for just one year and Nettleship for two years respectively, since all three had certainly left by 1st May 1872. Undoubtedly, they rapidly became bored by a learning process that epitomised the sad depths to which so many felt that 'traditional' British art had sunk by this time, if only by having distanced itself so effectively from the exciting developments on the continent. So, possibly feeling that they had at least 'given it a try' by going through the motions of

---

* The records of the RA do, indeed, record that Nettleship was admitted as a Probationer on 28th July 1870. However, at that time, the archives did not record when or if probationary students ever progressed to full time places. Since this would normally have happened after three months, presumably Nettleship (and Wilson and Yeats also) did become full-time students – albeit quite briefly.

† Well Road is situated only a stone's throw from the point in Heath Street at which Ford Madox Brown painted '*Work*'- the culminating opus of his P.R.B. period, and which took from 1852 till 1863 to complete. Evidently, if George Wilson originally stayed with his cousin, Jessie Thurburn Scott, when he first arrived in London, he must have found lodgings of his own fairly quickly – albeit still not far away from his cousin, who had no doubt been instructed to look out for him!

submitting to the ethos of the RA, the three decided together to enter the newly founded Slade School of Fine Art at University College, London.[*]

In this way, three of the 'Brethren' remained together again, but now they were studying figure drawing within the refreshing surroundings of the Slade – and under the keen tuition of the neo-classical painter, Edward Poynter. Poynter had been appointed first Slade professor when the school opened its doors in October 1871, and he retained the post through until 1876 when he handed over to Alphonse Legros (1837-1911). Poynter later became Director of the South Kensington Art Schools and, perhaps somewhat to the horror of his earlier students, President of the Royal Academy for twenty-two years, right through until the year before his death in 1919.

Poynter had been born in Paris and his successor Legros, in Dijon. Both had their formative training in Parisian studio art schools, rather than the formality of the RA and the École des Beaux Arts – although each did attend his relevant national institution for a while. If anything, Legros disliked the Royal Academy even more than his predecessor initially had, and between them they created a significant influence upon a generation or so of important British artists. That level of influence was to be continued dramatically from Legros' own retirement from the post in 1892 and on into the new century by his successor, Frederick Brown (1851-1941) and his renowned assistant, Henry Tonks (1862-1937). Legros was known to Degas (Edgar, 1834-1917) and some of the later French Impressionists, and so became a very useful link between Paris and the changing face of painting in England.

During the later years of his life, Poynter combined, most unusually, the Directorship of the National Gallery with his Presidency of the RA. In line with what became almost a custom of the times in honouring the accredited grand masters of painting, he was created baronet in 1902. And, as with his similarly honoured peers such as Lord Leighton, Sir Lawrence Alma-Tadema (1836-1912) and Sir Edward Burne-Jones, he was equally capable of producing enormous and spectacular canvasses.

In Poynter's time, the General Fine Art course at the Slade cost seven guineas (about £575 today) per term – although there were other options, such as a series of classes or drawing sessions at two guineas per course. It seems, however, that almost any combination of courses, time and relevant payment were possible – and maybe this was in deference to the impoverished status of so many of their students.

---

[*]   Felix Slade's beneficence in bequeathing £35,000 in 1868 (£2.73m today) to found two chairs in Fine Art at Oxford and Cambridge and, in addition, to found a Faculty of Fine Arts in London, could not have been better timed to capitalise on the current dearth of innovative teaching. And so University College, London, was quick to offer to incorporate the building of the Slade School within its new Gower Street site – where Edward Poynter (later 'Sir') was first elected to the chair. The chair in Oxford was first taken up by John Ruskin, whilst that in Cambridge went to the architect, Sir Matthew Digby Wyatt. These latter appointments created an interesting juxtaposition, since the two men held diametrically opposed views on many subjects concerning both art and architecture, and spent more than a little time criticizing one another's positions!

In the case of Wilson and his colleagues, it appears that they started their Slade tuition at the beginning of the summer term of 1872. They paid their fees in small instalments of £2-12s-6d at a time (£2.62½ in decimal terms – but approximately £205 today). George Wilson is recorded as having paid this amount on four occasions with his last payment being made on 30ᵗʰ April 1873. Nettleship made his last payment during the same week, but, rather true to form, the Slade archives mention that Yeats staved off making his final payment for a further month, on 19ᵗʰ May!

Although they only stayed at the Slade for four terms (and the strange amount each is recorded as having paid makes it impossible to know which courses or classes they signed up to), there is a probability that the group also subscribed to additional classes as well. In respect of this, Yeats mentions in a letter written to his wife Susan towards the end of 1872 (who by then had decided to remain in Ireland with the children), that he had 'paid £10 (equal to around £780 today) to Poynters' (i.e. the Slade).[113] This payment of yet another strange amount was made about halfway through Yeats's time at the Slade.

For Wilson in particular, and indeed for Yeats too, Poynter's tuition made a truly significant contribution to his development – in particular as a draughtsman. Although he always experienced some difficulty in transcribing his drawing skills into his oil paintings, he never experienced the same problems with his watercolour drawings. There exist a small number of fine figure study drawings within the British Museum's and the Victoria and Albert Museum's collections, as well as a few others resting in private hands. These drawings – as well as the sketches contained within his surviving sketchbooks – all show a continuous strong influence of Poynter's tutorship

This influence cannot be recognised to quite the same extent or in quite the same way in the early work of the other two young artists. In particular, Nettleship's early drawings (from his Heatherley days at least) often appear laboured in an almost over-exerted attempt to emulate the power of Blake. There is little in the way of drawing that can be identified to Nettleship's Slade days for comparison, but certainly Yeats's drawings, although demonstrating Poynter's influence, had a much more sensitive, relaxed and free style to them. Yeats continued to draw obsessively throughout his life – and almost always most delightfully, and sometimes quite exquisitely. A considerable collection of these drawings remains within his family descent and others are in the collection of the National Gallery of Ireland.

Of the three colleagues, Yeats had called Nettleship 'our genius.' However, he recorded in his *Memoirs* that Nettleship believed Wilson to be 'a born painter' to which Yeats had added that although they all might envy him, yet they could not imitate him as he simply knew too much.[114] Later, he debated with Samuel Butler (who he said didn't know how to sketch!) over his opinion of the inevitability that all great artists *can* sketch, since the sense of outline is the first that comes to them, following which they acquire and develop the sense of surface. He went on to remark that that was exactly the situation with George Wilson, who was 'richly endowed with all the artistic instincts', and who had 'an intellect and a judgement that was like sulight'.[115]

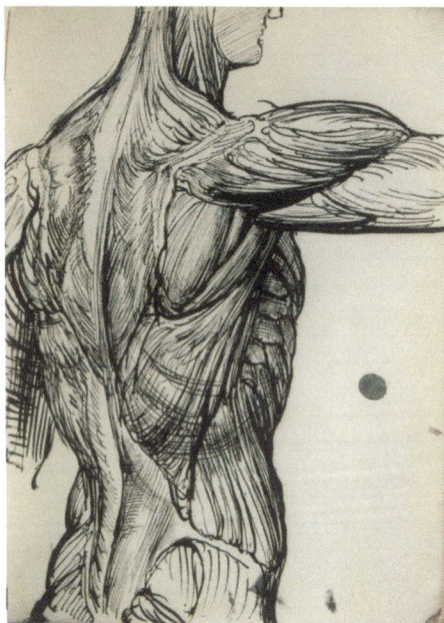

A brief sketch drawing from one of George Wilson's sketchbooks that illustrates the type of anatomical drawing that J.B. Yeats referred to in his unpublished *Memoirs*.

He recalled that when working in the art school, Wilson always had a book of anatomy beside him, which exposed in minute detail the underlying muscle construction.. This certainly displays the difference in approach, and outcome, of the drawings of the two friends – each delightful in its own way. But Yeats perhaps went to somewhat excessive extremes in his conjecture that when Wilson painted in life classes direct from the figure, or simply defined the single elements of a hand, arm, face, or even just a nose, that his painting of flesh compared with the 'palpitating quality' of a Michelangelo sculpture, which was both 'their delight' but which equally was beyond them.[116]

Whilst in the early days, Nettleship pursued avidly the style of Blake as his mentor, Wilson could be seen from his earliest days to be the pure romantic – whether through his chalk drawings, his charming woodland watercolour drawings, or in his allegorical paintings for which he employed either oil or watercolour, and sometimes tempera. Nevertheless, in these latter paintings, there is sometimes a harking back to Blake inspired concepts – such as in his study entitled *The Dance* for the eventual painting *Arcadia*. Whether intentional or not (and the subject is certainly completely different), just one work of which this composition is certainly reminiscent is Blake's illustration to *Nurse's Song* in *Songs of Innocence and Experience* (1789).[117]

Comparing the available drawings by each of these three aspiring artists from their student days, there is certainly a studied quality, but also a pure, if sometimes possibly a precise classicism, to Wilson's work (which sometimes became stilted when transcribed into a major oil-painting); but there is a greater and even more relaxed and natural freedom to Yeats's drawings. Yet the invariable, and seemingly only, comment ever made on Yeats's work was of his insecurity and lack of confidence. This could be an unfair judgement and might well reflect Yeats's own expressions of self-doubt, but it probably also played easily into Nettleship's indubitable desire to be hailed always as the natural 'ringleader'. Yeats's drawings may not always have been very strong, but they always have great sensitivity and charm. This cannot often be said about the few of Nettleship's drawings that are generally accessibly – which are usually imaginative and always strong – even heavy at times – but somehow lacking any great subtlety.

It has to be questioned then, whether the title of 'Genius' – awarded to him by Yeats as well as self-styled by Nettleship himself – was not more of a reaction to his attempts as quite a young man to emulate Blake, as an artist, and to pontificate about Browning, as an essayist, rather than a true reflection of his real ability! But without access to many of his major early works, it is presently impossible to know. In those early days, Yeats was evidently fascinated, if not infatuated, by Nettleship, so no doubt fell in easily with the required notion. Furthermore, no doubt the debate that would have surrounded any such discussion amongst these young and sometimes highly opinionated artists (and even more so whilst Edwin Ellis was present) would have had as much bearing as the quality of the works themselves. If one or another *appeared* to be pursuing the right vision, then that would have carried great weight. However, Wilson would most certainly have guarded his own opinion!

In July 1872, within the strained Yeats household, the somewhat inevitable decision had been made that Susan Yeats should return to the relative domestic shelter of her family in Sligo in order to raise their children.[118] And so that most unfortunate and unsuccessful excursion she had made to join her husband in London came to an end – at least for a couple of years. So when Yeats returned alone to London at the end of the summer of 1872, to take up his training at The Slade once more, he found it imperative to find someone else with whom to share the cost of the large, and now very empty, house in Fitzroy Road – at least until he could try to sublet it. He approached George Wilson, who happily agreed to move in and share the costs of rent and a maid. But of course no sub-let took place and so they enjoyed the best part of a year in each other's company. Yeats thought that Wilson was doing him 'a great deal of good'.[119]

Wilson was a very quiet and unassuming person. He was extremely economical with his words; but when he did speak, it was always well considered and perceptive. Yeats, in his unpublished *Memoirs* mentions that he was a good talker, but that he also had the knack of being able to stimulate and at the same time check the conversation through an interjected remark or a cautious question and a humorous chuckle. He found living with Wilson to be easy, and he also found him a delightful companion, as the Scot generally wished merely to be alone and quiet. He was very musical and, as Yeats remarked, he could remember the most complicated harmonies after hearing them just once and could then whistle them back straightaway. He enjoyed playing the piano, but 'nothing but the great masters and exercises'; but mostly, he worked away industriously at his art.[120]

There is one other amusing little tale that Yeats related to his wife, Susan, at this time in a letter dated 30th January 1873, when one of Yeats's Kildare tenants apparently arrived completely unannounced on the doorstep at Fitzroy Road to discuss a proposal to buy one of the Yeats estate farms. Yeats remarked that his own 'dismay and Wilson's delight were equal – an Irish tenant is not to be seen every day. He was much impressed by his bigness and hulking solidity'![121]

George Wilson had developed an interest in the work of Corot (1796-1875), and his influence can sometimes be seen in certain elements of Wilson's work. Corot not only shared his love for Italy, but equally his love of painting within forests – in Corot's case, painting in the forests of Fontainebleau. This evidently struck a strong chord with Wilson's own delight in the forests of his Scottish homeland. Corot's sometime treatment of the taut boughs of windswept trees, threatening to have the leaves stripped off them, such as in *The Gust of Wind* (Musée Saint-Denis, Reims), can often be seen reflected in a similar vein within Wilson's more imaginative woodland landscapes.

Corot's handling of water, and indeed, the light and composition in paintings such as the oil painting of *Le Pont de Mantes* (Louvre, Paris) can be seen as influencing Wilson's own similar compositions. The two paintings of *The Brig o' Balgownie* (The Old Bridge of Don in north Aberdeen), although both painted in watercolour, are good examples of this comparison.

Again, in Wilson's watercolour study for *Arcadia* entitled *The Dance* (already referred to above for its Blake-like design), the dancing figures similarly harken back to the dancing wood nymphs incorporated within Corot's several Renaissance-inspired experimental developments from Claudian landscape, variously entitled around *Danse des Nymphes* – a number of which hang in the Musée d'Orsay in Paris.

And yet again, in another Scottish woodland watercolour, *The Huntly Lodge Woods in Summer*, one might imagine Wilson chuckling out aloud in his characteristic way as he painted in the bright, 'typically Corot' single splash of red for the dress of one of the girls in the scene. But there the comparison broadly ends as, for instance, Wilson's treatment of sky and colour tone is somewhat removed from that of the French master.

In his manuscript *Memoirs*, Yeats recorded how, following a chance encounter with Wilson in a Bond Street shop where an exhibition of pictures was being held, Wilson seems to have managed to explain the work of Corot in a way that enabled Yeats to be able to appreciate it for the first time. Initially, Yeats first dismissed a 'brown looking picture' as being no good at all before Wilson told him who the artist was. Yeats's problem appears to have been an inability to refocus from their training that had been overseen and guided by the teachings of Ruskin, whereby they were taught to look for a carefully drawn and accentuated foreground and middle distance, whilst the horizon was of little more consequence than as a background for the rest of the composition. But above all they visualised life as always being bright and of pure colour, whereas Corot's pictures were all browns and greys.[122]

Wilson, on the other hand – and despite Yeats's assertion that they had both developed similarly – had evidently already transcended into a far more eclectic appreciation of the art around him at the time, possibly largely due to his travels abroad, which Yeats had largely lacked. The irony of this example is that Yeats's own development into portraiture in the succeeding years was to rely greatly upon the colours with which he was having so much difficulty at the Bond Street exhibition! But from Wilson's point of view, this may be the first intimation that he was looking beyond his earlier teachings to what had influenced the French impressionists.

At the Slade, all three students were making serious progress and getting on well with Poynter – albeit that Yeats sustained his continuing lack of self-belief. Poynter wanted them to progress to using oils, but Yeats demurred. It was at this point that Nettleship suggested that Yeats should give up his formal training and begin painting portraits – which was eventually to become, relatively effectively, the essence of his 'life's work' – but for the moment Poynter concurred that he should carry on with his basic development.[123] Yeats, the eternal student, needed no greater encouragement.

Some competition via a 'designing club' was introduced into their efforts when 'at homes' were held every two weeks at the house of the future actor, Johnston Forbes-Robertson (1853-1937; later to be knighted, but at that time a student at the Royal Academy). At these occasions, the members of the Brotherhood, along with some others, would submit 'designs' on assigned subjects, which Yeats referred to as 'ideas for pictures we proposed to paint'.[124]

In April 1873, Yeats invited Wilson to visit Sligo with him for Easter. Returning via Dublin, they stayed as the guests of the Dowden brothers: Wilson staying with Edward, whilst Yeats stayed with John. Edward Dowden, writing on 15th April of that year to Elizabeth West, his life-long correspondent who eventually became his second wife, mentioned their impending arrival. In a subsequent letter to Miss West, dated 24th April, he described their visit and their departure a few days later. In this letter, Dowden talks of a happy day spent walking to Howth, towards the Baily Lighthouse, where he read some of his poems to the two artists, whilst they, in all probability – or undoubtedly Wilson, at least – sketched contentedly from the landscape.[125]

In July 1873, the lease at Fitzroy Road came to an end. By 31st July, both Yeats, then aged 34, and Wilson, 10 years his junior at just 24, had also finished their last formal term at the Slade. Yeats, already developing the trait that would dominate throughout his lifetime, had half-finished portrait commissions in both Dublin and London at the time. His wife Susan returned to London to help him clear the house in Fitzroy Road, following which they both went back to Ireland – she to her family once again, but Yeats himself effectively without a welcoming home of his own. He therefore spent much of the time in Dublin and so, although he was back in his homeland once again, he found there that his young family had already grown apart from him. But at least in Dublin, he had a portrait of Edward Dowden to finish.[126]

George Wilson also moved on, but his address, and indeed what became of him for the next three or four years is not entirely clear. His brother John, writing to John Todhunter in May 1890, immediately after Wilson's death, reported that his brother had spent two years in Rome after finishing his studies in London. There is no reason to doubt that this is correct, since other references allude to his travels starting from this point. Furthermore, he did not commence his somewhat irregular submissions to London exhibitions until some years later in 1877. It would therefore have been both opportune and logical for him to have journeyed to Italy to further his education immediately after he left the Slade having, presumably, by then taken the decision that his formal training had at last come to an end.

It is not known whether he stayed in Italy for the duration or whether he returned home at intervals. The latter is the more likely, since he always liked to visit his family back in Scotland regularly each year. Certainly, it is believed that he was in Scotland sometime probably during 1875, when the formal photographs reproduced elsewhere in this book are calculated to have been taken. Although 1875 was also the date of the birth of his niece, Rachel, it is hardly likely that this would have been any sort of specifically memorable event in his brother John's calendar, since John Wilson's wife, Anna, produced a new child almost each and every year over a period of two decades – the last being born when she was in her 44th year!

CHAPTER EIGHT

Finally to work!

During the watershed years of 1873-74, and with Wilson understood to be abroad in Italy, the other two enduring members of the Brotherhood, J.T. Nettleship and J.B. Yeats, also drifted apart somewhat. Susan Yeats had come over to London to help her husband clear out the Fitzroy Road house following the termination of its lease, before they both returned to Ireland.[127] And by 1874, Nettleship had moved from his studio in 22, Newman Street to a new location at 233, Stanhope Street, near to Regent's Park and the Zoological Gardens, where he had already started to get on with producing his animal paintings that Rossetti had rather unkindly referred to as his 'pot-boilers'.

It was at this same Stanhope Street address that George Wilson was next to appear, and it was where both he and Nettleship settled into a concerted productive period over the subsequent several years, during which they both exhibited fairly regularly from that address. We don't presently know whether the property was leased by Nettleship or Wilson or by both of them, as there is a confusing array of correspondence and exhibition submissions, all generating from that same address. This includes at least one letter that, rather curiously, carries this address, but which was sent to Nettleship by his fiancée, Ada Cort Hinton, whilst he was away working in Andover! Whether Ada was merely using it as a convenient poste-restante address, or whether she was staying there temporarily herself, is not divulged.[128]

It is equally unclear whether Stanhope Street was the young artists' home or was purely used by them as a studio. It may be that Nettleship was living at the address during 1874; however, by 1875 he was living at 20a, Albert Street – no more than a few hundred yards north of Stanhope Street.[129] This may have been in anticipation of the event in April 1876 when Nettleship and Ada Hinton were married. Presumably then, after their honeymoon in Devon, they set up home and settled down in Albert Street. Nevertheless, Nettleship certainly continued to exhibit from the Stanhope Street address right through until 1879, so most probably he continued to work from there as his studio.

However, it would seem most unlikely that the itinerant George Wilson would see any logic or indeed any necessity whatsoever for two separate lodgings in London, and he could easily have simply made the Stanhope Street address his convenient London base for both work and sleep in between his travels. There is an amusing reference to the frugality of Wilson's life in a letter from Nettleship to Ada Hinton of around October 1877, sent while he and Wilson were away together painting in Surrey. He reported an incident that appears to have come about through there being no clean sheets awaiting them on the beds when they arrived, so they had to sleep 'elsewhere' for one or two nights. He went on to say that although he had immediately taken to the bed once the clean sheets had arrived, George Wilson had chosen not to do so, as he remained perfectly comfortable continuing to sleep 'elsewhere' – wherever 'elsewhere' happened to be![130]

Meanwhile, whilst Nettleship and Wilson were buttoning down to some serious work, Yeats had been in Ireland, where, ironically, during this brief period, he also actually completed and sold a number of commissions, and had started to make a bit of a name for himself – plus of course, some much-needed cash! Incredulously then, but equally also so typically, rather than building on what he had so far achieved, in October 1874, he took the shattering decision for his family, to abandon his Irish commissions and their related income and return yet again to London to resume his study courses 'to perfect his technique'. This time though, in true Yeatsian style, he performed a complete circle in his academic career by returning not to the Slade and Poynter's tuition, but back to Heatherley's once again, taking lodgings for all his family at 14, Edith Villas in West Kensington – a small and most uncomfortable house compared with what they had previously been used to.[131]

Both Dowden and Todhunter managed to obtain commissions for Yeats in London, but these also he postponed in favour of the furtherance of his revisited Heatherley studies. In any case, they would probably have been doomed to failure so long as his sole aim remained perfection in all his paintings – which of course he always failed to secure.[132] He was by then 35 years old, and back at art school once again. Not only should he have completed his studies long ago, but should have been exhibiting regularly and selling his paintings, whereas in fact he had signally failed to make his mark – or indeed, any real money!

In 1876, Yeats made one of his all too rare decisions to go out and solicit commissions for portraits and, indeed, he did at least secure one or two – including one of John Todhunter and another of Isaac Butt, the Conservative and Unionist politician turned Nationalist, who was at the top of his career. Butt had been a friend of Yeats's father and he deemed the commission would be a useful one to promote his own career.[133] However, once again, fate served to interrupt this small but positive surge forward. Some years earlier, at Christmas 1872, Yeats had made a visit to Ireland to see his temporarily estranged wife, Susan, and his family in Sligo, and to go on to a large commission to paint the Herbert family at Muckross House in Killarney. Almost immediately after he had arrived with the family, he was called back to Sligo on the news of the death of his youngest son, Robert. In a similar vein, in June 1876, Yeats's youngest daughter, Jane, fell ill and died before her first birthday.[134]

Once again, the grief-stricken Susan hastily moved her children back to the comfort of her own family in Ireland, where Yeats suddenly found that he also had to join her when his own mother died in Dublin shortly afterwards. Following this turmoil, to which were added further financial problems involving his property in Ireland, upon returning to England, Yeats took yet another of his totally irrational decisions to ditch his search for further commissions in London and to revert to working on refining his landscape technique. This was the occasion that led to the oft-recounted tale of his inability to complete a particular landscape painting at Burnham Beeches because the seasons kept changing faster than he could complete the work to his own contentment.

Thus, the Yeats predicament of effectively zero progress continued. To make matters worse, by 1877, the first year when both George Wilson and Nettleship together had pictures hung at the Royal Academy (although Nettleship had exhibited once previously at the RA in 1874 with *Not Dead Yet*), Yeats could only be thoroughly frustrated by his own singular failure to get any of his works accepted. By his own admission, he was going nowhere.[135] Since he had exhibited *Pippa Passes* at the Dudley in 1871, and *A Brunette* there in 1872, he had subsequently, in 1876, only had two small drawings accepted, again at the Dudley – one in black and white entitled *The Lute Player*, and the other a watercolour of *Mrs Barrington Orr*.

Sometimes in the case of intermingling lives, one year seems to turn out to be a joint watershed – and in respect of Wilson and Nettleship, 1877 was certainly a busy year that held many exciting developments; but for Yeats it held just more of the same old lack of progress and direction. Nevertheless, it was good that the friends hadn't entirely lost contact, and the earlier style of drawing 'competition' that had previously taken place at Forbes-Robertson's house back in 1872 evidently still appealed to them as, five years later on in 1877, when they were all back in London once again, they got together and formed another 'designing club' modelled on the earlier Forbes-Robertson association. This time Robert Catterson Smith, who had studied with them at Heatherley's, was included – although he wrote about this with a rather despondent element of doubt when describing it to John Todhunter on 2nd July 1877:

> *Wilson, and Nettleship are in the RA The former has a male head* [Study of a Head (No. 296) q.v.]. *The latter a large lion and a girl with a dog in her lap. I don't think Yates* [sic] *has anything any where. I believe he has been out of town painting – I called at his house and they said he was away – Wilson said the* [sic] *thought it was a mistake to be away so long – I think he is now back … Wilson, Nettleship, Ellis and others have formed a designing club – I think I am a member. They are to have periodical meetings to show the designs made to a given subject. There is a payment of 2s.6d.* [equivalent to £10 today, and a significant sum of money for the 'kitty' that Yeats could still ill-afford at that time] *to be made by each member at each of these meetings, and they are to vote for one of the designs, and which ever gets the most votes is to be purchased by the club and kept by it. The first of these meetings has taken place (28th June): and the subject was – There was a little city and few men within it, there came a great king against it and built great bulwarks against it.*

Now there was found in it a poor wise man, and he by his wisdom delivered the city; yet no man remembered that same poor man. I believe this subject was suggested by Yates [sic]. *Wilson's got the most votes – I had not got a design made, the greatest reason for that was that I could not see how to convey the absolute meaning of the verses. Nor do I at all believe that any one of the designs conveyed it. Wilson's and Kennedy's* designs were really fine. The subject for next time is, "That the sons of God saw the daughters of men and that they were fair: and they took them wives of all which they chose".*† *It is to be done in a fortnight – It seems such a tremendous subject to me. But I suppose there is no use in being ashamed of one's efforts...*[136]

In July of 1877, Nettleship made an excursion to Aberdeenshire along with Ralph Radcliffe Whitehead – perhaps to find out what it was that so enamoured George Wilson about the landscape. It is difficult to tell whether Wilson actually accompanied them as well, but it would appear probably not. However, it does appear from a letter Nettleship wrote to Ada in the form of a diary note made during his train journey, that they probably rested in Aberdeen with another of George Wilson's older brothers, Charles,‡ before journeying on to stay at Kildrummy Lodge, near Mossat, for a couple of months. It could have been that Wilson travelled with them, but then went on to visit his eldest brother John, in Huntly just 15 miles farther north, on his own; however, Nettleship's subsequent letter to Ada seems to indicate that Wilson had been left behind.

The date of that letter was 25th July when, in a mock grumpy tone that commenced with the endearment, 'All right Collywobbles...' he then carried on with a short numbered list of answers, apparently in response to a series of questions of Ada's concerning Wilson's plans for the summer – which Nettleship had clearly failed to answer to her satisfaction on a previous occasion! In this letter, he stated that,

1. George is going nowhere this summer unless he has altered his mind since I left you.

2. He would very much like to come to Haslemere with us – subject to his being able to afford it.

3. I want him to if he will.

4. Etc., etc.... [137]

---

* In all probability, this was Charles Napier Kennedy (1852–1898), who had also studied at The Slade under E.J. Poynter at the same time as the others mentioned here – and was considerably influenced by Poynter. Kennedy commenced painting portraits and genre scenes, but developed mainly into mythological subjects. He exhibited widely.

† The biblical subject chosen is from Genesis 6. v2. A watercolour drawing of this title was purchased from George Wilson by John Todhunter and was exhibited at both of the retrospective Wilson exhibitions, held in 1893 and 1903. Todhunter's watercolour (now assumed lost) was presumably developed from the concept proposed for this design 'competition'.

‡ Charles Wilson WS (1842-1927), Procurator Fiscal for Aberdeenshire, lived at Westfield Terrace, Aberdeen.

Ada's evidently persistent questioning may have been related to the fact that, in the previous March, she had produced their first child Ida (who was later to marry the artist Augustus John – much to her parents' horror!) Her previous letter that stimulated this reply is not available, but it would have been understandable for her to wish to know what precisely was being planned by her husband. It is also interesting to note here that all three are happily on first-name terms, which at that time is a clear indication that by then they must already have developed a very close personal relationship.

The Haslemere trip did indeed go ahead in October of that year, although Ada stayed at home with Ida – possibly because she would, by then, have discovered that she was in the very early stages of pregnancy with her second child, eventually to be named Ethel, and who eventually arrived on 17th May 1878. In two extant letters from John Nettleship to his wife, he describes in touching and comic terms some of the pranks that he and George Wilson got up to with some local friends by the name of Hutchinson and others who lived in the area.* On one occasion, Nettleship reports that they decorated the house with large quantities of ivy and greenery and painted rough sketches and symbols all over the walls, in theory for a send-off party for Wilson's impending departure. However, it seems from the second letter that the party was perhaps too much of a success, as Wilson in fact stayed on for several days more after that.

Between the evident buffoonery that he narrated to Ada, there are references to Nettleship hoping to complete a number of large paintings while Wilson was evidently deeply involved in painting his preferred woodland landscapes, much to Nettleship's expressed admiration.[138] These letters portray two very good friends at their most relaxed and enjoying themselves with very little in the way of day-to-day worries to hinder them. This was in sharp contrast to their old friend Yeats's continuing conundrums during that same period over finding commissions, achieving self-satisfying results from his work – and, of course, continually making ends meet.

It was at this point that Nettleship commenced a period of 24 years, leading up to his death in 1902, during which he exhibited prolifically.[139] His paintings were hung regularly at the Royal Academy – scarcely missing a year – but also predominantly at the Royal Institute of Oil Painters, the New Gallery and the Walker Art Gallery in Liverpool, as well as the Grosvenor and other London and provincial galleries. As previously mentioned, as early as 1874, he had commenced the submission of these paintings from the studio at 233, Stanhope Street, whereas by the time of Ethel's birth,

---

* It is not entirely certain what the relationship was between the Nettleships and the Haslemere area, but it seems probable that the link was (partly at least) through the same Hutchinson family. John Nettleship's brother Edward, who was equally a close friend of George Wilson, was, in his early medical career, assistant and close friend to Sir John Hutchinson, Surgeon at the London Hospital and Dean of its Medical School. In 1885, Edward had also bought some land in Hindhead, near to Haslemere, where he completed the construction of a new house called 'Nutcombe' in 1887. George Wilson often visited the Nettleships and painted a number of watercolour landscapes in the area.

his address was registered as 20, Giesbach Road, Islington – some two and a half miles farther north from the studio.

But by the time Nettleship had returned from his important trip to India, lasting from October 1880 to March 1881, when he painted a cheetah hunt and an equestrian portrait, both commissioned by the Gaekwar of Baroda, it seems that both he and George Wilson had given up the Stanhope Street address. From 1881 to 1883, Nettleship is recorded as having submitted paintings to exhibition (including the Baroda cheetah hunt painting, entitled *The Last Leap but One*, to the RA) from Park Road Studios in Haverstock Hill, Hampstead. George Wilson, in contrast, pursued his own frequent travels abroad during the early 1880s, particularly to Italy, although he had also in the meantime – and by 1883 at the latest – taken a studio of his own at 65, Newman Street, right back in the heart of the artistic area off Oxford Street that his colleagues had all aspired to in their earlier student days. This was undoubtedly the most prolific period of Wilson's short career, and he even submitted a number of his more significant works to exhibition from this Newman Street address during 1883 and 1884. Similarly, this address appears on the reverse of several of his still existent larger allegorical oil paintings. However, his tenancy was evidently quite short, since by 1885 he is also recorded as exhibiting from No. 1, The Mall, Park Road, Haverstock Hill, London. NW.

Unfortunately, there is no exact address quoted for Nettleship's earlier 'Park Road Studios' (and there were many artists' studio complexes in the area), so we do not know if this is indeed one and the same as Wilson's studio, and whether the two occupied the same studio either concurrently or even consecutively; but the similarity of address, and previous history would indicate the likelihood of this. we do have is a new address from which Nettleship was exhibiting regularly from 1884 (whilst Wilson was still based in Newman Street), and this was the previous address of the home of his mother-in-law, Margaret Hinton, at 35, Acacia Road in St. John's Wood – around the opposite side of Regent's Park from Haverstock Hill.[140]

Whether Margaret Hinton was still living at the address at the same time is not known. She was living in Hertfordshire when she died in 1888, but it may be assumed that Nettleship was only occupying Acacia Road as his studio since his own family was recorded as living at 2, Melbury Terrace in Marylebone for the 1881 census[*] through to when his third daughter, Ursula, was born in February 1886. The simple, but unproven, conclusion would be that when Nettleship went to India, both painters just gave up the Stanhope Street address, making their own arrangements until they joined up again later on, purely as it suited them both.

---

[*] John Nettleship was not in fact present at home during the 1881 census; indeed, both he and George Wilson do not appear to have been registered anywhere in the UK, so were presumably both out of the country or on their travels. Nettleship may still have been on his way back from India, whilst Wilson might have been in Italy that spring – which would have been quite customary for him.

It is not known how long Wilson retained use of the Mall Studio, since information about his life becomes very thin from this point up until the time of his death, just five years later in 1890. It is interesting to note, however, that there is an evident growing confidence, not only in the work that both Nettleship and Wilson were undertaking at this time, but also in the fact that they took on a studio of the nature of those in The Mall Studios complex, and in such a comparatively prestigious location.[*]

* * *

The most productive years of George Wilson's life are set out in as much detail as is presently known in following chapters. However, it is deemed appropriate to record at this point some facets of his life as it related to both Nettleship and Yeats in those intervening years. This also serves to conclude the entries related here in respect of his two earliest companions and their own work.

We presently have little further information at all as to George Wilson's whereabouts during these last five years of his life. But by 1889, the Nettleship family had moved to their final settled address of 58, Wigmore Street, and this may well have included numbers 56 and 60 as well, since the previous occupants had run a business occupying all three premises. It was from this address that Ada Nettleship was to expand and very effectively develop the dressmaking business that would largely keep the family's fortunes afloat. If indeed it were the case that the three properties were effectively one, it might also explain the curiosity of the letter written by John Nettleship to Halsey Ricardo in June 1891 following George Wilson's death, and bearing the address of Number 60 rather than Number 58 (q.v.).

At this point there is very little more to report of the life of John Trivett Nettleship, which has never been researched to conclusion. He had moved away from his stricter Pre-Raphaelite and Blake-inspired roots at a very early stage, but during his later

---

*   Park Road, later renamed Parkhill Road in 1897, runs off Haverstock Hill in Hampstead, an area noted in the late 1800s for good quality houses designed to be occupied by professionals and artists, and indeed a number of artists' studios existed in the neighbourhood. The Mall Studios (originally simply called 'The Mall'), are actually located off the adjoining Tasker Road, and were built by Thomas Batterbury in 1872. They do still exist today, although not specifically as artists' studios.

The studios were occupied variously by many now prominent artists – including, in the earlier days, George Clausen (1852 – 1944) and Walter Sickert (1860-1942); but during the 1930s they became home (specifically, No 7) to the influential abstract artist group that included Barbara Hepworth (1903-1975) and her first husband, John Skeaping (1901-1980), who was eventually replaced by her second husband, Ben Nicholson (1894-1982]. When the latter couple moved to St Ives in 1940, the studio was taken over by their friend and colleague, Henry Moore (1898-1986), although he also was forced to move out very shortly afterwards when the building received minor bomb damage during WWII.

It is of further interest that in the 1881 census, only three of the eight studios were actually occupied – at least, presumably, as residential accommodation.

enduring 'animal' phase, he certainly produced some prolific work, and his paintings do, infrequently, appear for sale or at auction. His accomplishment as a wild animal painter became well recognised, and this led to him being commissioned from time to time by other artists to paint in the animals into their pictures. It is understood that Henry Holiday (1839-1927) requested Nettleship's assistance to paint-in the pigeons in his most famous painting of *Dante and Beatrice* (Walker Art Gallery), completed in 1883. In 1894, Nettleship became a member of the Royal Institute of Oil Painters.

J.T. Nettleship never gave up his friendship and close affection for Wilson, and there is a poignant and emotional account in the letter from Nettleship to Halsey Ricardo, dated 15th June 1891, just over a year after Wilson's death, describing his painful difficulty in dealing with some packing cases containing a number of Wilson's larger oil paintings. This single letter (apparently written as Nettleship was about to depart on a trip to the Pyrenees with Ralph Radcliffe Whitehead, and shortly before the latter finally emigrated to the USA) brings home most succinctly the emphatic bond felt between these friends at the final loss of one of their number. This was in spite of their having led rather more separate lives for the past few years, and showed how little time had changed their fundamental empathy for each other and each other's work.

The circumstances of this letter appear to indicate that Whitehead – who at that time had just become divorced from his first wife in favour of Jane Byrd McCall – had placed his three major Wilson paintings into storage cases, and had asked Nettleship to look after them for him. The letter carries a postscript apologising for all the crossings out – due to the evident change in information Nettleship had received prior to sending it off. The relevant part of the letter is transcribed verbatim.

> *My dear Halsey,*
>
> *Many thanks for your letter; I shall be grateful if you will take charge of these 3 pictures of George's, for I have neither the space nor light to hang them properly, and moreover they are entombed in packing cases. I did unscrew the lids to show them to Todhunter, but in that half-exposed fashion they haunt me – like mummies.*
>
> *So I have screwed them up again – with the remorseful feeling of a half-hearted resurrectionist – whose courage has failed him at the uncovering.*
>
> *Now I had written to Sutton & Co the carriers who are coming to take some of the traps for the Pyrenean trip, asking them to take these 3 cases to your house, intending myself to call or write to you first. But as you are away ~~I don't suppose your servants want to take them without your asking. So if you will kindly give instructions at Bedford Square for the cases to be taken in, I'll have them sent there before I go.~~ ₓI called there this morning, and your parlourmaid said she would take them in. Sutton & Co have just carted them off this afternoon, so you will find them on your return tomorrow or whenever you do arrive.ₓ Before I go, which will be in about a fortnight ₓI hope to come and bid you and Mrs Ricardo goodbye.ₓ ~~It's awfully good of you to propose coming for them yourself, but they are too heavy~~*

for and big for the four wheeler (the Whiteheads thought the contrary) and this staircase is decidedly awkward, as I know from experience of hauling these and other bulky things up it and down it – So I hope you will let me have them taken to your house in your absence if you are not coming back before July. ₓNB The Persephone came loose in her box, but quite uninjured; so I put no screws in her back and took the risk of her reaching you in good condition, as she had travelled safely so, all the way from Styriaₓ [Austria].

There were never any Dryads in the Pyrenees, and not fernseed nor mandragora nor all the ---- rest of it; will ever medicine give [illegible] to such a vision. I am quite in suspense about the success of this trip, but Whitehead is bent on making everything very jolly and pleasant, and I rather check myself from expecting too much so that the pleasure when it comes may be a "shock of sweet respite". Pixies there may be and I trust your wish may prove a prophecy.

Are you down in Sussex on business, or taking a bitter-sweet revenge on Asolo and Venice? I hope the latter as well as the former, for it's princely weather now, -- I always hate this time of year in London, the streets are such pure futility, still, some of them lead to the zoo, and there's a grand young boy lion there with a girl mate, & they romp outside and make cub love beautifully; moreover he lets the other lions know that <u>he</u> can roar too, a little, and the grunt he ends up with is almost the real thing. Harry your boy would delight in that pair but in the male particularly.

I have been doing Samson drinking, partly to my own satisfaction, and I don't despair of your liking it; the thing had been in a rubbishy state for years {but / and} at any rate there is some intention in the canvas now. ...

... Your ever affectionate Jack

It may be assumed that two of the three paintings referred to were *The Spring Witch* and *Persephone (The Rape of Proserpine)*, but what the title of the third was remains uncertain.

Nettleship got a lot of his inspiration and the 'models' for the animal paintings for which he became best known, from regular visits to London Zoo in Regent's Park. In 1890, he was even elected fellow of the Zoological Society. It cannot be certain what the reference to Asolo and Venice means, but those concerned in every aspect of this correspondence had lost within four months two of their main connections associated with those idyllic Italian towns. Primarily, Robert Browning had died in December 1889, but subsequently George Wilson had also passed away just three months later on 1st April 1890 – although the latter would never have presumed to associate himself with any such pattern of thought.[141]

John Nettleship only lived for another 12 years after Wilson's death when he also died on 31st August 1902, aged 61 years, after a long and painful illness. He was buried in Kensal Green Cemetery. A memorial tablet in bronze, designed by the symbolist sculptor Sir George Frampton (1860–1928), was placed in the parish church of Kettering. This tablet was contributed to by both of Nettleship's more widely-known contemporary Kettering-born artists: the Pre-Raphaelite inspired Thomas Cooper Gotch (1854–1931) and the landscapist, Sir Alfred East (1849–1913). Apart from his regular showings at the RA and many other public exhibitions, a sole exhibition of Nettleship's paintings was staged at the Rembrandt Gallery in London in 1890.

What became of his personal collection of paintings is not presently known. In addition to his own works, the collection included a number by George Wilson. His wife, Ada, retained all his chattels until her own death in 1932, when she bequeathed just one of her husband's pictures to each of her

John Trivett Nettleship, ca. 1900, from a photograph courtesy of Mrs K.N. Protopapa and Northamptonshire Records Office (as custodians), The Nettleship Collection.

two remaining daughters (Ethel and Ursula, both of whom remained unmarried) and one painting to each of her grandchildren. These grandchildren were the five sons of her eldest daughter, Ida, who became the first wife of the painter Augustus John, and who had died in 1907. The rest of the collection was to be sold. It has not been investigated further to any extent, but it is understood that none of the John descendents is aware of the location of any of these bequeathed paintings. That would not be entirely surprising among the plethora of paintings and drawings left by Augustus John himself – who somewhat overshadowed his father-in-law as well as all of Nettleship's friends in every imaginable way.

The good intention here was originally to reproduce a number of Nettleship's works, but apart from those very few previously referred to in public galleries, very little of significance appears to be immediately available. That objective will consequently have to await another occasion.

* * *

From the above, it will be recognised that with the detailed life of John Trivett Nettleship and his works presently being very little known, he certainly deserves rather more research to enable him to become a better understood, defined and recorded artist.

Equally of course, the same applies, although rather more so, to George Wilson – and that is largely the purpose of this book. J.B., however, is a very different story. Much studied work has been undertaken in respect of his life and his work – but not always with both aspects of the subject discussed with the same degree of interest, in the same book, and at the same time. One exception to this – and which the author of this book has been most grateful to have been permitted to refer to frequently, has been William M. Murphy's exhaustively researched and comprehensive book, *Prodigal Father, The Life of John Butler Yeats (1839-1933)*.[142]

In addition, of course, extensive volumes have been written about J.B. Yeats's eldest son, W.B. Yeats, and those inevitably revolve at times around his relationship with his father. Then again, there is an ever-increasing interest in the work of the younger son, Jack B. Yeats, whose paintings seem, equally, to demand ever-increasing sums at sale. Add in the inherent interest in the lives of W.B. Yeats's own daughter, Anne, and his two sisters, Lily and Lolly, and this all adds up to a considerable amount of published information about the family. The only further comment, therefore, that is deemed necessary with reference to J.B. Yeats's life as it relates to time span covered by this present book, follows on here. However, for an extensive, erudite and detailed descriptive analysis of the artistic merits of three generations of that remarkable family, the exemplary book *Yeats, Portrait of an Artistic Family* by Hilary Pyle, Yeats Curator at the National Gallery of Ireland, is essential reading.[143]

The fact that John Butler Yeats's life is far better chronicled than his colleagues' is then, to a fair extent, due initially to the success of his two sons – to begin with, to W.B. Yeats, but more recently and increasingly so, to Jack B. Yeats. Yet despite their father's own failure ever to pursue his objectives with any degree of direction or concerted focus of ambition, it is not unreasonable to suggest that his own considerable proficiency as a portrait painter is still not as widely recognised today as it ought to be – although thankfully that would appear to be changing. In particular, this has been through the dedication of the National Gallery of Ireland and Hilary Pyle, who in 1999 brought to fruition their concept of a dedicated Yeats Museum to which she was then Curator until her recent retirement.

One enduring thread of communication that kept each of the Heatherley and Slade friends at least aware of the others' movements was the life-long interest of John Todhunter. In 1879, Yeats had had enough of the dingy crowded house at Edith Villas, which only served to remind everyone continually of the death of his daughter Jane. He therefore decided (with the customary non-consideration of any cost or other implications) that he really needed to move his family into the new 'model village' that was being developed for London's artistic and literary community in Bedford Park, west London. Bedford Park had been commenced in 1875 with 'Queen Anne' style houses primarily designed specifically for those interested in the arts. The community was almost completely self-contained with its own shopping, church and essential facilities. By the time the Yeats family moved into 8 Woodstock Road, 350 houses had already been built, largely designed by Norman Shaw, with wallpaper and other interior design features by his friend William Morris. William de Morgan's tiles were also used in abundance. It must therefore have seemed practically essential for Yeats that he should be part of this new aesthetic environment and, although the area was considered comparatively cheap to live in, he inevitably still found it extremely difficult to pay his way with the local traders.[144]

The Yeatses' move to Bedford Park coincided with Todhunter's remarriage and his own relocation into the same area, which immediately made him a near neighbour of the Yeatses. At the same time, Todhunter continued to correspond with all those involved or associated with the original Heatherley group, and as and when something interesting arose, he also continued occasionally to purchase paintings and drawings from members of this now increasingly disparate group. He thus became a life-long friend to them all, although he largely lost interest in purchasing the paintings of both Nettleship and Yeats once they had moved away from their early Pre-Raphaelite inspired roots. Nevertheless, he did continue throughout his life to collect in particular a significant number of George Wilson's works – and remained his close friend as well as enthusiastic patron to the end.

Yeats's later relationship with Wilson and with Nettleship is harder to judge. Whilst Wilson enquired after Yeats in correspondence to their other mutual friends, there is only infrequent evidence of Yeats returning such an enquiry – but it did certainly happen. That is not to suggest that the friendship largely foundered; but undoubtedly, and despite Yeats's earlier assertions from his student days as to how much 'good' Wilson was doing him at the time, he would always, rather inevitably, have seemed too quiet and unassuming a colleague to have featured highly in Yeats's longer-term priorities. It is indicative of the relative situations of the old friends that when Wilson had on occasions asked after Yeats, he had to add that he wasn't sure where to write to him or where he was currently living. However, to be fair, that applied equally to Wilson, the perpetual itinerant, although he did always return habitually to his various studio bases in London – which from a *poste-restante* point of view, he appears to have shared to a large extent with Nettleship throughout all but (possibly) the last few years of his life.

As with the very different styles of living that the three colleagues adopted during their working lives, and although they had followed virtually identical training paths, the artistic direction that each ultimately took was also fundamentally different.

Nettleship became an almost stereotypical Head of a largely conventional Victorian household. Artistically, he had effectively abandoned at a very early stage his exciting foundation in Blake and Pre-Raphaelitism for the comparatively staid occupation as specialist animal painter. This was supposed to produce the regular 'pot-boiler' income, but unfortunately never did, although largely thanks to his wife's successful dressmaking business and other income, they were always reasonably well-off.

Wilson was totally different. He was the only one of the three who never abandoned his early principles and was, to a significant extent at least, a Pre-Raphaelite follower to the end. That is not to say that he didn't progress and, as already alluded to, he was producing some almost impressionistic work towards the end of the 1880s. There can be very little doubt at all that, had he lived another 20 or 30 years, he would have made his mark in some form or other, with or without intentionally aiming to do so. From a lifestyle point of view, Wilson was also the greatest exception. He travelled regularly around Scotland, England

and Europe, and never settled down long in any one place – even in his *de facto* base city of London. He was the nomad of the group and therefore by far the most adventurous of the three; he never married, and lived as simple a life as it was possible to achieve. He was utterly unmotivated by commercialism and 'fame', but seems, nevertheless, to have generated sufficient income to just about keep his head above water.

Yeats, though, was a very individual and complicated mixture, and his character and lifestyle are almost impossible to précis with any brevity. He was married of course, but in a very complex relationship caught between his wife and his friends, and it was the relationship with his wife that largely lost out – indeed, even came close to being a disastrous failure. He was frequently saved from starvation in his early days by income from a variety of unplanned sources, all of which ultimately dried up. Rather than buckling down to hard work to support his expanding family, he chose almost anything else to pursue rather than income-generating work. However, genetically speaking he must have been the best-endowed of the three by far, in view of the remarkable dynasty of artistic endowment that descended directly from him.

Although Yeats, as with Nettleship, was also quick to abandon his earliest 'Pre-Raphaelite' principles, this comes as less of a surprise in that he had never in the first instance migrated in any one particular direction from which to veer later. Indeed, he found it almost impossible even to decide when he might have learnt enough at art school to enable him to move out into the real world of earning a living. As previously noted though, by the early 1870s, and long before Wilson had his first chalk *Study of a Head* accepted by the R.A in 1877, Yeats, without any such success himself, had moved almost entirely into the portrait painting arena at which he was becoming so accomplished – if never, of course, entirely satisfied. There is no question that he was a fine draughtsman and artist, who was badly let down by his own inadequacies of character and determination – although never by ability. His pencil drawings are always particularly sensitive, and his incessant sketching forms a continuing and delightful diary record of his children and family, as well as his friends and acquaintances.

That continual sketching is, of course, a very important element of Yeats's portrait record, and this book would be lacking if it failed at least to round off J.B. Yeats's relevance to the global picture in that short period within his life that related to Wilson's own short life. Yet it is actually true to say that his relevance to Wilson's latter years became relatively insignificant as they moved somewhat apart in every way. It might seem important to present an outline at least of how Yeats's particular work had moved on at that same time – and beyond. Similarly, it might appear incongruous only to reproduce in this book, as the sole examples of J.B. Yeats's work, just the one quick sketch drawing of John Todhunter and two of the very few existing early works (of *Pippa Passes*) as previously displayed. But in fact the central theme of Yeats's work from hereon – that of portraiture – bears little relevance to Wilson's remaining years, so those who wish to study the furtherance of Yeats's life and artistic career are recommended to consult those detailed publications devoted to this undoubtedly fascinating subject.

Although the decision is probably correct to exclude further works that are far removed from the central theme, there could still have been a strong incentive to include at the very least the striking portrait of J.B. Yeats's long-suffering wife Susan (National Gallery of Ireland), if only because she was such an important, if somewhat marginalised element of that earlier period in Yeats's life. They certainly had a most unusual and confused relationship, yet it was one that was still deeply devoted in many ways. He seems to have singularly failed to give any real consideration to her feelings at any of the critical decision points during her relatively short life of 59 years – the last 13 of which she endured as an invalid through the effects of the two strokes she suffered in 1887.

Susan was of course well known to the early 'Brotherhood', but Yeats seemed to consider her as somehow extraneous to his relationship with his artist friends. Ellis is reported as having been thoroughly rude and obnoxious towards her in her own home; however, it would not have been in the nature of either Nettleship or Wilson to be so, and undoubtedly the empathetic Wilson, in particular, would have felt most uncomfortable at Ellis's ungallant behaviour and would have worried deeply for her well-being. Hilary Pyle suggests that the early portrait of Susan, referred to above, was probably painted around 1875, following their being reunited as a family in London once again after two years effective separation whilst Yeats found work wherever he could.[145] It shows a somewhat reluctant and resigned Susan dressed in formal attire – possibly her 'Sunday best'. Nevertheless, it also shows a still striking and intelligent woman beneath the melancholy.

As already intimated, it is not deemed appropriate to pursue J.B Yeats's own life far beyond the extent of George Wilson's, as it is very well detailed elsewhere. It remains therefore, simply to record that J.B. Yeats died in New York City on 3rd February 1922, six weeks before his 83rd birthday and having outlived all his closer colleagues and friends from his early student days – both younger and older.

*   *   *

Having 'painted' something of the history of the earlier days of Wilson and his friends from the little that is recorded of those days, from hereon this book concentrates on the remaining, tragically few, final years of George Wilson's own life. In addition there is included as comprehensive a record as possible of everything that is currently known of his still extant works, as well as cross-references to some now lost but still identifiable works.

CHAPTER NINE

George Wilson's productive years

Following George Wilson's completion of his Slade studies and his subsequent departure from the Yeatses' Fitzroy Road home when the lease terminated in July 1873, he was understood to have spent the next two years between 1873 and 1874 broadening his studies in Rome, according to his brother, John.[146] Upon his return home, and although it is not known for sure, it would certainly have been logical for him to have taken a studio together with Nettleship, particularly since his arrival home probably coincided with about the time that Nettleship vacated his own Newman Street studio for new premises at 233, Stanhope Street, London, NW. It would be natural for the relaxed friendship between the two to have stimulated an agreement whereby they shared the costs of a studio, with Wilson drifting in and out as he wished and, in all probability, living there as well whenever he was in London.

Nettleship had exhibited for the first time at the RA in 1874 from this Stanhope Street address, with his earliest 'animal' subject to be hung, entitled *Not Dead Yet* . He next exhibited another similar subject *Who shall rouse him up?* at the RA in 1877, and then again virtually continuously thereafter throughout his life. Nettleship's 1877 painting was one of a number that he painted all through his career that perpetuated the Brotherhood's early penchant for illustrating biblical passages – in his case via the symbolism of his wild animals. In the 1877 painting, the passage was from Genesis Ch.49. v.9, relating Judah to a lion.

1877 was also the year when George Wilson had his first submission to the RA (the chalk *Study of a Head*) accepted as well – again from 233, Stanhope Street. How long the two retained the Stanhope Street address is not clearly recorded but can be reasonably estimated. As noted above, Nettleship, if he ever actually lived there, had certainly moved his personal living accommodation to Albert Street in 1875, the year before his marriage in 1876. Nevertheless, he exhibited from Stanhope Street right up until he went to India in October 1880, returning in March 1881, following which he used his Park Road, Hampstead studio address until 1883.

There is no record of where Wilson was during these three years, and he was not registered as being resident at any British address for the 1881 census, so he may well have been abroad for that event. It is of interest to note that Stanhope Street was not an area that was renowned as having been popular with artists, but since virtually the whole street was redeveloped in the urgent post-war desire for 'improved social housing' – ably abetted by the German bombing Blitz of London in the Second World War – it is difficult to know exactly what sort of premises these might have been. All we know from the 1881 census is that they must have been reasonably substantial buildings as there were 17 other occupants of No. 233 that were listed on that day. Wilson's next firmly recorded address was back in Newman Street (near Oxford Street), at number 65, by 1883.

In the meantime, in 1877, the *Study of a Head* was accepted and hung (no 296) at the Royal Academy Summer Exhibition. In the same year, he also submitted and had accepted at the Dudley Gallery 'Black and White' exhibition, the chalk drawing entitled *A Bacchante* that John Todhunter thought so highly of – and indeed, purchased. Both of these drawings clearly show the influence of Poynter's tuition.

In 1878, Wilson was accepted again at the RA (no 518) with his poignant oil painting entitled *The Quest from Shelley's "Alastor"*, an allegory from Shelley's poem *Alastor; or, The Spirit of Solitude*. Both *A Bacchante* and *Alastor* were purchased by John Todhunter[*] and were illustrated in his commemorative tribute to George Wilson's life, published in the *English Illustrated Magazine* in August 1891.[147] In this short and poetically written, if somewhat eulogistic article of just eight pages, Todhunter created a succinct and at the same time illuminating précis of Wilson's life. To a large extent, it is this one document that has been transcribed, often verbatim, in virtually every later publication in reference to George Wilson's life and work.

Although John Todhunter was well qualified to write this account, he is no longer particularly widely remembered for any of his own achievements. No doubt, he would have liked to be partially remembered, if only to a lesser extent, as a minor patron of the fine arts; but if at all, his legacy is mainly as a classical and pastoral poet and dramatist. Although he attained some real success in the 1880s and '90s with the new style of 'advanced absolute realism' to packed houses in the theatre – often including lead performances by the most celebrated actress of the time, Florence Farr – he failed to achieve enduring prominence as a playwright. Todhunter's version of Euripides' *Helena in Troas* was first performed in June 1886, and *A Sicilian Idyll* came on stage on 5th May

----

* In the exhibition catalogue to the 1961 exhibition '*W B Yeats, Images of a Poet*' held consecutively at the Whitworth Art Gallery, University of Manchester and The Building Centre, Dublin, *Head of a Bacchante* is listed as an exhibit, being a 'chalk drawing from Dr J. Todhunter's collection, now in the University of Reading.' However, the Keeper of Archives and Manuscripts at Reading confirms that neither the Todhunter collection (of purely literary items) nor the university itself contain any such drawings by Wilson. This exhibition statement therefore remains a mystery. The illustration may simply have been a copy from the *English Illustrated Magazine* article.

1890 – just one month after his great friend, George Wilson had died in Scotland. This latter occurrence must have caused Todhunter more than a little distress at such a busy personal time.

In 1894, Florence Farr persuaded Annie Horniman, the wealthy Manchester spinster who was to become the ardent and influential admirer of W.B. Yeats, to finance a series of new plays for her. John Todhunter's *A Comedy if Sighs* was performed at the Avenue Theatre in Bedford Park in conjunction with George Bernard Shaw's *Arms and the Man*, and with W.B. Yeats's *The Land of Heart's Desire* as a curtain raiser. Unfortunately, it seems that the 'absolute realism' may have been just too advanced for the audience, and the only play to survive more than three weeks was Shaw's!

But, in view of his close friendship with Wilson and both his intense interest in and considerable experience of his work, Todhunter was very well placed to be both admirer and critic of the sometimes erratic success of Wilson's achievements. In his *English Illustrated Magazine* article, he wrote constructively about Wilson's admitted faults, but also eloquently and authoritatively about the qualities of *Alastor* (q.v.) – the painting that was considered widely at the time to be Wilson's *chef d'oeuvre*, or certainly at least one of his best. It is therefore a very great regret, if indeed the common belief is correct, that *Alastor*, in particular, was destroyed along with the rest of Todhunter's art collection.

However, we have to be thankful at least that the Aberdeen Art Gallery has amongst its collection a well worked pencil and watercolour study for the final picture – although as a study this is inevitably relatively 'light-weight' and lacks some of the intensity of feeling (and reported strength of colour) that the final picture portrayed. Thankfully though, we do also have a good contemporary photograph of the final version of *Alastor*, and this was reproduced in Dr Andrew Cassels Brown's history of the Wilson family – albeit that this is inevitably in black and white, so the original colours still remain tantalisingly elusive.

In 1878, Frederic (later, Lord) Leighton was elected President of the Royal Academy, and it was hoped that through his more cosmopolitan outlook, the RA would become less insular and more tolerant of the younger painters who hated its restrictive teaching practices. Indeed, in 1879, The Academy Summer Exhibition achieved record attendances of nearly 400,000. Nevertheless, most of the damage had been done some while previously and the 'alternative' galleries, usually financed by private investors, continued to appeal and attract the disenchanted – including so many of the great names of the day.

Somewhat inevitably, Wilson too had taken a liking to these less ostentatious galleries, and again in 1879 he exhibited at the Dudley. This time, he submitted a watercolour entitled *Arise thou that sleepest!,* * which was priced for sale at £18.0.0 (equivalent to a little

---

* There is no known image to associate with this title so it is not known for sure what it depicted. However, it is reasonable to assume that this was probably another of the Bible quotations so liked by the Brotherhood – this time the well-known and oft discussed quotation from Paul's Epistle to the Ephesians 5. v.14. In fact, both the Authorised and Revised versions read as: '...*Awake thou that sleepest, and arise from the dead, and Christ shall give thee light.*' But the verse is often précised when quoted in theological discussion exactly as Wilson has stated it, so undoubtedly this slip (if indeed it is such) may be forgiven!

over £1,500 today). There is no traceable record of anyone having bought the painting, but since it is neither recorded elsewhere, nor listed in either of Wilson's retrospective exhibitions, it is a fair assumption that it must indeed have been sold and so, hopefully, might still survive somewhere today.

Wilson does not appear to have exhibited any more works until 1882, but in the meantime, he travelled extensively both at home and abroad. Indeed, on 10th April 1881, J.B. Yeats wrote to Todhunter from Dublin, and in a somewhat restless-sounding letter in which he also expressed his concern at not being able to find enough models in Dublin, he closed by saying, 'I wrote to Wilson some days ago but have not had any answer...'. [148] Wilson would most probably have been in Italy at that time in spring.

When not away travelling, George Wilson always returned home to Scotland for a few months each year to see his family, for the most part staying at Castle Park in Huntly with his elder brother, John, who was Factor to the Duke of Richmond and Gordon's Aberdeenshire estates. Whilst at 'home', he would paint avidly in and around Huntly, along the rivers Deveron and Bogie and among the forests, and along the north Banffshire coast of the Moray Firth. Occasionally, he made forays into the Nethy Bridge and the Spey valley to paint among the Cairngorm Mountains, or across to Aberdeen – where he had a further 'second home' with another older brother, Charles, who held the high office of Procurator Fiscal* for Aberdeenshire.

Sometimes Wilson also stayed with yet a third of his older brothers, James, at Arradoul House near Buckie on the Moray coast. In 1882, James had taken over from his uncle Alexander as Managing Director of the family's farming interests in the region when his eldest brother, John, removed the Wilsons' factorial allegiance from the Findlaters and Seafields to the Gordons. But more particularly, James managed their Inchgower malt whisky distillery – no doubt a greatly added incentive to George's visits! Ironically, James also suffered, and eventually died, from the same familial gastric problems that afflicted his younger brother.

Very few photographs of George Wilson exist, and the only known photo from later in his short life was probably taken in 1889, coincidentally within a very large formal family group, and from some distance outside his brother John's house, Castle Park in Huntly.[149] Because of the distance and size of the original group, the quality is not crisp, but modern optical technology has enabled considerable enhancement of this photograph. This reveals a gaunt, almost emaciated-looking man, aged somewhat beyond his true years from the rather dapper young man shown in the previously reproduced photograph from around 12 years earlier. Little more than six months after this scene, he had died.

Yet he is easily recognisable and still retains his drooping moustache, although the rakish hat of the younger man has been replaced by a topical formal tall 'bowler'.

---

*   Public prosecutor and coroner in Scotland

Castle Park, Huntly. probably 1889. Photograph of John Wilson, Factor to the Duke of Richmond and Gordon's Huntly estates, with his family and household entourage outside Castle Park – where George Wilson spent several months each year. George Wilson is sitting to the rear of the group, ninth from the left and next to his brother, looking to his right and left away from the photographer.

A gaunt George Wilson is depicted in this enhanced optical enlargement from the group photograph above. It is a credit to the quality of the original photograph that the section shown here represents an area of no more than 7 mm x 10 mm on the original print.

Indeed, this must have been an important family photograph as everyone is in their finest highland or dress attire. There are two horses on parade, plus a number of other 'status props' such as a penny-farthing, a goat-cart, bag-pipes and a tennis racquet – and the whole of Castle Park itself is included in the composition.

George Wilson appears to be holding a pose that indicates some unease and personal reluctance at being included at all. He is surrounded by his many nephews and nieces, and his brother John stands just behind him. The tallest of the children (standing just in front of John in the photograph) is George Wilson's niece Rachel, then aged 13 years. Rachel appeared in at least two of his paintings and eventually followed her uncle to become a proficient professional artist herself.

There is also, within one of Wilson's surviving sketchbooks, a charming pencil sketch (q.v.) that can be nothing other than a self-portrait. Again, the moustache is evident, but this time on a man probably around 20 years younger – and far less ravaged by the gastric disease that cursed him throughout his life, and which eventually was to kill him.

Apart from his homeland in Scotland, Wilson also much enjoyed the south of England, and particularly the area of the Sussex Downs around Arundel, where he painted a number of landscapes. He also ventured farther inland towards the Hampshire and Surrey rural county border areas around Petersfield, Midhurst and Haslemere. As already identified, Wilson had developed a connection with the Haslemere area through his contacts with the Nettleship brothers. Elsewhere in the region, the attractions of the Sussex Downs to painters over the years were well established; but in Wilson's case, he would undoubtedly have been aware that it was also just to the west of Arundel, in the small village of Felpham, that William Blake, the Brotherhood's great mentor and 'evangel', had lived for the few happiest years of his life. It was there that he is rumoured to have been inspired to write the opening lines of *And did those feet in ancient time,* the preface to his work *Milton: a Poem* (1804) – and best known today as the hymn *Jerusalem.*

Abroad in 1885, Wilson visited Algiers in north Africa – just on that one occasion, as far as we know. Apart from the odd letter, there is little to tell us what routes or modes of transport he used for his journeys abroad. Almost certainly, he would have travelled to Italy via Paris and would undoubtedly have made good use of his time there to take in the Paris exhibitions. Like many landscape artists, he was a great walker by force of habit, but presumably the long-distance journeys would have been made largely by train. Nevertheless, how he would have made his way to Algiers would be interesting to discover.

Many Victorian artists contributed to the general interest in *Orientalism,* largely directed (at least so far as the British artists were concerned) towards the eastern Mediterranean, which provided the backgrounds for their religious subjects. However, following the French colonisation of north Africa in the early 19th Century, there was a far greater interest in that area as well. This was principally led by legions of French artists from Delacroix (1798-1863) with works such as *Women of Algiers in their Apartment* (1834, Louvre, Paris), through to Renoir (1841-1919), who painted his *Mosque in Algiers* (private collection) in 1882, and so onwards. By the 1880s and '90s, they were crossing the Mediterranean in their droves to paint new and exciting subjects in the red gorges of El-Kantara and the arcades of the Place de l'Amirauté in Algiers.

So it probably was not at all a surprising place for Wilson to visit, especially since during the 1880s, Algiers had also become a fashionable place to visit for health reasons, due to its agreeable climate. This was something that Wilson constantly sought out for himself, and from his letters to Todhunter from Algiers, it becomes evident that he was going through a particularly bad patch in his health during and perhaps before this trip. From his work point of view in Algiers, Wilson's watercolour paintings displayed a new intense impression of heat and colour, and we have extant evidence of his own paintings from those 'red gorges' – whether at El-Kantara or elsewhere. In this respect, he does not tell us how far from Algiers he strayed.

Almost certainly, most of all Wilson loved to visit Italy – which he continued to do throughout the 1880s. He frequently wrote to Todhunter from Rome, Venice and, especially, from Robert Browning's (and his own) beloved Asolo. It was in Asolo that Wilson spent – almost as his closing pilgrimage – the last six weeks of his final visit to Italy in 1889, when he spent some time in the company of Robert Browning's close American friend Katharine Bronson. Wilson wrote later to Todhunter of this kindness when Mrs Bronson cared for him through a particularly bad bout of his sickness, which ultimately led up to his death a few months later.

However, earlier in January 1882, Wilson was wintering in Italy and wrote a long letter to Todhunter from Rome. This letter contains many interesting glimpses into Wilson's gentle character, as well as his occasionally mischievous sense of humour in one none too subtle expression, which in present day terms would be deemed completely 'politically incorrect'!. The almost childlike joie-de-vivre displayed in the letter contrasts starkly with Wilson's continual fight against his debilitating gastric disease, and may just highlight some brief period of respite from this condition – a malady that he chose to ignore as much as possible, and equally to hide as well as he could from his friends. Of interest also is that Wilson's style of correspondence with Todhunter differs widely from the 'deep and meaningful' debates that formed the major part of correspondence that Todhunter received from Yeats and the others within and around the 'Brotherhood' at that time.

However, there are a number of other more interesting references in this letter, which give us a good insight into his daily life and method of working; his delight in the surrounding light, and most importantly, his desire to paint-in the backgrounds and surrounds to his pictures from the most appropriate natural scenery he could find. Evidently he was perfectly prepared to take his canvasses to Italy to achieve this, which substantiates the understanding that he painted-in the strongly Renaissance inspired backgrounds to his larger oil paintings in situ in the foothills of the Dolomites to the north of Asolo. Wilson's letter is reproduced here in its entirety – complete with all its idiosyncrasies:

Via Sistina no 72.
Jan 15th
Roma

My dear Todhunter

It has been on the tip of my pen to write to you several times and now I'll do it –pat. I wont describe Rome to you since you have been here, and there are numerous guidebooks on the subject. I enjoy it much on its own account and also that one can paint with a roomful of daylight, and depend on its continuance.

The afternoons are so lovely, the day begins with hoar frost and sharp cold, but the conquering sun is too much for it, and in the afternoon one bathes in delightful *warmth, and Rome is so lovely then and onwards to evening ever lovelier. The other evening my friend[*] and I came from the outside into the city by the Vatican gate. Rome was a purple pall with flakes of gold on its edges where the last rays touched and behind, the hills were in a blaze, blue grey below but with radiant, gleaming heads. There is something in the air here which is depressing; the great age of the place, the strata so well marked of succeeding civilizations which overlay each other, one devouring the other as if Zeus devoured Saturn; and the Colossal landmarks of these events are awful as well as curious or beautiful. I find myself rather inclined to hate the Catholic Church or at least Popedom. The way these popes swagger in every church on every hill almost under every green tree and encourage art – to worship beast gods & make images thereof is curious to see but rather heart rending to the artist : for the spurns that patient merit from the unworthy takes shouldn't be exemplified by the quiet severe and lovely work of the early rennaisance [sic] having to give place to the ludicrous swagger and blattant [sic] foolery of the seventeenth and eighteenth century men. What clever ranters <u>they</u> were though. Picturesque black guards too sometimes – [here are inserted two small ink drawings of 'swaggering' and 'fooling' saints, with the caption against them...] These are feeble attempts to do 18th Century saints, but no – they aren't like, all the better.*

Again the afternoons though; when one has worked hard from 9 till twelve, comes lunch and then a delicious loaf maybe to the forum or as far as the colliseum [sic], <u>guide book less</u>, unhurried by thoughts that there is only a week to see it all. Hurried by nothing except that the light will go and then is work to be done. What a sky and how beautiful the city looks wherever one gets a point of vantage. Don't think that a delicious loaf is the regular, matter of course sequel to lunch by no means: but once or twice a week at the most. I'm not idling. I've got well on with a picture that I took out with me – a dance of young men and maidens in a woody place in Crete see Iliad[†]. Im going to paint Cretan scenery from what material I can find in the Roman campagnia or maybe Tivoli. Ive also got another started of Winter and Spring. A

---

* Unfortunately, we have no idea who this friend might have been. It is possible that Todhunter understood to whom this referred without having to mention a name, or maybe it was simply someone whom Todhunter would not have known at all, so was irrelevant to name and explain.

Wilson's address at Via Sistina No 72 is of some interest. The now rather more chic 'Via' had then for long accommodated the abodes of artists and literary persons. 100 years earlier, No 72 had been the lodging of the famous Swiss portrait and allegorical subject painter, Angelica Kauffmann (1741-1807), who painted her portrait of her friend Goethe at the address.

† From Wilson's description, this painting can fairly certainly be identified as *Arcadia*, which was exhibited at the Grosvenor Gallery in 1883. The painting was loaned, along with another unidentified oil painting entitled *Eros*, by Mr Herbert Young to the 1903 exhibition, but the whereabouts of both is no longer known. Fortunately, however, the study for the painting (called *The Dance*, and at that time belonging to Russell Scott), was printed in the published set of photogravures taken by George Washington Wilson & Co. to commemorate the 1893 Aberdeen exhibition. Thus, we know what the painting broadly looked like. The second picture mentioned is, with very little doubt from the description, the commencement of his major oeuvre now entitled *The Spring Witch*, that safely resides today in the collection of the Delaware Art Museum.

good old subject that I hope to make something new of it. I've got Spring young and radiant (if I can) . rising out of the cerements of the dead winter wondering at herself but seeing her kingdom before her and glad thereof: golly massa Todhunter if I can paint it as well as I sometimes think it, it will be a picture. I have spoken and the gods will have at me. It will never get painted at all. "There shall no swaggerers come here" is written over the gate of the palace of art.

How goes it with you altogether. Have you been doing any work lately, poetry or criticism? Is the new house getting well into shape? Are Mrs. Todhunter and the baby both well : I hope they are. I should be so very glad if there were any chance of seeing you out here this winter but I know it won't happen.

Have you seen what Nettleship has been doing I should like to hear from an independent outsider. He has begun something in a new genre for him which promised well and I should like to hear that they had turned out well. Yeats-? if you know anything of him tell me.. I would write but I fear he may have changed his address.

Yours in haste somewhere

ever sincerely

George Wilson

very kind regards to Mrs Todhunter. [150]

There is a wonderful irony in Wilson's last paragraph, where he worries that any letter addressed to Yeats might not find its mark in case he had moved on yet again! In fact, this was not an unreasonable assumption, since towards the end of 1881, when the lease at Woodstock Road had thankfully ended, Yeats had indeed moved his family back to Ireland. Once there, they moved from one address to another in Howth in the first six months – although he did in fact remain in the area for two of his happiest years.[151]

Similarly, and despite the continual nagging of his gastric disease, this period in Wilson's life also appears to have been one of his most contented and productive in relation to the figurative oil painting area of his work. He appears to have produced, or at least to have commenced alongside his continuing regular output of watercolour landscapes, a significant number of larger allegorical oil paintings between approximately 1880 and 1885.

Upon his return from Italy later in 1882, Wilson submitted a watercolour entitled *On the Banffshire Coast* for exhibition for the first time outside London. He sent the picture – one of a number that he painted bearing the same subject title – via the Glasgow agent, James MacClure and Son, to the Royal Glasgow Institute of the Fine Arts Annual Exhibition. The exhibit number was 905, bearing a sale price of £10.0.0 (now about

£830). It is not known if this picture was sold, but several similar titles still exist in private collections.

By 1883 at the latest, Wilson had taken his studio at 65, Newman Street; this time, right in the heart of one of the traditional artists' communities, and close to the art school of his early mentor and teacher, Thomas Heatherley. This address appears against his exhibited works from 1883 to 1884, but prior to that he could either have retained the Stanhope Street studio for his own use after Nettleship left for India in 1880, or he could equally have moved into Newman Street two years earlier to coincide with the time that Nettleship left. Two of the exhibited works from '83 and '84 were the oil painting *Arcadia* (referred to above), shown at the Grosvenor Gallery's Summer Exhibition in 1883, and *Summer and the Winds* – a tempera painting that was illustrated (no 92) in the 1884 catalogue of the Sixty-Sixth annual Exhibition of the Royal Institute of Painters in Water Colours.

Summer and the Winds was originally in the possession of Mr H.H. Young, who loaned the picture to the 1893 exhibition, but by the time of the 1903 exhibition, it had apparently been purchased by Halsey Ricardo, George Wilson's architect friend and collector. Ricardo bequeathed the painting in his will of 1928 to his daughter, Esther. The picture was then described for probate as being 'in carved gilt frame glazed' and was valued at £5.5.0 (equivalent to ca. £230 today). Esther was married to Walter Howarth F.R.C.S., who was an important collector of English post-impressionist paintings – and in particular, those of Walter Sickert (1860-1942). Unfortunately – and maybe in some way due to Walter Howarth's particular interest – *Summer and the Winds* is now no longer traceable.

It is assumed that H.H. Young must be the same as the Herbert Young who, in addition to *Arcadia* as noted above, also loaned another oil painting entitled *Eros* to the 1903 exhibition. Nothing further is known of the detail of this latter painting – or indeed of the present whereabouts of either *Arcadia* or *Eros*, but the H.H. Young referred to is believed to be the artist, photographer and philanthropist of that name (1854-1941)[*] who lived at Carlton Lane in Horsham. Like Wilson, Young had a very close attachment to Asolo, where he owned a villa that he subsequently donated to his God-daughter, the renowned traveller, explorer and writer (and eventually, centenarian) Dame Freya Stark (1893-1993). Young could well then have met Wilson in Asolo – or it could possibly have been through his southern counties contacts such as the Nettleship family or Halsey Ricardo. It is interesting to note that Herbert Young was once the owner of three of Wilson's most important works – regrettably all now missing.

Once again, in 1884, Wilson exhibited outside London when he sent the allegorical oil painting entitled *The Song of the Nightingale* to the Autumn Exhibition at the Walker Art Gallery in Liverpool. The painting was exhibited simply as *The Nightingale* (no. 259)

---

[*] H.H. Young is recorded as having exhibited once each at the RA and at the Grosvenor Gallery in 1885 and 1886.

and the price sought was £70.0.0 (about £6,000 at today's prices). It appears though, that the picture did not sell at this significant sum, since it still remains in Wilson family descent today.

The Song of the Nightingale is still housed in its handsome original gilt frame, which also bears exhibition labels for the Scottish National Exhibitions of 1908 and 1911, in Edinburgh and Glasgow, respectively. The owner of the painting throughout that period of time was Charles Wilson WS, Procurator Fiscal for Aberdeenshire, and one of George Wilson's many older brothers – with whom he often stayed when visiting or travelling through Aberdeen – and a devoted collector of his paintings.

The last painting that appears to have been exhibited by Wilson during his lifetime was again at the Royal Institute of Painters in Water Colours, in the following year of 1885. This was the Sixty-Seventh Annual Exhibition in which number 336 was the watercolour entitled *The Lost Paradise* from the poem by John Milton. It was accompanied by the quotation that it depicted, just four lines from the end of that epic work:

> *They looking back, all the Eastern side beheld*
> *Of Paradise, so late their happy seat,*
> *Waved over by that flaming brand; the gate,*
> *With dreadful faces thronged, and fiery arms:*
>
> *-- Milton*

Although *The Lost Paradise* must presumably have been an allegorical work, it is yet another painting of which we have no information as to how Wilson depicted the quotation from the poem for his composition, since no further record of it appears to exist. As the watercolour didn't appear at either of the retrospective exhibitions, it may be assumed that it was bought at the Royal Institute exhibition by a now anonymous purchaser. The present whereabouts of the painting is not known.

Although George Wilson had suffered all his life from a very severe debilitating gastric disease – which in more modern times has been accorded various diagnoses[*] – it was during this last decade of his short life that he found it particularly agreeable to spend more time in warmer climes. At the same time, this very much suited his passion for experiencing the historic art of Italy, as well as the countryside and light that had inspired it.

---

[*]   In his history of the Wilson family, *The Wilsons, A Banffshire Family of Factors*, Dr Andrew Cassels Brown (husband of Rachel (née) Wilson q.v. – one of George Wilson's nieces, who appears in at least two of his paintings) diagnosed Wilson's complaint as being a duodenal ulcer. Others have suggested cancer – but Dr Cassels Brown's book records that many of the Wilson family suffered to varying degrees of seriousness from a similar disease, which sometimes took their life at an early age. George Wilson himself always referred to it somewhat dismissively as his 'dyspepsia' – which mild complaint of course it most certainly was not. His death certificate stated 'stricture and ulceration of the pylorus' broadly agreeing with Cassels Brown's diagnosis.

He once wrote to Todhunter from southern France as he seemingly wandered through various towns on his way to Italy. In this letter, he describes the medieval town of Sisteron, nestling in the Haute Provencale foothills of the Alps. He refers initially to it in a surprisingly unkind fashion in view of its historic appeal – yet quickly, and almost apologetically, follows this up with the same romantic expression of the beauty of its surroundings that ruled his painting – and his life:

> *Sisteron, which is a squalid, stenchy little hole of a town, which no man of the tourist order ever heard of before, or stopped in, is flopped down in as lovely a country as you can conceive of, the kind of country that I like better than all the others, and have seldom seen – a rich, smiling valley under the highest cultivation, vines, figs, almonds, mulberries, wheat, maize, a whole cornucopia of richness, with two winding rivers fresh from the Alps meeting in the midst thereof, and behind, fierce, threatening, ragged peaks, blue and snow-crowned.*[152]

Why the town of Sisteron itself should have dismayed him quite so much is a mystery, but in fact, all of Wilson's few remaining letters portray a refreshingly transparent style – almost naïve, yet at the same time wholly down-to-earth; emulating the poetic romanticism that dominated the life he followed and which totally encompassed his very *raison d'être*. From Venice, he once wrote:

> *There is nothing like Venice anywhere. Yesterday and yesternight were given over to processions. Two festas came together. I wish, oh! I wish you had been here to have seen. There was a thing at the end that was amazing beyond description. It was like a vision out of the Revelation. Fancy briefly, two mighty walls of dusky flame, fretted with golden traceries in colour of molten metal. Between these walls, which are made by the close walls of palaces on the Grand Canal, advances a thing in shape of a temple made of a thousand different coloured fires, out of which flows music (which might be better, and as it is, spoils the thing a bit). Behind, comes on in perfect silence a great throng of gondolas, with their great steel beaks all aglow, and the men looking like statues cut in sunset clouds. You should have seen it. Then the water, you know, was like something never seen out of Venice. Ah, well, once again I wish you had been here to see it! Then the religious procession in the afternoon, or rather evening, with all Venice to see. Again golden fires above and golden waters below. But it was the sun himself this time. To see the white dresses of the little St. Johns and the Baa-lambs, and gorgeous priests and wonderful canopies and censers,* and all against the sky as they crossed a bridge, with the huge disk of the setting sun spotting itself through everything and, setting the water on fire, is—to get into difficulties with the English language.*[153]

---

*   One wonders quite what George Wilson's strict Scottish Presbyterian family would have made of this remark!

The aura of romanticism with which Wilson described his surroundings might have come directly from one of the titles that were dreamed up by him and his colleagues for their drawing competitions. One is almost persuaded to imagine this self-deprecating and most modest of painters experiencing these sights in something approaching a child-like wide-eyed wonderment! The contrast between the drenching light in which he found he could paint in Italy and north Africa and that which he experienced in the north of Scotland was unquestionably considerable. Certainly, the watercolour landscapes that can be related to these very different climes exhibit a strong response to the available light and the prevailing climate. However, in all his paintings, colour was vital to him and the results are almost always vibrant. In the paintings from Italy and Algiers the colours are sometimes astounding; from Scotland, the ever-present luxuriance of his woodland landscapes in particular, shows an intrinsic understanding not only of what he was painting, but also the very fundamentals of the nature that created these surroundings. In Italy and Africa there is the ubiquitous dryness and crispness, whilst in Scotland there is an all-pervading lushness that permeates Wilson's paintings to the extent that one might almost be able to squeeze the water out of the moss-covered trees and banks.

However, in his later watercolours (and it is essential always to differentiate between the two media and Wilson's technique in respect of each) from around the mid 1880s onwards, something of a change appears. Regardless of wherever they are painted amongst his favourite locations, there is sometimes a clear indication of some movement towards the impressionism that had swept through France during the previous decade, and which, by then, was already in its second phase. This change appears to have commenced broadly around the time of his visit to north Africa in 1985, only falteringly so to start with, but increasingly boldly through the final five years leading up to the end of his life.

None of this should be particularly surprising. Undoubtedly, since he usually travelled to Italy via central France, this would inevitably have taken in Paris. Wilson would therefore have been fully aware of what was going on in France, yet maybe to a somewhat lesser extent in England. He had been trained in the shadow of the Pre-Raphaelites and had readily adopted and adhered to their ethos. He was already a convinced and practising *pleinairist* and colourist; he was consistently representing colour and light and the visual sensations created by light; he often utilised tiny brushstrokes to great effect in depicting the image of what he saw, and he certainly appears to have been influenced by Corot, as were several of the French Impressionists. Finally, as with the greatest colourists of his age, and those from before and following after, he also became experimental with time.

And, in truth, *were* these two movements so very far apart in their basic philosophy? No less an advocate for the Pre-Raphaelite movement than Ruskin – who had no empathy whatsoever with any French painting of his time – could not have constructed a more expressive and precise statement of the fundamental aims of the Impressionists when he wrote in *The Stones of Venice:*

The whole function of the artist in the world is to be a seeing and feeling creature; to be an instrument of such tenderness and sensitiveness, that no shadow, no hue, no line, no instantaneous and evanescent expression of the visible things round him, shall either be left unrecorded, or fade from the book of record. It is not his business either to think, to judge, to argue, or to know. ... The work of his life is to be twofold only: to see, to feel.[154]

Whereas the Pre-Raphaelites painted subjects from classicism, medievalism and romanticism, the Impressionists tended to paint simple everyday people in everyday scenes. However, neither philosophy tolerated 'studio tricks' with arranged lights and colourless shadows. So whilst all the above statements of comparison are bland and simplistic, and whilst volumes have been written elsewhere on both subjects and in far greater and more erudite detail, that is certainly not the intention here. But it does, nevertheless, highlight the demanding question as to where George Wilson was heading with his painting towards the end of his life.

In May 1885, Wilson was in Algiers when he wrote to Todhunter:

How lovely the country is just now there are no words to say. I had never dreamed of such a paradise of wild flowers. There are most of ours, but much bigger than with us. And innumerable others as new to me as the queer jewel-stones in the new Jerusalem would be -- marvellous cups and trumpets and bugles. ... I have had a bad turn of it with the arch-fiend, Dyspepsia, which has taken the colour out of life generally a good deal, but I hope for better things before long.

This unusually open reference to his perpetual and debilitating illness was written five years before his death, yet shows his equally perpetual optimism that the problem would always just go away, permitting him to do better and better work. A few days later, from the same place he wrote again to say,

I wish you were here. How you would delight in the lovely evenings. The day seems to swoon away into night under glorious opiates of incense from a world of flowers.[155]

This alternating between the highs and lows of one moment being laid low by a stomach problem that would eventually become so serious that it would kill him, and in the next dismissing it with his over-riding optimism that he would eventually get over it, would have been enough to demoralize the very strongest of wills. However, that is what Wilson endured, and it therefore seems remarkable that he produced as much work as he did in his short life. Indeed, it was such a short life that beyond his training years at Heatherley's, the Royal Academy schools, and finally the Slade, which terminated in 1873, he had little more than 15 years of productive work. Since he neither signed nor dated any of his pictures, so far as we know, we only have exhibition records, and the occasional label on the reverse of a painting to catalogue his development – and that has made the task very difficult.

From the small amount of documentary evidence that has survived, backed up by anecdotal family recollections, we know that Wilson did, indeed, lead a generally nomadic life. He visited Scotland for some months every year, and he had friends whom he visited in Sussex quite frequently. But most of all, he loved to visit Italy, with Venice and Asolo in the north as his favourite haunts, followed by Florence and Rome in central Italy. All in all, of the three friends who started out from art school together, it was Wilson, the least assuming and pretentious of them all, who turned out to be by far the most adventurous. Despite his continuous debilitating illness, he was prepared to travel far and wide in Europe to further his knowledge of traditional historic art and modern trends. And that was something that neither Nettleship nor Yeats ventured to do – even, as in Yeats's case in both 1907 and 1909, when someone else was prepared to pay for the travel.[156]

Although we cannot be sure of all of Wilson's addresses in London – particularly during the last five years of his life, it does appear that he became fairly settled with London as his home base. It also appears that he managed to support himself adequately in digs that would include something of a studio, and, whilst he was based in the Mall Studios in Hampstead, he was actually based in comparatively 'prestigious' surroundings within the art world. By this premise, it must be assumed that he also succeeded in selling sufficient of his work to maintain this at least adequate lifestyle. He certainly had a small number of reasonably well-to-do patrons who, equally as importantly, also became his good friends as well. Apart from his lone trips to Italy to paint, he also travelled there in sociable groups with friends as well – and in particular, with the Nettleship brothers. But to the end, whether due to the combination of his medical training with his vested interest in someone he considered to be exceptionally gifted as an artist, it was John Todhunter who never left him out of his thoughts.

CHAPTER TEN

The last months

As previously stated, there is a regrettable dearth of documentary record surrounding George Wilson's life. In order to compensate for this, and in an attempt to elicit the greatest possible insight into the man and his *raison d'être*, a more than usual amount of what has been saved is reproduced verbatim here. It is hoped that the reader will tolerate this in the best interests of the study – and will feel that it is a valuable contribution towards creating the clearest global picture of George Wilson.

Reference has been made to John Todhunter's good personal understanding of Wilson's work – and of the underlying reticence, yet at the same time emphatically over-riding principles, that formed the character of the man himself. Their close friendship and Todhunter's significant collection of Wilson's work in all the various different media that he from time to time employed enabled Todhunter to utilise his own considerable descriptive powers to great effect. Todhunter's scrutiny of the method and variable success of Wilson's achievements through those very different media of oil, watercolour and chalk drawing, as described in his *English Illustrated Magazine* article of 1891, probably cannot be bettered. Any attempt to re-define the original in new terms would be entirely pointless since there was probably no-one who knew or understood Wilson better. The limited quotations here are therefore transcribed directly and without further justification from Todhunter's original published text:

> *... That Wilson's genius received but scant recognition during his life was largely due to his own modest, reticent, retiring temperament. He was not especially ill-used by either Providence or his fellow men, and did not feel himself so ill-used. He buried himself in his art, and lived happily enough, without making much effort to rise to the surface. He never could have been a popular painter. His art was too refined, idealistic, visionary; and in this age of blatant self-assertion he seldom took even the most ordinary means of making himself known. ...*

... If he had obtained a wider recognition, it would, no doubt, have been both pleasant and beneficial to him. His art has some of the faults as well as the merits of recluse art. But he was spared that sordid struggle with poverty which has warped many a man of genius. It is doubtful whether he could have painted "pot-boilers", but it is certain that he never did paint them, unless a rare portrait could be so designated. He remained poor; but he had a small circle of admirers, who bought his pictures because they loved his art and as he never married he managed to live comfortably enough. The art-critics molested him but little. They may occasionally have "damned him with faint praise", but he troubled himself little about them, whether they spoke or remained silent. ...

... He was singularly sensitive, shy, and reticent, even with his most intimate friends, and he was always a silent man, with the gift of silence which might have delighted Carlyle himself, had he known him. If betrayed into expressing an opinion about anything, he would often suddenly stop, as if he felt that nothing he could say could have the slightest interest for any one. But if he even ventured to say of some beautiful thing that it was "awfully jolly", it was worth something to hear him say it, such a depth of enthusiastic appreciation he managed to convey in so conventional a phrase. He was, however, a delightful letter-writer, expressing himself easily and racily, so that even his briefest notes had a charming individuality. ...

... He had several little knots of friends whom he loved, and who loved him, and among whom he would appear and disappear, as the spirit moved him, like a migratory bird. He lived an innocent, impulsive, vivid life, balanced by an inward harmony; shrinking from everything coarse and ugly with a morality which was instinctive rather than of conventional principle. He loved music, children, and flowers. Music was, indeed, his spirit's native air; he seemed to inhale it like a satisfying perfume, and to pasture his imagination upon it.[157]

In support of this latter description, Andrew Cassels Brown, husband of one of George Wilson's nieces, Rachel, also records in the Wilson family history a note about George Wilson's placid nature, and his love of music and flowers and children – and how children loved him. He recollects how Wilson's nieces and nephews would remember the shouts of laughter that used to follow upon his discovery that they had squeezed the valuable paint out of his tubes, or poured out the water from his container, when he was far away from any source of replenishment![158] It is easy, from these anecdotes, to understand how Wilson would have been attracted to Blake's poetry, and particularly perhaps his *Songs of Innocence*. He would equally, no doubt, have wished to beware of the dangers posed in the antithetical poems within *Songs of Experience* – the second counter-element of that 'two-part' publication. Blake's preoccupation with Good and Evil is no more clearly defined than in the two counter poems – one from each part – entitled respectively *Nurse's Song* and *NURSES Song*.[159]

In seeking to place Wilson's art into the context of the day, Todhunter comments:

At the present day the technique of painting in the presentation of the various aspects of nature has been carried to a pitch of perfection never before attained. The unpaintable is becoming every day more paintable; and sometimes the vanity of technique leads men into a self-conscious display of skill, a posturing for the plaudits of the smart spectator who has learnt the latest cant of art-criticism. Such art as this is rhetoric, not poetry, and as such must take a lower place. Wilson's art has none of this rhetorical quality. He painted to please himself, painted what he loved because he loved it. His work is full of a brooding delight in beauty for its own sake, full of a poetic quality which has been somewhat rare in our most modern art, though there are signs of better things of late. It is poetic not merely in subject, but in sentiment and handling; and it is this poetic quality which gives Wilson his distinction. He is, it might almost be said, a Keats among painters. There is a lyrical sensuousness in his work which recalls Keats: that noble sensuousness in which sensation and vision are one, the senses being touched and informed with high imagination. His favourite subjects were poetical or mythical designs, in which ideal figures were set in the background of ideal landscape. His development as a painter was very gradual, and tortuous rather than straightforward. His powers grew by their exercise, but they grew almost imperceptibly. In his painting of the figure especially he won his way forward by slow degrees. In his landscape work his progress was much more evident, as he advanced from slight sketches to finished studies, rich in detail, and so on to finely balanced compositions. In his most laborious, as in his most rapid studies, he painted his own vision of nature; nature seen in the glamour of an emotional moment. From first to last he was a master of colour, and the charm of even his slightest sketches is largely dependent upon delicate harmonies of colour.

He was singularly diffident about his work, always pursuing his ideal, and never, in his own opinion, coming within measurable distance of attaining it. The strange faults of drawing the figure, perceptible in some of his compositions, and contrasting with the delicate freedom of his preliminaries studies in chalk, are largely due to over-labour. He was constantly seeking the exact attitude or gesture which should perfectly express the sentiment he wished to express, and he worked and re-handled until his eye lost something of its delicate perception. The power and beauty of his draughtsmanship of the human figure is best seen in his school studies from the nude, and in his preliminaries studies for pictures. In these it is easy to see the same instinctive idealism that characterises his landscape work. In some nude studies the human form is approached without reverence, and painted with base cynical cleverness, and without any true feeling for beauty. Mere nakedness is gloated over, with something like a debauched or inverted Puritanism. Wilson's drawings, so tenderly touched with ideality, so full of delight in the beauty of lines and delicacy of modelling, are at the opposite pole from these. He came of a good old Puritan stock; yet there is not a trace of Puritanism, inverted or otherwise, in his work. It has the innocent unconsciousness of Greek work. ...[160]

... Wilson may not have been a great, but he was an exquisite painter. He had the secret of beauty as few men in this generation are given to have it. He dreamed of beauty, and painted what he dreamed, imperfectly no doubt, but always delightfully. He did not follow the usual methods or arrive at the usual results. What the average man does easily, he either could not do or did with difficulty; but then he did what the average man cannot do. He painted poems because he lived in them. He painted trees divinely, because he loved them and felt through all their life, from the firmly planted roots to the intricately woven branches, bending and springing to every wind that plays through their leaves. His drawing of stems and branches, sometimes rapid and suggestive, sometimes elaborately studied, always vital, cannot easily be matched. He painted the sunned spaces of grassy glades, seen through and under the trees, deliciously; and steep grassy slopes in sunshine or shadow, and the wild tangle of long grass and weeds and flowers, inimitably, because he loved these things too, and loved to let his spirit bask and wander among them. In all his landscape work there is a sweet idyllic quality, which perhaps recalls Mason* more than any other of our painters, though Wilson's compositions and handling were widely different from his. Many of his landscape studies soothe yet quicken the mind, like fine pastoral poetry. One might imagine these sunny or twilight lawns and leas trodden by the feet of that shepherd-boy in Sydney's Arcadia who lives on in our imaginations "piping as if he would never grow old". Wilson's pictures have this quality of eternal youth. They never grow old; and they are most pleasant things to live with. They are the outcome of the best hours of a life which, in spite of much suffering, was essentially a happy one.

And to complete the tribute, Todhunter closes by saying:

One might indeed venture to apply to George Wilson the noble lines written by Landor of himself, except the last :

"I strove with none, for none was worth my strife,
Nature I loved, and after Nature, art,
I warmed both hands before the fire of life,
It sinks, and I am ready to depart."[161]

Todhunter's words may appear to display those of a man still feeling the emotion of the loss of a very good and long-standing friend whom he had seen suffer continually if with fortitude during most of his life, and in particular over the last few years. However this is almost all we have available to us in the way of contemporarily written commentary – and his words have consequently formed the basis of almost every other brief reference to Wilson thereafter in general biographical entries. Nevertheless, Todhunter's description of the man is certainly borne out within the limited amount of

---

*   There were a number of artists by the name of Mason working at this time. It is not immediately clear which Mason Todhunter is referring to here

evidence available from the small number of additional recorded and anecdotal sources that it has been possible to research.

So far as the description of Wilson's work is concerned, then – yes; almost certainly, Todhunter's opinion is biased by his subjective and strong personal admiration for what he believed Wilson had achieved, and for what was undoubtedly continuing to improve and mature even while the incapacitating illness that was slowly starving him to death, effectively destroyed much of the last few, and most productive, years of his short life. However, Todhunter is honest about Wilson's faults and, interestingly, when he re-wrote the *English Illustrated Magazine* article some 12 years later on as an introduction to the 1903 retrospective exhibition of Wilson's work at the Baillie Gallery in London, he amended and added the following in order to emphasise Wilson's own rigorous response to various perceived inadequacies or dissatisfaction with the results of his endeavours:

> *He was constantly seeking the exact attitude or gesture which should perfectly express the sentiment he wished to express, and he worked and rehandled until his eye lost something of its delicate perception, the final result sometimes being so unsatisfactory to himself that he destroyed in disgust many pictures which contained beautiful passages, but in which one or more figures did not satisfy him. One of these was "La Belle Dame sans Merci", which in its unfinished state promised to be fine; but which mysteriously disappeared from his studio as the face of the Belle Dame herself did not realise his conception of the "wild-eyed fairy's child" of Keats's poem.*[162]

It has often been advocated that Scottish art is all about colour and light. If that indeed is true, then Wilson also did indeed fulfil what would have been expected of him. Nonetheless, his last letter from Venice, sent at around Easter-time in 1889, the year before he died, still displays, in parallel with his poor health, some of the frustrations and self-disbelief that plagued him about transcribing his sketches into finished works:

> *I have done a good deal of painting here, but oh! it's so poor! I don't mean as compared with a real thing but with what I feel I can do. Forgive these groans of egotism, neither believe that I think nature poor compared with my sketches.*[163]

This was certainly the last time that Wilson visited Italy. We know that he was due to go there that Easter, because one of John Nettleship's brothers (Richard Lewis), who had maintained a regular correspondence with Ralph Radcliffe Whitehead since his student days, had written to the latter on April 9th saying:

> *I wish I could have come to Italy this Easter … I am glad that you will see Ned [Edward Nettleship] and Wilson. They are going to have a Miss Peters with them, a nice creature. I think they are right not to accept your hospitality. I mean that four people can never feel <u>quite</u> comfortable when they are quartering themselves on two. But I don't suppose you will see the less of them.*[164]

George Wilson seems to have become about as close to Edward Nettleship as he had to any of his friends. To have travelled to Italy at that time in such a foursome would normally have required a close affinity (or complete formality) between all of the members of the group. It may be presumed that Edward Nettleship was, quite naturally, accompanied by his wife. The 'Miss Peters' referred to as the fourth member of the party then becomes something of an enigma. Although her Christian name was not mentioned, the lady in question was almost certainly a Miss Caroline Peters, who was a close friend of the Nettleships.

Caroline Peters was a spinster who lived in Surrey 'on her own means', but who also stayed from time to time with the Nettleships at their house in Wimbledon and later on at 'Nutcombe' in Hindhead, Surrey. She was a fine linguist and carried out secretarial work for Edward Nettleship from time to time. She was nine years younger than George Wilson, making her just 32 at the time of this trip, and she eventually lived to a good age, dying in 1939.[165] Since George Wilson never married, it might be tempting to surmise that, in view of their trip to Italy together with the Nettleships, he could have borne some sort of attachment towards this Miss Peters. Unfortunately though, there are no specific references at all to any women of such import in Wilson's life so the question remains unanswered.

As previously suggested, the only woman to whom he may have been quite close was his particular favourite model who sat for the majority of his figurative paintings and to whom it is evident from the empathy shown in his paintings that he must have had at least a fair degree of attachment. Yeats may well then not have been entirely correct when he surmised that, 'Notwithstanding his interest in drawing naked women ... None of us, not even his intimate friend Nettleship, was able to discover a peticote [sic] in his lonely life...'[166] But whether any such female friendships did, in fact, ever prosper further, we certainly do not know at this time.

As something that would be no more than a convenient (and somewhat mischievous) conjecture, it might be suggested that Miss Peters could perhaps have been one and the same as Wilson's model, journeying with him to sit in location before a Dolomite backdrop. But contemporary photographs of Caroline Peters bear no resemblance whatsoever to Wilson's model. And in any case, in all reality, and particularly in view of the fact that Wilson's models in his figurative works were seldom more than partially clothed at the most, it would have been far more likely at that time for his model to have been a working girl or even a prostitute, since sitting to painters was a well-recognised secondary source of income for members of the 'oldest profession'. It would also have been most unusually bohemian behaviour for an extremely well-bred young lady to take her clothes off so regularly, even for the sake of art – whether for money or even free of charge – so all we may presume is that both Wilson and Miss Peters were probably just equally good mutual friends of Edward Nettleship and his family.

In a similar vein, there is another completely unproven anecdote handed down in the Wilson family that, although he never married, George Wilson was reported to have been the propagator of a 'by-blow'. This now archaic expression is normally understood to mean an illegitimate child, however the somewhat more genteel interpretation passed down within the family never stretched beyond this alluding to him having taken a mistress! Although such anecdotes often carry at least some small element of truth (the 'no smoke without fire' maxim), one feels that, had there really been a child involved in his life, there would probably have been a stronger record of this in correspondence and the family history written nearly 50 years after his death, and it would certainly have been most surprising if the family were to have abandoned such a child. Nevertheless, a mother does not give up her child easily, and the hypocrisy of Victorian values could equally have swept such knowledge into the proverbial skeleton's cupboard, so it is both expedient and enticing to leave the matter in abeyance for the future!

It was in late 1889 and early 1890, during the last few months of his life, that Wilson wrote, in a series of letters to John Todhunter, some of the lines that epitomised his own character even more succinctly than those written by anyone else. That character was reflected so naturally in the gentleness of his work, and in tandem with his eternal (yet thoroughly misplaced) optimism that he would eventually get over his debilitating disease. Again, much of the content of these letters has been transcribed here verbatim in order to convey the extraordinary sensitivity of the man – which again can be so easily and similarly recognised in his work. Another point of interest is that, despite the long association between the two men, Wilson never became quite so affectionally close to Todhunter as he did to friends like the Nettleships and Ricardo, and his written form of address in *My dear Todhunter* remained in the style of relaxed formality of close professional friends. This may well in fact have been with some deference towards Todhunter's continued patronage of Wilson and his work.

Late in 1889, Wilson had suffered a severe relapse in his health – which evidently knocked even his own eternal optimism backwards. It is not known precisely when he went to Scotland that year, but one of the last watercolours that he must have been working on just before he died was painted (probably) on the sands of the Moray Firth, depicting two figures in summer attire and ascribed as Gertrude and Walter, his niece and nephew. As Walter could certainly not have been less than three years old at the time of the painting, this clearly dates the painting to the summer of 1889. It seems then that Wilson probably stayed on at Huntly after the summer, perhaps when his health started to deteriorate; but, whether fortuitous or not, it was certainly most fortunate that he was staying in Huntly, as usual with his brother at Castle Park, when this deterioration occurred.

He first wrote to Todhunter during this, his last, period in a letter dated simply, and somewhat unhelpfully, as 'Thursday 1889' (probably late November or early December), to thank him for sending him £10 (about £600 today) '...so promptly.' He continued:

> I am not in straits for money but it will be useful. I am most kindly nursed by my sister in law in whose house I am staying. No one could be more kindly looked after. My brother has a very large family* and is not rolling in wealth tho', so that I am very glad to pay when I can.

---

* John Wilson and his wife Anna produced 16 children in just 21 years, three of whom did not survive their first year. None of the 13 surviving children had left home permanently at the time of their uncle George's death, so the house must have been very crowded in accommodating an invalid in his own room as well.

I got on so extremely well for some days after the breaking of the blood vessel & the fainting that I thought I was going straight on to recovery. I have not been so well the last two days however & evidently recovery is not to be so easily got at. I will write you very shortly about what you ask me as to pictures of mine...[167]

By this time Wilson had evidently become quite weak and was spending most of his days lying in bed. His writing had become somewhat of a scrawl; added to which, he was generally using a pencil – undoubtedly in deference to his devoted, but on occasions, most formidable sister-in-law, Anna. His letters, therefore, are not always entirely easy to decipher. He next wrote to Todhunter in early December 1889, again in no more than a short note of self-deprecation, but also with a quite positive statement that he did not want any exhibition of his work:

I still find myself unable to do more than scrawl short notes. For the £10 you must take whatever you think of adequate value. I trust you absolutely in the matter only for heavens sake dont [sic] stint yourself.

I daresay I could give you a pretty complete list of people who have work of mine but I think you had better abandon the idea of a little show. It would be such a <u>very</u> little one and I really and truly feel that in my time I have done little little [sic] that is worth showing but have still hopes & glimpses of a time that will justify my existence to myself & maybe one or two others. Most foolish most vain of hopes this will seem to most men who know me, but I feel like Lear that "it is a chance that doth redeem all the sorrows ever I have felt." I do not alude [sic] to any mysterious ripening of powers of new birth of any kind but I still feel such joy in art & life & the way to better use of both is somehow made clearer & clearer. So I think we wont [sic] have any show, for to come to more immediate reasons it means expense which I am not up to at present & should be ashamed to have fall on you.

Many thanks dear Todhunter for all you have done for me...[168]

Although we haven't a copy of John Todhunter's reply to this letter, he evidently did respond immediately, since Wilson wrote to him again on 12 December. It also seems that Todhunter had for some while been planning to encourage George Wilson to compile an exhibition and sale of his work, as he appears to have ignored Wilson's objection to any exhibition and enclosed with his letter a draft 'catalogue' for such an exhibition. He also evidently sought to elicit Wilson's views on suitable pricing for some of his works, but this merely produced the same old basic disbelief that Wilson owned that anyone would actually pay 'good money' for his efforts! But, rather ominously, he was also just beginning to acknowledge the severity of his disease, and more surprisingly, to refer to it.

By now have you set me down as a careless, thankless ruffian, or as a man impassive & calm as an Egyptian god to the labours of others on his behalf? The real fact is though I've been rather iller than normal since your last letter came and I waited for a rather better time to come. It's dreadfully destructive to any energy

I ever had this Dyspeptic sickness. I am writing in bed, and if I were tedious as a king I could find it in my heart to bestow it all on your worship, but my position must put limits to my good intentions that way. Your notion of exhibiting my things seems to me "rum" seeing what a tiny core of finished work there is in them, I am quite willing to leave you as judge & arbitrator in the matter though – too willing. As money is a considerable object now I should have taken your suggestion of a sale now & again to the appreciative if casual inspector as an admirable one, you putting such prices as seemed to you good. This though thrusting the office of shopman on you would save the more serious business of getting them framed &c. Either way or any way & every way I seem to be evading [sic] you with trouble & wrong such as I have no right whatever to ask you to take. Your kindness really overwhelms me, but do whatever you will. I recognized almost every thing in your catalogue, but for pricing I see no clearer than before. <u>Do</u> that for me.

I will write more intelligently by and bye. I have been passing blood from the stomach both ways which made me very weak for a bit...[169]

Once again, Todhunter must have replied very quickly, as George Wilson again wrote to him on December 23rd 1889. It seems that Wilson's illness was rapidly getting worse, with only minor improvements in between, and undoubtedly John Todhunter's medical training allowed him to sense that some urgency was needed if the proposed exhibition was ever to come to fruition.

Thank you much for your very kind letter. I am getting on or rather creeping on little by little, I think; though I am still far below par. When I think most that I am doing well & just going to stride on to health the enemy gives me a shove & down I go into the abyss again to begin once more a laborious painful climbing. Its only very bad Dyspepsia. There isn't any abcess [sic] or the like. The doctor seems to think I will probably get over it in time. In eternity, it seems more like some times.*

It is a very great pleasure to me to think that my drawings give you pleasure. I thought the portfolio wd only be an incubus to you when I left them first. In my lone & lorn estate its really very heartening to get a little praise. You wouldn't believe how it has worked in my veins & noddle to have your words of praise – what encouragement it has given me. I should be only too happy to sell some of these things. but as far as I remember, they are merely scraps, studies hints, inklings of ideas in red chalk, disarrangements in dirt & black chalk & the like. However if it pleases you to buy & to get others to buy it will please me much to sell. You can use your discretion about prices; I can say nothing about that without being on the

---

*   These two statements reflect either Wilson's over-optimistic nature, or a simple hiding of the truth by his doctor – who was to pronounce death from ulceration and stricture of the pylorus only three months later.

spot but I'm content to take what you can get. Your letter though ver [sic] welcome came too soon. I had thought to send you some record of my feelings over your book. I find my ideas on the subject not worth giving at present so I wont say more than that I feel attracted greatly by the Celtic mythology & hope to convey to you by & bye my more complete thanks for the book...[170]

John Todhunter seems to have been working quite quickly to arrange an exhibition of Wilson's work, but this letter also intimates that he has now proposed the direct sale of a number of items from a portfolio of Wilson's drawings and sketches that had been left with him at some time. A sceptic might seek to cast aspersions on his motives. Did he, for instance, see this perhaps as being opportunistic to his own ends as a collector? But without the other side of this correspondence, it is impossible to gauge which pictures he was trying to sell on George Wilson's behalf – and to whom. Nevertheless, everything within the evidence to date indicates that John Todhunter had nothing but the greatest affection for George Wilson; the desire to enhance his standing, and to draw-in towards him the proper interest in his work that Wilson had always so harshly dismissed himself. On 7th January 1890, Wilson wrote again to Todhunter:

I am very grateful to you for your trouble in working these sales for me. I perfectly approve of the prices. I also leave you to do whatever you like in the future. I fear most of my best things are difficult to get at. Asia belongs to Mr Ricardo 13 Bedford Square W.C. I think Arcadia is in Austria. Spring is in Asolo, where Browning was at the last.

Summer & the winds is also in Austria I think. Russell Scott 1 the Chestnuts Hampstead Heath has the Singing Girls.

I am still in bed and don't know when I may be up again. I don't have much pain, but I dont have much digestion either so that I am very weak. However I am endowed with a good deal of patience & hope to be my own man yet. The weather is provokingly mild. I feel as if I might be out.

The warmest good wishes to you & all yours...[171]

To some extent, Wilson was right in his concern that some of his better works might be inaccessible abroad, as neither *Spring* (presumed to be Ralph Radcliffe Whitehead's *The Spring Witch*) nor *Arcadia* were procured for the eventual 1893 exhibition, although *Summer and the Winds* (by then owned by Mr H.H. Young) was certainly exhibited. Since Whitehead lived at various times both in Austria and Asolo, as well as in Florence (which is actually more likely to have been where *The Spring Witch* would have resided by then) it may well be that all these paintings belonged to Whitehead at one time or another – but there is presently no evidence to support this theory. In addition, Herbert Young also owned a villa in Asolo, so there may simply have been some confusion in Wilson's suffering mind by this time. 'The Singing Girls' undoubtedly refers to Russell Scott's *A Spring Song*.

Wilson's letter is also slightly confusing as to Todhunter's intentions. On the one hand, he seems to intimate that Todhunter was arranging sales of his works, yet on the other hand, it would appear that his friend was already planning a fairly major exhibition of works to include many that were already in private hands. However, the next letter dated 16th January, seems to confirm that Todhunter had forwarded at least a small deposit towards some sale or other.

> *I have to acknowledge with much thanks the £3. Perhaps your friend will make the greater jump later. I'm still in bed uncertain whether to get in or not. There is no going back either. Only a kind of dead look* [sic].
>
> *I have a feeling that an energetic Doctor wd get me out of this impasse. Mine is a very very old man, good in his time but beginning to dote.*[*] *I have read a good deal of the Banshee*[†] *& of the others too but I am reserving any serious reading of the book till I am in possession of my faculties. My poor head is not up to the level of reading new work except very little at a time...*[172]

A short while later, in early February, Todhunter tells us that Wilson wrote to him again, reminiscing about his love for Italy. This letter displays a still less optimistic note and perhaps his first realisation of what was in store for him. It also hints at the great dilemma caused to him by his love for visiting Italy, and the hope that the climate would help his ill-health, against the lack of any long-term improvement.

> *...The mere sound of the South acts as a charm on me, though, alas! it loves me only but little. I sometimes think Italy to be, emotionally, more in me, less separate from my existence of pleasurable thought, than any other part of my life. It isn't so of course really, but it does count for a lot, and will be to me always only half real, half a dream, as of the ante-natal country with its "clouds of glory". I wonder if I shall ever see it again. ...*[173]

The inevitable answer would of course be 'no'. But less than two weeks later on February 17th, Wilson next wrote again to Todhunter, and in this letter he displayed once again the eternal optimism that he always held for a full recovery whenever he experienced the slightest improvement in his health. There is also an interesting reminiscence of what would turn out to have been to be his last trip to Italy:

---

[*] George Wilson's doctor was in fact his uncle, also named George Wilson, who was the Godfather who had witnessed his (presumably) erroneous baptism certificate. George Wilson MD had an extraordinary life that is not directly relevant to this book; however, it is of passing interest to note that on the occasion of his final retirement in 1892, at the grand age of 81, he sat to James Cadenhead (1858-1927) R.S.A. for a reportedly fine portrait that was donated by his patients and friends.

It is not surprising that the much younger George Wilson should have suggested that a 'more energetic' – by which he presumably meant 'younger' – doctor than his uncle, who, when still practising at the age of 79 would undoubtedly have been 'beginning to dote', might have had some more modern ideas about his condition! Still, this 'doting' old doctor would be responsible for signing not only his nephew's birth certificate but also, sadly, his death certificate.

[†] Todhunter had presumably sent Wilson a copy of his most recent book *The Banshee, and Other Poems*, published in 1888.

I daresay you will be pleased to hear from me -- even such a bedridden scrawl is I am capable of. I am just a little better than when I wrote you last. And hope that you may be. I am on the upward plane again, but it is really no good being anything but 'umble' over the state of one's health. I gather from many sides that such a case as mine is common enough & complete recovery common enough too, so that I retain a good hope of doing well in time. Meanwhile boredom sits heavily on me I must confess and I feel that to be at work again would be heavenly sweet. I haven't head enough generally for reading except novels & I have got oh so sick of them! Therefore I still defer finishing your book till I can give it fair play.

Do you know that my last six weeks in Italy were spent in Asolo & partly in the society of the lady to whom R.B. dedicates his last book. She was kind to my invalid condition. I lived with a friend who hitherto had been the only Englishman or person there of the English race.

It's one of the sweetest beautifullest [sic] places you could ever imagine with still a legend or so of silk mills such as Pippa worked in but no real mills...[174]

Robert Browning (the R.B. referred to in the letter) had, of course, spent his last autumn in Asolo, and final days in Venice where he died at the Palazzo Rezzonico, the magnificent Venetian palace on the Grand Canal that belonged to his artist son Pen (Robert) Browning. Browning died on December 12th 1889 – the very day that his last book of poems, *Asolando*, was published to excellent reviews in London.[175] He had written many of the poems for this work in Asolo, where he stayed with Mrs Katharine Bronson, the widowed American who had been his close friend of the past ten years, and to whom he dedicated *Asolando*.

George Wilson's description of Mrs Bronson as having been 'kind to his invalid condition' was typical of this lady's generosity. She owned a fine house in Venice, where she first settled in 1876 as one of the earliest of the wealthy American expatriates, and where she quickly became known for her generosity as a hostess to artists of all nationalities. She had more recently also purchased a property in the lovely Treviso town of Asolo, where she had made a summer retreat out of one of the towers of the tiny city's walls. There she created rooms for her many guests. These rooms faced in towards the city, whilst a loggia on the outside of the tower overlooked the Lombardy plain.

Wilson doesn't state that he actually stayed with Mrs Bronson during his visit, but evidently he met her socially through that small community – and she always liked to entertain her visitors in the evenings. Robert Browning was not present at this time, since he didn't travel to Italy that fateful year until the autumn and we know that Wilson's last visit took place around Easter. The reference to 'the Englishman' friend with whom he was staying presently remains a mystery, but he could of course, quite conceivably, have been Herbert Young.

Robert Browning's son, Pen, loved Italy and Italian life as much as his father did; and in particular, he also came to love Asolo, where he later invested in a lace factory (but no new silk mills!) to bring employment to the city in which he died and was buried in 1912.

122

George Wilson's last letter to Todhunter finally came a month later than the previous one, on March 29th. Unsurprisingly in the circumstances, this seems a very depressing letter, and for once Wilson appears to have lost some of his eternal optimism for better times to come, but he still looks forward to better times, and deprecates his 'selfishness' for even thinking of himself when others have been so kind to him.

> *Here I am, still a prisoner to my bed. Isn't it a long business? I seem to neither lose nor gain much on the whole, now going on a little, now falling back in a disheartening manner. I look forward with much hope & comfort to the approach of warmer weather to set me up for I think to sit outside in the sun & simmer wd suit me better than anything. The kindness of one's friends is a thing to be eternally grateful for. My room is a bower of daffodils & anemones & such like and smells of Araby.*
>
> *Well after this selfish outflowing let me hope that you are well & all of you, that you haven't had what the folks here call the 'Fluency' and that if you have you hadn't a relapse which seems to be the Devil -- the real devil -- the first a mere make believe.*[*]
>
> *From this sick bed of mine I groan to think of all you men busy, doing work after your kinds. When shall I get to work again?*
>
> *Have you any news of Ellis or Yeats or others that I know?*
>
> *What is Paget[†] doing for the RA or other exhibitions...*[176]

Wilson's pleadingly simple: 'When shall I get to work again?' has a distressed poignancy attached to it, which is borne out by the next very brief letter that Todhunter was to receive from Castle Park, dated just three days later on 1st April 1890 (Tuesday) – this time from George Wilson's sister-in-law, Anna Wilson, who had nursed him so caringly through the past six months.

> *Geo Wilson died this morning quietly & without suffering at 4.30.*[177]

George Wilson's funeral took place on the following Saturday in the pretty, ancient village churchyard of Fordyce, after a long procession from Huntly that left at 11.00 a.m. and, perhaps rather curiously to us in modern times, travelled via Portsoy Station at 12.00 noon.[178] The distance of the first 'leg' to Portsoy was around 18 miles, so presumably the coffin must have travelled by train in order to arrive at Portsoy anywhere near in time for 12.00 noon. This would have been followed by a further three miles by road cortège

---

* This is presumed to be a topical reference to the widespread and drastic influenza epidemic that swept the UK in 1889 and 1890, as part of a worldwide pandemic, reaching Scotland from England in mid December 1889.

† There were several Pagets exhibiting at this time – many related – but this comment almost certainly refers to Henry Marriott Paget (1856-1936). However, it could just possibly be his brother, Sidney Edward Paget (1860-1908). Henry Paget was a good friend of J.B. Yeats, living close to him in Bedford Park. He was another member of the Calumet Club, and was brother-in-law to the actress, Florence Farr.

to Fordyce. George Wilson was buried in the area of the churchyard where Wilson family members had been buried since the mid 1700s. His name appears upon an imposing Aberdeen pink granite headstone, on which is recorded a memorial to his father John and his mother Helen, plus nine of his parents' thirteen children, added chronologically following their deaths prior to 1911.[*]

One week after Anna Wilson's letter, and in response to Todhunter's predictable letter of condolence, Anna wrote again:

> *... His life seems to me to have been rather a sad one but he did not think so, and he never seemed to lose heart either of success in his profession or recovery of his health. He died without ever saying that he had given up hope, and the day before he told me if he could tide over this attack he wd. pull through yet -- he was perfectly sensible up to the last moment the last he said was "Good bye, goodbye" not 2 minutes before the end – Yr. kind appreciation of his work seemed to gratify him, and he asked me to read what you said of it -- My husband writes with me in thanks for yr. kind sympathy.*[179]

This is the last of the family correspondence that we have concerning George Wilson; however, it is worth recording a couple of parallel references from the enduring correspondence between R.L. Nettleship and Ralph Radcliffe Whitehead that demonstrate the affection in which Wilson seems to have been held by all who were acquainted with him: Towards the end of the 1880's, Whitehead and his first wife had made their home in Florence. On Christmas Eve, 1889, Nettleship wrote to Whitehead, saying that he could not join him over the Christmas vacation, adding that his brother Jack (J.T. Nettleship) had given him 'bad news of Wilson:' adding,

> *... it doesn't seem as if he could last long (though why should one identify "him" with a poor failing piece of flesh and bones, which, if one did not identify with something with which it has nothing to do, would be felt to have its own proper life and beauty, as much as autumn leaf or a lichened trunk).*[180]

This interesting (but apparently unintentional) analogy towards the sort of woodland vision that Wilson had so frequently painted in his watercolour landscapes is somehow quite endearing. Evidently, from the tone of this letter, though, there was a far gloomier prognosis being widely discussed concerning Wilson's eventual prospects than he was personally prepared to accept at this same time. In the event, that prognosis turned out to

---

[*]   It is a curious anomaly that when Andrew Cassels Brown wrote the Wilson Family History in 1936, he recorded only an epitaph on a tombstone that had been erected (apparently solely) to the memory of George Wilson's father, John (d. 1852). He does not mention the additional 10 names showing today, so it is not clear if this is the same stone referred to by Cassels Brown or a new one erected some time after 1936 when the book was published. If the latter, which appears most unlikely, then it would seem strange that the further three children who had also died by 1936 were not included on the stone as well. The last of John Wilson senior's children (Jessie – known to all as 'Great Aunt Janet') died at the great age of 96 in 1946.

be the more accurate one, despite Wilson doggedly hanging on to his frail life for a further three months. So it was, those three months later on April 4th 1890, that R.L. Nettleship wrote again to Whitehead, once more regretting that he could not visit him in Italy that Easter either, and querying whether he had heard of George Wilson's death, saying that his brother Ned (Edward) had written to tell him of it two days earlier. He went on:

> *... As he said, one feels that a bit of sunshine is gone out of life. I don't think I ever knew a man who was so utterly unpretentious and unadorned, and yet who was such a real force whenever he found himself.*[181]

Edward Nettleship had shown the remarkable depth of his own personal affection for Wilson by taking the considerable trouble to travel up to Huntly to visit him during his final days. Their close friendship and this particular event were recorded by Nettleship's widow in her notes towards her husband's own obituary some 23 years later.

The final reference we have from Ralph Whitehead was written from an enduring personal memory, again some 20 years later, on July 11th 1910. He was writing to his wife Jane Byrd (McCall), who appears to have been away on a recuperative sailing trip. They were then living at their Byrdcliffe Art Colony at Woodstock, Ulster County, New York. After various leading opening comments on the weather, he continues:

> *...This is a wonderful Summer and you are very wonderful in it. You are more like your old dear self! And you know I often think of you as Summer – I suppose because of the suggestion of that picture of George Wilson's "Summer & the Winds" in which Summer is something like you. ...*[182]

It may seem strange that Whitehead should have made this connection over 20 years after George Wilson's death, and again epitomises the deep impression that was left on Wilson's friends by what to them would undoubtedly have seemed to be his untimely, if inevitable, death. A photograph in Cornell University Museum of Art of Jane Byrd McCall in her mid-twenties shows her as being a strikingly beautiful woman.[183] However, the likeness of Jane to the girl who sat for the subject in Wilson's painting of 'Summer' (and, incidentally, for at least one or two of the other 'Winds' in that painting as well) is not immediately obvious. There is certainly a vague similarity, but the girl who poses for these elements in the painting appears, as usual, to be George Wilson's favourite model – who continues to remain, most inconveniently, totally anonymous.

Summer & the Winds was a tempera painting of unknown size since it is now missing. As surmised above, there is no firm record at present that it ever belonged to Whitehead; however, George Wilson did tell Todhunter that he believed *Summer & the Winds* and *Arcadia* were both in Austria (which is presumed to mean that he thought that they were both in Whitehead's possession at that time).[184] So this may be why he had such a particular memory of the painting.

CHAPTER ELEVEN

George Wilson's retrospective exhibitions

John Todhunter took up the reins of his idea for an exhibition of George Wilson's work with some speed following Wilson's death, and he had contacted the bereaved family again on 19th May. It seems that this time he must have first proposed the idea of writing an article about Wilson's life for publication. Without doubt, this would have been the article that was eventually published in August 1891 in the *English Illustrated Magazine*. As always, the Wilsons replied immediately by return, on 20th May – but by this time, the family had clearly closed ranks as far as any further dispersal of George Wilson's work was concerned; so his brother John replied directly:

> *... George died, leaving no will, and no instructions with regard to anything, and we have no ideas of what articles, -- paintings, drawings or other, -- there may be in London belonging to him.*
>
> *We have asked my brother-in-law, Mr. Russell Scott,* a kind friend of George's, to make some enquiry among his friends, and to obtain what possessions he can, & forward them to my Mother, at Aberdeen. -- We do not wish to sell any-thing.*

---

*   This is the Russell Scott previously referred to, who was married to George Wilson's first cousin, Jessie (née) Thurburn and with whom George probably first stayed when he arrived in London in 1868. Russell Scott was actually John Wilson's brother-in-law by marriage, in that Jessie Scott and John Wilson's own wife Anna were sisters (née Thurburn). John and Anna Wilson (and Jessie Scott also, of course) were also first cousins and, unusually, second cousins at the same time – their respective fathers having also been first cousins!

The ancient Scottish family of Thurburn was almost inextricably linked to the Wilsons for four generations, and by first cousin marriages (occasionally more than one) in the last three of these. Surprisingly, this does not seem to have created any real problems, although some of these marriages avoided having children. However, from those who did decide to procreate, the prolific number of offspring produced included many fine academic, artistic and successful business people, many of whom spread their wings to the four corners of the earth.

Mr. Scott has full authority from the family to act for them. -- There can be no objection to your using the drawings for the purpose you name, and I have written to Mr. Scott to that effect. -- May I trouble you to get a copy of the Review sent to me by the publishers in which your article appears. -- [185]

Following this, on 24th May, John Wilson again wrote to Todhunter – who had himself replied to John Wilson's previous letter on 21st May, by return – on the matter of what to do with Wilson's work lying in London – and which George Wilson had previously instructed Todhunter to sell as he deemed fit. He also enclosed a note with some information about his brother's early life:

I duly received your note of the 21st inst, and have since seen my Mother.

She has so little of George's work that she is not willing to part with any specimens of it now remaining. – She desires me to say that she would be sorry to disappoint you, but you can understand her desire to retain them. –

Choose any one you like from those in your possession, and accept it as a present from her & a souvenir of George. –

I have written to Mr. Scott to tell him we should like you to do this [186]

From this response, it is difficult to tell where all the pictures were then located. It isn't known where George Wilson lived when in London during his final years, but Todhunter of course knew, and it seems that he certainly had access to some of his work – possibly during the months before Wilson died and while Todhunter was attempting to arrange their sales. However, at John Wilson's request, Russell Scott evidently seems to have stepped in and collected up what remained of the pictures, and it was Scott who took up the correspondence towards the end of the year. After commencing with some further anecdotal information about Wilson's life, much of which would undoubtedly have been well known to Todhunter already (but some of which was in fact erroneous!), he added one or two more intimate insights into Wilson's character:

... In after life [following on from his art studies] *his own want of technical facility was, I think, a constant source of hindrance & discouragement to him -- But there is no doubt that bad health, during the years that should have been the most fruitful of his life, greatly marred the amt. of his work, and often its completeness. He inherited a family delicacy of the digestion & suffered much more than most of his friends knew -- and it was this I think, as much as his naturally unsystematic and tentative way of working that, with all the fine qualities of his genius, prevented him from producing more work, & more complete work. He lived like a child, & worked like one -- not looking beyond the present, and satisfied with the exercise, in his art, of his own faculties. He had too I think a childlike simplicity & purity of nature –*

As a friend of his perhaps you may be interested by an expression of his feeling that occurred shortly before his death --

His brothers wife, who devoted herself to him all thro' his last illness with the greatest possible kindness, was at his bedside with the nurse when he worn [sic] to a shadow, appeared quite unconscious, & rapidly sinking. She said something to the nurse about the need, at such a time, of religious faith -- on which George murmured "I believe in God, good bye" and, almost at that moment, died.

Of course in a life like his, there is hardly anything beyond his work, of an external character to relate -- I never was a correspondent of his, & probably, tho' I have known him & his family so long, I knew him less intimately, a good deal, than some of his other friends -- Whenever I hear from you, I will send his pictures to whatever interest you may give...[187]

John Todhunter's efforts in persuading the Wilson family to allow him to organise a retrospective exhibition of George Wilson's works eventually met with success. With the co-operation of the several members of the family who possessed so many examples of his work, and with the ardent support of his small circle of friends and patrons in London, it was decided to hold the exhibition in his native Aberdeenshire at the Aberdeen Art Gallery, hosted by the Aberdeen Artists' Society as part of their annual exhibition.[*]

First of all, however, he immediately wrote and published the eulogistic account of George Wilson's life and works, which appeared in the *English Illustrated Magazine* of August, 1891 – and which has been previously quoted here. This article, whether directly or indirectly, also became the basis for almost every other account that has since been published about George Wilson – including, to a significant extent, the entry in Percy Bate's *The English Pre-Raphaelite Painters; Their Associates and Successors.* However, despite Bate's still somewhat eulogistic style, he did make an effort to re-write some of the text, and certainly added a number of original comments of his own. One of these is worth quoting as an amusing comparison with those Pre-Raphaelites to whom Wilson was deemed a 'Successor' – but one that indeed still holds some truth. However, it can only apply in general to Wilson's figurative oils and other allegorical works and considerably less so to the majority of his watercolour landscapes, albeit not without exception. Certainly the reference to the refreshing 'open air' atmosphere of Wilson's work would have appealed to the painter immensely:

... in conclusion, it may be again noted that throughout the work of George Wilson the atmosphere is essentially ethereal. The rare air is that of a poet's world, the sun-bathed Arcadia of nymph and faun, the mystic land of faërie; but the air

---

[*] It is worth noting that all the works that were exhibited at Aberdeen were listed as being owned by various individuals and that none were from Wilson's studio. Presumably therefore, all the works that Todhunter had been trying to sell before Wilson died had indeed by then been sold – even if only to himself, perhaps. However, there is an anomaly here in that press reports at the time (q.v.) record that seem to indicate that certain sales of Wilson's work were made at the exhibition. There is presently no explanation to this anomaly.

is the open air, and not the perfumed incense-laden breeze, that haunts the mind when one thinks of Rossetti's superb conceptions...[188]

It took two years to organise the Aberdeen exhibition. This entailed pulling together the works that were all in the private hands of friends and family that were widespread across the country; but evidently some from abroad as well, since several of those mentioned in Wilson's letter of 7th January 1890 were shown at this exhibition. Eventually 73 works were hung under the title *The Wilson Collection* in Gallery III of the 1893 Annual Exhibition of the Aberdeen Artists' Society. These works were representative of every medium in which Wilson worked.

In the same exhibition were hung another group of works by several other well-known Aberdonian and Scottish artists – including around 50 by James Cassie, RSA (1819-1879), and a number also by John Phillip, RA (1817-1867), John Pettie, RA (1839-1893), and James Campbell Noble, RSA (1846-1913). Undoubtedly, this must have been quite a spectacular exhibition all round, and it is therefore a fine tribute to the immediate recognition of the quality of George Wilson's work that from the press reports that followed the exhibition, it was this section that appears to have caught the attention of all.

In addition to the exhibition itself, the Aberdeen Artists' Society commissioned George Wilson's renowned namesake, George Washington Wilson, Queen Victoria's Royal Photographer in Scotland, to photograph and publish a limited edition of 100 numbered sets of 'phototypes' (photogravures) of 12 of the pictures in the exhibition. These early photographs are the only record we have of a small number of important George Wilson pictures that are presently believed to be lost.

The 12 plates were printed onto 10 sheets of fine wove paper, which bear a delightful watermark depicting an early open-cab steam engine, with the date of 1889 inscribed on its tender, and bordered at each end by a monogram of the letters 'G O G'. Each set of 10 sheets is enclosed within an apparently hand-made paper folder, on which is inscribed on the two sides of the front page the title and publishing information; a list of the plates and their owners; the limited edition statement and date of Nov. 1893, plus a handwritten unique number for the set and the manuscript company signature of George Washington Wilson and Co Ltd. On the inside of the back page is an account of the life of George Wilson, based largely, once again, on John Todhunter's *English Illustrated Magazine* article of 1891, and signed with the initials 'W.K.' for William Kelly, the renowned Aberdeen architect.*

George Wilson's sister-in-law, Anna – who had nursed him so carefully and devotedly during his final months – was equally renowned within the family (and even more so

---

* Dr William Kelly was an eminent Aberdeen architect and antiquarian, who designed, amongst other buildings, the Aberdeen Savings Bank head office at 19 Union Terrace. However, he is undoubtedly best remembered for the parapet on Union Bridge supporting the splendid bronze leopards that are still known locally as 'Kelly's Cats'.

beyond!) as being a real 'tartar' when she chose to be – which apparently was quite frequently; but she always kept in close, regular, and affectionate correspondence with her many children, wherever in the world they might have landed. During the lead-up to the exhibition, letters from Anna to her second-eldest son, Alan, then aged 18 and studying in France and Germany, record some fervent activity towards the selection of paintings for the Aberdeen exhibition. This exhibition eventually opened on February 14th of that year with the final picture selection having been made by a Mr Sheriff.* On or around 4th January, Anna wrote to Alan Wilson:

> ...*About the pictures Mr Sheriff came out and saw the pictures on Saturday He selected about 15 of ours and seemed very much pleased with some of them ...*[189]

She went on to describe some of the paintings that were selected. A week later, possibly on 11th January, she wrote again that:

> ... *Papa and I have had a busy day preparing 16 of Uncle Dodie's pictures for the exhibition. We have had a great changing of frames [.] The woman gathering sticks has been put into a handsome frame that hung over the drawing room door with an old ruined castle by moonlight -- a bought thing. The new frame improves the picture so much and we have done the same to the one of the Kinnoir park hanging below Mahomet.† ... We have had [no] end of labels to tie on and schedules to fill up but now they are really to be sent off. ...*[190]

On 10th of February, Anna wrote again to Alan to tell him that the exhibition of paintings was to open on Wednesday (14th), and that:

> ... *Papa had a letter from Auntie Janet today and she told him that Uncle Charlie‡ had gone to the Art Gallery to see Uncle Dodie's pictures hung and he was very much pleased with them. They have given him a capital position on one side of the room and Uncle Charlie says some of his pictures that have been sent down from London are very fine and much admired. The one of "Asia" that Dr Todhunter illustrated is a very fine picture Uncle Charlie says. I must try and let you see what is said about them at the opening. ...*[191]

As we know from the newspaper reports at the time, the Aberdeen exhibition was deemed a great success. But at the same time, and although it was heralded in his home county, and by the press and his family and friends, in the eyes of the adopted Londoner,

---

* The identity of the Mr Sheriff referred to here has presently not been ascertained.

† 'The [Old] Woman Gathering Sticks' was the familial name for *The Fall of the Leaf.* 'Kinnoir park' is understood to refer to *The Huntly Lodge Woods in Summer,* whilst 'Mahomet' presumably refers to the sole Algiers painting that was loaned by John Wilson to both retrospective exhibitions, simply entitled *A View in Algiers.*

‡ George Wilson's brother, Charles Wilson, WS, Procurator Fiscal for Aberdeenshire.

John Todhunter, Aberdeen was simply 'not London' – and he had always felt that a significant George Wilson exhibition in London was fully justified. In the event, it took him another 10 years to achieve his aim, but in 1903 with the enthusiastic support of John Baillie's Gallery at 1, Princes Terrace, Hereford Road, in west London, he succeeded in launching an exhibition of Wilson's work as the first of what was intended to be a series of exhibitions at the gallery to be devoted to 'Neglected Artists'.

It seems certain that Todhunter's original intention at the time that Wilson's health was finally failing, was to try to organise an exhibition and sale of some of the works that still lay in his studio, as well as showing many of those items that hung already on the walls of his patrons – and his family, of course. Wilson's early death ensured that the family would certainly never part with any of their paintings, but what actually happened to the remaining unsold works is not clear. His studio was finally cleared by his friend Russell Scott (the husband of his cousin Jessie), with the help of Todhunter, no doubt. Unfortunately, Russell Scott's own significant collection is also now untraceable through the descendents of his family.

As with the Aberdeen exhibition, all the works shown in London were already in private hands. Nevertheless, there is a reference (whether accurate or not) that some of them – in Aberdeen at least – *were* offered for sale, since the *Aberdeen Free Press* of February, 1893, reported that:

> *...among the purchasers of pictures have been the Marquis of Huntly* [who had formally opened the exhibition]*, Mr Ogston of Ardoe, Mr James Ogston of Norwood, and Mr Wilson of Albyn Terrace.*[*]

Although this remark was made within the specific report on Wilson's exhibits, the overall press report referred elsewhere to the whole exhibition, so there is some ambiguity as to whether these bought works were by Wilson or perhaps by others exhibiting.

So, ten years on, Anna Wilson was again put to the task of preparing their collection of George Wilson's paintings for yet another exhibition, and on September 6th 1903, she wrote again to her son, Alan – who was by this time working in the Chinese Customs Service:

> *... We have very empty walls at present, for all Uncle Dodie's paintings are off to this London exhibition, and the dining room and Drawing room look very dismantled*[.] *There is to be ab* [sic] *article on his works in the Oct Studio by some lady, I forget her name, I must try to remember to send you a copy. It is Dr Todhunter and some of his old Artistic friends who are moving in the matter*[.] *They seem to*

---

* The suggestion of sales being made from among the Wilson exhibits is difficult to relate to the owners listed – none of whom would have been very likely to wish to sell. Although the *Aberdeen Free Press* column referred specifically to the Wilson exhibition alone, it may be that the reporter was mistaken and that the purchases were made from other areas of the overall gallery exhibition.

think his work has never been sufficiently known so they are getting his paintings exhibited along with some others, at this Exhibition. ...[192]

In another letter to Alan, after the exhibition had closed, there is a brief mention that Anna had safely received back the box of paintings, but she complains that it will take them a whole day to re-hang them. She further comments that the reviews have, once again, been good.

Of the reviews received, one was the article published in the 1903-04 volume of *The Studio* (referred to by Anna Wilson) and written by Leonore van der Veer, which appeared in Vol. 30 covering October 1903 to January 1904. It was a four-page account plus illustrations from the exhibition, which incorporated, once again, the same basic facts that John Todhunter had first written in 1893, but with a new set of critiques of Wilson's workmanship generally. In addition, there were illustrations included of a few of the pictures on show – including a fortunate full-colour reproduction of *Study of an Oak Tree* and some other previously unseen items from Todhunter's collection.[193]

There was one other insignificant (in size) but important mention of the exhibition that was included in the *Art Journal* of 1903. This was the briefest of records within the general report by the Journal's critic, Frank Rinder, on the London exhibitions that had opened in September and October of 1903 and, whilst including nothing of a new commentary nature, there was included one small illustration of one of Wilson's preliminary works *Study for A Spring Song* (q.v.) that has not been reproduced elsewhere.[194] This was evidently an early pencil or chalk sketch for the figures in the final composition, and therefore must have been one of the two studies with this same title (Nos 98 and 99) within the three items that were loaned to the exhibition by George Haité.†

In the catalogue that accompanied the Baillie exhibition, simply entitled *George Wilson 1848-1890*, Todhunter had revised and précised an abstract of his earlier *English Illustrated Magazine* article as an introduction to the exhibition. Baillie also included on the frontispiece of the catalogue, just one illustration (q.v.) of a very typical red chalk sketch by Wilson, depicting in fine detail a hooded and cloaked female figure, enclosed within an arched outline frame for some unidentified design. This drawing is not referred to in

---

* Anna Wilson's information here may not be correct – or perhaps not the final decision concerning the exhibition. No reference can be found from catalogues or other references that the Baillie Gallery showed works by any other artists at the same time as the Wilson exhibition.

† Although there is no other reference to George Haité elsewhere in the researched records relating to George Wilson, it is an unusual name, and so it is a reasonable assumption that this was the English painter, textile designer and author, George Charles Haité (1855-1924). Among his numerous publications on design, the most important was *Plant Studies for Artists, Designers and Art Students*.

Confusingly, his father was also called George Haité, and was the even more renowned Victorian textile designer who was essentially responsible for introducing the ubiquitous Paisley Pattern designs that became used with great popularity in shawls and elsewhere. Haité's 'Cashmere' patterns were derived from woven shawls made in the Indian province of Kashmir.

the text of the catalogue and is not specifically recognisable from the listed chalk studies exhibited, of which a number are simply described individually as being a '*Study*'.

A few years later, in 1908, appeared James (later Sir James) L. Caw's still definitive and reliable book entitled *Scottish Painting, Past and Present, 1620-1908.*[195] Again, like Percy Bate before him, and just a few after him, Caw relied heavily on the very few well known facts about George Wilson, as originally recorded by Todhunter. But yet again, he adds a few of his own comments about some of the pictures that he must have noted from the later Baillie exhibition. No doubt then, as the then Director of the National Gallery of Scotland, Caw would have been much pleased were he to have known that, nearly 70 years later on in 1976, the National Gallery in Edinburgh would at last receive just one George Wilson watercolour, entitled *A Fallen Beech*, within the excellent Helen Barlow Bequest.

Three years after receipt of the Barlow bequest, the National Gallery of Scotland staged an exhibition in 1979 of all 56 bequeathed works, entitled *English Watercolours and other Drawings: The Helen Barlow Bequest.* *A Fallen Beech* was exhibit No. 53 and was accompanied by a half page colour illustration in the catalogue. More recently, in 2004 to 2005, the painting has toured with the exhibition of Scottish landscape drawing entitled *A Picturesque Pursuit: Scottish Landscape Drawings from the National Gallery of Scotland*, at the Robert Fleming Gallery in London, followed by its home gallery in Edinburgh where the exhibition was renamed *A Journey Through Scotland,* then finally on to the Richard Feigen Gallery in New York.

The only other small gallery exhibition of George Wilson's work of which we are aware, was staged once again by the Aberdeen Art Gallery, from 9th April to 7th June 1990. This exhibition, compiled to mark the centenary of Wilson's death, was entitled *Poetic Vision* and comprised just 17 paintings, plus two sketchbooks and a number of loose drawings, all from the collections of the Aberdeen Art Gallery and just one private owner.

Since the date of this latter exhibition, prior to which there was no co-ordinated knowledge of the present owners of George Wilson's work, a further significant number of pictures by Wilson have been located – many in the hands of the few remaining descendents of his family and friends. Happily, these do now include one or two of his larger allegorical oil paintings – which, although to some they may not necessarily represent his most enchanting works, do represent a very important element of his life's aspirations and are especially impressive in their own right.

From this latter area of his work, just one painting has appeared in a major exhibition, and that was the larger figurative oil painting, *The Spring Witch,* that toured for two years between 2005 and 2007 along with the majority of the most significant works from within the Bancroft Collection of the Delaware Art Museum. This touring exhibition, entitled *Waking Dreams – The Art of the Pre-Raphaelites from the Delaware Art Museum,* has appeared at exhibition locations in eight states across the USA and, in the summer of 2005, at just one European location – the Castle Museum in Nottingham, England. The exhibition was accompanied by a magnificent catalogue that is a veritable work of art in itself, and which incorporates a full-page illustration of *The Spring Witch.*

CHAPTER TWELVE

Influences on a future that was never to be

So what direction was Wilson's work taking towards the end of his short life? In such a relatively short productive period of little over 15 years, and particularly since he never, ever, signed or dated his work, it is not possible to be precise about the dating of any of his work, except those that were exhibited or referred to at particular times. Thankfully, there are just about enough of these to identify the general trend in his development. As previously suggested, he never really lost his earliest Pre-Raphaelite principles, but latterly there was a distinctive change towards an even bolder use of colour and light in his painting (although we can only experience this through the predominant medium of watercolour paintings that remain). This appears to have intensified following on from his later trips to Italy and to north Africa and is evidently inspired by the strength of the natural light and heat in those climes. At the same time, Wilson would inevitably have encountered the modern French paintings that were on show as he journeyed through Paris, and some influence of this movement must certainly have rubbed off onto him as well.

Unfortunately, there are only four of his larger allegorical oil paintings still known to exist – or, at least, that have so far been traced. The order or progression towards completion of these works is not absolutely certain, so can only be calculated. Two of these paintings (*Asia* and *The Song of the Nightingale*) are primarily figurative compositions depicting scenes from the poetry of Shelley and Keats. The other two may have been commissioned or conceived as a pair, although they are not particularly close in their execution. These are *The Rape of Proserpine* (also known as *Persephone*) and *The Spring Witch,* depicting the initial abduction and the annual return in spring of Proserpine from the underworld. *The Spring Witch* stands out as being certainly the most detailed and thoroughly finished of these works, where the figure of Proserpine as she emerges from the underworld is surrounded to a far greater degree by detailed symbolist elements. The painting also shows a greater measure of confidence in execution than the others and is probably the last to be completed. *The Song of the Nightingale*, although a charming composition, is in some ways possibly the least successful, whilst *Asia* and *The Rape of Proserpine* bear a number of closer similarities than their subjects might naturally signify. Wilson's use of the same model for all four of these Paintings, with her piercing blue-green eyes and varying tones of reddish hair, gives them all something of a feeling of 'sequence', somehow.

One might wish to believe that, had he lived to a somewhat greater age, Wilson would have progressed to even greater achievements – and indeed, significant recognition. However, there is always that nagging feeling that he probably simply would not have allowed this to happen and would have tried to walk away from it all! The seeking of fame and fortune was fundamentally not in his character. Nevertheless, with evidence of increasing interest in his work, the corresponding resultant increase in recognition would probably have been largely taken out of his hands – if only by Todhunter's 'direction' of his affairs. Similarly, there is equal evidence that, towards the end of his life, he appeared to be quite capable of maintaining himself (albeit only very frugally by all contemporary accounts) in a studio within the artistically fashionable north London suburb of Hampstead, so perhaps a change in his fortunes was already underway in any case.

It is now to be hoped that a revived growing recognition of his work, perhaps even with a little help from this account, might uncover many more of his paintings that presently remain 'lost'. From the two retrospective exhibition lists of his work, in 1893 and 1903, plus a number of other pictures that are still known about in public and private hands, we can now compile a first catalogue raisonné of around 150 works. However, this is certainly nowhere near a complete list of all George Wilson's once extant works.

For instance, it is known that Wilson's youngest brother, Hugh, was an ardent collector of his brother's work, and that he took a collection of his paintings out to Australia with him when he emigrated to Melbourne in 1877. Later in 1888, Hugh became one of the founders of the reconstructed Royal Bank of Australia (subsequently absorbed into ANZ), retiring as its General Manager in 1923.[196] None of his collection of paintings returned to the UK after his death in 1933, and although he became a great benefactor to the arts (both visual and musical) in his adopted city, there is presently no evidence as to how, or to whom, the paintings were dispersed.

Hugh Wilson was a great traveller, and on one of his return visits to tour through Europe he wrote from the Neues Union Hotel in Dresden on 23rd June 1928, a few months after the death of George Wilson's old friend and patron, Halsey Ricardo, to the executors of Ricardo's will in an attempt to purchase the painting *Asia* from the estate. There had been a small announcement in the newspapers that Ricardo had bequeathed a 'De Morgan lustre dish' to the British Museum, and the painting *Asia* to the National Gallery in London. Hugh Wilson had heard about this from his family, and wrote to ask if he might bid for the painting should the National Gallery not accept it.[197]

The National Gallery did not in fact accept the picture, nor indeed is there any apparent evidence in their archives of the Selection Committee having discussed the matter at the time. This may have been a pity from the point of view of Wilson's future recognition; however, the late 1920's were not at all a good receptive period for pictures painted in the Pre-Raphaelite style.

It was probably also somewhat more providential that the executors did not take up Hugh Wilson's offer, since he died in Australia five years later and, had he taken the painting home with him, it would almost certainly now be lost along with the rest of his significant collection of his brother's work. Thankfully, *Asia* has remained safe within Ricardo family descent.

George Wilson undoubtedly lived at an extraordinarily bountiful time for painters who were both gifted and, equally importantly, were also prepared to promote themselves. He certainly featured amongst the former, but equally as certainly was not interested in being considered in any way akin to the latter; and since it inevitably needed both facets (at least) to achieve a prominent reputation, he signally failed to achieve such eminence. Wilson, however, would scarcely have considered this failure – or indeed important – since it wouldn't even have occurred to him to try to compete in the first place. Quite simply he was not interested.

As a blunt indication of this chasm between those who were 'in demand' and those who didn't so register, it is recorded that Millais reputedly earned between £20,000 and £40,000 a year (an astonishing modern-day equivalent of £1,750,000 to £3,500,000) at the height of his fame. At the same time, it is recorded that Holman Hunt (who was apparently advised by Dickens as to what to charge for his paintings!) achieved one of the highest sums ever paid directly to a living British artist for a painting, when he sold the second 1904 replica of the original *The Light of the World* (St Paul's Cathedral, London) to Charles Booth for £12,000 (£1 million today).

This differential was entirely reflective of the gap that existed at the time between the extremely rich and 'the rest'. George Wilson and J.B. Yeats were delighted to receive £5 or £10 (£400 - £800) for a small painting during their post-student Brotherhood days – as indeed might any good aspiring young artist today. Even towards the latter years of his short life, Wilson was only asking £70 (£6,000) at exhibition in the Walker art Gallery for his larger figurative oil painting *The Song of the Nightingale* – and it is unlikely even then that such a sum would have been his idea, more likely being applied on the advice of others.

Another, rather more oblique outcome of the later Victorians' passion for grand art, equally encouraged by State patronage, was what became almost a plethora of titles bestowed upon many of the greater names. Knighthoods and baronetcies became almost commonplace, and even occasional peerages – Millais, Burne-Jones, Poynter, Leighton … and so on. Behind, and indeed, amongst all of this were hundreds of aspiring and very competent artists, all struggling to be seen. George Wilson did not even consider positioning himself amongst this latter group. To him, the argument was inconsequential! He painted purely for the love of painting and to depict in the best way that he was able his interpretation of Nature that he loved so much, and the poetry that encompassed that love. He was never quite happy with the results – probably because he held the fundamental belief that Nature simply could not be truly emulated or effectively depicted – only merely impersonated.

George Wilson drew and painted in many different media. In drawing, he used pencil or ink, charcoal, and particularly, chalk – of which red and brown was a common favourite combination; but (unlike Nettleship's later drawings) no pastel work has been found so far as we are presently aware. To paint, he used watercolour, with and without body colour, and occasionally tempera or gouache, all to great effect; and of course, he used oils. His more complete drawings tend to be mainly studio figure and head studies, but with occasional sorties into allegorical subjects. In all his drawing, Poynter's influential teaching had a marked affect, and some of these small works are the most sensitive and effective of all he achieved. There is no doubt that he was a very accomplished draughtsman. With very few exceptions, his oil paintings portrayed almost entirely poetic and romantic symbolism by way of subject. Just very occasionally, he painted an oil landscape or a portrait. However, it was when he came to use watercolour that his work became most relaxed and finished.

Frequently the subject figures in Wilson's oil paintings have technical faults in draughtsmanship; but then so did those in so great a man as Rossetti's oil paintings – such as the hands in *The Day Dream* (1880, Victoria and Albert Museum) or *La Bella Mano* (1875, Delaware Art Museum), which appear to be somewhat contorted. But this has usually been acknowledged – even from so early a critique as Percy Bate's *The English Pre-Raphaelite Painters*, in which Bate pointed out that it seldom detracts from the appreciation of the finished work.[198] Bate further suggests that Rossetti's technical faults might be partly due to the P.R.B.'s inherent obduracy towards traditional academic art teaching. In Wilson's case, the faults are not dissimilar to Rossetti's, and although the later 1869 'Brotherhood' professed the same objections to the Royal Academy teaching curriculum, he certainly did at least work hard on his draughtsmanship. In particular, hands and feet caused him problems, but seldom faces and torsos. However, unlike Rossetti, Wilson habitually lacked general confidence in his oil work.

He was an inveterate sketcher and took a great deal of trouble in trying to perfect his figure drawing. From his sketchbooks we can see that he evidently recognised his difficulty with limbs and he always worked very hard at his preliminary sketches. It certainly seems that his difficulty lay in transcribing his preparatory work into the finished oil painting. This is far less the case for his watercolours, so it seems that it was both the medium and the scale of the work that was the main problem, with repeated re-working of areas leading sometimes to an inconclusive result. These minor and not necessarily offensive faults apart, his larger oils certainly present visionary poetic interpretations, and always contain his same boldness in colouring.

The foregrounds of these larger allegorical works (and similar smaller watercolours or tempera works) will be found to be filled with minutely detailed flora, and sometimes small animals, indicative of Wilson's underlying Pre-Raphaelite leaning. However, the figures and the backgrounds of the four (known) remaining allegorical oils all contain the far stronger influences of the Italian Renaissance. Even Wilson's smaller pastoral studies in tempera or watercolour, such as *Summer and the Winds,* are reminiscent of Botticelli's *Primavera* (Uffizi Gallery, Florence) and Mantegna's *Parnassus* (Louvre, Paris); and it is Botticelli again that one sees in the pose of Persephone in *The Spring Witch.* Perhaps most illuminating are the rocky mountainous backdrops in all four oil paintings, which are so readily inspired by the works of Mantegna (Andrea, 1431-1506),

Botticelli (Sandro, 1445 – 1510) and Leonardo da Vinci (1452-1519), and which so strongly portray those influences.

Wilson's careful and continuing study of Italian High Renaissance Art is evident in these compositions; but where his watercolours were concerned, he appears to have had two completely separate missions. On one hand he carried his same symbolist visions into a number of often more successfully accomplished allegorical works; whilst on the other, he pursued what was probably his greatest love of all, or at least his most relaxed and natural ability – his landscapes, and particularly, his woodland landscapes.

It is in his treatment of trees and branches, both in his watercolours and in his oil backgrounds, that some influence of Corot might be seen. As Todhunter observed, 'His drawing of stems and branches, sometimes rapid and suggestive, sometimes elaborately studied, always vital, cannot easily be matched.[199] The finest detailing from the central point of a tree, or trees and branches, migrates towards its extremities into brilliantly formed, yet almost ethereal, shapes. The appeal of Corot's work should hardly be surprising: his reported comment to a pupil that 'Beauty in art is truth bathed in an impression, the emotion that is received from Nature.' ... 'If you have been sincere in your emotion you will be able to pass it on to others.' succinctly epitomises Wilson's own raison d'être.

A further point of influence from pre-impressionist French artists can be detected in the series of coastal scenes painted mainly on the north Banffshire Moray coastline around the small towns of Buckie and Cullen. In these paintings, there continually appears a particular reminiscence of Gustave Courbet (1819-1877) and his 1860s *Wave* series of paintings (National Gallery of Scotland; Fine Arts Museums of San Francisco, and – more properly known as *The Stormy Sea* – Musée d'Orsay, Paris, etc.). But yet again, from Courbet's statement of realistic principles, published in the *Courrier du Dimanche* in 1861 that, 'The art of painting should consist solely of the representation of objects visible and tangible to the artist',[200] it is hardly surprising that Wilson might find inspiration from Courbet as well.

However, the apparent French influence doesn't stop there because, whilst Wilson's figurative oil paintings never lost their Pre-Raphaelite roots, he became much more adventurous with his later watercolour landscapes, and following his later visits to Italy and to north Africa, his use of colour and light become quite bold indeed. He never quite used the impressionist technique of breaking down the inter-relationship of light and colour, but in some of these later paintings he came quite close, and managed to relate some of the sensations caused by light, whilst at the same time, line perhaps became slightly less important.

However, the theme that never left the forefront of Wilson's work was his absolute devotion to the outstanding and (literally) never-ending colours in nature. He worked from nature, and could only ever be considered to be a *pleinairist*. His evident love of certain particular colours dominated his work throughout the early and middle periods of his short life. Seldom do these paintings *not* contain swathes of colours based on vivid shades incorporating Cadmium Red and Vermilion and Prussian Blue. It was only during the latter years of his life that the brilliant light of Italy and North Africa seems to have influenced him towards employing a much greater variety of colours together to create a mildly more impressionistic yet equally radiant result.

John Todhunter wrote that Wilson's favourite subjects were 'poetical or mythical designs, in which ideal figures were set in a background of ideal landscape.'[201] This may well be correct – and Todhunter probably knew Wilson better than almost anyone else did. But one can't help feeling that Wilson saw the allegorical pictures to which Todhunter was referring, to be an 'objective' in life – his 'daily labour' – whilst his landscapes were his 'pure relaxation' – almost even his 'leisure pursuit'.

* * *

Earlier reference has been made to George Wilson's favourite model, who appears in so many of his allegorical works and studies. The previous reference alluded to both the recorded and the anecdotal evidence of Wilson's attachment to his model. It is, nevertheless, an interesting and relevant subject that demands further exploration.

There is little doubt that this young woman, whoever she was, and who appears so frequently in his paintings, was extremely important to George Wilson, and remained so over quite a long period. She appears throughout his two surviving sketchbooks and is the principle model for all his allegorical works – both in oil and occasional other media. She was evidently extremely responsive to Wilson's demands for dramatic poses as she appears with consistent regularity in the sketchbooks in a variety of such poses – both clothed and unclothed. Not only is she easily recognisable, with her astonishingly blue-green eyes and her mass of auburn hair, but one can also easily sense the very close rapport between artist and model that is essential for the outcome of their co-operation to be at once both relaxed and also dramatically effective. But somewhat further than this, frequently the result in Wilson's case is also very sensual, whilst never quite verging on eroticism.

In contrast to the striking and overtly promiscuous beauty of the Rossetti models, with their cupid's-bow lips, Wilson's model appears more akin to Burne-Jones's softer and more 'homely' and 'sisterly' conceptions – although her build appears somewhat 'heavier' than Burne-Jones tended to employ, or at least portray. And, like Burne-Jones, sometimes the same countenance may appear more than once in different figures within the same composition.

Just two of Wilson's sketchbooks remain in existence, in which he depicts, in the main, passing moments, situations or studied poses. One of these books is quite small and the other actually no more than a lined exercise notebook. Both include a number of more developed posed studies that are, once again, of his favourite sitter. It seems that this young woman was very adept at responding to Wilson's demands for the classic countenance that is portrayed in so many of his allegorical works. She is able to depict, as demanded, the tragedy, joy, horror, or shear terror for the required pose with apparent ease; yet all the time she retains a voluptuous sensuality that would have delighted any figure painter.

While she may not have been a naturally classic beauty, she had the charming homely good looks that one feels must have epitomised not only her real persona, but also everything that a quiet and reticent young Scot would find very alluring. Perhaps the most fascinating element to this is that this reportedly shy Scot apparently had absolutely no qualms about persuading his model to pose in the nude – and not just occasionally, but almost invariably! Apart from her evidently full and nubile figure, she had those penetratingly blue-green eyes that Wilson depicted in shades of startling ice blue through to aquamarine. Her hair appears to have been of auburn red, again depicted in a variety of shades but never losing the basic tone range, and with her full lips, she seems to have been an exciting and attractive sitter – even if no more than that – whom Wilson utilised throughout much of his short professional life.

It is of course mischievous even to intimate that we have no knowledge if it was to this young woman that the familial anecdotes of George Wilson having a 'by-blow' referred, and it is completely unfair to suggest such a thing in the absence of proper evidence. However, it also has to be said that it certainly would not have been at all unusual at that time if it were – when very many of the very much grander artists of the day were carrying-on with, and even occasionally getting around to marrying, their models – or, as in one or two most famous instances, the modelling wives of their best friends! In parallel with John Todhunter, John and Edward Nettleship and with Halsey Ricardo, this young woman *visibly* held a level of importance in Wilson's life that was paramount. As we have said, she appears everywhere in what remains of Wilson's work; it is just such a very great pity that, because he felt neither the desire nor the need to diarise his work or his progress, we presently have absolutely no idea who she was!

*   *   *

It has already been stated that the principle reasons for researching and compiling this book were firstly to record the life of George Wilson and how this related to the Victorian art scene and those around him, in particular to his two closest artist friends, J.T. Nettleship and J.B. Yeats; and secondly it was important, at the same time, to try to locate and to catalogue as many of George Wilson's pictures as possible as an enduring illustrated record.

Inevitably, this process became extended through research into a much broader additional insight into John Nettleship's life and work as well and, whilst the prime objectives always remained, it has been pleasing to be able to raise at least to a small extent the profile of Nettleship as well, and even to add, albeit only nominally, to the already considerable amount that has been written about J.B. Yeats.

An additional outcome that must be hoped for from this exercise is to raise the public's awareness of George Wilson as one of our most perceptive and natural, but at the same time, now 'neglected' Victorian artists. This may even enable one or two fortunate owners to put a name at last to some previously anonymous paintings. To aid this process if possible, there are appendices included with cross-referenced listings of the original owners of the various paintings that were exhibited at the two immediately post-contemporary retrospective exhibitions, first in Aberdeen in 1893, and subsequently in London in 1903. Also referenced is the second small exhibition in Aberdeen in 1990, plus those very few pictures that Wilson ever bothered to exhibit in contemporary public exhibitions. Other pictures that were known about elsewhere during Wilson's lifetime and shortly thereafter are similarly included with as much information that it has been possible to find.

The section immediately below, displaying the paintings and drawings by George Wilson of which we have pictorial evidence, represents the major portion of those pictures whose whereabouts are established, or which have more recently been traced. But also included, for their value in revealing the widest account of Wilson's work, are some of his paintings and drawings the present whereabouts of which are regrettably no longer known. In these cases, we are lucky to be able to rely on good quality contemporary photographs, as well as the privately published set of George Washington Wilson phototypes (Photogravures), to record them for posterity.

Where a title has at some time changed, the original or earliest title recorded or known has been shown in the first instance, with the later name(s) shown in brackets. In some instances, where a title is not known, some 'educated' suggestions have been offered as to possible, and even occasionally probable, identification or title. These are recorded as being subjective wherever they arise and should not be taken as anything more than that.

CHAPTER THIRTEEN

Illustrated catalogue of the works of George Wilson

The most appropriate ordering for this catalogue has proved somewhat of a challenge. The chronological dating of the majority of the George Wilson's works is largely no more than a best logical estimate, except for when contemporary exhibition is recorded. Nonetheless, estimated chronological order has broadly been used here, with some flexibility for medium and subject matter, and this produces an actual progression through some initial drawings that lie mainly in museum collections, into the very few larger figurative oil paintings that either still exist or of which (as in one 'lost' instance) we have a photographic image.

Since there is no clear evidence of any figurative oil paintings having been completed much later than around the middle of the 1880s, this in fact allows us to migrate easily into the area that Wilson evidently enjoyed most – that of his (mainly) landscape watercolour drawings. These have been divided into groups for a variety of reasons that should, hopefully, be apparent as the catalogue progresses – some by location; others by subject matter, etc. – however, this does mean that even estimated chronological order has had to be abandoned on occasions.

Although it is of minor importance within Wilson's oeuvre, it seems appropriate to commence with the only known (or at least confidently assumed) self-portrait sketch of Wilson himself. There are just two of George Wilson's sketchbooks presently known to be in existence – generally referred to for convenience simply as the 'large' and the 'small'. They both appear to commence from a fairly early date, and to have been used (probably concurrently) over quite a long period. At least one other third portfolio of sketches (recorded within the papers accompanying the Helen Barlow Bequest to the National Gallery of Scotland in 1976) cannot now be traced, and undoubtedly there would at some time have been many more as well.

1   **Self Portrait drawing
(from a sketchbook –
without title)**

Date not known;
probably ca. 1868-70
Pencil on feint ruled paper
8⅛ in x 6½ in (irregular)
(207 mm x 166 mm)

Private Collection

*Provenance: George Wilson;
Wilson family descent to
current private collection*

Few of the sketches within the two remaining books display more than early preliminary ideas – but one or two are recognisable through the existence (or photographic evidence) of the eventual finished paintings. This small sketch is one of two or three that are certainly self-modelled sketches. The reproduction here appears to be a deliberate self-portrait sketch (possibly somewhat surprisingly, in view of George Wilson's reserved nature), whereas others are more evidently draft poses for future design ideas. The sketch probably dates from George Wilson's earliest years in London whilst attending Heatherley's. It shows no overt influence of Poynter's tuition, which became so positive after Wilson's Slade days. It does, however, show an endearing face that well fits the various written images of Wilson's persona.

The similarity of the sketch to the formal photograph shown here is distorted to a certain extent by the presence of the rather smart hat. The photo is from a family group that is inscribed but not dated. It is estimated to have been taken in around 1875 – i.e. around five to seven years after the sketch was made. Both these images may be compared to the previously reproduced photograph, probably taken some 14 years later in 1889 when, even allowing for the gauntness caused by the ravages of his illness that had deteriorated over the intervening years, his characteristics still remain evident.

Following the 1903 exhibition held at the John Baillie Gallery in West London, four interesting drawings and studies were donated personally by John Baillie, two each to The Victoria and Albert Museum and The British Museum respectively. It is unclear whether these drawings formed any part of the main exhibition, since they don't appear to have been clearly listed in the catalogue, but the bequests were apparently made in the personal name of John Baillie.

It is not known when any of these drawings were made, but they are all on quite large dimension sheets of paper. It might be argued that the two well-resolved studies (nos. 2 and 3 below) were very much the product of Poynter's direct tuition at the Slade, but they could quite equally be from one or two years later than that – although they would still evidently seem to be studio works. The other two studies (nos. 4 and 5) are working drawings for presently unidentified works. Figure 5 is also represented several times within the surviving sketchbooks, generally in rather more primitive form, although in one instance filled out in watercolour.

The fact that the four drawings were presented separately to the British Museum and the V&A – albeit at almost exactly the same time – may indicate an attempt to register Wilson's art with important libraries or collections. This would very much concur with John Todhunter's own desire to elevate Wilson's reputation in the eyes of the world as a 'Neglected Artist'. Clearly Baillie shared this view, and evidently he must personally have owned some of Wilson's works. Although the London exhibition did not take place until 10 years after that held in Aberdeen, it might possibly have been through Baillie's good offices that Todhunter was trying to arrange the sale of some of Wilson's work during his last terminal months of illness in Scotland.

2   Study of a female nude figure, back view

Date unknown; may be ca. 1872-75
Black chalk on paper
21 in x 10½ in (533 mm x 267 mm)
May have been exhibited with the John Baillie exhibition of 1903

© Victoria & Albert Museum, London

Provenance: Donated to the Victoria and Albert Museum, 18th November 1903, by John Baillie following the 1903 exhibition at Baillie's Gallery

This fine drawing demonstrates a quality that has all the hallmarks of being instructed by Poynter, and is very probably a life class drawing from the Slade, although it could possibly be later. It is impossible to tell who the model is, but from the build and stature, this could alternatively be a rear view of his same particular favourite model who appeared in so many of his figurative works – in which case it would probably be a year or two later.

The composition is very finely drawn with great attention to the detail of the underlying muscle structure of the lower and middle back and the shoulders in particular. Although Wilson seldom painted his nudes from behind, the single slightly bent knee with raised calf and heel was a favourite stance that he adopted successfully, if not always with such fine draughtsmanship, within some of his allegorical oil paintings.

3   Study of a nude man

Date not known;
probably ca. 1872-73
Red chalk, over charcoal,
on paper
21¾ in x 14¾ in
(554 mm x 375 mm)
May have been exhibited
with the John Baillie
exhibition of 1903

© The British Museum

*Provenance: Donated
to the British Museum,
10th November 1903, by
John Baillie following
the 1903 exhibition at
Baillie's Gallery*

145

This drawing shows a young male nude in full length, facing down to the front, with his arms held behind his back, and his legs slightly apart in a casual stance, with one raised as if on a small step. This appears to be another studio work, possibly left unfinished – although Wilson may merely have been paying greatest attention deliberately to just the main features of the torso and head, with one arm and both legs fading, unresolved, towards their extremities. This drawing is again, in all probability, a Slade period work.

4   Two studies of a nude woman

Date not known; possibly ca. 1880- 83
Black, red and white chalk, on brown paper
13¼ in x 21¼ in (336 mm x 539 mm)
May have been exhibited with the John Baillie exhibition of 1903

© The British Museum

Provenance: Donated to the British Museum, 10th November 1903, by John Baillie following the 1903 exhibition at Baillie's Gallery

The multiplicity of often quite minor alternative variations to a pose, frequently superimposed one upon another, is typical of Wilson's sketching technique – and his determination to arrive at exactly the desired result. The model in these sketches is Wilson's favourite girl once again. It would appear that these might be very early sketches for *Asia* – in which the same model appeared. The high stretched-out arms possibly demonstrate this, but in the final picture, *Asia* appears full face on. The facial expression, that is so essential to the painting, is not dissimilar.

5   Study of a female figure carrying a bowl; with additional studies of hands etc

Date unknown
Red chalk on paper
(with splashes of
watercolour paint on
the paper)
20¼ in x 15¼ in
(514 mm x 388 mm)
May have been
exhibited with the John
Baillie exhibition of
1903

© Victoria & Albert
Museum, London

*Provenance: Donated
to the Victoria & Albert
Museum, 18th November,
1903, by John Baillie
following the 1903
exhibition at Baillie's
Gallery*

It is not known what this figure represents – except that she possibly appears to be casting seed or flowers. There are numerous similar preliminary sketches within Wilson's sketchbooks, but it is not known whether that composition was ever carried through to fruition, or what the title might have been. There is one tiny design drawing carried through to watercolour as well (reproduced here). This latter may give a clue towards an idea for a painting owning some influence of Botticelli's *Primavera* (Uffizi Gallery, Florence). The second drawing on the same sketchbook page relates to the drawing below.

147

6   Study of a female figure in a cloak and hood

Date unknown
Red chalk
Size unknown
May have been exhibited first at Aberdeen in 1893, then again at the John Baillie exhibition, 1903

Present whereabouts unknown

Provenance: Not known, but possibly Mrs Eliza Thurburn, now presumed lost

This study appeared as the only illustration on the frontispiece of the catalogue published to accompany the John Baillie exhibition of 1903. Unfortunately, there was neither title given nor any reference within the text to identify the drawing to any one of the exhibits. It is therefore, once again, not known for certain exactly what this figure depicts; nor is it known to whom it belonged at the time of the Baillie exhibition. There was, however, a drawing entitled *Figure of a Woman in chalk* among three chalk studies loaned to the Aberdeen exhibition by Mrs Eliza Thurburn (one of George Wilson's elder sisters), although the (same?) three chalk works that she loaned to the Baillie exhibition were each entitled simply *Chalk Study*. There are some sketches of the same design in Wilson's sketchbooks, one in watercolour (see above) in which the figure is carrying flowers.

This chalk drawing appears to be a well-resolved study, and the outlined frame with its arched top indicates perhaps that it was either an element of something larger that was planned – perhaps a triptych – or part of a series of illustrations. Again, there is the strong influence of Poynter's Slade tuition, and even a small and relatively unusual element of Burne-Jones. As a simple study, it shows the exceptional power of Wilson's draughtsmanship from the finely detailed face out to the less important extremities via some typically careful attention to the drapery. It is also typical of Wilson not to have included the whole of the subject in the composition, leaving the focus very specifically on the pose and attitude of the figure itself.

7   Study of a Head

1876-77
Red, brown and
black chalk, over
pencil, on heavy
weight paper
13 in x 11in
(330 mm x
279 mm)
First exhibited:
Royal Academy,
1877 (296)

Private collection

Provenance:
Charles Wilson;
descended through
Wilson family to
current private
collection

It has frequently been stated, erroneously in fact, that George Wilson only exhibited once at the Royal Academy – with *Alastor* in 1878. That is not so. The previous year, in 1877, he exhibited for the first time with his chalk drawing entitled *Study of a Head.*

This drawing is a strangely enigmatic, principally red and brown chalk study. The influence of Poynter's tuition is clear. Part of the enigma lies, curiously, in the gender of the sitter, which by no means would be entirely certain without the description by Robert Catterson Smith in a letter to John Todhunter that Wilson's submission to the RA that year was a study of a man's head. [202] Additionally, the expression on the face is about as enigmatic as that of the *Mona Lisa*!

There are no highlights at all in the eyes, giving the subject an even greater degree of ambiguity as to the sitter's mood, although the mottling of the irises is drawn with fine detail. Added to this, the tiniest vague, yet almost grimly determined, smile on the face (which runs through from the eyes to the mouth) creates an expression that is quite confusing – indeed, almost worrying, whilst at the same time giving an opposing impression of an extremely sensitive and kindly person who has perhaps been badly treated by life. It is a most interesting piece of drawing.

The picture has suffered some minor foxing to the paper, which at some time had been overlaid by pastel. This has subsequently been removed and the drawing is now restored to its near original state. It is still framed in its original dark brown stained oak frame with gilt inner frame and plain white mount.

8   **The Quest from Shelley's "Alastor"**

1876-1878
Oil on canvas
Size unknown
First exhibited: Royal Academy, 1878 (518)

Whereabouts not known, believed lost.

Provenance: purchased by Dr John Todhunter direct from the artist, for an unrecorded sum. The painting remained within his collection until this was apparently lost (possibly to fire) after his death

This is the second painting that Wilson exhibited at the Royal Academy (in 1878), and was probably his first major allegorical work. The title given above is the full title of the painting under which it was originally exhibited at the RA. In later exhibition, this was commonly abbreviated simply to *Alastor*. Regrettably though, it is now believed lost along with the remainder of the Todhunter collection; so it is at least fortunate that we have available the good black and white photograph, previously published in the Wilson Family History, [203] and now reproduced here. It is not recorded who originally took the photograph, but it is most likely that it was the same image that was taken by George Washington Wilson & Co for their published set of phototypes, where it was listed as No. 2.

The design is based upon Shelley's didactic narrative poem '*Alastor; or, The Spirit of Solitude*', which was first published in 1816, and which (as Mary Shelley later commented) was largely believed to be the outpourings of her husband's own emotions in expectation of his recently predicted death from consumption. Shelley employed his most brilliant imagination to paint the delicate tones that embodied both the highs and the lows of the passion and struggle of the emotions of the poet who is at centre of the poem, despite the transcending solitude that results in his inevitable death. George Wilson's depiction of the poet's coming to terms with the scene predestined for these last moments is a monumental success.

> *Dark, gleaming, and of most translucent wave,*
> *Images all the woven boughs above,*
>
> *...*
>
> *Between one foliaged lattice twinkling fair,*
> *Or painted bird, sleeping beneath the moon,*
> *Or gorgeous insect floating motionless,*
> *Unconscious of the day, ere yet his wings*
> *Have spread their glories to the gaze of noon.*
>
> *Hither the poet came. His eyes beheld*
> *Their own wan light through the reflected lines*
> *Of his thin hair, distinct in the dark depth*
> *Of that still fountain; as the human heart,*
> *Gazing in dreams over the gloomy grave,*
> *Sees its own treacherous likeness there. He heard*
> *The motion of the leaves—the grass that sprung*
> *Startled and glanced and trembled even to feel*
> *An unaccustomed presence—and the sound*
> *Of the sweet brook that from the secret springs*
> *Of that dark fountain rose. A spirit seemed*
> *To stand beside him—clothed in no bright robes*
> *Of shadowy silver and no enshrining light,...*
>
> *When on the threshold of the green recess*
> *The wanderer's footsteps fell, he knew that death*
> *Was on him. ....*

Sometimes referred to as George Wilson's chef d'oeuvre, *Alastor* is in fact just one of several allegorical oil paintings that stand out. Not only is Wilson's depiction of the emotions of the poet in this time of crisis most succinctly portrayed, but he also manages the clever parallel allegory recognised in the biographical nature of Shelley's poem.

Percy Bysshe Shelley (1792-1822). Stipple engraving by W. Finden, after the portrait by Amelia Curran, with facsimile signature beneath.

There is only one well-known portrait of Shelley, now in the collection of the National Portrait Gallery in London, painted in 1819 by the comparatively little-known artist, Amelia Curran (1775–1847), while still a student.* Wilson has employed a subtle similitude to this portrait that is, at the same time, unmistakable. To this end, the painting may be seen as Wilson's own dedication to the poet who, perhaps beyond all others, impressed and affected his life and work.

John Todhunter bought *Alastor* at or before the Royal Academy exhibition, for an unknown price. He always considered it to be one of his finest purchases. Unfortunately, the painting is now believed to be lost, along with virtually the entire Todhunter collection. There are reports that these paintings were lost in a fire in an Army and Navy Stores repository where they were being stored; however, the Army and Navy have no record of such a fire.

Todhunter is eloquent in his description of the painting in *The English Illustrated Magazine* of August 1891, and it is an eternal pity that we do not have a coloured image to respond to. However, we do know how Wilson treated the sort of undergrowth and background detail that is evident in the painting, so it is not difficult to imagine what a vibrant painting this must have been. By way of further description, Todhunter wrote:

> The "Alastor", exhibited many years ago at the Academy, represents the Poet
> of Shelley's poem as he comes to the lonely spot in the woods where he is to die at
> moonrise. He puts aside the branches of thicket, through which he has to force his way,
> with his right hand, peering through them with wistful, melancholy eyes, while with his
> left he presses his scanty drapery to his breast, as though his heart itself were a wound.
> The last faint afterglow of sunset is seen through the trees above his head, and a single

---

* In fact, it seems unlikely that Wilson would have seen the actual painting by Amelia Curran, since Shelley's widow Mary begged her to let her have it following his death just three years later in 1822. It then stayed within the family's descent until the end of the century. Both Wilson and Todhunter are rather more likely to have seen the engraving of the portrait by W. Finden that is reproduced here. This was first reproduced as an engraving in Volume 2 of *Finden's Landscape & Portrait Illustrations to the Life and Works of Lord Byron*, John Murray, London, 1832.

white moth [the 'gorgeous insect'], *disturbed by his coming, flutters away by his left shoulder. A few withered leaves, whose brown tints are of great value in the scheme of colour, mark the time as late autumn. The likeness of the poet's face to the well-known portrait of Shelley will be evident to everyone. In this exquisite picture Wilson has embodied the very spirit of Shelley's poem—the spirit of solitude. It is genius making its way alone through the wilderness of the world. This is one of the most perfectly finished of his pictures. The figure is a masterpiece of expression; and the lovely branch-drawing is at once true to nature and subtly composed. As a piece of rich and delicate colour it is beyond praise; and the whole has a haunting intensity, yet is full of the decorative quality which runs like music through all this painter's work.*

To some extent, *Alastor* may be seen as a transitional painting between the detailed woodland scenes that Wilson so loved to paint, principally in watercolour, and the small series of increasingly symbolist oil paintings that followed *Alastor* over several years.

During the researches for this book, a strange curiosity appeared within the very helpful information that was provided by the Head of the Department of Special Collections at the State University of New York at Stony Brook, where the microfilmed W.B. Yeats Manuscripts lie. One of the boxes of materials containing *Still Pictures and Portraits* relating to *Friends and Associates of W.B. Yeats* included an item entitled *Alastor*. This item turned out to be an envelope containing a single aged photograph (reproduced here), in poor condition, of a man again broadly emulating the pose of George Wilson's picture of the same name, but in an overtly ominous and sinister way. The faded text at the bottom of the photo is difficult to decipher, but appears to state: *"ALASTOR" — MYSTIC, Portrait ? ? Margravine Gardens, Barons Court, UK.* The front of the envelope bears the handwritten words *Prophetic Man Alastor*, whilst on the rear flap of the envelope was stamped the address *Coole Park, Gort., Co. Galway.*

Coole Park was, of course, the property belonging to Lady Augusta Gregory, the Irish playwright and promoter of the Gaelic movement, who was so much the collaborator and mentor of W.B. Yeats. There has been made (but not clearly explained) a conjectural connection between the white swans on the lake at Coole Park and Shelley's poem *Alastor*, but it is impossible to hazard a guess as to quite who the 'Alastor' character in the photograph is. It may well emanate from W.B. Yeats's mystic and occult interests – but, apart from the name and apparent visual similarity, what possible relevance this has to George Wilson's *Alastor* (or indeed to Shelley's poem), presently remains a total mystery!

9   Study for "Alastor"

Probably ca. 1875-77
Pencil and some watercolour on paper
13¾ in x 9¾ in (348 mm x 249 mm)
First exhibited: Aberdeen Art Gallery (Aberdeen Artists' Society), 1893 (573)

© Aberdeen Art Gallery and Museums Collections

Provenance: Charles Wilson; bequeathed either direct or via his estate to Aberdeen Art Gallery

As with so many of the presently identified paintings, this study for *Alastor* lay in the possession of one of George Wilson's close relatives. In this case, it was his older brother, Charles Wilson, Procurator Fiscal for Aberdeenshire and an ardent collector of his brother's paintings, who possessed a significant collection at the time of the artist's death.

This well-worked preliminary sketch for the eventual painting is, if anything, even more reminiscent of Amelia Curran's portrait of Shelley – in that it displays the similarly faint and deceptive near smile of that painting, rather than the very much more emphatic look of resigned foreboding that dominates the finished work of *Alastor*. Between the sketch and the final oil painting, Wilson evidently paid great attention to perfecting the apprehension and solitude of the poem and its poet.

The sketch shows an alertness of head, and hands that are alive to the branches through which he is peering. The poet looks somehow safe where he is, within a cage of undergrowth – if only he could remain there. In the eventual picture, the poet's head is inclined and displays resignation towards the fate that he perceives. His right hand makes no attempt to get to grips with the unprotecting branches; rather it almost seeks to gain support from them, while the left hand grasps desperately onto the remnants of his clothing.

The sketch for the painting appears to be in its original simple wooden frame. It is recorded as having been gifted to Aberdeen Art Gallery, along with other works, by friends of the artist – but with no date recorded. In view of the family distribution of the unmarried Charles Wilson's effects following his death, this gift would most likely have been carried out at around that same time (in 1927). His many of other paintings were similarly distributed among his several nephews and nieces at that time.

This work appeared (No. 3.) in the small exhibition entitled 'Poetic Vision' staged at the Aberdeen Art Gallery in 1990 to commemorate the centenary of Wilson's death in April 1890.

It has been convenient to display consecutively above both of the only two works that Wilson ever exhibited at the Royal Academy, along with the well-resolved study for the second of these for comparison.

Alastor certainly represented George Wilson's first successful, and somewhat larger, allegorical oil painting, and we presently know of just four other such paintings that progressed from this area of his work. It is impossible to be sure of their actual dates of completion – indeed, it is not even certain that the following order of events is entirely correct. However, in the absence of any firmer evidence, it is a based upon best intuition from the surrounding evidence available. The reader should take it as no more than a guide.

From the various labels or references that still exist on the reverse of some of these paintings and on their original frames, they all appear to have emanated from Wilson's studio address of 65 Newman Street, off Oxford Street, London W. (now W.1.) This would place them broadly between the dates of 1880 to 1885 – these being the last and first dates outside which there is evidence of previous and later studio addresses. The period would, therefore, quite probably be at least slightly narrower than the five years identified, but we only have firm evidence for the years 1883 to 1884 at the Newman Street address. However, since *Alastor* was completed (from Wilson's previous Stanhope Street address) before the 1878 Academy exhibition, it would be logical to assume that one or two of these paintings are likely to have been commenced, at least, from the late 1870s to early 1880s.

10   The Song of the Nightingale

Probably ca. 1880-84
Oil on canvas
24 in x 36¼ in   (610 mm x 920 mm)
First exhibited: Walker Art Gallery, Liverpool, 1884   (259)

Private Collection

Provenance: Charles Wilson; descended through the Wilson family to current private collection

In Wilson's eyes, and apart from Blake of course, the three great romantic poets were Shelley, Keats and more latterly, Browning. The lives of the two earlier poets – Shelley's in particular, but also Keats's – closely pre-empted Wilson's own lifelong fight against chronic illness, resulting in his early death. Shelley wrote *Alastor* in the late summer days of 1815, which were warm and dry. He worked on the poem under the shade of the massive oak trees in Windsor Great Park whilst enjoying some months of comparatively good health, in stark contrast to the subject of his poem.

Interestingly, but in complete contrast to *Alastor*, Shelley wrote his poem *To a Sky-lark* in a tone of uplifting joyfulness. Symbolically, he uses the soaring flight of the bird, with its continuous accompaniment of frantic, twinkling song to portray through multi-sensory images the joy that mankind should be able to learn and experience through such a bird. But yet again by contrast, it is Keats's *Ode to a Nightingale* that is far more akin to the subject of *Alastor*, with the poet of the ode in a drowsy, lethargic and sad frame of mind. Keats reverts to using the equally beautiful song of the nightingale to contrast his solitary depression and despair. He appears almost to be wandering in a drugged daze. Somewhat predictably, therefore, it is Keats's *Ode to a Nightingale* rather than Shelley's *To a Sky-lark* that George Wilson chose to depict in another of his allegorical oils paintings.

It may seem ironic that the mood swings in Keats's ode emulate more the soaring flight and fall of a Skylark than the continuous piping joyfulness of the Nightingale. But it is the contrast of his despair with this beauty that Keats symbolises. The first three stanzas of the poem are given over to the poet's despair with the songbird hidden out of reach. It is from the second half of the first stanza and also from the second stanza that Wilson finds the opportunity to set the scene for his painting:

...That thou, light-winged Dryad of the trees,
In some melodious plot
Of beechen green, and shadows numberless,
Singest of summer in full-throated ease.

...

O for a beaker full of the warm South,
Full of the true, the blushful Hippocrene,
With beaded bubbles winking at the brim,
And purple-stained mouth;
That I might drink, and leave the world unseen,
And with thee fade away into the forest dim:

In the fourth stanza, there is suddenly a glimmer of hope and, with the bird's help, for escape from his pain. But this dies quickly within the fifth stanza, which gives Wilson greater detail for his picture:

I cannot see what flowers are at my feet,
Nor what soft incense hangs upon the boughs,

...

White hawthorn, and the pastoral eglantine;
Fast fading violets cover'd up in leaves;
And mid-May's eldest child,
The coming musk-rose, full of dewy wine, ...

The sixth stanza is the turning point in the poem: the poet's despair is wide open, but there are also signs of self-reconciliation and hope through the two final stanzas. Wilson appears to be using Keats' vision of Ruth (in the 7th stanza) *Through the sad heart of Ruth, when, sick for home...* to symbolise all the poet's confusion of feelings, as she listens intently at daybreak for a gleam of hope from the nightingale, which is completely hidden from her, yet boldly silhouetted for the viewer of the painting to see. For such a beautiful songster, the nightingale is a very drab bird, and this fact is lost neither in the poem, nor in the painting.

Wilson didn't attach one specific quotation from the Ode to his painting when first he set out with his depiction. He appears to have endeavoured to encompass all the elements of interpretation of the poem and its symbolism into one simple portrayal of the scene. The model for the picture is, once more, his model with the penetrating blue eyes. Her expression is one of intense foreboding. From within the dense thicket to her side escape strands of the eglantine (sweet briar) of the poem – in itself the very symbol of poetry – and a circlet of this is also entwined around her head. Rather more curious is the classic stone relief that stands by her knee and which appears to depict a male figure carrying a water jar or perhaps an ephah. The symbolism of this figure, and how the common symbolic meaning (egotism or vanity) of the small clutch of narcissi beside the stone should be interpreted, is not immediately obvious. It has been suggested that the relief might depict Ruth in the cornfield – but the figure appears to be male, so perhaps it is Boaz instead!

Wilson's treatment of the early light of sunrise reflected on the sea, and the colour of the sea and the sky themselves, is almost impressionistic. Yet, at the same time, there may be some influence of Corot in the painting as well – even down to the small surprise splash of an unidentifiable red blossom within the undergrowth! The 'cotton-wool' clouds are typical of Wilson both in their simplicity and in their mode of display in their Renaissance inspired background. The painting shows all the signs of the dissatisfaction and overworking for which the artist was recognised. In various areas, the painting-out of minor details is evident: part of the model's hair; an extra stem of the briar; even the outer three fingers of her left hand appear revised and indistinct.

The exact date that Wilson painted *The Song of the Nightingale* is not known, but the indications are towards the earlier years between 1880 and 1884. He submitted the painting for exhibition (simply listed as *The Nightingale*) to the Walker Art Gallery, Liverpool, in 1884 from the address of 65 Newman Street, London, where he first took his studio from late 1879-80 (at the earliest), until early 1885 (at the latest).

The painting still resides in its attractive original gilt frame of two different bands of gesso leaf formations separated by a broad plain board of gilded oak. Although when hung at the Walker *The Nightingale* bore a price tag of £70.0.0, the picture appears not to have sold – unless it was bought then (rather than acquired later) by Wilson's brother Charles, who certainly owned the painting at the time of both retrospective exhibitions in 1893 and 1903. Charles Wilson subsequently loaned *The Song of the Nightingale* twice to the Scottish National Exhibitions of 1908 (Edinburgh) and 1911 (Glasgow) but the frame bears one further torn hand-written exhibition label in Charles Wilson's ownership as *"11 Subject unknown"*. This may simply have been the sequential numbering that he appended when forwarding the painting along with his numerous others to one of the exhibitions.

It is a curiosity that probably relates to this label in that the correct title of the painting doesn't actually appear in the 1893 Aberdeen exhibition list – although it does appear properly described as No. 7 in the George Washington Wilson set of phototypes photographed at that exhibition. There were, however, two paintings in the 1893 list lent by Charles Wilson entitled '*Subject Unknown*', and it appears that the title was not recognised somehow in relation to the catalogue. Nevertheless, from a contemporary account of the exhibition in the *Aberdeen Free Press* in February 1893, it is undoubtedly this painting which was clearly described as hanging below *Asia* and which was exhibited as number 560.

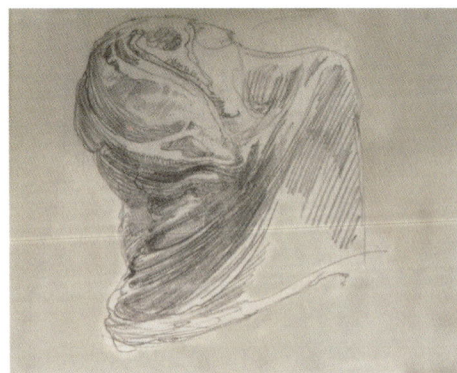

There are numerous sketches in Wilson's sketchbooks, depicting the fall of drapery over limbs in various different poses – something that Wilson continuously aimed at perfecting. Some of these relate to the composition for *The Song of the Nightingale,* as do several other design sketch ideas.

11   Asia

Probably ca. 1881-84
Oil on canvas
37½ in x 29¼ in (950 mm x 745 mm)
First recorded exhibition: Aberdeen Art Gallery (Aberdeen Artists'
Society), 1893 (561)

Private Collection

Provenance: Halsey Ricardo; by family descent to current private collection

Without doubt, one of George Wilson's most successful oil paintings, and although not purchased by John Todhunter, but by the architect Halsey Ricardo instead, Todhunter still considered it to be Wilson's chef d'oeuvre. Again, because Todhunter was, more than anyone, in regular contact with Wilson and would have discussed his paintings in great detail with him, there is little point in projecting any description other than his contemporary narrative on this painting.

Asia depicts a moment from the beginning of Scene I in Act II of Shelley's lyrical drama *Prometheus Unbound*, which Todhunter describes:

> *The moment chosen by Wilson is that when Asia, waiting in solitude in her vale in*
> *the Indian Caucasus for news of the final struggle of Prometheus, sees her sister Panthea*
> *approaching as the dawn breaks:--*

> *"This is the season, this the day, the hour;*
> *At sunrise thou shouldst come, sweet sister mine,*
> *Too long desired, too long delaying, come!*
> *...*
> > *Hear I not*
> *The Æolian music of her sea-green plumes*
> *Winnowing the crimson dawn?"*

> *In this noble picture Asia stands with both arms stretched upwards in an ecstasy of*
> *longing. Her lovely face is upraised, her cheeks slightly flushed with roseate colour, as if*
> *she herself were the very spirit of dawn, the liquid blue eyes gazing into the eastern sky, the*
> *lips tremulous with expectation. The wind of dawn seems to play through the diaphanous*
> *golden-red drapery which half veils her figure, and echoes the rich note of colour in her hair.*
> *Her left breast is bare, and under her bare feet flowers are springing. In the background is*
> *a great wall of rugged mountain-peaks, their bases still steeped in dusky twilight..*[204]

Wilson loved painting in the Dolomites, to the north of Asolo where he made his base camp, undoubtedly because of the direct relationship of the natural mountainscapes to the backgrounds in so much of the Renaissance art that influenced him so. Quite how he discovered Asolo in the first place is not known, but the town's association with Browning could well have been

instrumental. He took his current canvasses with him on his trips to Italy, and so it is most probable that the background to Asia was painted 'on location' in this way.

Again, Wilson has some minor trouble with the painting of the hands and feet of his subject, but to a far lesser degree than in *The Song of the Nightingale*. However, there is no problem at all with the rest of the figure drawing and, as Todhunter points out; the painting of the diaphanous drapery that scarcely covers her body is very cleverly executed. Similarly, the background and foreground of the surrounding landscape is painted true to Wilson's dedicated following of the Renaissance form, and even more particularly to depict the scene described by 'The Echoes' in the poem as:-

> *Through the many-folded mountains;*
> *To the rents, and gulfs, and chasms,*

Wilson introduces much symbolism into the painting – in particular, one of his favourite devices, that of the flowering Almond as the first flower of spring to denote here the welcoming of the return of Asia's sister Panthea. This reference is in direct response to the later lines in the same scene, when Panthea says:-

> *It passes now into my mind. Methought*
> *As we sate here, the flower- infolding buds*
> *Burst on yon lightning-blasted almond tree; ...*

The presence of the somewhat overt pair of white rabbits is rather more curious. The usual symbolism attached to rabbits is that of fertility or lust, or is associated with lunar figures such as Moon goddesses, so this would appear unlikely here. The positioning of the rabbits, facing each other some distance apart, more probably displays a simple but clever device employed by Wilson to mirror the meeting of the two sisters, where, in the picture itself, Panthea's place is taken by the artist and thus she cannot be seen. Alternatively, and since there is sometimes a temptation to try to read more into paintings than maybe the artist originally intended, allowing for Wilson's innate sense of humour, he may merely have inserted them just for fun. The model is once again his same anonymous favourite.

The painting still retains its striking original Morris inspired frame, heavily moulded with stylised gilt acanthus leaves raised above a black ground and gilt outer surround. This is a relatively splendid frame and probably indicates that it was rather more likely to have been commissioned directly by Ricardo rather than the artist. The painting was reproduced as No.9 in the set of George Washington Wilson phototypes commissioned from the 1903 Aberdeen exhibition.

12 Study for Shelley's "Asia"

Probably ca. 1880-83
Chalk
Size unknown
First recorded
exhibition:
John Baillie Gallery,
1903 (94)

Whereabouts
unknown

*Provenance: Purchased
by Dr John Todhunter
direct from the artist.
Present whereabouts not
known; presumed lost*

This preliminary sketch for Asia has unfortunately been lost with the rest of Todhunter's collection. It shows a rather different treatment for the background, which was not carried through to the final painting, in that '...the darker lake Reflects it [the sunrise – as referred to in Asia's speech]; ...' – a seemingly rather charming and effective backdrop to the figure – has been replaced by the mountainous chasms in the final version.

Similarly, Asia's face lacks the sense of expectation and gladness that is so strong a feature of the finished painting. The model also appears to be different The image shown here is reproduced from the only recorded copy of the sketch, as attached to Leonore van der Veer's article about George Wilson in Volume 30 of The Studio, 1903-04.[205] *Asia* was evidently some while at the composition stage, as there are innumerable working sketches in a variety of poses and stages of resolution within the extant sketchbooks.

13   The Rape of Proserpine (Persephone)

Probably ca. 1881-84
Oil on canvas
30 in x 27 in (760 mm x 685 mm)
First recorded exhibition: Aberdeen Art Gallery (Aberdeen   Artists' Society), 1893 (566)

Private Collection

Provenance: Ralph Radcliffe Whitehead to Halsey Ricardo; by family descent to current private collection

The Rape of Proserpine, or *Persephone* as she has simply been referred to rather more delicately in recent times, is the second large allegorical oil painting purchased by Ralph Radcliffe Whitehead – almost certainly direct from the artist. But while *The Spring Witch* (q.v.) travelled with Whitehead when he emigrated to America, he appears to have sold *Persephone* to Halsey Ricardo at around that time of his departure. The painting still retains its original frame, which bears verso a portion of a label that advises that the painting – as with all the Newman Street studio oils – must have been exhibited together in some formal, or informal, setting, although it is not known where. This painting bears the number and script: *3 / The Rape of Proserpine / painted by the la[te] George Wilson / lent by R. Radcliffe Whitehead Esq.* The bottom line referring to the lender has subsequently been crossed out heavily in pencil – presumably when it changed hands.

This label may well have been the owner's reference to his listing of the paintings being sent to either the 1893 or 1903 exhibitions – except that this doesn't accord with the ownership of the other similarly labelled paintings, so the reason presently remains obscure. The design of the wholly gilt frame in this case is a rather simpler flat affair, surrounded on either side by an outer and (narrower) inner ribbed moulding, broken at regular intervals by a variety of small incised geometric circular devices. The painting has remained behind glass since its original framing, and retains much of the vibrant colours of its inception.

As usual with Wilson's allegorical paintings the figure is largely *déshabillé*, and the upper torso displays some of Wilson's accustomed difficulties associated with oil-painting draughtsmanship. But again, as with *Asia*, we find the clever execution of the remaining diaphanous veil about her lower limbs. The carpet of flowers – each of which is minutely detailed – is again typical of these works. This time it is the narcissus-like flowers that were reported to have attracted Persephone away from her companions in the fields of Enna in Sicily that predominate. The employment of the menacing hand of Hades emanating from a fiery fissure in the land is an effective device to depict the opening up of the earth and to symbolise the 'rape' or abduction of Proserpine. This counterbalances the story being related, without detracting from Wilson's prime subject in the figure itself. This is more an expressive portrait of Proserpine in a predicament from which she cannot escape, rather than an attempt to tell the full story of the 'First Act' in one picture. Again, the background to this picture was probably painted in the Dolomites, following Wilson's adherence to Renaissance scenery, and we find the same model posing once again, as in all his other significant works (although in this painting she has slightly more of a 'Burne-Jones' air about her).

This is certainly the painting referred to so emotionally by John Nettleship, when he wrote in June 1891 to Halsey Ricardo asking him to look after Whitehead's pictures in his own absence. *The Persephone came loose in her box, but quite uninjured; so I put no screws in her back and took the risk of her reaching you in good condition, as she had travelled safely so, all the way from Styria* (Austria). As we know, Ricardo took in the three paintings – so it may be that he never returned them all but instead purchased one or two of them from Whitehead. But nevertheless, *Persephone (Proserpine)* was still listed as being in Whitehead's ownership at the time of the 1903 exhibition at the Baillie Gallery, although he no longer lived in the UK himself. One must assume therefore that the picture was merely still only being guarded by Ricardo at that time, whilst *The Spring Witch*, that appeared in neither of the retrospective exhibitions, had been uplifted by Whitehead and removed to the USA when he emigrated in 1901.

When Whitehead first purchased both *The Rape of Proserpine* and *The Spring Witch*, he was, in effect, purchasing depictions of the two critical events at either end of the story of Proserpine's abduction to the Underworld and her annual return to the Earth in springtime. Indeed, it may well have been that he did, in fact, commission either or both of the paintings for this purpose.

14   The Spring Witch

Probably ca. 1882-85
Oil on canvas
42 in x 31½ in (1067 mm x 800 mm)
First recorded exhibition: 2005 'Waking Dreams: The Art of the
Pre-Raphaelites from the Delaware Art Museum' (91); a touring
exhibition to locations in the USA and the UK (Nottingham Castle)

Delaware Art Museum, Wilmington, USA

Provenance: Ralph Radcliffe Whitehead; through family descent, from thence presented as a partial gift to the Delaware Art Museum, 1992

Of the just five larger allegorical oil paintings that have been identified (but of which only four are still known to exist) it was *Alastor* and *Asia* that were each heralded independently as George Wilson's *chef d'oeuvre*, at the different times of their exhibition. *Alastor* is now feared lost, but since the 'rediscovery' (at least in the author's knowledge) of the existence of *The Spring Witch*, it is this painting that would certainly seem to represent – or at least share – the pinnacle of Wilson's achievement in this area of his work.

The previous general non-awareness of the existence of *The Spring Witch* was largely due, so it seems, to the painting never having been publicly exhibited before its current location in the Delaware Art Museum. It is ironic therefore that this is (again, as far as we know) the only painting of its style by George Wilson that is now hanging in a public gallery.

It is probable that it was purchased directly from the artist, either as a commission or upon sight. This would indicate that the painting was purchased new by its first and only recorded owner and family descent (prior to the Delaware Art Museum) – the philanthropist Ralph Radcliffe Whitehead – who also purchased *The Rape of Proserpine*, probably also directly from the artist.

Certainly, it would seem that *The Spring Witch* was in Whitehead's hands in January 1890, when Wilson mentioned in a letter to John Todhunter that it was residing in Asolo. This location is, however, inconclusive, and may have been a simple mistake by the then very sick Wilson, since Whitehead was by that time actually living in Florence – where in fact Wilson had visited him on the way to or from Asolo in the previous summer of 1889. The fact that Whitehead also owned *The Rape of Proserpine* at an early date intimates that perhaps the two pictures might have been commissioned as a pair – i.e. the dual subjects of the abduction (the classical meaning of 'rape') and spring return of Persephone (or Proserpine in the Latin) from Hades in the Underworld. However, it is believed that *The Rape of Proserpine* was probably painted a year or two prior to *Spring Witch*. If this latter assumption is correct, then it is perhaps surprising that the pair were split up when Whitehead left *The Rape of Proserpine* in Ricardo's care at the time that he emigrated to America – but maybe this was a logistical decision at the time.

So far as we can establish, *The Spring Witch* was the only painting that Whitehead took with him to America in 1901, following his second marriage to Jane Byrd McCall. The painting remained with Whitehead's descendents until it was part-gifted by them to the Bancroft Collection of the Delaware Art Museum in Wilmington in 1992.

The mythical story of the abduction of Persephone by Hades, the God of the Underworld, and her mother Demeter's subsequent fight to get her back, was a favourite subject of artists through the ages. Apart from Rossetti's well-known picture of *Proserpine* (1873-77; Tate Gallery and others), holding the bitten pomegranate within the halls of the Underworld, probably one of the better recognised images of the subject returning from the Underworld is Frederic Lord Leighton's *Return of Persephone* (painted in 1890-91; Leeds City Gallery). In that painting, the subject is depicted as a rather fragile romantic form, in typical flowing neo-classical attire, ostensibly floating down towards her mother's outstretched arms. It might seem a somewhat curious extension of 'artistic license' that Persephone appears to be descending from on high like an angel, rather than emerging from six months underground! Leighton's painting displays the far removal of symbolism and allegory into decorative commercial art. In stark contrast, George Wilson's painting shows his elemental adherence to traditional Pre-Raphaelite principles – very much still at a second phase level rather than the much more diluted and stylised third phase. Although no doubt in unintentional reflection of this, *The Spring Witch* was indeed painted centrally between the dates of the two other paintings of the subject referred to above.

Wilson's *Persephone* is much more down to earth. She is shown emerging back into the world for the first time following the negotiation of her 'release'. She appears wide-eyed and evidently dazzled by the brilliance of the light of a bright spring dawn that is emphasised by the fiery sunrise on the horizon. She emerges from a dark, roughly-constructed black hole of an archway within an ancient rock-face, bordered by a sharp mountainous background – all of which owes more than a little to the influence that the Italian Renaissance exerted upon Wilson's work, and perhaps in particular by Mantegna's *Crucifixion* (Louvre, Paris) or Leonardo's *Virgin of the Rocks* (National Gallery, London and Louvre, Paris).

Once again, Wilson has used his favourite model – this time completely nude – and makes much of her piercing blue eyes, as she emerges from the bowels of the Underworld. The symbolism of her nudity depicts the virgin state of nature and innocence, unconcealed reality and pure truth, thus emphasising the force of her abduction against her will. She holds what might instantly appear to be the traditional mythical pomegranate whose pulp and seeds Hades tricked her into eating, and which enforced the deal for her to spend six months of each year in the Underworld. However, the fruit is of slightly uncharacteristic shape so the late Rowland Elzea, Curator of the Collections at Delaware until 1993, suggested that there might be the alternative interpretation of it perhaps being a poppy seedpod instead.[206] In Christian symbolism the poppy denotes sleep – perhaps the sleep from which nature awakens every spring.

The strange mystic vapour or fiery stream emanating from the fruit is quite difficult to understand. Elzea described it as the 'mystic stream of life' – and that is probably as good an interpretation as any. But in that case, the fruit would more realistically have to be confirmed symbolically to be the pomegranate – which, in itself, would also certainly be more traditional. One further suggestion for the encircling stream is that it represents the light from the torch of the magical and dark Goddess Hekate, who guided Persephone back to the Earth.

Whatever the explanation, the semblance of Wilson's Persephone to Botticelli's Venus in *The Birth of Venus* (Uffizi Gallery, Florence) is worth consideration. The poses are somewhat different, but the stance and the degree of trepidation shown by each figure have a common theme. To some extent even, there is a similitude between Persephone's encircling 'stream of life' and the hair of Botticelli's Venus that entwines her so modestly. As Venus approaches land, she knows she will have to lose her divine nakedness as she comes amongst humankind. Similarly, Persephone will immediately have become aware of her own comparable position and new responsibilities at her first sight of the land before her that her mother Demeter has deliberately neglected in her absence.

Where and how the title of *The Spring Witch* for the picture arose is quite unknown. It is not, so far as the author is aware, a title that has previously been adopted for the subject – but the painting was certainly referred to contemporarily as *Spring* by both George Wilson and his colleagues. One possible curious explanation of the *Witch* element of the title could relate to the magical effect that spring, in the personification of Persephone, has upon the land. The connotation being that of a white witch using her power for the good of the Earth.

The world into which Persephone steps so gingerly is not the one she left previously. Her mother, Demeter, the Goddess of earth and harvest, was so distraught at losing her daughter that she gave up looking after the crops to search for Persephone. The story is well known, and when Demeter discovered where her daughter had been abducted to, she pleaded with Zeus to instruct Hades to release her. The condition laid down for this, that she should return so long as she had not eaten any food in the Underworld, was of course broken through Hades' cunning in tricking her to eat the seeds of the pomegranate, and so a compromise was struck whereby she had to stay for six months in the Underworld, but could return to Earth for the other six months. So every year from thereon, Demeter, through anger or sadness, allowed the plants to wither or die during the winter months, only to be brought gladly back to life again in the spring.

And it is with this symbolic reawakening of Nature in spring that Wilson quite simply fills his canvas. The most obvious symbol of hope is the flowering almond tree – widely recognised also as the first flowering tree of the year, the blossom is The Awakener. Then at her feet, we find the first bulbs of spring in the crocuses, and, tucked away also close to her foot is a small toad – symbol of resurrection and rebirth. Nearby, again, we find a cluster of toadstools depicting good fortune and rapid growth. All these symbols of new life and hope are intermingled with the relics of the previous year that have died away. Amongst the dead poppy heads that denote the sleep of winter, there are also a number of dead stems of the yarrow or sheep's parsley type, which carry their seeds so effectively into a new year. There is also the entwined dead growth of the previous year's Morning Glory, which again symbolises the beginning of life. The extent to which Wilson has detailed the foreground is, as usual, meticulous; but rather less usually, the figure draughtsmanship does not display the usual faults and evidence of much reworking so often seen in his previous figurative oil paintings.

In correspondence, Wilson referred to having taken a large canvas to Italy to work on in the early 1880's – and it may well have been *The Spring Witch*, although the painting of the small wood copse in the background bears all the evidence of being painted as much in the beech forests of north Banffshire as north Italy.

He also referred specifically to working on this painting in a letter dated 15th January 1882 to John Todhunter in which he said, *I've also got another* [painting] *started of Winter and Spring. A good old subject that I hope to make something new of it. I've got Spring young and radiant (if I can). rising out of the cerements of the dead winter wondering at herself but seeing her kingdom before her and glad thereof: golly massa Todhunter if I can paint it as well as I sometimes think it, it will be a picture.* [207]

The gilt frame holding the picture is original and similar in its simple Arts and Crafts influenced design to those that Wilson (or his patrons) had made for the majority of his other larger oil paintings. In this case, the flat section between the internal and external mouldings is broken up by regularly placed small incised circular designs, with crossed lines within. These designs are placed equilaterally around the frame, with one in each corner and with one placed centrally at top and bottom, and two on each side. The design of the frame is therefore not at all dissimilar to that surrounding its 'sister' picture, *The Rape of Proserpine*.

The back of the stretcher has an early label affixed denoting *George Wilson/Oxford St. W. / No. 1 The Spring Witch*. Wilson's studio at the time was at 65, Newman St., off Oxford St., London W (now W.1.). A number of Wilson's pictures within their original frames have similar labels attached denoting an apparent exhibition or hanging number. Those seen all fall between 'No 1' and 'No 4', although some numbers are duplicated. It is not assumed that they represent unknown exhibition entries, but nor it is known what these numbers do refer to. The dates assumed for the painting represent the latest that could have been possible from the Newman Street studio, since by 1885 Wilson was exhibiting from No. 1, The Mall, Park Road, Hampstead.

The Spring Witch is not listed as having appeared in either of the retrospective exhibitions of 1893 and 1903. As we know, in 1901, Halsey Ricardo took into care three of Wilson's paintings belonging to Whitehead, including for certain *The Rape of Proserpine*, but also presumably *The Spring Witch*. A third Whitehead-owned title has never been identified, so presently remains anonymous. Thus, it may be that Ricardo eventually (and after the 1903 exhibition) purchased one or two of them from Whitehead, including *The Rape of Proserpine,* whilst *The Spring Witch* was uplifted by Whitehead later in 1901 and exported to America when he emigrated. This would explain its absence from the 1903 exhibition at the Baillie Gallery. It may be that Wilson himself gives the explanation for its absence from the 1893 exhibition, when he wrote to Todhunter in January 1890 with a reference to *Spring* as being located in Asolo – although it would actually be more likely by then to have resided in Florence, which is where Whitehead was living at the time – and indeed, with whom Wilson stayed on his last Italian journey in 1889.

There are a number of small preliminary sketches for the design of *The Spring Witch* within the remaining sketchbooks, including the relatively finally resolved idea reproduction here. As can be seen from this, the sketchbook is no more than a lined school exercise book.

15   'Portrait of a Very Young Lady'

1877
Gouache on board
10 in x 7 in (254 mm x 178 mm)
First recorded exhibition: Not known

Private Collection

Provenance: George Wilson personal collection; via John Wilson, via Wilson family descent to current private collection

The sitter in this charming portrait painted in profile is George Wilson's niece, Rachel Wilson, at the age of two years. Painted in gouache, with much white bodycolour, the technique used is more akin to an oil painting. There are two strong distractions within the composition of this painting; firstly from the cat which stares fixedly at the artist and viewer, and secondly, the bright orange in the child's hand. But both fail to overcome the continual leading of the eye to her rosy face and, more particularly, her gleaming hair – which has been painted with the finest of detail and skilful use of body colour. The sandy tint portrayed was retained by Rachel until late in her life when the inevitable silver-grey took ove.

There are two interesting comparative pencil drawings by John Butler Yeats, illustrated in *Prodigal Father* William M. Murphy's essential biography about George Wilson's early colleague.[208] Both of these sketches represent his younger son, Jack B. Yeats aged three and five years respectively. On each occasion, not only does Yeats depict the similar style of dress adopted for children of both sexes at that age and time, as also evidenced by Wilson in his *Portrait of a Very Young Lady*, but also, more importantly, the enduring influence of Poynter's tuition is unmistakable for both of the recent Slade students.

The painting is still in its original simple gilt ribbed frame, with gilt mount under glass. There are two labels verso. The main title label appears to be an exhibit label. It is in Wilson's hand and notes the number 'No 2'; the title; and contains his signature and address shown as 233, Stanhope Street, Hampstead Road, N.W. The second label is now no more than an irrecoverable very fragile scrap, but appears to indicate (not in Wilson's hand) that the painting had, at

Jack B. Yeats, 1874, pencil, by John Butler Yeats, as published in *Prodigal Father* (Murphy), p.98 (see acknowledgements), from the collection of the late Michael Yeats.

some time, been offered for sale. There is now only one remaining word 'price' that is reasonably discernable, although until recently, the actual price being sought was still visible at £2.2.0 (about £170 today). There is no evidence as to where this painting was exhibited, and somewhat inevitably it ended up in the possession of George Wilson's brother, John, who was the father of the sitter – who inherited the painting herself in due course. Why such a close family subject should have been offered for sale is curious. It may simply be that Wilson did not wish to burden his brother with the cost of yet another painting – and hence the anonymous title rather than a named portrait.

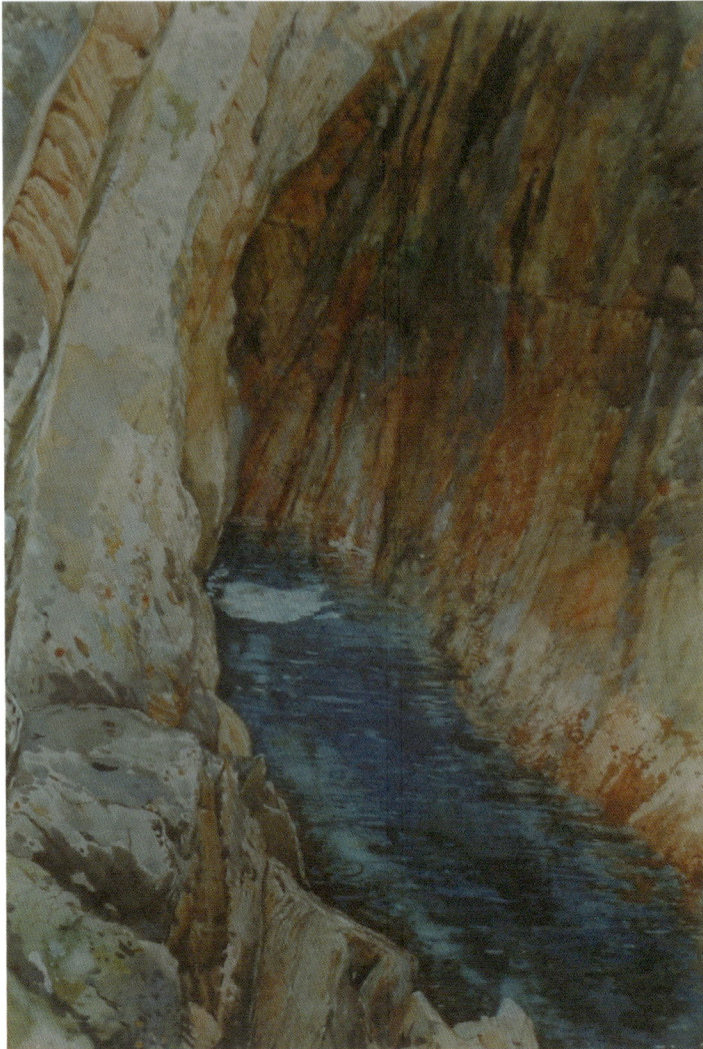

16 The Whale's Mouth

Probably ca. 1875-80
Watercolour with some body colour on heavy weight wove paper
13½ in x 9½ in (343 mm x 242 mm)
First recorded exhibition: Not known

Private Collection

Provenance: Wilson family; via family descent to current private collection

The Whale's Mouth is an interesting study in many ways. At the outset, it could be deemed a pure 'Ruskinesque' study of the typical rock formations that are found along the north coastline of the Moray Firth, around Portknockie and Cullen. Wilson frequently painted in the area over the years, whilst visiting his uncle, Alexander and then subsequently his brother, James, who were successive managing directors of the nearby family whisky distillery of Inchgower.

Two of the main rock formations that are regular modern-day visitor attractions along this beautiful stretch of coastline are the even more curious 'Bow Fiddle Rock' and this, 'The Whale's Mouth'. The Bow Fiddle Rock is the more prominent feature, as it is farther out to sea and so is a more obvious 'sight'. It is also far less accessible. The Whale's Mouth is easily accessible from the land side, but as may be seen from the almost contemporary photograph shown here, the far side juts well out into the sea. However, as with all the rock features in the area, the stratum the rock lies, somewhat incongruously, in the opposite direction to that depicted in Wilson's composition. This means that, unless for some obscure reason he deliberately reversed the formation, he must have painted it from the seaward side, and the small wave surge must be the effect of the water being drawn out again over the rocky floor rather than breaking into the land, as shown in the photograph.

It was previously deemed a mystery as to how this painting could have been made – unless from a boat – until through the local investigations of the Editor of Portknockie's village magazine, aptly named *The K'nocker*, it was discovered from some of the older inhabitants that at one time it had indeed been possible. There had once been a fisherman's pathway to the far end of the cave, which long ago became too dangerous to remain passable and has now virtually disappeared.

The Whale's Mouth, near Portknockie, Banffshire, photographed in 1897 by Rachel Cassels Brown (née Wilson)

The fact that Wilson has ignored within his composition the fascinating shape of the open cave mouth, and has 'cropped' the whole formation of the cave, is indicative of his concentration on the pure depiction of the surface of the rock features themselves – which he has portrayed in the finest detail.

17   An Old Oak (Study of an Oak Tree)

Probably ca. 1878 – 82
Watercolour
Size unknown
First exhibited: Aberdeen Art Gallery (Aberdeen Artists' Society), 1893 (548)

Whereabouts unknown

Provenance: John Todhunter; now believed lost

Although now believed lost, we are fortunate that a full colour print of this finely detailed painting was published with Leonore van der Veer's article about Wilson in Volume 30 of The Studio, 1903-04. [209] It is from that illustration that the copy shown here is reproduced. The quality of reproduction is quite impressive despite the limitations of processing available at the time, over 100 years ago; however, in all probability, some of the vibrancy of the greens and browns, as well as the yellow of the apparent sunset sky, are lacking

It is not known where Wilson painted this picture, but it seems quite likely to have been during one of his visits to the south coast of England, in all likelihood around the West Sussex South Downs town of Arundel, and possibly in the ancient Arundel Castle Park. The magnificent old oak, with its rent side – perhaps from a lightning strike – and uppermost main boughs and reaches slowly dying off, is mirrored by a number of similarly afflicted trees in the background. It is evidently wintertime, so the small splash of evergreen colour presented by the dwarfed bush to right of the oak's trunk gives a feeling of continuity to the scene.

Apparently painted in a parkland setting and, equally, in an evidently ancient one as well, one might imagine Wilson pondering, as he painted, about Shelley writing his narrative poem *Alastor* – which was so important to Wilson – in Windsor Great Park under just such an oak. His treatment of the heavily stressed boughs, dragged down by the weight of their branches and leaves over centuries, is reminiscent once again of certain aspects of Corot. However, the clever definition of the central tree asks more questions than it answers. Is this tree like those that surround it? In a typical composition, Wilson has only allowed us to see the bottom half, so should we assume that the ravages of the elements have treated it in the same way as the other trees that linger behind it? We may assume that it is one amongst many, yet we shall never know – but the majesty of the tree would make any passer-by slow or stop to pay it homage.

18   The Fall of the Leaf   (commonly known as 'The Old Woman Gathering Sticks')

Probably ca. 1878-82
Watercolour on heavy weight wove paper
9¾ in x 13½ in (247 mm x 343 mm)
First recorded exhibition: Aberdeen Art Gallery (Aberdeen Artists' Society), 1893 (570)

Private Collection

Provenance: John Wilson; via Wilson family descent to current private collection

The Old Woman Gathering Sticks – as this powerfully-coloured watercolour has always been affectionately known within the Wilson family – epitomises Wilson's ability in this medium at its very best. Painted in a strong Pre-Raphaelite style with fine detailing of foreground interest, one feels that it should almost be possible to squeeze the water out of the moss on the tree roots!

The composition is believed to have been painted in the beech forests in the north of old Banffshire, to the east of Cullen. The placing of the old woman well to the bottom left of the painting leaves Wilson scope to develop the immense detail of the forest floor; but all the time, the small gulley that runs diagonally across the picture draws the eye back to the woman. This effect of pulling the picture together is further emphasised by the denser woodland to the top right of the picture and the clear fence effectively curtailing further movement in that direction, as well as the evident steep ravine that disappears over the ridge to the rear. This deep dropping away of the effective horizon behind the thinning trees allows the artist to bring the sky down to a low level, with only the hint of more distant hills glimpsed through the trees. This enables Wilson to filter more light into the picture over the important left hand side.

The quite stunningly vibrant colours used are typical of Wilson's confidence in this medium, maximising the contrast between the extensive autumn reds of the fallen leaves and the bright green of the moss covered banks and roots, and even the multitude of colours depicting the lichen covered trunks and the remaining evergreens.

19   The Huntly Lodge Woods in Summer

[Verso: Unresolved watercolour of hills and water meadows with
sheep in the foreground]
Probably 1889
Watercolour on heavy weight wove paper
10 in x 14 in (254 mm x 356 mm)
First recorded exhibition: Aberdeen Art Gallery (Aberdeen Artists'
Society), 1893 (551)

Private Collection

Provenance: John Wilson; via Wilson family descent to current private collection

This watercolour must be one of the last of a number that Wilson painted of his beloved Highland
Scots Pine forests – painted in the minutest detail, and with an exquisite observation of the
myriad of colours that make up the under-canopy of these dense forests. Although the title
refers to 'Huntly Lodge Woods', there are no obvious woods now identifiable to this name, so the
location for this painting is almost certainly the Kinnoir Wood that stretches to the east of Huntly
Lodge – at that time the home of the Duke of Gordon in Huntly, but now a luxury hotel. Kinnoir
Wood covers two small pine-covered hills close to Pirriesmill Farm, one of George Wilson's brother
John's farms at Castle Park in Huntly, where he painted many woodland subjects. The painting

was originally owned by John Wilson. His wife Anna was almost certainly referring to this work when she wrote to her son Alan in 1893, describing the upheaval of sorting all their paintings for the Aberdeen exhibition: ... *Papa and I have had a busy day preparing 16 of Uncle Dodie's pictures for the exhibition ... The woman gathering sticks* [see above] *has been put into a handsome frame ... and we have done the same to the one of the Kinnoir park hanging below Mahomet.* ...

In this painting, Wilson has incorporated the increased extra interest of two figures – one taking advantage of the shade from the evident heat, while the second approaching figure, as she trudges up the slope, draws the viewer continually back to speculate what, perhaps, the recumbent woman might be doing. She certainly appears to be reading, but Wilson sees no need to complicate the composition by showing a book, which is 'understood' to be hidden in the grass.

Although Wilson has once again employed the same tactic of placing the main figure to the bottom left of the scene, this time the emphasis is changed – both by the background hillside sloping away towards the bottom right from behind the older woman, naturally drawing the gaze away from the centre of focus, and by the striking prominence of the second girl. There becomes a split in attention between the two figures, but this is resolved by the positive steps that the younger approaching girl is making towards the other – who appears oblivious of her approach – making the eye rebound between the two in anticipation of their meeting.

The figures are two of Wilson's numerous nieces – the daughters of his brother John. The older woman is probably the 20-year-old Gertrude (Gerty) Wilson,[*] while the younger girl is Rachel once again – this time aged 13 years. Although the composition here is entirely typical of Wilson's own technique, the scarlet colouring of Rachel's dress could not be more focal – perhaps just another example of fun by Wilson in emulation of Corot. Either way, it is a blatant and totally unexpected statement of colour in the midst of an otherwise tranquil scene. As usual, Wilson has made no attempt to capture the vastness of the woods within the composition, and the canopy of the closest trees is way above the composition. This in itself serves to frame the scene. There is also a clever bright area of light filtering through a rare break in the density of the woods, immediately between the two figures, which emphasises the density of the rest.

Verso, there is a partially resolved landscape study with a wooded hill behind, perhaps, a river in the middle distance and with sheep grazing in the foreground scrubland. Certain elements of this composition are clearly stated; all that remains is the detailed work for which Wilson is consistently recognised.

---

[*]   It is of interest that a family photograph exists from this date, in which Gerty Wilson appears to be wearing exactly the same dress and hat. It is also probable that, since George Wilson usually only made one visit each year to stay at his brother's house in Huntly, the painting was made around the time of that photograph (previously reproduced) that depicts the whole family in front of Castle Park house. This would have been during his last summer, when he appears to have remained at Castle Park, as his health deteriorated towards his untimely death in the spring of 1890

**20   Untitled   (inscribed verso 'Gerty and Walter Wilson on the Sands').
May possibly be either 'Sea Beach near Buckie' or 'The
Aberdeen Beach'**

1889
Watercolour, heightened with bodycolour, on heavy wove paper, laid
onto board
10 in x 14 in (253 mm x 355 mm)
First exhibited: Not known (unless under a different title)
Private collection

Provenance: John Wilson; Walter Wilson and by family descent to current collection

It is of valuable significance that family record has ascribed the names of the figures in this
painting to those of a specific nephew and niece of George Wilson's – again two of the children
of his brother John, with whom he stayed at Castle Park in Huntly each year. John had a very
large family and his occasionally rather formidable wife, Anna (who nursed George Wilson so
considerately during his last few months), seemed to be in almost continuous production of the
16 children who were born to them throughout the 21-year period from 1865 to 1886. Of the first

five born, all were girls, although two died at birth. Gertrude (Gerty) was the third eldest surviving daughter and was born in 1869. The much younger child in the painting is her youngest brother, Walter who, as the last of John and Anna Wilson's children, did not arrive until August 1886; so although not dated, the painting could not have been made any earlier than the summer of 1889 – six to nine months before George Wilson died. One again, it also appears that the work remains unfinished.

Gertrude Wilson was married in 1902 to Frederick (Fritz) Carpendale, who eventually became a commander with the P&O line. In contrast to her parents, they had just one daughter of their own but she sadly died when only one year old. Gerty herself died at Aberdeen in 1932. In 1910, Walter Wilson represented the third and last generation of the Wilson family to manage the Inchgower malt whisky distillery, where he remained as Managing Director until the decision was taken in 1929 to sell off the entire business, 'lock, stock and barrel', as a direct result of the Depression. In 1914, Walter had married Helen Stalker, and they had three children – all of whom served in the Second World War, but only one survived – via whom this painting descended.

The date attached to the painting would certainly make it one of the last to have been commenced by George Wilson – possibly towards the end of the summer of 1889, following which he is believed to have remained at his brother's house in Huntly when his health took a serious turn for the worse. The painting certainly appears, as is rather often the case, to be not very finished, and although the girl's head is painted with quite simple, but delicate skill at such a small scale, there remain a number of early pencil strokes showing quite visibly through the transparency of the paint. To some extent, these pencil lines mar the overall effect close up – but not so much from a viewing distance. However, it is hard to envisage how these might have been extinguished, in view of the delicate translucent layers to the rest of the face, so maybe the painting was simply executed with some speed.

The treatment of the waves is typical of Wilson's many coastal scenes. However, the inclusion of the figures is rather less usual, which might indicate that it was no more than a spontaneous opportunity on a family trip to the beach. The fall of the fabric of Gerty's dress harks directly back to Wilson's earlier Pre-Raphaelite works and to his student days. The effect of the body structure beneath clothing never ceased to fascinate him and appeared in a profusion of studies within his two sketchbooks. The pose adopted is almost identical to that of one of the girls in Wilson's

earlier allegorical work, *A Spring Song* (q.v.), albeit depicted from a slightly different angle. Similarly, the almost translucent effect of Walter's 'dress' is clearly reminiscent of Wilson's larger scale oil paintings – such as the diaphanous raiment of the central figure in *Asia* (q.v.) The overt use of the pure white body colour to create the bright highlights in both figures' clothing, as well as in Gerty's hair and the breaking waves, is again quite commonplace in Wilson's work.

The two alternative recorded titles offered as possibilities for this work are no more than speculative, but either is quite feasible. Neither title has been identified to other works elsewhere, so the works attached to these may otherwise be lost. However, from family correspondence, we know that John Wilson apparently virtually cleared his walls of his brother's paintings to send to both the retrospective exhibitions, so although it is known from photographic evidence within the house that there were a few other works not sent, probably very few were omitted. However, there is one discrepancy to this that might counter the argument, and that is that *Sea Beach near Buckie*, the most likely option of the two titles suggested, did not in fact, for some unknown reason, go to the Aberdeen exhibition, unless under a completely obscure title.

21   Trees (A Fallen Beech)

[Verso: Unresolved watercolour landscape study]

Date unknown, possibly ca 1880-85
Watercolour on heavy weight wove paper
11¼ in x 15¼ in (286 mm x 388 mm) – irregular
First exhibited: Aberdeen Art Gallery (Aberdeen Artists' Society),
1893 (545)

© National Gallery of Scotland, Edinburgh

Provenance: Dr Anderson (1893); Dr Thomas Barlow; through family descent, bequeathed via the Helen Barlow Bequest to the National Gallery of Scotland, Edinburgh, 1976

There is some curiosity attached to the provenance of this picture. In the Aberdeen Exhibition catalogue, and also in the list of plates printed in the George Washington Wilson phototypes from that exhibition (where it appeared as No. 10[b]), the painting was shown with its original (if somewhat generic) title simply of *Trees*, and was identified as belonging to a 'Dr Anderson' of London. The painting did not feature in the subsequent 1903 Baillie exhibition.

The next time that this particularly fine woodland watercolour appeared in public (when it had become rather more explicitly entitled *A Fallen Beech*) was in the list of 56 paintings that were bequeathed to the National Gallery of Scotland in April 1976, within the wonderful private collection from the estate of the late Miss H. A. D. Barlow. Amongst the documentation that accompanied the bequest was a list of the paintings and the locations where each originally hung in the Barlow family home at No. 10, Wimpole Street, London. Additionally, there was included the following illuminating memorandum relating to the Wilson picture:

George Wilson was an Aberdeen artist. A portfolio of his drawings [alas, apparently no longer traceable] *accompanies this collection. He was a great friend of John Nettleship the animal artist, a patient of Sir Thomas Barlow's who suffered from alcoholism. Wilson took Nettleship away on a painting tour and never left him for six months at the end of which Nettleship was permanently cured. This picture was a gift to Sir Thomas from Wilson.*[210]

It is strange that it would appear from this account that the painting was always owned by the Barlow family from the date of Wilson's gift through to the bequest to the National Gallery of Scotland. Whether the Dr Anderson of 1893 was merely a mistake, or whatever else might have transpired, is not known. It is equally difficult to place a date on Wilson's 'painting tour' with Nettleship, and the note does not say whether the painting was an immediate gift after the event or was given somewhat later. Certainly W.B. Yeats recorded that Nettleship was cured long before the later 1880s, but one would have imagined that the enforced abstention would have been more likely, in fact, to have taken place before his marriage, a good 10 years earlier in 1876. However, the painting appears to be rather too late in style for such an early date, so the mystery will remain unsolved for the time being.

The Wilson family were highly respected as long-time factors, as well as landowners in their own right, in the Cullen region of north Banffshire. Local respect for the family has remained strong in the area even well over a century after the majority had left the locality. Even so, it seems quite strange that there should have been real local interest when the knowledge was made public that this painting had been bequeathed to the National Gallery of Scotland. But once known, it appears also to have been very much welcomed in this very parochial part of the country. Local anecdotal evidence ascribes the central tree in the painting as having been a well-known local landmark in Crannoch Wood, a beech-wood forest to the east of Cullen, both at the time it was painted and for many decades afterwards.[211] And while no-one has been prepared to try to identify it, it is said that this once magnificent tree still remained at least until quite recently as a severely decayed relic within those forests. When the author visited Crannoch Wood some years ago, he discovered many such fallen and heavily decayed trees, some of considerable girth and evident age, within these now effectively unmanaged woodlands. The idea that any one of these might have fit the bill is of course attractive, but the real likelihood of its existence after over 100 years is probably slight – despite local enthusiasm for such a notion!

Somewhat different in treatment to the *Study of an Oak Tree* (q.v.), the finely detailed painting of the bracken and vegetation, and the last vestiges of life displayed in the leaves of the beech itself, suddenly give way to another swirl of an ethereal wind-swept Corotesque tree to the rear of the fallen tree – perhaps denoting the younger emerging tree that will take centre stage in the coming years. This vibrant young tree is harshly offset by the particularly finely detailed treatment of the decaying stump in the foreground, apparently previously destroyed by an earlier incident, and which is a masterly piece of watercolour drawing in itself. In contrast to Wilson's 'cotton-wool' treatment of the clouds in his allegorical oil paintings, the sky in this watercolour, although almost incidental to the dominant subject that spreads its web of branches across the whole span of the picture, is a fine depiction of a Scottish spring day.

In somewhat typical Wilson fashion in utilising both sides of the paper, verso there is an unresolved landscape study. The location of this view is not clear, but may be a taken from just south of Huntly, looking west towards Clashmach Hill in the distance.

Following the Barlow bequest, the National Gallery of Scotland staged an exhibition in 1979 of all 56 donated works, entitled *English Watercolours and other Drawings: The Helen Barlow Bequest. A Fallen Beech* was exhibit No 53 accompanied by a half page colour illustration.

More recently, from 2004 to 2005, the painting has toured with the exhibition of Scottish landscape drawing entitled *A Picturesque Pursuit: Scottish Landscape Drawings from the National Gallery of Scotland*, first at the Robert Fleming Gallery in London, followed by its home gallery in Edinburgh, where the exhibition was renamed *A Journey Through Scotland*, then finally on to the Richard Feigen Gallery in New York.

22 Old Bridge of Don (The Brig o' Balgownie)

Date not known, possibly ca. 1876-80
Watercolour on heavy weight wove paper
10 in x 15 in (254 mm x 381 mm). One inch is added to the left
side of the painting to extend the width of the composition
First recorded exhibition: John Baillie Gallery, London, 1903 (62)

Private Collection

Provenance: Charles Wilson; via Wilson family descent to current private collection

These next two paintings of the north Aberdeen landmark, the Old Bridge of Don, or the Brig o' Balgownie as it is commonly known, are almost identical – except that one is only about one quarter the size of the other. The smaller painting certainly doesn't seems to be a preliminary sketch for the other, but at the same time, it is most unlike Wilson to repeat an identical scene – even down to the autumnal season and detail such as the boat on the left bank, so perhaps one was a commission from the other.

There are in fact minor differences in the two paintings – such as the extra figures near the boat in the larger picture being replaced by just one child nearer to the house in the smaller one. There are also differences to the perimeter of the larger painting as this encompasses a slightly greater perspective all round – and to the extent that there is a very ill-concealed addition of about one inch to the width of the paper along the left hand edge. This serves to bring in yet another figure carrying a small baby (that is only hinted at in the smaller painting) who appears to be watching the artist at work, and also the water-edge hut to the right of the picture that is essential to the balance of the wider perspective. Wilson's technique in painting the perfectly still water is quite masterly – and is an excellent example for other students of the medium.

In addition to the two paintings reproduced here, there is a contemporary photograph of the interior of John Wilson's house, Castle Park in Huntly, which appears to include, indistinctly, one further painting of the bridge, drawn from a slightly lower perspective that is more akin to the G.W. Wilson & Co. photograph also reproduced below. This latter painting now appears to be lost.

23   Old Bridge of Don   (The Brig o' Balgownie)

Date not known, possibly ca. 1876-80
Watercolour on heavy wove paper
4¾ in x 6⅞ in   (120 mm x 175 mm)
First recorded exhibition: 'Poetic Vision', Aberdeen Art Gallery,
1990 (13)

Private Collection

Provenance: Wilson family; via family descent to current private collection

The impressively high single Gothic arched Brig o' Balgownie, one of the oldest bridges in Britain, was commenced in ca. 1290 and completed in 1320. It still stands (and probably will for ever now that it is closed to traffic!) to the north of Aberdeen, where it is now a popular tourist attraction.

The bridge looks deceptively low and small through the perspective of the paintings, and the roadway is indeed very narrow. But the bridge actually boasts on a plaque that it has a massive single arch span of 12 mtrs (40 feet) that claims to be a record for such a stone bridge, and at low water, reaches 17 mtrs (56 feet) above the deep salmon pool beneath, which itself has the curious name of 'The Black Neuk'.

The view that Wilson painted is impossible to see clearly today, since the river banks have become completely overgrown by a dense thicket of sycamore trees – which could have emanated from the twin trees that stand in the paintings on the right bank beside the bridge. Both those trees are still there today; the main trunk of the larger tree to the rear is now stunted as if struck by lightning, and only supports a few large side branches, but the smaller tree in front of it is now a fine mature sycamore. Since the painting, the rural surroundings are now inevitably quite built up. The shore-side fisherman's 'cot' to the left, well protected behind its own flood walls appears to have been replaced by a larger property built higher above the flood plain level. The hut on the right bank (showing only in the larger picture) has now completely disappeared without trace.

The depiction of the placid water, apparently almost unmoving below the arch of the bridge and reflecting a fine late autumn day, belies a river that can quickly become a storming torrent descending from the mid-Grampian heights many miles away. Both paintings display a masterly technical quality in the execution of the water that renders the equally detailed attention to the surrounding trees and river banks almost secondary.

George Washington Wilson, Queen Victoria's royal photographer in Scotland, inevitably photographed the picturesque Brig o' Balgownie on numerous occasions during the last quarter of the 19th century. The George Washington Wilson archive collection in Aberdeen University Library contains a number of prints from a range of similar viewpoints to that which George Wilson painted, with many of them

Brig o' Balgownie photographed by George Washington Wilson & Co. Ltd., between 1880 and 1904 (when this print was listed in the latter year's catalogue). © University of Aberdeen Library G.W. Wilson Collection.

evidently photographed at around the same time, since these are listed as being included in the firm's 1877 catalogue.[212]

It is of particular interest that the small skiff beached on the left bank in both paintings is clearly visible in many of the archive photographs and, although not entirely clear from that reproduced here, it is of exactly the same shape and design as was depicted by Wilson. However, also of interest is that although the waterside 'cot' with its surrounding flood protection wall, near the left side base of the arch, is clearly evident in the paintings and many of the earlier photographs, the building appears to have become completely dilapidated in slightly later photos (as shown here). Indeed, there is no evidence at all today of either the cot or the shed sited on the opposite bank. Otherwise, apart from the obvious seasonal differences, the view is little different – either then or now.

The smaller work appeared (No. 13.) in the small exhibition entitled 'Poetic Vision' staged at the Aberdeen Art Gallery in 1990 to commemorate the centenary of Wilson's death in April 1890.

If one single location could be identified as George Wilson's favourite place above all others, then purely through the number of paintings that he created along the short stretch of the River Deveron as it runs in a deep gulley between the Old Castle of Huntly and Huntly Lodge, this would lay a strong claim to be that spot. Undoubtedly, had he been in a position to reside more permanently in Italy, he might well have found an even greater landmark attraction, perhaps around the environs of Asolo, but assuredly he would still have longed for his native Aberdeenshire as well.

The following are those examples of this series of paintings that are currently still known to be in existence. In themselves, they demonstrate in a microcosm the development of Wilson's technique in landscape painting over a relatively short period of time, from his Pre-Raphaelite roots through to some really quite bold and almost impressionistic influences.

24   'A Bit' On the Deveron, near Huntly

Date not known, possibly ca. 1880-85
Watercolour on heavy weight wove paper
9¾ in x 13¾ in (248 mm x 349 mm)
First recorded exhibition: Aberdeen Art Gallery (Aberdeen Artists'
Society), 1893 (550)

Private Collection

Provenance: Mrs Eliza Thurburn; via Wilson family descent to current private collection

The first two pictures shown here are typical of Wilson's numerous paintings along the reaches of the Deveron. There are 10 metres or so descent to the river's edge from the road that leads from the town, past the old Huntly Castle and up to Huntly Lodge (then the seat of the Dukes of Richmond and Gordon, but now a comfortable hotel), where the road sweeps over the narrow stone bridge into the house driveway. At the river's edge, one can turn either left or right along the riverbank and come across dozens of views like those depicted here by Wilson. They are almost unchanged in the 120 years since the pictures were painted, and the trees (mainly beeches) are effectively the same. There are of course many younger replacements, but the majority are now simply quite vast. A 'bit' here simply means a 'spot' along the river bank.

Again, there is a masterly execution in the water, whether rough and tumbling down the gently sloping reaches perhaps in spring, or entirely placid in early autumn, as are depicted differently in these two paintings. From an early date, and whether or not in observance of the earlier doctrine of Ruskin, Wilson's attention to the painting of rocks and boulders showed that he evidently loved painting these in their multitude of tones, as can be seen in many of these river's edge paintings. Similarly, there is continued evidence of the 'ethereal' treatment of the trees that may be seen as being somewhat reminiscent of Corot's wind-swept studies. The bold use of colour in depicting the bluish cold stone against the warm auburn red of the bed of fallen autumnal leaves is a typical Wilson treatment.

The first painting (above) was included as No. 3^b in the set of phototypes commissioned from George Washington Wilson following the 1893 Aberdeen exhibition. It also appeared (No. 15.) in the small exhibition entitled 'Poetic Vision' staged at the Aberdeen Art Gallery in 1990 to commemorate the centenary of Wilson's death in April 1890.

25   On the Deveron (may be On the Deveron, Autumn)

Date not known, possibly ca. 1878-83
Watercolour with some body-colour on heavy weight paper
9¾ in x 13¾ in (248 mm x 349 mm)
First exhibited: Unconfirmed, but possibly one of four paintings
exhibited with the same simple title (543, 546, 558, or 569) at
Aberdeen Art Gallery (Aberdeen Artists' Society), 1893

Private Collection

Provenance: Probably Charles Wilson; via Wilson family descent to current private collection

The second painting of these two, which appear almost to be a 'pair' in geographical terms, may indeed simply be facing up-river instead of down-stream – and in a different season. Stylistically rather 'freer' in execution; this may be intentional in depicting the evidently blustery seasonal conditions resulting in a rather rougher stretch of riverbank. However, in contrast, there is a very delicate application of body-white to highlight the finely drawn branches and twigs that reach out centrally over the river, some carrying only the remaining vestiges of autumnal leaves. Only one of George Wilson's Deveron paintings bore the 'Autumn' subtitle, and it is purely surmise in relation to its descent that suggests that this could be the relevant work.

26   On the Deveron

Date not known,
possibly ca. 1875-80
Watercolour on heavy
weight wove paper
13¼ in x 9½ in
(337 mm x 241 mm)
First recorded
exhibition:
Unconfirmed, but
possibly one of four
paintings exhibited with
the same simple title
(543, 546, 558, or 569)
at Aberdeen Art Gallery
(Aberdeen Artists'
Society), 1893

Private Collection

*Provenance: Probably from
the collection of Charles
Wilson; via Wilson family
descent to current private
collection*

This watercolour is an interesting and unusual variation of the above Deveron pictures, in that Wilson did not often paint his landscape paintings in a 'portrait' format. Here it is a clever device, particularly for this autumnal composition, which relies heavily upon the height and strength of the trees to the left of the scene to create the scale of the picture. However, the principal trunk – depicted in very much greater and more vibrant detail than its more background neighbours – melds directly into the mossy and rocky bank below, and from there tumbles straight into the boulders of the river.

From this point, the eyes are drawn into a short circular promenade to clamber across the rocks in the shallow river, and then follow the bank on the farther side away towards the less prominent supporting trees of the composition. Once again, these 'background' trees hold no more than an ethereal impression of their true detail and stature that allows the foreground to dominate. In some ways, the river itself might appear to be almost insignificant to this composition; but in fact, it plays a critical rôle in dividing the two very different banks and in creating the revolving interest of the composition.

As always, Wilson has paid great attention to the composition, and has painted the picture looking upwards towards the rising bank opposite, which effectively precludes any higher background landscape and thereby allows the sky to bring light right down to what would otherwise be the dark centre and foreground portions of the painting. The shadowy image of the solitary crow flying through the trees must have been an opportunistic moment that brings life (albeit of a rather sinister nature) to the scene at a predominantly 'dead' time of year.

27   On the Deveron

Date not known, possibly ca. 1883-87
Watercolour with some body-colour on heavy weight wove paper
6¾ in x 13¾ in (172 mm x 349 mm)
First recorded exhibition: Unconfirmed, but possibly one of four
paintings exhibited with the same simple title (543, 546, 558, or
569) at Aberdeen Art Gallery (Aberdeen Artists' Society), 1893

Private Collection

Provenance: Probably Charles Wilson; via Wilson family descent to current private collection

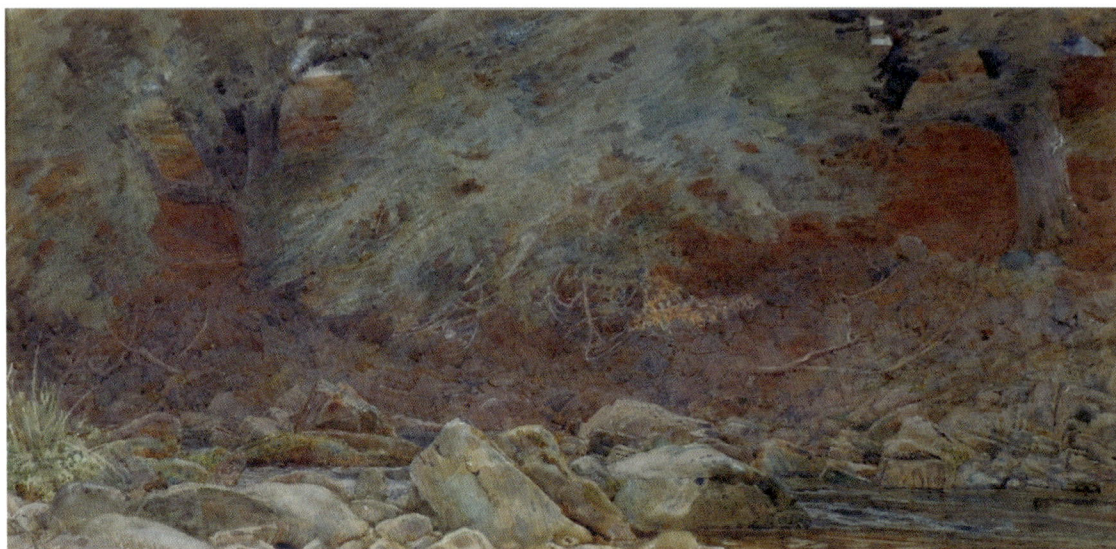

Following on from the previous painting, this next is a quite small, but extremely detailed view of the Deveron – and one that portrays the river itself in an even more secondary rôle to the trees and (most particularly) the rock formations that border and traverse the river.

Along with the early watercolour painting of *The Whale's Mouth* reproduced below, this study owes some degree of allegiance to the Ruskinian dictum for the painting of rock formations. However Wilson's small composition here is far more than a pure technical study of the strewn rock strata, and depicts yet again, in a simple but effective multitude of brushstrokes, the sweeping beech covered banks of the Deveron. The colours in the trees, and the shallow and comparatively quietly behaved, low water, indicate that it is probably painted in late summer.

Again, the rising bank permits the sky to filter through the trees – but only just, as a hint above the rise of the bank, which in this painting is very much secondary to the dense canopy of the vegetation that forms the top half of the composition, but of which only the base can be seen. The light for the foreground in this case comes from the evidently blue sky directly above the river expanse, which in itself contrasts with the density of the dark canopy over the bank.

190

28   Title unknown (possibly one of 'On the Deveron')

Date not known, possibly ca. 1885-1888
Watercolour with some bodycolour
9¾ in x 13¾ in (247 mm x 348 mm)
First recorded exhibition: Unconfirmed, but possibly one of four
paintings exhibited with the same simple title (543, 546, 558, or
569) at Aberdeen Art Gallery (Aberdeen Artists' Society), 1893

Private collection

Provenance: Charles Wilson; via Wilson family descent to current private collection

The next painting shown here is one of many that Wilson painted that succinctly epitomise the love that he never lost – despite the stated and undoubted attractions of Italy and elsewhere – for the forests of his native Scotland. It could not be more typical in its rendition of a Highland river heading down from the snowy mid-heights of the Grampians, through overcrowded pine forests, towards an eventual but still distant sea. That sea could be anywhere between the eastern Moray Firth and Aberdeen – but the river's upper inland course from the central Highland mountains would always be inexorably similar.

This is a classical Wilson scene and composition. The detailing of the fir trees and their branches to the minutest detail of their pine needles and the individual blades of grass below, contrasts directly to the often ethereal depiction of Wilson's other great love – the magnificent beech forests of northern Banffshire in all their winter glory.

Wilson has used a very limited palate of blues, greens and browns with some white to great effect, and once again, the composition ignores any panorama in lieu of the finer detail of the foreground and middle ground. The important tree trunk to the far left shows in subdued shadow no more than the bole of what is evidently a lofty pine, but yet it is a major constituent of what is a purely natural and thoroughly uncontrived snapshot that might be taken at almost any point in a walk through such a forest.

Although it is mooted that this might also be one of the Deveron paintings, it would be unusual to find that river falling between evidently steep banks with significant hills behind – that is, until one reaches a point some miles farther inland to the west of Huntly, perhaps past the Haugh of Glass. Here the gorges and banks are indeed crowded by Scots Pines and become much more of a feature. An alternative location is not immediately obvious from available evidence, but that in itself neither confirms the Deveron nor precludes other options.

Finally, in the two remaining Deveron paintings that are presently available, George Wilson appears to have progressed quite significantly forward in his approach both to composition and to colouring, in a relatively short period of time. Whilst there is still a fundamental adherence to some Pre-Raphaelite principals, there is additionally an apparent movement towards a degree of impressionistic treatment of light and colour.

The location again, as with the first two Deveron paintings shown above, appears to be very similar in both paintings. Equally the season appears to be high summer in both. The main difference lies in the colouring of each – the one demonstrating perhaps the heat of midday, while the other seems to indicate a cooler early evening.

Both of these views, in the less common portrait format, display an extraordinary effect in light and colouring, from the trees and rock formations, to deep into the water – with the second composition appearing perhaps to be a perceptible evolution from the first. They both demonstrate really quite impressionist qualities and probably represent work that is developmentally about as late as any of Wilson's surviving watercolours – or, indeed as late as any of his paintings in any medium, since he appears to have concentrated on watercolour for the latter years of his life.

29   On the Deveron

Date not known, possibly ca. 1886-88
Watercolour with some body-colour on heavy weight wove paper
13½ in x 9¾ in (343 mm x 248 mm)
First recorded exhibition: 'Poetic Vision', Aberdeen Art Gallery,
1990 (7)

Private Collection

Provenance: Wilson family; via Wilson family descent to current private collection

30   On the Deveron

Date not known, possibly ca. 1887-89
Watercolour with some body-colour on heavy weight wove paper
13¾ in x 9¾ in (348 mm x 247 mm)
First recorded exhibition: Unconfirmed, but possibly one of four
paintings exhibited with the same simple title (543, 546, 558, or
569) at Aberdeen Art Gallery (Aberdeen Artists' Society), 1893

Private Collection

Provenance: Probably Charles Wilson; via Wilson family descent to current private collection

The first of these two paintings above (29) appeared (cat. No. 7.) in the small exhibition entitled 'Poetic Vision' staged at the Aberdeen Art Gallery in 1990 to commemorate the centenary of Wilson's death.

Although not exactly the same view as the second painting, it is evidently painted from a similarly close viewpoint. It is, somewhat unusually, painted at the height of, or late in summer, which was not a regular time for Wilson to visit his brother in Huntly. This alone leads one to suspect that it might have been painted during the summer of 1889, when it would appear (from the evidence that supports the dating of the beach painting above, depicting Gerty and Walter Wilson) that Wilson was, indeed, in the area – and, additionally, there in summertime.

The second painting in this comparison is also painted in summer, but is composed in quite astonishing colouring that produces an effective masterpiece. Again, this is believed to be one of the last paintings that Wilson made during that late summer, and is further thought to demonstrate the firm direction that he was pursuing in (at least) his watercolour drawing. Yet somehow, he seems to have crammed a major leap forward in quite daring colouration into just the last few months of his painting life – almost as a pre-emption of what was to befall him within those few months.

Nevertheless, he adheres religiously to the doctrine of carefully painting the beautifully weathered granite rock formations. Elsewhere, he has used a device, typical to much of his woodland landscape work, in making the effective horizon the middle distance undulation (in this case the top of the river bank and only the merest glimpse of sky). This serves to allow him to bring the background sky down to the same level, creating both light through the woodland and interest to the dense foliage.

In both paintings there appears to be a slight turn in the leaf colour, lending support to the time of year to be late summer. This is reiterated by the calmly flowing waters that exude the very essence of the peaty-coloured clarity that epitomises their birth in the middle heights of the Grampians. These are waters that would be a raging torrent for many months of the year.

As identified above, there is an interesting contrast to the Deveron paintings – which all represent pure landscape painting – from the compositions that George Wilson also frequently painted along the Deveron's smaller, and very different natured sister river, the Bogie. The two rivers ultimately join up at a place called rather logically 'The Meetings', about one mile north of Huntly Castle. The Deveron carries water from numerous tributaries that emanate from the lower-to-middle reaches of the Grampian Mountains to the west of Huntly and, somehow, these origins are reflected in the frequently rugged nature of the river itself.

The Bogie, in quiet contrast, is born of streams that commence life in the gentler Correen Hills to the south, from where the river meanders quietly towards Huntly through water meadows bordered by the much slighter and softer lower hills. It is a very different river in nature, and George Wilson treats it so in his paintings, which generally depict pastoral scenes that sometimes contain figures enjoying equally pastoral or rural pastimes.

31   On the Bogie—Clashmach in the Distance

Date not known, possibly ca. 1882-86
Watercolour
6¾ in x 13¾ in (170 mm x 348 mm)
First exhibited: Aberdeen Art Gallery (Aberdeen Artists' Society),
1893 (585)

© Aberdeen Art Gallery and Museums Collections

Provenance: Charles Wilson; either bequeathed directly to The Aberdeen Art Gallery, or indirectly via his estate

This painting appears to be set some distance south of Huntly town, where the Bogie becomes quite narrow and meandering, and may possibly be painted from the water meadows between the main road (now the A97) and the main Huntly to Aberdeen railway line, in the region of the Mains of Collithie and Millhill Farm.

The attention to the detail of the grass and wild flower meadows would give any modern day environmentalist courage for the future! The placid foreground is dramatically offset by the grim and bleak stormy horizon over the Grampians, behind Clashmach in the distance to the north. This sky is cleverly reflected in the only very small area of water that is visible – and which is in itself contrasted heavily by the blaze of colour within the grasses adjacent to it. One imagines that the impending storm probably made Wilson very wet whilst walking home to his brother's house at Castle Park in Huntly after painting this picture!

This work appeared (No. 2.) in the small exhibition entitled 'Poetic Vision' staged at the Aberdeen Art Gallery in 1990 to commemorate the centenary of Wilson's death in April 1890.

32   Landscape, Bogie Bridge—Sunset

Date not known, possibly ca. 1880-85
Watercolour
6½ in x 13½ in (165 mm x 345 mm)
First exhibited: Aberdeen Art Gallery (Aberdeen Artists' Society),
1893 (536)

© Aberdeen Art Gallery and Museums Collections

Provenance: Charles Wilson; either bequeathed directly to The Aberdeen Art Gallery, or indirectly via his estate

In contrast, this placid, bucolic summer evening's view is painted in the opposite direction from the painting above, and from the opposite side of Huntly's Bogie Bridge, on the water meadows to the north of the town. This point is just a few hundred yards from the 'Meetings' – the confluence where the Bogie meets the Deveron and thence flows out to reach the sea between Banff and MacDuff. Castle Park, the home of George Wilson's brother, John, with whom he came to stay every year, lies just a quarter of a mile to the north-west and just to the right of this view on the opposite side of the river.

The modern day photograph from the artist's viewpoint shows just how little this view has changed over the last 120 years. No doubt the young saplings along the riverbank are relatively new replacements for those that were still young in the original painting. Hidden in the middle foreground

The River Bogie with the Bogie Bridge at Huntly in the background. Photograph taken by the author in 2002.

of the photo, below the houses, is now the town's curling pond. Although there has inevitably been significant new growth in the town, none has affected this particular view, except that the old stone road bridge over the river is now more grown-over and hidden, but otherwise it is little changed. There is a fair level of artistic licence in the painting, which clearly displays the Clashmach Hills towering quite predominantly in the background, whereas in reality, and as can just be seen in the photograph, they are actually little in evidence and only predominate somewhat farther to the south-west (right of the view), and far too distant to dominate in such a manner. In order to get the authentic outline of these hills, it was probably necessary for the artist to paint that element from the opposite (south) side of the bridge. Although probably not a particularly late painting, the early evening light and colouring employed appear to display some elements of an almost impressionistic effect behind a very Pre-Raphaelite foreground.

This work appeared (No. 4.) in the small exhibition entitled 'Poetic Vision' staged at the Aberdeen Art Gallery in 1990 to commemorate the centenary of Wilson's death in April 1890.

33 Title unknown (believed to be 'The Bogie at Huntly in Summer')*

Probably ca. 1884-86
Watercolour with some body-colour
9 in x 6⅜ in
(228 mm x 162 mm)
First exhibited: Unconfirmed, but if * then Aberdeen Art Gallery (Aberdeen Artists' Society), 1893 (556)

Private collection

Provenance: John Wilson; via Wilson family descent to current private collection

This most vibrant and in many ways delightful familial scene depicts (according to family record) Norman Wilson, one of George Wilson's several nephews, fishing on the River Bogie – necessarily within reasonable walking distance of Castle

Park. The hills behind are undoubtedly the Clashmach Hills again, and so the position for the painting is probably around the Burnend and Greenhaugh area, approximately   mile south of Huntly. Nonetheless, the proximity of the hills to the scene has again clearly been enhanced quite significantly by the artist to enclose the subject more fully within the foreground, and to eliminate the distraction of a distant view of the hills. The figure of the fisherman has been placed subtly to the extreme right of the frame, which leaves the splendour of the exquisite wild flower and grass painting in the left foreground without competition.

Although quite a late painting in Wilson's life, the whole composition, with the figure study, the dozens of swallows and martins that swoop and dive on the midges that infest every Scottish river in summer, and the very detailed painting of the foreground wild flowers and grasses, all hark back strongly to Wilson's earliest Pre-Raphaelite principles.

The likely age of the young fisherman would certainly bear out the family record that it is the eldest of John Wilson's sons, Norman (born in 1871), since he was the oldest boy in the family by three years. Norman, like so many of his Scottish kindred, emigrated abroad to make his life (and no doubt his fortune, as he would have hoped). However, at the age of just 24, he received an appointment in the Ugandan Government Service, in charge of a district called Usoga, whose populace was in a state of considerable discontent with British rule and with its Sudanese soldiery – which in itself was largely quite out of control. When the latter mutinied a year later in 1897, Norman and two other Europeans were captured and taken hostage by the Sudanese under the guise of negotiation, but were then summarily executed by them in cold blood. There is a memorial cairn to the three men at the spot of their murder, but due to subsequent depopulation, this is now well off the beaten track and may, or may not, still be in existence.

34   Title unknown   (Possibly 'On the Bogie, Huntly in the distance')*

Date not known
Watercolour
5¼ in x 8¼ in (133 mm x 210 mm)
First exhibited: Unconfirmed, but if * then Aberdeen Art Gallery
(Aberdeen Artists' Society), 1893 (584)

Private collection

Provenance: John Wilson; via Wilson family descent to current private collection

This painting features in a contemporary photograph of the interior of John Wilson's house, Castle Park in Huntly. It is one of a number that still exist that were left unfinished to a greater or lesser degree. In this case, the river to the foreground stage. This means that the title of this painting certainly has to fall into the category of having some element of doubt. Nevertheless, descent of the painting would be correct and the title is attributable to no other composition now identifiable.

The location is almost certainly on the River Bogie at a point somewhere to the south of Huntly town. There are any number of possible locations where the river would meander sharply across a northerly view with Huntly town only just glimpsed through the trees to the background far right. However, the painting remains too little resolved to be entirely sure of this claim.

The painting is interesting as an indication of how Wilson composed and built up his technique. The cattle on the ridge of the horizon are no more than coloured patches – yet it is obvious what they are, and what colour they would have been painted. Similarly, the tone of the picture has been set with an evident evening sky and light that suggests recovery from a recent downpour.

35   The Bogie, with Huntly Castle in the distance

Date not known possibly ca. 1880-85
Watercolour
9½ in x 13½ in (242 mm x 343 mm)
First exhibited: May have been Aberdeen Art Gallery (Aberdeen
Artists' Society), 1893 (583)

Private collection

Provenance: John Wilson; via Wilson family descent to current private collection

36   Huntly Castle

Date not known possibly ca. 1885-88
Watercolour
8 in x 13 in (203 mm x 330 mm)
First exhibited: May have been Aberdeen Art Gallery (Aberdeen
Artists' Society), 1893 (537)

Private collection

Provenance: Charles Wilson; via Wilson family descent to current private collection

These two views of the ancient ruined Castle at Huntly, although painted in completely different styles and in contrasting moods, were both painted from almost exactly the same position to the south-east of the castle, and north-east of Huntly town. The view is directly across the area between the two rivers, Deveron and Bogie, just before their confluence at the point known as The Meetings. This land was to become designated for the Huntly Golf Club in 1892, only a few years after the paintings were made.

The first composition does appear to be quite autumnal, whilst the second shows all the signs of being a frosty spring day. But the greatest difference is in the vibrant and almost impressionistic light and colouring of the later composition. In the first painting, the River Bogie is clearly visible in the foreground, so this must have been painted on the south-east bank of the river, adjacent to Pirriesmill Farm. However the second and later painting appears to be from the opposite north-west bank of the river, as the river doesn't appear to feature and the focus of the painting is consequently quite different. Both works show a road or track as no more than a thin line running across the foreground, although in the earlier picture this is merely glimpsed through the trees bordering the river. This retains the focal interest of the composition in the foreground detail, with the river almost encapsulated by the surrounding undergrowth and bushes, and with the distant castle no more than a shadowy backdrop – as the title suggests. The clarity of the water reflecting the sky is cleverly emphasised by the surface area farther to the left that appears to be quite murky – perhaps covered with a coating of weed.

The later work, however, has only one point of focus – and that is evidently the old castle, with everything else either leading towards it or indeed marking it out, such as the pair of solitary ethereal 'Corotesque' wind-swept trees in the foreground. These continually draw the attention to the evident focal point of the castle itself, somewhat like finger-posts pointing the way, but also by almost enclosing the castle in a frame of their branches. The sheep are painted in no more than an indicative manner, but give the whole picture a sense of great calm.

The earlier work appeared (No. 5.) in the small exhibition entitled 'Poetic Vision' staged at the Aberdeen Art Gallery in 1990 to commemorate the centenary of Wilson's death in April 1890.

37   Title unknown   (possibly 'Near Nethy Bridge')*

Date not known
Watercolour
6½ in x 13½ in (165 mm x 343 mm)
First exhibited: Unconfirmed, but if * then may have been at
Aberdeen Art Gallery (Aberdeen Artists' Society), 1893 (577)

Private collection

Provenance: Wilson family, possibly Mrs Eliza Thurburn; via Wilson family descent to current private collection

It is not at all certain as to what is the title of this painting. It is painted from high up in the Scottish Highlands, and in the knowledge that Wilson painted occasionally in the region of Nethy Bridge and the Cairngorms, the suggestion that this might be one of his recorded paintings of the region is no more than fair speculation. The provenance and exhibition history of the proposed title do, however, lend some weight to the possibility.

It is probably quite an early landscape study, as the depiction is indicative of the backdrops to many of Wilson's allegorical oil paintings that relied so heavily on the Renaissance influence. The cloud formations are very similar, and the mountain range to the backdrop is simply bleak. However, apart from the main tree just off-centre, there is no real focal point to the composition – which leaves one guessing as to its purpose beyond being a simple attractive landscape. It is unusual in this respect in that it doesn't hold any great clarity of subject – and may simply have been the sketch developing a background idea for something more substantive. There are a number of interesting subjects that fit this bill – such as the 'lost' figurative watercolour *A Spring Song* (q.v.)

This work appeared (No. 16.) in the small exhibition entitled 'Poetic Vision' staged at the Aberdeen Art Gallery in 1990 to commemorate the centenary of Wilson's death in April 1890.

38   Unfinished Picture of Tree and Cot   (Study of Tree and Cottage)

Date not known, possibly 1880-1885
Watercolour with some body colour on heavy wove paper
9¼ in x 9¾ in (235 mm x 248 mm)
First exhibited: Aberdeen Art Gallery (Aberdeen Artists' Society), 1893 (582)

Private Collection

Provenance: John Wilson; via Wilson family descent to current private collection

Probably painted in Sussex or the South of England in the early to mid 1880s, there is an interesting use of light playing upon the mossy roof of the barn adjoining the cottage, whilst the foreground is more reminiscent of a William Morris wallpaper!

It is not known why this painting was specifically referred to as 'unfinished' at the 1893 Aberdeen exhibition – more than any others on display. At the 1903 exhibition in London, it was simply described as Study of Tree and Cottage.

The centrepiece of the composition is, as so often, a fine specimen of one of Wilson's beloved beech trees. The light glimpsed on the trunk is a minor reflection of the broad swathe of bright low sunlight swamping the thatched roof, and the viewer's focus is neatly caught between the two central points of interest. There is at the same time, an interesting glimpse of the bright summer sky caught through the leafy branches of the tree, and reflected onto the bracken in the foreground. As so often, the composition centres on a small portion of a far greater perspective – which, had it all been included, would have rendered the whole to be a much more bland picture.

39   Title unknown (may be 'The Cairngorms, from Abernethy')

Date not known, possibly ca. 1883-88
Watercolour
6¾ in x 9¾ in (172 mm x 247 mm)
First exhibited: Unconfirmed, but may have been at Aberdeen Art Gallery (Aberdeen Artists' Society), 1893 (541)

Private collection

Provenance: Wilson Family; via family descent to current private collection

Although the provisional title above has been suggested for this painting, there is no proof to support this, and there are indeed one or two alternative, albeit more generalist titles, such as *Evening* or *Twilight* that could fit from alternative routes of family descent. Wilson also painted a number of pictures with the simple title of *Sunset*, and this again could certainly be another alternative title for the painting. However, from the records available, none of the recorded paintings with that name would have descended through to the present-day owner.

On the other hand, there are no other recorded titles that refer specifically to the Cairngorms, or indeed, to any other significant mountain. There is no doubt that a view of Cairn Gorm itself is possible from the Abernethy Forest, but probably not quite as starkly as this painting depicts; however the suggested title refers only to the mountain range in general and this certainly does contain a number of other more appropriate peaks.

Anyway, whatever the title, it is certainly a dramatic – and quite surprising – composition. The foreground, in particular, displays the use of a wet-on-wet technique, which is unusual in any paintings that we know of that are to any great extent finished. However, this method from Wilson is certainly not unique to this work. He utilised the technique particularly in the early stages of building up the background in his work, and evidence for this exists in the several works that were left at differing stages of completion, from the earliest outline onwards. This may appear to be an unfinished painting, although equally, it might simply be a sketch of a particular moment. Either way, it is a successful and vibrant study as it stands.

The next three painting are representative of Wilson's English landscape work. The paintings shown here demonstrate a very different light and colour – somehow more muted, perhaps by the additional brightness, although it is difficult to be clear in this assumption, as there is an element of some being unfinished in those works that are available in this area. There were one or two paintings exhibited with titles relating to the Arundel area, but none that can be directly related accurately by title or descent without further provenance or descriptive detail – which is not presently forthcoming.

40   Title unknown   (may be 'Wood near Arundel')*

Date unknown, possibly ca. 1880-85
Watercolour
9¾ in x 13¾ in (247 mm x 349 mm)
First exhibited: Unconfirmed, but if* then Aberdeen Art Gallery
(Aberdeen Artists, Society), 1893 (539)

Private collection

Provenance: Possibly Charles Wilson; via family descent to current private collection

This picture of an open stretch of woodland with a small pond in the foreground does indeed appear to be somewhat unfinished. The composition alone lends some weight to the opinion that it is probably one of George Wilson's English woodland landscapes painted in the South Downs near to Arundel in West Sussex – possibly at the perimeter of the Park at Arundel Castle, along the very minor road leading north-east out of the town that runs parallel to the Arun River. If this is correct, then the title proposed becomes a distinct possibility, since the descent of the painting would also be appropriate.

It is an interesting example of Wilson's technique in building up his watercolours – showing, in this case, how the detail has been commenced at quite an early stage. Once again, he has stopped the composition well below the canopy of the trees, creating a frame to the painting – particularly to the top centre right, where an important focal element of the design is being built up.

41   View in Arundel Park

Date unknown, possibly ca. 1880-85
Watercolour with body colour
9⅝ in x 13¼ in (245 mm x 337 mm)
First exhibited: 'Poetic Vision', Aberdeen Art Gallery, 1990 (12)

Private collection

Provenance: Wilson Family; via Wilson family descent to current private collection

This painting bears a label verso that is typical of a number of such labels – but, unusually, this one does not appear to be in George Wilson's own hand. The label bears the title of the painting and Wilson's name and his London Newman Street address, which puts the painting into a period of between around 1882 to 1885, when Wilson rented his studio at 65, Newman Street (off Oxford Street in London).

Arundel Park is the extensive area of parkland estate that circles out broadly from Arundel Castle towards the Downs to the north and which also contains the handsome large Regency style house of the same name as well as the many other estate properties belonging to the Dukes of Norfolk. There are numerous public footpaths and walks throughout the estate, many of them leading up into the Downs. This picture appears to have been painted possibly not far from the previous painting, but higher up where the track meanders from the Arun riverside road up into the Downland hills before turning back along a ridge towards Arundel town again, and past Arundel Park House.

The inclusion of the dead deer in the foreground, with the carrion crows circling above it, is an unusual observation by Wilson – and not the sort of subject that he would often have chosen – or chosen lightly. It must have moved his gentle nature considerably to have incorporated such an image – although he would have been well accustomed to such sights, both in his native Scotland as well as in the South Downs, where deer are still in great abundance today.

The carcase of the dead deer is mirrored and emphasised by the two 'supporting' dead tree trunks on either side and the sentinel dead stump starkly outlined in contrast by the depths of the woods behind. The right hand trunk even emulates the shape of the deer, whilst the left hand timber appears to be rearing up in its last throes before death. All in all an apparently morbidly symbolic painting, but yet somehow it is still not an entirely gloomy one, with the refreshingly crisp blue autumnal sky of the heavens above, making the death below seem quite paltry by comparison.

This work appeared (No. 12.) in the small exhibition entitled 'Poetic Vision' staged at the Aberdeen Art Gallery in 1990 to commemorate the centenary of Wilson's death in April 1890.

42   Title unknown (may be 'An Opening in the Wood')*

Date unknown, possibly ca. 1880-85
Watercolour
8½ in x 13¾ in (216 mm x 350 mm)
First recorded exhibition: Not known, but if *, then Aberdeen Art
Gallery (Aberdeen Artists' Society), 1893 (555)

Private collection

Provenance: Possibly Mrs Eliza Thurburn; via Wilson family descent to current private collection

This again is another of Wilson's English woodland landscapes, probably painted in the Sussex Downs near to Arundel. Indeed, it could possibly be painted on the ridge away to the front of Arundel Park House, overlooking the Arun valley. The more distant hills in the background would then be the next outcrop of the rolling Downland countryside directly to the east of Arundel town at the village of Crossbush. No exhibition is certain for the painting, but Mrs Thurburn loaned a watercolour entitled simply *An Opening in the Wood* to both the 1893 and 1903 exhibitions. This title cannot be identified for sure, but is suggested, only tentatively, as the most likely of those that she loaned at the time.

The leafless trees and very long shadows superimposed on brightly lit turf suggest an early winter evening. To some extent, the picture appears unfinished in the midground areas, although, the treatment of the foreground may well be intentional with the pale ground forcing the eye ever backwards towards the copse of young woodland birches – and the shadows have already been painted-in in quite sufficient detail. The brief detailing of the upper branches along the top of the picture and in front of the sky is a typical Wilson ploy to avoid the distraction of what might become overwhelmingly intense foliage, when a hint at least of what lies behind is essential to balance the composition. This again forces the eye back towards the important central patchwork of brighter coloured grass, which is criss-crossed by trunks and shadows, but then continues to spread right across the composition.

This work appeared (No. 11.) in the small exhibition entitled 'Poetic Vision' staged at the Aberdeen Art Gallery in 1990 to commemorate the centenary of Wilson's death in April 1890.

The following section of paintings represents (unfortunately, so far as we are aware) virtually all that remains from George Wilson's originally extensive portfolio of paintings made abroad – in Italy (Rome; Siena; San Giminiano; Venice, and Asolo) for the most part; but also in Algiers, North Africa.

43   A Scene in Italy

Date unknown, possibly ca. 1885-89
Watercolour with some body colour
10¼ in x 14¼ in (260 mm x 363 mm)
First recorded exhibition: Aberdeen Art Gallery (Aberdeen Artists'
Society), 1893 (544)

Private collection

Provenance: John Wilson; via Wilson family descent to current private collection

Very few of George Wilson's paintings from Italy have survived, since it appears that these were mainly purchased by friends from outside the family, and so most have become lost today. As always, attribution here has been difficult, but since out of the few that have survived, only one painting with a 'non-specific' Italian title was loaned to both of the exhibitions by any member of the Wilson family – this time by John Wilson – so the given attribution is probably sound. Anyone who has visited and experienced the remarkable, and unmistakable, mountain formations in the Dolomite region of northern Italy will recognise that without doubt this picture was painted in that area, during one of Wilson's increasingly frequent visits to that region.

Throughout the last active decade of his life, Wilson made regular pilgrimages to Italy, where he reported that the weather suited his frail constitution so much better. These trips usually took in central Italy, with Florence and Rome, either on the way out or back, where he painted in Siena and San Giminiano, as well as in Venice, and of course his (and Robert Browning's) beloved Asolo and the Dolomites.

Certainly, Wilson recorded in his letters that he took canvasses with him on these trips for his larger oil paintings in order to paint-in the backgrounds, using the Dolomites as his model, to emulate the Renaissance scenery to which he was so dedicated.

In this watercolour, the bold treatment of light and colour indicates that the picture was probably painted towards the end of Wilson's life. The colours employed in the mountain range, which create the light and shadows, are particularly exciting, and are emphasised by the clever lightening of the sky itself. This is brighter in the centre of the painting, which helps draw the eye towards that focal point – from where the attention meanders in a circular motion via the prominent bush, the rock in the foreground, and thence via the darkened strip of foliage to the right, and up towards the mountain range once again.

This work appeared (No. 10.) in the small exhibition entitled 'Poetic Vision' staged at the Aberdeen Art Gallery in 1990 to commemorate the centenary of Wilson's death in April 1890.

44   Title unknown   (probably painted in north Italy)

Date unknown, possibly ca. 1885-89 Watercolour with some body colour
6 in x 10 in (152 mm x 254 mm)
First recorded exhibition: Not known

Private collection

Provenance: Halsey Ricardo; via family descent to current private collection

Until it was rediscovered during the researches for this book, there had previously been no record anywhere of Halsey Ricardo's ownership of this painting. It neither bears a title, nor is there any similar painting recorded as having been lent to exhibition by Ricardo. It is thought probably to have been painted in North Italy, but this time possibly in the hills around the town of Asolo, and is probably of a similar period to the previous painting. The bright colouring and treatment of the hot, dry hill scrub and gorse is very alike in both paintings, but in this case may not be completely finished.

There is a further small sketch illustrated later below that probably falls into either this group of Italian paintings, or it may possibly be in Algiers. This is purely a deduction as the painting forms part of a collection of variously complete and incomplete works within an inherited portfolio.

45   Venice

Date unknown, possibly ca. 1875-80
Watercolour
3¾ in x 7½ in   (95 mm x 190 mm)
First recorded exhibition: Unconfirmed, but probably Aberdeen Art
Gallery (Aberdeen Artists' Society), 1893 (535)

Private collection

Provenance: Probably Charles Wilson; via family descent to current private collection

From the two exhibition lists, it would appear that the main lender of Italian paintings was Edward Nettleship, and (after his death) his widow. Again, the only Venetian scene loaned by the Wilson Family came from Charles Wilson, so it is surmised that in all probability this small watercolour drawing of Venice, which may not be entirely finished, is one and the same.

The scene is painted looking north-east from the most north-westerly point on the Fondamente Nuove – which now accommodates a marine refuelling station! Apart from this, very little has changed in over a century. The view looks towards the Chiesa San Michele on the cemetery island Isola di San Michele, with the island of Murano farther behind to the left. Today the cemetery is more built up and the tree-covering is greater. Murano is also similarly a bit more

The cemetery Isola di San Michele (right), with the island of Murano beyond (left); photographed from the Fondamente Nuove in Venice by the author in 2003.

developed; however all the principal landmarks remain. Artistic licence has given rather greater scale to the church, and may also have omitted the various obtrusive sea markers and marine tethering posts that would probably have been present then just they are as now.

This work appeared (No. 9.) in the small exhibition entitled 'Poetic Vision' staged at the Aberdeen Art Gallery in 1990 to commemorate the centenary of Wilson's death in April 1890.

46   A View in Algiers

1885
Watercolour
7⅛ in x 13½ in (180 mm x 343 mm)
First recorded exhibition: Aberdeen Art Gallery (Aberdeen Artists' Society), 1893 (578)

Private collection

Provenance: John Wilson; via Wilson family descent to current private collection

In May 1885, George Wilson made his one and only recorded painting trip to north Africa, sailing to Algiers and spending a few weeks revelling in the light and colour of the land. Reference to this trip is recorded elsewhere, but to reiterate the enchantment he felt for this new experience, he wrote to John Todhunter: *I had never dreamed of such a paradise of wild flowers. There are most of ours, but much bigger than with us. And innumerable others as new to me as the queer jewel-stones in the new Jerusalem would be – marvellous cups and trumpets and bugles...*[213]

This small watercolour is the only known surviving painting from this evidently exciting experience and equally stimulating trip. Although a few Algiers subjects were recorded at exhibition in the ownership of others from outside the Wilson family, only one was recorded from within the family ownership of George Wilson's elder brother, John. John's wife Anna refers in a letter, contemporary to the 1893 exhibition, that, *The new frame improves the picture so much and we have done the same to the one of the Kinnoir park hanging below Mahomet.* [214] Although the title *Mahomet** was not carried through to either exhibition, such 'pet' names were not an unusual occurrence, and certainly no other paintings of Algiers were loaned by John Wilson, so the assumption regarding identity appears strong.

Some of the left foreground of the painting may not be completely finished if compared to the right, and Wilson may simply have left it once he had returned home with no further chance of finishing the painting *in situ*. The very bold colouring of the orange-red escarpment, evidently reflecting heat against the background cypress and closer foreground trees is dramatic. Similarly, the fine detail paid to the small citrus tree to the far right would indicate that there might be more to be done to the painting.

---

* Although there is no obvious place name that relates to Anna Wilson's description, Mahomet is, of course, an alternative spelling for Muhammad, though why she should use this is not known – unless it was merely just another 'pet' name adopted by the family.

It is not known exactly where the painting was made and although the colour of the escarpment might veer towards an assumption that it could be the famed red gorges at El-Kantara, there is no evidence to support this.

This work appeared (No. 8.) in the small exhibition entitled 'Poetic Vision' staged at the Aberdeen Art Gallery in 1990 to commemorate the centenary of Wilson's death in April 1890.

With the following group of paintings, we return to the north shores of the Scottish Banffshire coastline along the Moray Firth and the eastern sands at Aberdeen. The north coastline in particular was a subject that Wilson visited over and over again. He knew the region intimately, having been to school in Cullen at a young age, and having many relations who farmed along the fertile coastline and, of course, distilled their malt whisky at Inchgower near Buckie. The shoreline at Aberdeen also featured on occasions, when Wilson stayed in the town with another older brother, Charles, who was Procurator Fiscal for Aberdeenshire.

Wilson seems to have been fascinated by the breaking of waves on the shoreline, as he painted many scenes that centred on this ever-changing subject. The incessant breaking of waves, as with burning flames in a fire, both share that same fleeting momentary occasion, never again to be repeated exactly – and both are equally difficult to capture with total satisfaction. Maybe Wilson simply enjoyed the challenge; but equally, it is a subject in which he achieved some real success.

Most of these views concentrate on the breaking waves filling the major central element of each painting, with any added interest forming a secondary peripheral 'frame' to the edges. In this respect, some of these paintings can be somewhat reminiscent of Gustave Courbet's 1860s series of paintings entitled *The Wave,* (National Gallery of Scotland; Fine Arts Museums of San Francisco, and – more properly known as *The Stormy Sea* – Musée d'Orsay, Paris, etc.). These are paintings that Wilson could very well have seen as he travelled via Paris on his way to Italy.

Rather like his numerous studies painted along the River Deveron, Wilson's Moray Firth and Aberdeen coastal paintings are almost impossible to differentiate from title alone, or to attribute accurately to the relevant recorded exhibition titles of the subject. Only very few remain of a once fairly extensive array of such studies. Those that we know of are depicted below, but with no attempt to relate them all individually to exhibition titles. Additionally, a similar, but now missing painting is reproduced later amongst the George Washington Wilson phototypes from the 1893 exhibition.

47   Title unknown (possibly On the Moray Coast, Banffshire; or may alternatively be Aberdeen Sands, or The Aberdeen Beach, or Sea Beach near Buckie)

Date not known
Watercolour with body colour
4 in x 8⅝ in (100 mm x 220 mm)
First recorded exhibition: 'Poetic Vision', Aberdeen Art Gallery, 1990
(6)

Private collection

Provenance: Wilson family; via family descent to current private collection

The first of these paintings (above) is a very small sketch that could have been painted almost anywhere along the sandy stretch of coastline around Buckie and Cullen – or indeed at Aberdeen. It is not identifiable either as a specific location or as an exhibited work. Nevertheless, it is a typically simple and effective portrayal of the subject, and works very well as such.

This second work (below) is a much clearer subject and has been identified locally today as a very little changed view of the rocky outcrop of coastline at Ianstown, about half way between the fishing villages of Buckie and Findochty. This is the painting that was exhibited at both the 1893 and 1903 exhibitions and which was recorded then as being in the possession of George Wilson's eldest sister, Mrs Eliza Thurburn – from whom the present descent emanated.

Both these above works appeared (Nos. 6. and 14.) in the small exhibition entitled 'Poetic Vision' staged at the Aberdeen Art Gallery in 1990 to commemorate the centenary of Wilson's death in April 1890.

216

48   On the Shore at Ianstown

Date not known, possibly ca. 1883-88
Watercolour with body colour
9½ in x 13¾ in   (242 mm x 350 mm)
First recorded exhibition: Aberdeen Art Gallery (Aberdeen Artists'
Society), 1893 (571)

Private collection

Provenance: Mrs Eliza Thurburn; via Wilson family descent to current private collection

Although probably painted quite late in Wilson's career, the attention to the rock formations continues (as it did whenever he painted such features) to reflect an earlier Ruskinian doctrine; whilst the sea and sky take on a rather more impressionistic approach. It is a delightfully relaxed composition, contrasting the passive, yet heavily weathered rocks against the (temporarily) placid seascape, with an impending severe change in weather looming on the horizon – a very recognisable scene to those who live and work in the area.

49   **On the Moray Coast, Banffshire**

Date not known
Watercolour with body colour on light brown coloured paper
6 in x 10 in (152 mm x 254 mm)
First recorded exhibition: Not known

Private collection

Provenance: Halsey Ricardo; via family descent to current private collection

This is another painting that was 'rediscovered' within the descent from the architect, Halsey Ricardo's original ownership, and of which there was no previous record or exhibition note. As a first reaction, it might appear from the amount of toned paper that remains visible through the paint upon close inspection that this painting is quite unfinished. However, it was purchased and mounted and framed by Ricardo, Wilson's friend and patron; so unless this happened after Wilson's death, then we have to deduce that the effect may well have been intentional.

In fact, and indeed either way, the device works most effectively – both to enhance the stormy evening sky, and also to give the translucent effect to the receding water from the breaking waves over the sand in the foreground. From a practical point of view, it is difficult to imagine how, or what, Wilson would have painted onto the bare areas of paper when the other areas had been so extensively worked. It is just not the way in which he worked up his compositions. He has very successfully achieved the reflections of sky, unbroken wave, foam and the sandy sea-floor – all at varying depths of water – without the need for further attention to the painting. This is another painting that certainly has some reminiscences of Courbet's *Wave* paintings.

50 Title unknown (may be on the Moray Coast, Banffshire, near Cullen Bay)

Date not known
Watercolour with some body colour
6¾ in x 9¾ in (170 mm x 247 mm)
First recorded exhibition: Not known

Private Collection

Provenance: Wilson family; via family descent to current private collection

Both the painting above and the one following below (and indeed the five thereafter) all form part of the previously mentioned portfolio of loose paintings, sketches and drawings. The work above is a particularly effective study, of which the title is again no more than an assumption, since there is no anecdotal family or recorded reference to its history. In fact, two paintings ascribed as being related to Cullen Bay were exhibited at both retrospective exhibitions by Wilson family members; however, it is not apparent that this work has ever actually been framed.

The view is certainly reminiscent of parts of the Moray coast, where the rolling hills become sharply eroded where they meet the ferocity of the sea. Perhaps this is painted from the east end of Cullen Bay, looking towards Logie Head, but this is by no means certain. The treatment of the rock strata and the low light, possibly of late afternoon, have been cleverly handled and continually lead the eye round to the tip of the promontory. However, the ad-hoc positioning of the small burst of cumulus cloud (curiously reminiscent of a group of allegorical figures) above the hill serves to interrupt any relaxing of the viewer's attention.

51   Title unknown (may be along the Moray coast, Banffshire, or on the sands near Aberdeen)

Date not known
Watercolour with body colour
6¾ in x 9¾ in (170 mm x 247 mm)
First recorded exhibition: Not known

Private Collection

Provenance: Wilson family; via family descent to current private collection

Here again, Wilson has achieved all the basic principles of a successful water's edge seascape without over-working the painting. The light is curious, but works well to enforce the transparency of the receding surface water over the sand to the bottom right corner of the painting. The wind is evidently directly off the sea, which is choppy rather than stormy. The broadly straight line of the coast is identified by the wave lines, which lead directly to the peninsular to the right. This in turn 'points' directly to the two or three small boats sailing across the horizon and one large schooner that appears to be at anchor. The twin lighthouse and beacon may indicate that the promontory could be Girdle Ness and the entrance to Aberdeen harbour.

Again, there is an interesting patch of cloud to break up the monotony of the cloud blanket, and by offsetting this to the right and above the peninsular of land, Wilson creates a far more interesting composition than by simply balancing left and right evenly. The painting may possibly be not entirely finished.

52   Study of cloud formation

(recto to A river landscape q.v. No 54)

Date not known
Watercolour with body colour
3⅜ in x 5 in (87 mm x 126 mm)
First recorded exhibition: 'Poetic Vision', Aberdeen Art Gallery, 1990
(17)

Private Collection

Provenance: Wilson family; via family descent to current private collection

In George Wilson's earlier figurative oil paintings, which were so strongly influenced by the painting of the Renaissance period, there often appears to be an almost careless inattention to the formation of the clouds – which so often appear as small 'cotton-wool tufts'. As if to endorse Wilson's far greater attention to cloud formations in his later works – and particularly his watercolours, we find in the small portfolio of sketches, this attentive study of a billowing cumulus cloud structure, with small strata of other formations running through it. Apparently an evening scene, which Wilson so often liked to paint, the clouds are lit up by the sun both directly from its sinking over a distant horizon and also as a rosy evening reflection from below. At the same time, the earth's shadows also reflect the greater evening darkness that is descending under the threat of the underlying layer of rain clouds.

Painted recto to the landscape study shown below, this work appeared (No. 17.) in the small exhibition entitled 'Poetic Vision' staged at the Aberdeen Art Gallery in 1990 to commemorate the centenary of Wilson's death in April 1890.

The final few sketches included below generally appear to be little more than preliminary studies towards areas or categories of work that are variously represented above – with the possible exception of the second sketch reproduced below. This is tonally of a most unusual range for George Wilson to have employed. It appears to be almost inherently East Anglian in subject matter, landscape, colour and light – yet, as far as we are aware, Wilson never ventured in that geographical region of England. As an observation aside, this might be deemed something of a pity, since he would inevitably have rejoiced in the same characteristics that had originally so absorbed Thomas Gainsborough (1727-1788), John Crome (1768-1821) and John Constable (1776-1837), and more latterly, Sir Alfred Munnings (1878-1959) and Edward Seago (1910-1974), spanning two and a half centuries of quintessential English painting.

Other than this slight anomaly, the first study below is a simple well-resolved preliminary to a finished work (which is now believed lost), whilst the final two studies are typical of landscape scenes that Wilson painted over and over again – but here demonstrating his very different approach to very different countries and their relative environments.

53   Study for Letterfourie Bridge

Date not known, possibly ca. 1873-78
Watercolour
4⅜ in x 6¼ in (110 mm x 160 mm)
First recorded exhibition: Not known

Private Collection

Provenance: Wilson family; via family descent to current private collection

The strange Romanesque 'bridge – upon - bridge' construction of the Letterfourie Bridge, properly called the Craigmain Bridge, spans the deep and picturesque Findlater Gorge along the Letterfourie Burn. It lies to the south of Letterfourie House and is in fact a folly to that fine Adam designed building – renowned for its connections with Bonnie

Prince Charlie. All the same, the bridge is a splendid, if now somewhat obscure, tourist attraction and obviously appealed much to George Wilson's sensibilities.

He would of course have known very well of the bridge's existence as the (then) Gordon family-owned Letterfourie House was a very close neighbour, no more than half a mile away, from both the Arradoul Distillery House and the Wilson family-owned Inchgower Malt Whisky Distillery itself. Arradoul was the home of George Wilson's uncle Alexander, and subsequently of George's brother James, who successively ran the distillery, and with whom George frequently stayed on his annual sojourns back to his homeland. From local news reports, by the early 1880s George Wilson was very well-known locally for his depictions of local life and scenes – his association with his very well-respected brother and the Wilson family no doubt having been much heralded locally.

This small watercolour sketch, torn from the pages of Wilson's smaller sketchbook, is probably the preliminary work for a recorded watercolour of the bridge, which was owned and loaned for exhibition by James Wilson at both the 1893 and the subsequent 1903 exhibitions. Although only a small preliminary sketch, the style is typically reminiscent of the Deveron riverside paintings – both in colouring and construction, and is probably quite early.

54   A river landscape

(verso to Study of cloud formation, q.v. No 52)

Date not known
Watercolour
5 in x 3⅜ in (126 mm x 87 mm)
First recorded exhibition: Not known

Private Collection

Provenance: Wilson family; via family descent to current private collection

An unfinished composition, painted verso to the cloud study above. If anything, it might appear to be East Anglian in light and colour, but in view of the belief that Wilson never visited that part of England, there is no clear evidence as to where this small sketch might have been painted.

With no record of Wilson ever having visited East Anglia, the most likely alternative location would be somewhere where we know he painted in Sussex – possibly farther inland along the River Arun, above the tidal reaches. This could well accord with the higher stretches of the river as it descends through the South Downs. The painting depicts a very slow moving, almost stagnant, stretch of river at the height of summer, with its surface becoming blanketed in weed, whilst still reflecting the intermittent patches of sky. Reflection in water was something in which Wilson excelled. The delightful hint of the cottage hidden amongst the trees lining the riverbank, and indeed the whole subject, is somehow somewhat reminiscent of Constable and could well be no more than an experiment by Wilson in a different direction.

55 Subject unknown (a wooded landscape)

Date not known
Watercolour
5⅜ in x 10⅜ in (138 mm x 265 mm)
First recorded exhibition: Not known

Private Collection

Provenance: Wilson family; via family descent to current private collection

The curiosity of this sketch is that it is of a not entirely dissimilar tonal range to the previous sketch – although it could in fact have been painted almost anywhere within Wilson's 'territory'. It might possibly be Sussex with the South Downs in the background – but the heathery purple colouring of the hills indicates less general light and possibly greater height than the south of England, so the likelihood veers much more towards Scotland, or just possibly an evening or a dull day in northern Italy. The sketch is evidently only a preparatory work, but shows promise towards an interesting painting of light and shade with the semi-transparent screen of young trees, and the very brightly lit crowns to the shrubs in the middle foreground, before the very strong backdrop of dark hills and perhaps the evening sky.

56   Subject unknown   (possibly in Algiers or Italy)

Date not known, possibly 1885
Watercolour, heightened with some body colour
7½ in x 13⅞ in (190 mm x 351 mm)
First recorded exhibition: Not known

Private Collection

Provenance: Wilson family; via family descent to current private collection

This small painting appears to be an unfinished work, possibly from Wilson's Algiers trip, or alternatively maybe north Italy. It is not dissimilar in various ways to earlier-shown works from either region: The nature of the foreground scrub is repeated in both locations, but the trees rather more reflect the northern Italian compositions; however it is the red soil escarpment that hints towards it being somewhat more akin to Wilson's only other known North African work.

The typical brushwork depicting the scrub in the foreground and the middle distance belt of vibrant green trees is, in this instance, almost overwhelmed by the very powerful sky. Wilson is evidently in the process of achieving something that he did so very well – that of turning a view that initially seems to be scarcely of very great interest into one that will become full of much, eye-catching, detail. Inevitably, the result will equally demand great attention from the viewer in order to take it all in as the artist intended.

The following series of monochrome images are reproduced from a variety of archival sources; the quality is therefore not always ideal. However, they do serve as a useful (and presently unique) record of some of George Wilson's compositions that are currently believed lost. Where we have clear evidence, these compositions have accurate, or at least contemporary, titles ascribed to them, whilst others have suggested titles from available records. Others still – and in particular the 'generically' described landscapes from various countries and locations – cannot be identified with any great certainty at all and this is made clear.

Of the first two designs shown, we have clear evidence of almost everything about them except their sizes, since they were reproduced in contemporary publications either shortly after Wilson's death, or around ten years later following the 1903 *Neglected Artist* exhibition at the John Baillie Gallery in London. Although the majority of the other works in this section were also published around these same dates, this was without clear identification as to title, so some degree of assumption has been made. This again is made clear and, as with all supposition relating to Wilson's oeuvre, is open – and welcoming – to future clarification and correction.

57 **A Bacchante (Head of a Young Bacchante)**

1877
Chalk
Size unknown
First exhibited: Dudley Gallery, 1877

Whereabouts unknown

Provenance: Dr. John Todhunter, probably purchased at exhibition; now believed lost

Of *A Bacchante*, Todhunter wrote in *The English Illustrated Magazine* of 1891:

> *Of the two chalk studies here reproduced* [the other being the *Study for the Knight in "La Belle Dame sans Merci"* q.v.], *by far the most important is the splendid head of a young Bacchante, so fine in its handling and so rich in tone. It has qualities only to be found in the work of a great colourist.*[215]

The reproduction of *A Bacchante* attached to this article was in black and white; however, a red-brown coloured reproduction (from which the illustration shown here is reproduced as faithfully as possible) was published in Leonore van der Veer's article about George Wilson in Volume 30 of *The Studio*, 1903-04.[216] It is still impossible to tell whether this was originally a single colour chalk drawing, but it might be presumed from Todhunter's description that this was indeed correct; however that surmise is also backed-up to some extent by the inclusion of other full coloured reproduction where required within this later publication. The model for the drawing is, as usual, the young woman who appears in the majority of Wilson's important figurative paintings. Here she depicts that curious phenomenon of one of Bacchus's female accomplices, displaying just the right degree of mischievous humour, tinged with an observant, questioning air, as if daring the viewer to join in some off-scene fun and games – all highly emphasised by her wildly flying hair.

It is a masterly piece of drawing that concentrates and guides the viewer's focus in towards the detail of the facial features, leaving the surrounding features much to the viewer's own interpretation of the events of the moment. Indeed, there is (as with the *Study of a Head* q.v.) a certain enigma to the expression. Drawn just four years after leaving Poynter's tuition at the Slade, and originally exhibited in 1877 at the Dudley Gallery, *A Bacchante* displays significant influence from that instruction. In describing this drawing, van der Veer reiterated Todhunter when she considered this to be *the most masterly piece of modelling left by the artist.* She completed her account of the exhibition by concluding that *the truth is forced home to one that much of the world's best work is done by such quiet, unassuming natures as his.*[217]

58   Head of Knight in 'La Belle Dame sans Merci'

Date unknown
Chalk
Size unknown
First recorded exhibition: Aberdeen Art Gallery (Aberdeen Artists'
Society), 1893 (527)

Whereabouts unknown

Provenance: Purchased direct from the artist by Dr. John Todhunter. Still owned by him in 1893 and 1903; whereabouts now unknown

Keats's poetic ballad *La Belle Dame sans Merci*, originally written in 1819, must be one of the most frequently illustrated poems during the Victorian era. Representations exist by Walter Crane (1845-1915], Sir Frank Dicksee (1853-1928], John Waterhouse, Frank Cowper (1877-1958) and D.G. Rossetti, among many others.

George Wilson commenced a composition on this subject, which seems to have interested John Todhunter more than a little (perhaps because he had commissioned the painting). He was evidently not happy that Wilson had destroyed the canvas before its completion. The chalk study that is illustrated here was in Todhunter's possession, but this has also now disappeared along with the vast majority of his collection. He wrote of this study for the final picture in his 1891 article about Wilson for the *English Illustrated Magazine*, mentioning in relation to it that:

> *A large easel-picture of this subject was begun, and destroyed before completion. It was an embodiment of the lines [in stanza VI]:--*

"*I set her on my pacing steed,*
    And nothing else saw all day long,
For sidelong would she bend, and sing
    A faery's song."

The knight leads the horse by the bridle, and gazes up into the lady's face.[218]

Evidently, the canvas must have been in a fairly well developed state from Todhunter's succinct description, and one can envisage from the chalk study of the knight's head the general demeanour of the composition that Wilson must have had in mind. In Todhunter's introduction to the Baillie exhibition, which is broadly an amended version of his 1891 article for *The English Illustrated Magazine,* he added that Wilson, *destroyed in disgust many pictures which contained beautiful passages, but in which one or more figures did not satisfy him. One of these was "La Belle Dame sans Merci", which in its unfinished state promised to be fine; but which mysteriously disappeared from his studio as the face of the Belle Dame herself did not realise his conception of the "wild-eyed fairy's child" of Keats's poem.*[219]

There may just be some small hope that perhaps some of Todhunter's extensive collection of pictures were not in fact all destroyed by fire, and that this might then include the study for the knight in *La Belle Dame sans Merci*. Nonetheless, it seems there is very little doubt that we shall have to live with the knowledge that the final painting certainly did not survive Wilson's own disappointment with it, and his consequent attention to ensuring its demise.

228

59   Title unknown (possibly 'The Sons of God saw the Daughters of Men that they were fair')*

Date unknown. If *, then possibly ca. 1877-1880
*if so: Watercolour
Size unknown
First recorded exhibition: Aberdeen Art Gallery (Aberdeen Artists' Society), 1893 (586)

Whereabouts unknown

Provenance: Purchased direct from the artist by Dr John Todhunter. Still owned by him in 1893 and 1903; whereabouts now unknown

The title of this painting is not known for sure. The suggestion above is subjective and is based purely upon the knowledge of various possible titles that were recorded for exhibition, but for which we now have no ascribed illustration. Following this theory, the composition would have been based upon the Bible passage from Genesis Ch.6. v.2 that led to God recognising the developing wickedness of man; then subsequently to His sending down the Great Flood and of course to His covenant with Noah.

On 2nd June 1877, Robert Catterson Smith wrote to John Todhunter about the new 'designing club' that Wilson and his friends had re-established, and that the next subject to be portrayed was to be of this title. It is assumed that the eventual watercolour purchased from Wilson by Todhunter was the product, or at least the eventual outcome, from this design competition.[220]

The figurative design is strong in its Renaissance-inspired background – particularly if it is drawn in watercolour as suggested. However, the overall effect does not seem to be quite as successful as much of Wilson's work. There are several preliminary sketches for the design in Wilson's smaller sketchbook, which might endorse the earlier date for the painting, but that again is by no means certain.

The illustration here is taken from an old mounted photograph that lies within a private collection of Wilson descent. The only photographs that are known to have been taken at the time of the first Aberdeen exhibition were those made by George Washington Wilson & Co. for the commemorative sets of phototypes from that exhibition. It seems quite probable that the photographers took plates from more paintings than they finally utilised, and that this is a print that was discarded from the final selection. Presently, the George Washington Wilson archives have no record of the original plates; so again, this can only be broad, if rational, speculation.

60 Title unknown (believed to be 'Caritas')*

Date unknown
*if so: Watercolour
Size unknown
First recorded exhibition: Aberdeen Art Gallery (Aberdeen Artists' Society), 1893 (549)

Whereabouts unknown

Provenance: Purchased direct from the artist by Dr John Todhunter. Still owned by him in 1893 and 1903; whereabouts now unknown

This is possibly quite a late painting, in that George Wilson may have utilised his later developments in painting style, adopted along the Deveron reaches and elsewhere, to portray the backdrop to the picture. If this surmise is correct, then we may assume that the colouring of the painting would have been quite vivid. Although this reproduction is in black and white, it is possible to interpret the shading as being reminiscent of that bright colouring of the late portrait format paintings made in the Deveron location. However, the figure composition shows some reminiscences of Blake as well as Wilson's rather earlier Pre-Raphaelite and Poynter influenced empathies.

The title of the picture is not known for certain, but by process of elimination and some logical assumptions, *Caritas* is the only title from the works that Todhunter loaned to the later 1903 Baillie Gallery exhibition that could reasonably be appropriate to this composition. The painting was illustrated in Leonore van der Veer's article published in *The Studio* Volume 30, which covered the Baillie Gallery exhibition; however, the title inscription merely referred to the work somewhat unhelpfully as *From the Painting*! [221]

61   Title unknown (believed to be 'Eve's last look at Paradise')*

Date unknown
*if so: Watercolour
Size unknown
First recorded exhibition: John Baillie Gallery, 1903 (17)

Whereabouts unknown

Provenance: Purchased direct from the artist by Dr John Todhunter. Still owned by him in 1893 and 1903; whereabouts now unknown

As with the proposed designation for *Caritas* above, this title falls into the same category – and for the same reasons. It is believed that this painting is probably as described, and although there is no factual evidence for the claim, once again, there is no other title from Todhunter's loans to the Baillie exhibition that possibly fits the composition. Assuming the title to be correct, then once again, Wilson will have been illustrating events from the Book of Genesis, although not a specific passage this time. Unfortunately, also once again, Leonore van der Veer only referred unhelpfully in the inscription to the illustration in *The Studio* as being *From the Painting.* [222]

The composition shown here is mildly reminiscent of George Wilson's painting of *Asia*, with the Renaissance-inspired backdrop, typically of Dolomite origin, and the flower-strewn foreground, together with the treatment of the drapery worn by the figures. Wilson would undoubtedly have seen Michelangelo's ceiling in the Sistine Chapel in Rome, in which Adam is portrayed in *Genesis, The Fall and Expulsion from Paradise - The Expulsion* as appearing to be somewhat reticent – almost truculent – as he is ejected at the point of the sword. Here however, Wilson depicts Eve as cowering and ashamed. Indeed, Wilson's composition is altogether a more gentle and compassionate rendering of the expulsion from Eden. He has chosen a much softer approach; there is no sword and the angel appears almost reluctant as he ushers away a pitiful and wholly dejected Eve. She holds in her left hand a very slender shepherd's crook, the symbolism of which is not clear, although she does appear to be using this to try to gather towards her one last bloom from the typically flower-strewn foreground. Adam is nowhere to be seen!

231

62   Landscape near Harting, Sussex

Date unknown, possibly 1885-89
Tempera
Size unknown
First recorded exhibition: John Baillie Gallery, 1903 (83)

Whereabouts unknown

Provenance: Purchased direct from the artist by Halsey Ricardo; still owned by him in 1903. Present whereabouts unknown

It is not entirely clear quite how or why George Wilson should have discovered this particular area around the villages of South, East and West Harting, just to the south of the main road between Petersfield and Midhurst. He did, however, also paint some five miles to the north-east near the village of Milland, where he produced a watercolour drawing entitled *Pond in Borden Wood*, which was owned by Edward Nettleship and was exhibited at both retrospective exhibitions.

Then about another five miles farther to the north-east from Milland, one arrives at Haslemere and Hindhead, where Wilson stayed on several occasions throughout his painting lifetime with both John and Edward Nettleship, so neither spot would in fact have been far at all for the itinerant Wilson to reach from a friendly base.

In fact the ancient South Downs Way meanders through the area of Harting Down and, although not particularly high, the area does demonstrate the type of rolling downland countryside that is portrayed in Wilson's picture illustrated here – which is certainly painted at some height. There is a nice pastoral touch with harvesting or perhaps haymaking going on in the mid region of the composition. This activity, although relatively incidental to the scale of the painting, is brought into focus by the frame that is created by the foreground thickets, which the artist is apparently peering over, and the wooded downland hills behind that are typical of the area.

Unfortunately, the only illustration that we have available for this landscape is the etching that was made by the Paris born, but London-based etcher and portrait painter, Leon Daviel (fl. 1890-1928) for the *English Illustrated Magazine*.[223] Yet even this medium manages to portray effectively an image that is wholly Wilson in form and composition. Recorded as having been painted in the less common medium of tempera, we may assume that the colouring would probably have been very bright and depicting well the summer composition. It is also a painting for which we have an accurate title, and this in itself is also relatively unusual, since so many of Wilson's numerous landscapes, painted in various countries, merely bore a generic title at exhibition that makes clear identification virtually impossible today.

Previous reference has been made to the set of phototypes (photogravures) that was commissioned by the at the time of Aberdeen exhibition in 1893 from the firm of George Wilson's namesake, George Washington Wilson & Co. Ltd., Queen Victoria's royal photographer in Scotland. We are fortunate that a number of these sets of prints have survived, as they show images of several of Wilson's most important works that are presently believed lost.

Already shown above are modern reproductions of those paintings which either still exist, or for which an image is available that is of better quality than the equivalent printed phototype. These include *Alastor; Asia; The Song of the Nightingale; Trees (A Fallen Beech)*, and *'A Bit' on the Deveron*. The other seven paintings are reproduced below, direct from the phototypes. Although there is a major archive collection of George Washington Wilson's photographic plates at the Aberdeen University Library, unfortunately it has not so far been possible to locate the plates for these phototypes. The pity of this is that, almost undoubtedly, they would have originally included a greater number of photographed paintings that would have been omitted from the finally selected list for printing.

The phototype sets were commissioned by the Aberdeen Artists' Society in an opportunistic (and, thankfully, providential) move while such a significant collection of Wilson's paintings were all located within one place – and was aimed precisely at achieving an enduring record of some of his best work. This they did indeed achieve – as is evidenced by their inclusion here as well. However, there were only 100 sets of the phototypes published, so these in themselves are now a great rarity. Each set is dated Nov. 1893; is hand numbered and signed (by G. W. Wilson & Co. Ltd.), and contains 12 plates printed onto 10 individual sheets of irregular but similar dimensions. These are contained within an untrimmed folded sheet of an obscure overall size of approximately 11¼ in x 14⅝ in (one sheet containing the print of *Asia* is, curiously, in fact too wide for the folded cover sheet!). In turn, ten each of these sets were themselves enclosed in an outer 'artist's portfolio' with hard board covers, and embossed with the title.

The inside back page of the folded cover of each set has a brief introduction that comments on the reasons for the exhibition, with the acknowledgement that it was supported by *the generous assistance of Dr. Todhunter and Mr. Halsey Ricardo, and other friends of the painter*. It further includes a very brief précis of Wilson's life extracted from Todhunter's 1891 article for *The London Illustrated Magazine*. This introduction was initialled W.K., and was written by Dr. William Kelly, the eminent Aberdeen architect and antiquarian, who is probably best remembered for the parapet on Union Bridge that supports the delightful bronze leopards, known as 'Kelly's Cats'.

TEN PHOTOTYPES

OF THE WORKS OF

GEORGE WILSON

EXHIBITED AT THE

ABERDEEN ARTISTS' SOCIETY'S EXHIBITION

1893

AND PUBLISHED BY PERMISSION OF THE OWNERS OF

THE PICTURES UNDER THE AUSPICES

OF THE SOCIETY

GEO. W. WILSON & CO. LIMITED,

HER MAJESTY'S PHOTOGRAPHERS IN SCOTLAND,

25 CROWN STREET,

ABERDEEN

LIST OF PLATES.

		Present Possessor of Picture.
1.	"The Dance," Study for the unfinished picture "Arcadia,"	Russell Scott, Esq., London.
2.	"Alastor,"	Dr. J. Todhunter, London.
3ᵃ.	The Moray Firth, on the Banffshire coast,	John Wilson, Esq., Huntly.
3ᵇ.	On the Deveron, near Huntly,	Mrs. Thurburn, Keith.
4.	Scotch firs, near Huntly,	E. Nettleship, Esq., London.
5.	Summer and the Winds,	H. H. Young, Esq.
6.	"A Spring Song,"	Russell Scott, Esq., London.
7.	"The Song of the Nightingale,"	Charles Wilson, Esq., Aberdeen.
8.	Subject unknown,	
9.	"Asia,"	H. Ricardo, Esq., London.
10ᵃ.	Trees,	Dr. Anderson, London.
10ᵇ.	Beech trees (unfinished),	Russell Scott, Esq., London.

ONLY *one hundred sets of these prints*
published. Nov. 1893.
No. 40.

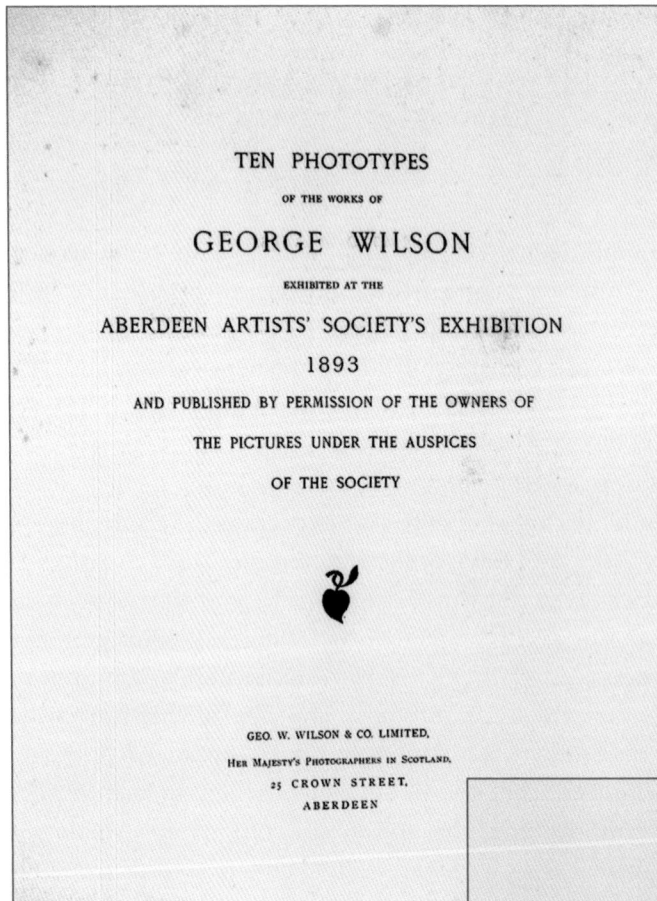

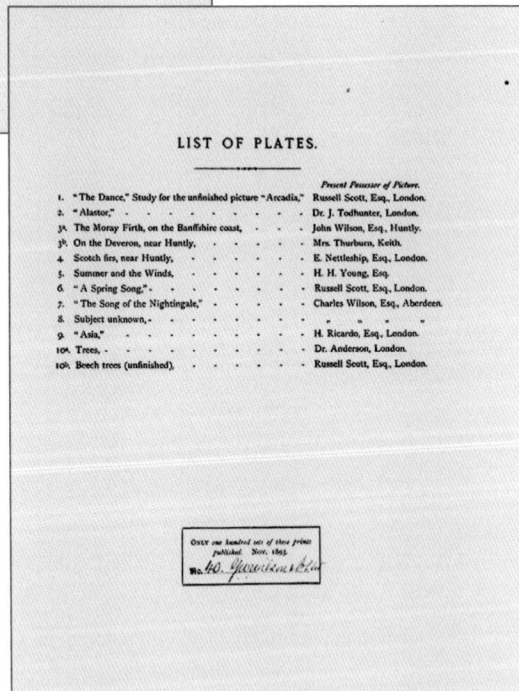

From *The Wilson Collection*. Front cover and inside front cover of the wrapper enclosing the George Washington Wilson & Co. sets of 10 Phototypes (photogravures) of 12 paintings, taken at the 1893 annual Aberdeen Artists' Society Exhibition at Aberdeen Art Gallery

63   "The Dance" – Study for a picture   (Study for the unfinished picture "Arcadia")

Date unknown, probably 1880-83
Watercolour
Size unknown
First exhibited: Aberdeen Art Gallery (Aberdeen Artists' Society),
1893 (568)

Whereabouts unknown

Provenance: Russell Scott (1893; 1903); whereabouts no longer known

This image is a reproduction of No. 1 in the set of phototypes commissioned by the Aberdeen Artists' Society from George Washington Wilson and Co Ltd, following the Aberdeen exhibition of 1893.

On 15th January 1882, George Wilson wrote to John Todhunter from Rome, describing a number of canvases that he had taken out to Italy with him to paint-in the appropriate areas on the spot. Amongst these, one can clearly be identified from his description as being *Arcadia*. It is a trifle amusing to note that, never having visited the Greek Peloponnese or the Greek islands, so far as we know, he is having to paint his Cretan back ground from what is available around Rome or Tivoli!

235

I've got well on with a picture that I took out with me – a dance of young men and maidens in a woody place in Crete see Iliad. Im going to paint Cretan scenery from what material I can find in the Roman campagnia or maybe Tivoli.[224]

Todhunter, in his eulogy on Wilson's life and work in *The London Illustrated Magazine* of 1891 wrote,

Many of his landscape studies soothe yet quicken the mind, like fine pastoral poetry. One might imagine these sunny or twilight lawns and leas trodden by the feat of that shepherd-boy in Sydney's Arcadia who lives on in our imaginations "piping as if he would never grow old".[225]

This was not in direct reference to Wilson's painting of Arcadia, but he and his friends – as with most of those Victorians who were immersed in Renaissance art and poetry – would certainly have been well versed in Sir Philip Sidney's (1554-1586) novel of pastoral ideals, entitled *The Countess of Pembroke's Arcadia*. This volume was first published in 1590 after Sidney's death by his sister Mary, Countess of Pembroke, for whom it had been written.

However, we know from Wilson's own letter to Todhunter exactly what his painting purports to represent, since he refers him directly to Homer's *Iliad* in describing the composition. But in fact, Wilson would appear to have been confused here since, in the *Iliad,* Homer only refers in militaristic terms to the real area of Arcadia situated in the arid central Peloponnese, whereas it was Virgil, in his *Eclogues*, who first developed the qualities of the imaginary and idealized landscape of the literary Arcadia. This is the gentle and luxuriant land of virtuous shepherds and rustic deities that was represented by the 17th century French painters Nicolas Poussin (1594-1665] and Claude Lorraine (ca.1600-1682].

But in Wilson's case, it was to some extent Blake but perhaps more the mid-19th century French painter, Corot, who influenced him in his interpretation. We now only have the phototype of the watercolour study for the final painting to refer to, but Wilson's circle of dancing figures is certainly reminiscent of Corot's Renaissance-inspired 'experimental developments from Claudian landscape', variously entitled around *La Danse des Nymphes* (Musée d'Orsay, Paris, etc). And again, and as so often, his trees bear that other Corotesque element of ethereal wind-driven branches and foliage that appear in the latter's many stormier landscape compositions such as *The Gust of Wind* (Musée Saint-Denis, Reims). Yet Wilson goes further in this allegory by including Pan, whose mythical home was the classic Arcadia, leaning casually against a tree as he plays on his pipes for the dancers.

By 1883, Wilson had taken a studio at 65, Newman Street, right in the heart of one of the traditional artists' communities, and close to the art school of his early mentor and teacher, Thomas Heatherley. This address appears on his exhibited works from 1883 to 1884, and those works included the oil painting of *Arcadia* that was shown at the Grosvenor Gallery's Summer Exhibition in 1883. This latter fact casts some doubt on the title accorded to the watercolour study (illustrated here) in the index to the George Washington Wilson phototypes, where it was referred to as *"The Dance", Study for the <u>unfinished</u> picture "Arcadia"*. Interestingly, in the exhibition catalogue itself, the title was simply *Study for a picture – "The Dance"*. The reference to the unfinished picture of Arcadia was repeated by Leonore van der Veer in her account of the Baillie exhibition of 1903 in Vol. 30 of *The Studio* of 1903-04. It is strange that the phototypes index should have referred to the oil painting of *Arcadia* as being unfinished, since it is assumed that Todhunter was involved in compiling the information used. However, it is much stranger that this remark was repeated in 1903, since the final oil painting was actually shown at that exhibition! But since much of what van der Veer wrote of Wilson's life and work was taken from John Todhunter's earlier account, this may simply have been a response to Wilson's own continual worry that, however much others liked his paintings, for him they seldom reached the standard that he himself would wish.

In one of his letters, written to Todhunter from his sick-bed in January 1890, concerning the latter's proposal for an exhibition, Wilson advised him, *I think Arcadia is in Austria* and that *Summer & the winds is also in Austria I think.* [226] This proves to be slightly mysterious and could be erroneous in view of Wilson's sickness. However, the only patron of Wilson's whom we know to have lived partially in Austria was Ralph Radcliffe Whitehead, during his first marriage up to around 1890-92. But there is no specific record of him having owned *Arcadia*, although he certainly might well have done so. It would also solve one other mystery if *Arcadia* were in fact the third, unidentified, subject that was referred to by John Nettleship when he wrote to Halsey Ricardo in 1892 asking him to take into storage Whitehead's three large boxed Wilson paintings. We may be almost certain that the other two were *The Spring Witch* and *The Rape of Proserpine* (the *Persephone* that is named in the letter). [227]

It is not surprising that *The Spring Witch* did not appear in Aberdeen in 1893, since Whitehead had by then taken the painting with him to America; yet *The Rape of Proserpine* was certainly exhibited (No. 566) in Aberdeen. And although the final oil of *Arcadia* also certainly did not appear at the 1893 exhibition (although its study did, of course), *Summer and the Winds* was indeed also exhibited there (No. 533), but then in the ownership of Mr H. H. Young. The curiosity here is that it is logically assumed that this H. H. Young is the same person as the Mr Herbert Young who loaned *Arcadia* to the 1903 exhibition, but who had by then (presumably) sold *Summer and the Winds* to Halsey Ricardo (see below). It is presumed that Whitehead left the other two paintings in England when he emigrated, so it is a possibility that Young bought *Arcadia* from Whitehead around this time, as indeed Ricardo bought *The Rape of Proserpine* from him – although in his case this could not have taken place until after the Aberdeen exhibition, since the painting was listed at that time as still being owned by Whitehead.

64   **The Moray Firth, on the Banffshire coast**

Date unknown, possibly 1883-88
Watercolour
Size unknown
First exhibited: Aberdeen Art Gallery (Aberdeen Artists' Society),
1893 (581)

Whereabouts unknown

Provenance: John Wilson (1893; 1903); whereabouts no longer known

This image is a reproduction of No. 3ª· in the set of phototypes commissioned by the Aberdeen Artists' Society from George Washington Wilson and Co Ltd, following the Aberdeen exhibition of 1893 and, as already noted within the section above that revolves around his Moray coast paintings, this is just one that we are aware of that is currently lost. Additionally, this painting features in a contemporary photograph of the interior of John Wilson's house, Castle Park in Huntly.

Painted at an entirely anonymous spot somewhere along the north shore of the Scottish Banffshire coastline of the Moray Firth, it was a subject that Wilson visited repeatedly. He knew the region intimately, having been to school as a youngster in Cullen when he lived nearby at the family farmstead of Tochieneal, and later on when he still had relatives who lived in the region – notably at the Inchgower Distillery and farm near Buckie, where he frequently stayed to paint in the area.

Reference has previously been made to Wilson's apparent fascination with the ever-changing subject of incessant breaking waves on the shoreline, which he painted on many occasions. The moment of the breaking of the waves fills the major central portion of this painting. The eye is drawn fleetingly to the small fishing boat on the horizon, but the pull of the waves against the undertow on the beach quickly drags the interest back to the central focus of the painting. This is another of the 'series' of Moray coastal paintings that appear to be somewhat reminiscent of Gustave Courbet's *Wave* paintings, made in the 1860s – paintings that Wilson could very well have seen in Paris whilst travelling through on his way to Italy.

65   Scotch Firs, near Huntly   (Pines and Rocks at Huntley)

Date unknown, possibly 1885-88
Watercolour
Size unknown
First exhibited: Aberdeen Art Gallery (Aberdeen Artists' Society),
1893 (572)

Whereabouts unknown

Provenance: E. Nettleship (1893); Mrs E. Nettleship (1903); whereabouts no longer known

This image is a reproduction of No. 4 in the set of phototypes commissioned by the Aberdeen Artists' Society from the George Washington Wilson and Co Ltd, following the Aberdeen exhibition of 1893.

The scene is another typically 'generic' composition that evidently appealed to Wilson somewhere around the Huntly area. Again, typically, the view demanded no specific title and, indeed, the descriptive title accorded to it changed mildly between the two exhibitions. Wilson's good friend, the optical surgeon Edward Nettleship, loaned the painting to the 1893 exhibition; but quite why it was catalogued later in 1903 as being loaned by Mrs E Nettleship (along with 10 other works) is not clear, since Edward Nettleship himself was still alive then and did not in fact die until some 10 years later, in 1913.

As so often with Wilson's compositions, the two tall central Scots Pine trees are cut off from their full height, allowing their canopies to form a frame to the composition. The eye is continually drawn down the trunks of the trees to the magnificent, heavily weathered, outcrop of rock, with its very cleverly painted lichen and moss covering. We have

239

no specific evidence that Wilson responded particularly to Ruskin's dictum about the drawing of rocks in nature, but he certainly took great care in their treatment and Ruskin should well have been pleased with his results. It is not known exactly where the painting was made, but it is quite possible that it was on one of the small wooded hillsides in the Kinnoir Wood or Battle Hill above Pirriesmill Farm – one of John Wilson's farms near Castle Park in Huntly, where George Wilson stayed with his brother for some months each year.

66   Summer and the Winds

1883-84
Tempera
Size unknown
First exhibited: Royal Institute of Painters in Watercolours, 1884
(92)

Whereabouts unknown

Provenance: H.H. Young (1893); Halsey Ricardo (1903); via family descent. Now believed lost

This image is a reproduction of No. 5 in the set of phototypes commissioned by the Aberdeen Artists' Society from George Washington Wilson and Co Ltd, following the Aberdeen exhibition of 1893.

This purely fantastic allegorical work, painted in the comparatively rare medium of tempera, would undoubtedly have been a very bright and striking work. Originally incorrectly titled *Summer in the Winds* in the 1893 Aberdeen Exhibition catalogue, this was corrected (probably by Dr Todhunter) before the index to the series of George Washington Wilson phototypes produced later in the year from that exhibition. It has always been assumed that H.H. Young, the owner of the picture at that time, was the contemporary artist of George Wilson's who exhibited once at the RA in 1885 and again at the Grosvenor Gallery in 1886. H.H. Young lived in Carlton Lane in Horsham, Sussex, and is understood to be the same person as the artist and photographer Herbert Young, who owned a villa in Asolo. Young may have known George Wilson from Asolo or via his travels in the mid Sussex area – possibly through Halsey Ricardo or the Nettleships – and Todhunter evidently knew him well enough to persuade him to exhibit this picture in Aberdeen. Herbert Young did also exhibit two oil paintings, *Eros* (of which no further information is available) and *Arcadia* (q.v.) at the Baillie exhibition of 1903. Young appears to have sold *Summer and the Winds* to Ricardo sometime after the Aberdeen Exhibition, as the latter is recorded as being the owner when the painting was loaned to the 1903 Baillie exhibition.

Ricardo eventually bequeathed the painting in his will of 1928 to his younger daughter, Esther. The picture was then described as being 'in carved gilt frame glazed' and was valued for probate at £5.5.0 (equivalent to ca. £230 today). Esther Ricardo was married to Walter Howarth F.R.C.S., a well-known collector of English (then modern) post-impressionist paintings – and in particular, of Walter Sickert. Important examples of Sickert's work that were either within (or had previously been in) Mr Howarth's collection are frequently represented in publications concerning the artist. Unfortunately – and maybe in some way due to Walter Howarth's particular focus of interest – *Summer and the Winds* is now no longer traceable within his family descent.

Summer and the Winds was originally exhibited (no. 92) in 1884 at the Sixty-Sixth Annual Exhibition of the Royal Institute of Painters in Water Colours, in which it was illustrated within the catalogue. The allegorical composition appears to be pure fantasy and is about as far as Wilson ever reached from the style of his landscape works. Nonetheless, it is a fascinating painting, utilising his usual model for the central 'Summer', also for the right hand 'Wind', and possibly for that to the far left as well. The other background model for the central 'Winds' may be the same as appears in *A Spring song* (q.v.) but the male model to the left is not known. Unusually for Wilson, the figures virtually fill the composition, leaving little space for other features. Nevertheless, he still manages to cover the foreground with a typical carpet of flowers, from which 'Summer' has collected a bowl full of petals that she is broadcasting amidst the flurry of activity that surrounds her. The petals are being blown by the Winds frantically all around the composition, while from a table beside her as she kneels, another pot is falling, leaving a trail of somewhat inexplicable 'vapour'. There are many sketches of 'angels' wings' within the remaining sketchbooks, and these are an element that Wilson seems to have enjoyed incorporating into such fantastic compositions.

Some 20 years after George Wilson's death, Ralph Radcliffe Whitehead referred back to this painting when he wrote in a letter to his wife, Jane, that he always 'likened her to summer', because she reminded him somewhat of the central character of 'Summer' in Wilson's painting of *Summer and the Winds*.[228] This purported likeness is not at all evident, however, from a contemporary photograph of Jane Byrd Whitehead.[229]

67   A Spring Song

Date unknown, possibly 1878-83
Watercolour
Size unknown
First exhibited: Aberdeen Art Gallery (Aberdeen Artists' Society),
1893 (562)

Whereabouts unknown

Provenance: Russell Scott (1893; 1903); whereabouts no longer known

This image is a reproduction of No. 6 in the set of phototypes commissioned by the Aberdeen Artists' Society from George Washington Wilson and Co Ltd, following the Aberdeen exhibition of 1893.

This is a charming and – in sharp contrast to *Summer and the Winds* – gently pastoral, but equally powerful Pre-Raphaelite composition. The general style of the composition and the treatment of the central figures with the almost 'incidental' sheep that are only partially included in the design and appear to be simply passing through the picture, indicate that it could be quite an early work, perhaps from the late 1870s to early '80s. In relation to the comparatively bleak background, the foreground is

242

strewn with flowers – as so often in Wilson's figurative works. The sheep are no more than maturing lambs, perhaps used to indicate late springtime without resorting to the distraction that newborn lambs would cause to the composition. These animals are meticulously painted, and show a distinct recollection of the work of Thomas Sidney Cooper (1803-1902). The models for the two singing girls in the painting are not generally seen elsewhere in Wilson's work, although the girl on the left may well be the same model as for the central 'Wind' to the rear of *Summer and the Winds* (q.v.).

John Todhunter remarked in his introduction to the 1903 John Baillie catalogue that Wilson's *studies in drapery are singularly beautiful*, and that view is easily endorsed by this work. Sketches of the drapery for the lower torso of each of the girls are repeated a number of times in the sketchbooks. And in addition to the watercolour sketch drawing *Study for 'A Spring Song'* (q.v.) and the finished painting referred to here, two rather more detailed pages of figure studies in pencil and chalk were included (Nos. 98 and 99) in the Baillie exhibition. One of these chalk studies (reproduced here - see also catalogue raisonné ID095 or ID096) accompanied the *Art Journal* critic Frank Rinder's brief 1903 article about the exhibition.[230] Both studies were loaned by Mr George Haité, who is presumed to be George Charles Haité (1855-1924), the English painter, textile designer and author.

It is not specifically recorded what Wilson was illustrating with this painting, although the two main contenders would both have been from Robert Browning. Browning wrote one of his lesser-known, very short poems (just three verses of three lines each) with the title of *Spring Song*; but the lines carry no immediately obvious relevance to Wilson's composition. The second contender, which we know to have been a favourite not only of Wilson's, but also of his student colleagues, J. B. Yeats and J. T. Nettleship, was the long dramatic poem, *Pippa Passes*. This contains the well-known *Pippa's Song*, which is also equally referred to as *Pippa's Spring Song*, or again, just simply as *Spring Song*. Whether usage of this latter form of the name was widespread in Wilson's time is not clear, but certainly the well-known lines would appear to be somewhat more appropriate to his composition:

> *The year's at the spring*
> *And day's at the morn;*
> *Morning's at seven;*
> *The hill-side's dew-pearled;*
> *The lark's on the wing;*
> *The snail's on the thorn:*
> *God's in his heaven---*
> *All's right with the world!*

The final composition for *A Spring Song* was in the collection of Russell Scott, elder brother of C.P. Scott, the renowned proprietor of the Manchester Guardian. Russell Scott was a good friend to George Wilson and had married his cousin, Jessie Thurburn. Regrettably though, it has not been possible to trace the present-day whereabouts of any of Russell Scott's collection of Wilson's paintings. This is particularly of concern because Scott acted as Wilson's *de facto* executor and took charge of the sorting out of his unsold studio paintings following his death. It is perhaps somewhat invidious – and certainly subjective – to pick out particular missing paintings as being of a greater loss than others, but the taunting images left for us by George Washington Wilson's photographs of both *A Spring Song* and the preceding painting, *Summer and the Winds*, would certainly place them into that category.

68   Study for 'A Spring Song'

Date unknown; possibly 1877-80
Watercolour
Size unknown
First recorded exhibition: John Baillie Gallery, 1903 (19)

Whereabouts unknown

Provenance: Purchased direct from the artist by Dr John Todhunter. Still owned by him in 1903; whereabouts now not known

As already mentioned, there was also exhibited at the Baillie exhibition the comparatively well-resolved watercolour *Study for 'A Spring Song'*. Although this painting was listed at the Baillie exhibition, it was not listed as such in the earlier Aberdeen exhibition. However, there was an otherwise unidentified work listed in Aberdeen under the title of *A Folk Song* (No 596), and it has been suggested that this might well be one and the same, perhaps having been another example of the occasionally casual misnaming of some works at that exhibition.

Regrettably, this painting also follows the continuing unfortunate account of the plethora of lost or missing paintings from Wilson's oeuvre, being yet another work from within the John Todhunter collection that is believed lost.

69   The Wounded Knight

Date unknown, possibly 1876-80
Watercolour
Size unknown
First exhibited: Aberdeen Art Gallery (Aberdeen Artists' Society), 1893 (576)

Whereabouts unknown

Provenance: Charles Wilson (1893; 1903); whereabouts no longer known

This image is a reproduction of No. 8 in the set of phototypes commissioned by the Aberdeen Artists' Society from the George Washington Wilson and Co Ltd, following the Aberdeen exhibition of 1893. In that exhibition, and also in the index to the later phototypes, this painting is entitled *Subject*

Unknown. Although the painting was owned by George Wilson's brother, Charles – the Procurator Fiscal for Aberdeenshire – it is surprising that the correct title was not used in view of John Todhunter's understood involvement with both the Aberdeen exhibition and the commissioning of the phototypes. When shown at the London Baillie exhibition in 1903, the correct title was certainly used.

There is, however, no more information available as to what Wilson was portraying specifically through this painting, although it quite possibly relates to one of the references to the wounded knight in Tennyson's *Idylls of the King*. The title has frequently been painted, but more usually with a 'caring maiden' attending the knight rather than what appears here to be the countenance of death. Perhaps in emulation of Shelley's *Alastor*, this is Wilson's own contribution towards pre-empting his own frail mortality. The overall demeanour of the painting indicates that it was probably painted in the mid to late 1870s.

70   Beech Trees – unfinished (A Beech Wood)

Date unknown
Watercolour
Size unknown
First exhibited: Aberdeen Art Gallery (Aberdeen Artists' Society),
1893 (590)

Whereabouts unknown

Provenance: Russell Scott (1893; 1903); whereabouts no longer known

This image is a reproduction of No. 10[b.] in the set of phototypes commissioned by the Aberdeen Artists' Society from the George Washington Wilson and Co Ltd, following the Aberdeen exhibition of 1893.

This painting is yet another from Russell Scott's missing collection. The watercolour appears to be something of a sister composition to the painting now in the collection of the National Gallery of Scotland in Edinburgh, generally known as *A Fallen Beech* (q.v.) – but originally entitled simply *Trees* for the 1893 Aberdeen exhibition. The date is probably similar too, or may be a year or two later, so is left as unattributed in view of the lack of clarity over the date of *A Fallen Beech*. Both works were illustrated in the George Washington Wilson sets of phototypes on the same sheet as numbers 10[a]. and 10[b] – possibly endorsing their association as a pair. Why *A Beech Wood* was described in 1893 as unfinished is difficult to tell without access to the original painting itself, but by 1903 that qualification had been dropped, which would certainly seem appropriate from the evidence shown here.

The composition was probably painted within the same general location as *A Fallen Beech*, in the beautiful Crannoch beech woods to the east of the town of Cullen. The colouring and general aura of the painting can probably therefore be well gauged largely from the previously reproduced illustration of *A Fallen Beech,* now resident in the National Gallery of Scotland in Edinburgh.

* * *

George Wilson remained the true Scot at heart and was never averse to making maximum use of his materials: After all, every sheet of paper has two sides! So, as will already have been noted from the descriptions throughout this book, one quite often finds interesting sketches, partially resolved to varying degrees, drawn or painted onto the back of his completed watercolour paintings. There also remain a few such works on new paper, at varying stages of completion, and these are of academic interest in demonstrating Wilson's technique in building up his watercolour compositions.

In addition, of course, there still exist the two sketchbooks to which previous reference has often been made. Although it is not possible to date the two sketchbooks accurately, since they appear to cross over to some extent both in subject matter and style, the smaller of the two (both in dimensions and number of pages) would appear generally to be the earlier, and does indeed, contains some quite naïve drawings. This book measures just 6⅛ in x 4⅜ in (156 mm x 110 mm) and contains 86 pages of sketches. The larger book, however, contains 346 pages of sketches and is approximately twice the overall dimensions as well, measuring 8⅛ in x 6½ in (207 mm x 166 mm). In general terms, both of the sketchbooks contain an array of subjects drawn in pencil, ink, charcoal, coloured chalk and occasionally in watercolour. There are botanical drawings in precise detail; figurative ideas and designs; anatomical details; facial expressions that largely appear to be self-modelled, and dozens of versions of minor details that appear to a greater or lesser extent in Wilson's finished works.

To a large extent, both the sketchbooks and Wilson's consistent use of every square inch of available medium as an opportunity to improve continually upon his technique are just one and the same thing. This accords entirely with his lifelong ethos that he painted purely because he loved to do so, and had little interest in the views of critics – unless these were his closest and most reliable friends.

These final comments effectively bring to a close the current body of available material, so far as we know it today. There is undoubtedly more information, and hopefully also there are some missing works hidden 'out there'; and maybe others will either pursue the theme or produce valuable information that could lead to possible future editions. It is certainly hoped so and, as stated at the outset, if a few fortunate owners who find they have previously anonymous 'lost' George Wilson works hanging on their walls can now successfully place Wilson as the artist, then that will be a very great bonus to all concerned. It goes without saying that the author will be very pleased to hear from anyone with a contribution to make – whether large or seemingly small – towards either the betterment or the extension of what has so far been included here about the life, work and associates of George Wilson.

Dr John Todhunter commenced his 1891 article in *The English Illustrated Magazine* about the life and work of George Wilson with the comment that Wilson was only 'known to a small circle as a painter of rare gifts … leaving behind him a considerable amount of very lovely work. *Pictor Ignotus !*' [231] This latter phrase (the 'Unknown Artist') is a direct reference to the poem of the same name by Robert Browning. Taken broadly out of its poetic context, this is an entirely appropriate reference in so many ways. Wilson loved the poetry of Browning, just as he shared with the poet his love of the Italy of Venice and Asolo. Furthermore, the monastic painter of the Renaissance immortalised in the poem suffered the same fate as Wilson of not having his paintings widely admired because he did not bother, or wish (in the poet's case), to submit them to public scrutiny. But there the parallel ends. Browning's painter was grieved by missing the fame that had passed him by because of this reticence; Wilson, however, could not have cared less! And while Browning's painter then retreated further into the shell of his 'repetitive' monastic painting, Wilson's work was anything but repetitive. It always continued to be poetic, visionary, colourful and entirely original to the end.

The Preface to this book set out by saying that it was hoped that by the end of the account, some of the greater depths and attributes of Wilson's character, as well as his work, would have become more important than just simply the overstated unobtrusiveness of his persona. This should now probably be so. Yes; he was certainly a quiet, dedicated and methodical worker, who had a strong and religious disinterest in worldly fame or wealth. He was also, like so many painters, usually left unfulfilled as a perfectionist.

But rather than being the introverted recluse that contemporary documentation tended to repeat, he appears to have made friends readily and easily wherever he landed. He regularly travelled great distances in comparison to all of his closer artist colleagues, and far more frequently than the vast majority of those within the general art circles of the time. The latter may have subsequently produced the greatest and grandest works from their studios, but Wilson never failed to bring a delightfully fresh and vibrant quality to the frequently innovative results of his widespread search for new subjects, perspectives and interpretations, to commit to canvas or paper.

He maintained his devoted adherence (at least to a very large extent) to his earliest Pre-Raphaelite ideals and his persistence in working *en plein air,* so far as this was practicable. This objectivity wavered no further than in response to what he saw and learnt (and was equally prepared to experiment with or develop to his own ends) from those working in the different countries and cultures through which he passed on his travels.

Just maybe, then, if this book can serve to raise the profile of George Wilson, as well as a wider interest in his work, to even a small extent, then he might become, with time, just a bit less the *Pictor Ignotus!*

CHAPTER FOURTEEN

Catalogue Raisonné of the recorded works of George Wilson

This catalogue has been drawn from every source of information currently believed to be available, including: family collections and family archival material; public exhibition lists; public collections; university and other library archive material; published text, and private correspondence.

What will quickly become evident is the sad fact that over half of all George Wilson's *known* paintings are presently believed to be missing. This percentage excludes, of course, all of those other works that he painted or drew and passed on, but were never recorded elsewhere. For instance, we have interior photographic evidence of several unknown apparent works hanging on the walls of Castle Park, Wilson's brother John's house in Huntly. But in other cases (such as the whole Todhunter collection), there is anecdotal evidence of assumed permanent loss due to catastrophe; but without firm evidence of any such fate, we must always reserve some hope of future discoveries. This catalogue, then, is deemed (and hoped) to be no more than a first edition of what may, with luck, develop over time into a much more precise and complete list.

However, there will be significant difficulties attached to the future identification of Wilson's lost works: The principle of these difficulties is that, so far as is presently experienced, George Wilson never, ever, signed (or dated) the face of any of his work. Only very occasionally are there labels appended to the rear stretcher or frame, sometimes in Wilson's own hand, ascribing a title or numbering a work apparently for exhibition. In this respect, there is at least one (or maybe more) incidence of labels – mainly, but not exclusively, attached to larger oil works – bearing a low series of numbers that appear to be intended exhibition numbers. The reason or purpose for these labels is presently not known.

In respect of the works listed below, only those that reside in public collections are identified as such. The remainder, by default, lie in private collections. The first 70 ID numbers (in either bold or standard type) for the works listed below correspond to those reproduced within the previous section of this book. Those images represent the full list of works for which we presently have clear identification and/or good reason to attribute the reproduction of that work to the specific or generic title shown. The first 56 works of these (with ID numbers in **bold** type, and excepting numbers 6, 8, 12 and 17 – which cannot be traced) are all still in existence. From ID 057 to 070 (ID numbers listed in normal standard type) the works listed have been illustrated from other sources or records, but are presently all believed to be missing. Finally, those remaining works with ID numbers listed in *italics* are the remaining works for which we have documentary evidence, but no image available to reproduce.

Self-evidently, and whilst greatest care has been paid to trying to pin down these latter works as accurately as possible, there will always remain some element of doubt as to their identification or possible duplication with other similarly described titles – which are often generic, or at best only broadly descriptive – such as *On the Deveron*. However, every attempt has been made to make clear any such doubt or possible alternatives within these listings. Finally, additional groups of items (such as portfolios and sketchbooks, etc.) are similarly listed and identified as extant or missing, but with the separate series of numbers commencing from ID901.

The author will, of course, be most grateful to receive any corrections and, in particular, any additions to this list for future reference and (hopefully, in due course of time) improved editions.

ID Ref.	Title of picture; Medium; Size	Original owner; of address; [Existing/Lost]	Main Exhibitions (see Note 1)†	Notes; Current public ownership
001	Self portrait drawing [extract from a sketchbook]; Pencil on paper; 8⅛ in x 6½ in (207 mm x 166 mm)	George Wilson's effects; N/A; [Still existing]	None	
002	Study of a Nude Female Figure, Back View; Chalk on paper; 21 in x 10½ in (533 mm x 267 mm)	Mr John Baillie; London; [Still existing]	Not known	V&A Museum
003	Study of a Nude Man, looking down; Chalk on paper; 21¾ in x 14¾ in (554 mm x 375 mm)	Mr John Baillie; London; [Still existing]	Not known	British Museum
004	Two Studies of a Nude Woman; Chalk on paper; 13¼ in x 21¼ in (336 mm x 539 mm)	Mr John Baillie; London; [Still existing]	Not known	British Museum

ID Ref.	Title of picture; Medium; Size	Original owner; of address; [Existing/Lost]	Main Exhibitions (see Note 1)†	Notes; Current public ownership
005	Study of Female Figure carrying a Bowl, with additional studies of Hands; Chalk on paper; 20¼ in x 15¼ in (514 mm x 388 mm)	Mr John Baillie; London; [Still existing]	Not known	V&A Museum
006	Study of a Female Figure clothed in a cloak and hood; Chalk on paper; Not known	Not known - may be Mrs Eliza Thurburn; Keith ?; [Believed lost]	Only illustration to John Baillie exhibition catalogue	May be ID135 [AA(525)] or any one of ID132; ID133; ID134 ID136; [JB(85); JB(86) or JB(87) etc]
007	Study of Head in Red Chalk; Chalk on paper; 13 in x 11 in (330 mm x 279 mm)	Mr Charles Wilson; Aberdeen; [Still existing]	RA(1877/ 296) AA(547) JB(88)	
008	The Quest from Shelley's 'Alastor'; Oil on canvas; Not known	Dr John Todhunter; London; [Believed lost]	RA(1878/ 518) AA(552) JB(8)	
009	Study for 'Alastor'; Pencil and watercolour on paper; 13¾ in x 9¾ in (348 mm x 249 mm)	Mr Charles Wilson; Aberdeen; [Still existing]	AA(573) JB(89) PV(3)	Aberdeen Art Gallery
010	The Song of the Nightingale; Oil on canvas; 24 in x 36¼ in (61 mm x 92 mm)	Mr Charles Wilson; Aberdeen; [Still existing]	WAG(1884/ 259) AA(560) JB(1)	
011	Asia; Oil on canvas; 37½ in x 29¼ in (950 mm x 745 mm)	Mr Halsey Ricardo; London; [Still existing]	AA(561) JB(13)	
012	Study for Shelley's 'Asia'; Chalk on paper; Not known	Dr John Todhunter; London; [Believed lost]	JB(94)	

ID Ref.	Title of picture; Medium; Size	Original owner; of address; [Existing/Lost]	Main Exhibitions (see Note 1)†	Notes; Current public ownership
013	The Rape of Proserpine; Oil on canvas; 30 in x 27 in (760 mm x 685 mm)	Mr Ralph R Whitehead; London; [Still existing]	AA(566) JB(15)	
014	The Spring Witch; Oil on canvas; 42 in x 31½ in (1067 mm x 800 mm)	Mr Ralph R Whitehead; London; [Still existing]	WD(91)	Delaware Art Museum
015	'Portrait of a Very Young Lady'; Gouache on paper laid onto board; 10 in x 7 in (254 mm x 178 mm)	Mr Charles Wilson; Aberdeen; [Still existing]	Not known	
016	The 'Whale's Mouth'; Watercolour on paper; 13½ in x 9½ in (343 mm x 242 mm)	Mr John Wilson; Huntly; [Still existing]	Not known	
017	An Old Oak; Watercolour on paper; Not known	Dr John Todhunter; London; [Believed lost]	AA(548) JB(22)	
018	The Fall of the Leaf; Watercolour on paper; 9¾ in x 13½ in (247 mm x 343 mm)	Mr John Wilson; Huntly; [Still existing]	AA(570) JB(69)	
019	The Huntly Lodge Woods in Summer; Watercolour on paper; 10 in x 14 in (254 mm x 356 mm)	Mr John Wilson; Huntly; [Still existing]	AA(551) JB(67)	
020	Untitled. (Gerty and Walter Wilson on the Sands) [could be 'The Aberdeen Beach'; or 'Sea Beach near Buckie'] Watercolour on paper, laid onto board 10 in x 14 in (253 mm x 355 mm)	Mr John Wilson; Huntly; [Still existing]	Not known	May be ID107 [AA(533) JB(64)]; or ID105 [JB(74)]
021	Trees (A Fallen Beech); Watercolour on paper; 11¼ in x 15¼ in (286 mm x 388 mm)	Dr Anderson; London; [Still existing]	AA(545)	National Gallery of Scotland

ID Ref.	Title of picture; Medium; Size	Original owner; of address; [Existing/Lost]	Main Exhibitions (see Note 1)†	Notes; Current public ownership
022	Old Bridge of Don (The Brig o' Balgownie); Watercolour on paper; 10 in x 15 in (254 mm x 381 mm)	Mr Charles Wilson; Aberdeen; [Still existing]	JB(62)?	JB(62) could alternatively be ID023
023	Old Bridge of Don (The Brig o' Balgownie); Watercolour on paper; 4¾ in x 6⅞ in (120 mm x 175 mm)	Wilson family; Not known; [Still existing]	JB(62)? PV(13)	JB(62) could alternatively be ID022
024	'A Bit' on the Deveron; near Huntly (Scene on the Deveron at Huntly); Watercolour on paper; 9¾ in x 13¾ in (248 mm x 349 mm)	Mrs Eliza Thurburn; Keith; [Still existing]	AA(550) JB(78) PV(15)	
025	On the Deveron; (may be 'Autumn'); Watercolour on paper; 9¾ in x 13¾ in (248 mm x 349 mm)	Mr Charles Wilson; Aberdeen; [Still existing]	AA(543) JB(54)	* see Note 2. below
026	On the Deveron [in portrait]; Watercolour on paper; 13¼ in x 9½ in (337 mm x 241 mm)	Mr Charles Wilson; Aberdeen; [Still existing]	AA(546) JB(55) *	* see Note 2. below
027	On the Deveron; Watercolour on paper; 6¾ in x 13¾ in (172 mm x 349 mm)	Mr Charles Wilson; Aberdeen; [Still existing]	AA(558) JB(56) *	* see Note 2. below
028	Title unknown [possibly on the Deveron]; Watercolour on paper; 9¾ in x 13¾ in (247 mm x 348 mm)	Mr Charles Wilson; Aberdeen; [Still existing]	AA(569) JB(57) *	* see Note 2. below
029	On the Deveron [in portrait]; Watercolour on paper; 13½ in x 9¾ in (343 mm x 248 mm)	Wilson family; Not known; [Still existing]	PV(7) *	* see Note 2. below
030	On the Deveron [in portrait]; Watercolour on paper; 13¾ in x 9¾ in (348 mm x 247 mm)	Mr Charles Wilson; Aberdeen; [Still existing]	Not known *	* see Note 2. below

ID Ref.	Title of picture; Medium; Size	Original owner; of address; [Existing/Lost]	Main Exhibitions (see Note 1)†	Notes; Current public ownership
031	On the Bogie - Clashmach in the distance; Watercolour on paper; 6¾ in x 13¾ in (170 mm x 348 mm)	Mr Charles Wilson; Aberdeen; [Still existing]	AA(585) JB(60) PV(2)	** see Note 3. below; Aberdeen Art Gallery
032	Landscape; Bogie Bridge – Sunset; Watercolour on paper; 6 ½ in x 13½ in (165 mm x 345 mm)	Mr Charles Wilson; Aberdeen; [Still existing]	AA(536) JB(50) PV(4)	Aberdeen Art Gallery
033	Title unknown [probably 'The Bogie at Huntly in Summer']; Watercolour on paper; 9 in x 6⅜ in (228 mm x 162 mm)	Mr John Wilson; Huntly; [Still existing]	AA(556) JB(68)	
034	Title unknown [possibly 'On the Bogie – Huntly in the distance']; Watercolour on paper; 5¼ in x 8¼ in (133 mm x 210 mm)	Mr John Wilson; Huntly; [Still existing]	AA(584)	
035	The Bogie, with Huntly Castle in the distance; Watercolour on paper; 9½ in x 13½ in (242 mm x 343 mm)	Mr John Wilson; Huntly; [Still existing]	AA(583) JB(73) PV(5)	
036	Huntly Castle; Watercolour on paper; 8 in x 13 in (203 mm x 330 mm)	Mr Charles Wilson; Aberdeen; [Still existing]	AA(537) JB(51)	
037	Title unknown [possibly 'Near Nethy Bridge']; Watercolour on paper; 6½ in x 13½ in (165 mm x 343 mm)	Mrs Eliza Thurburn; Keith; [Still existing]	AA(577) JB(82) PV(16)	
038	Unfinished picture of Tree and Cot (Study of Tree and Cottage); Watercolour on paper; 9¼ in x 9¾ in (235 mm x 248 mm)	Mr John Wilson; Huntly; [Still existing]	AA(582) JB(72)	
039	Title unknown [possibly 'The Cairngorms, from Abernethy'] ; Watercolour on paper; 6¾ in x 9¾ in (172 mm x 247 mm)	Mr John Wilson; Huntly; [Still existing]	AA(541) JB(65)	

ID Ref.	Title of picture; Medium; Size	Original owner; of address; [Existing/Lost]	Main Exhibitions (see Note 1)†	Notes; Current public ownership
040	Title unknown [possibly 'Wood near Arundel']; Watercolour on paper; 9¾ in x 13¾ in (247 mm x 349 mm)	Mr Charles Wilson; Aberdeen; [Still existing]	AA(539) JB(53)	
041	View in Arundel Park; Watercolour on paper; 9⅝ in x 13¼ in (245 mm x 337 mm)	Wilson family; Not known; [Still existing]	PV(12)	
042	Title unknown [possibly 'An Opening in the Wood']; Watercolour on paper; 8½ in x 13¾ in (216 mm x 350 mm)	Mrs Eliza Thurburn; Keith; [Still existing]	AA(555) JB(80) PV(11)	
043	A Scene in Italy; Watercolour on paper; 10¼ in x 14¼ in (260 mm x 363 mm)	Mr John Wilson; Huntly; [Still existing]	AA(544) JB(66) PV(10)	
044	Title unknown [Probably in north Italy]; Watercolour on paper; 6 in x 10 in (152 mm x 254 mm)	Mr Halsey Ricardo; London; [Still existing]	Not known	
045	Venice; Watercolour on paper; 3¾ in x 7½ in (95 mm x 190 mm)	Mr Charles Wilson; Aberdeen; [Still existing]	AA(535) JB(49) PV(9)	
046	A View in Algiers; Watercolour on paper; 7⅛ in x 13½ in (180 mm x 343 mm)	Mr John Wilson; Huntly; [Still existing]	AA(578) JB(70) PV(8)	
047	Title unknown [On the Moray Coast, Banffshire; or could be 'Aberdeen Sands'; or 'The Aberdeen Beach'; or 'Sea Beach near Buckie']; Watercolour on paper; 4 in x 8⅝ in (100 mm x 220 mm)	Wilson family; Not known; [Still existing]	PV(6)	May be ID087 [AA(529) JB(48)]; or ID107 [AA(533) JB(64)]; or ID105 [JB(74)]

ID Ref.	Title of picture; Medium; Size	Original owner; of address; [Existing/Lost]	Main Exhibitions (see Note 1)†	Notes; Current public ownership
048	On the Shore at Ianstown; Watercolour on paper; 9½ in x 13¾ in (242 mm x 350 mm)	Mrs Eliza Thurburn; Keith; [Still existing]	AA(571) JB(81) PV(14)	
049	On the Moray Coast; Banffshire; Watercolour on paper; 6 in x 10 in (152 mm x 254 mm)	Mr Halsey Ricardo; London; [Still existing]	Not known	
050	Title unknown [believed to be on the Moray Coast, near Cullen Bay]; Watercolour on paper; 6¾ in x 9¾ in (170 mm x 247 mm)	Wilson family; Not known; [Still existing]	None	
051	Title unknown (may be on the Moray Coast, Banffshire, or the sands near Aberdeen; Watercolour on paper; 6¾ in x 9¾ in (170 mm x 246 mm)	Wilson family; Not known; [Still existing]	None	
052	Study of cloud formation [recto to 054] Watercolour on paper; 3⅜ in x 5 in (87 mm x 126 mm)	George Wilson's effects; N/A; [Still existing]	PV(17)	
053	Study for Letterfourie Bridge [extract from sketchbook]; Watercolour on paper; 4⅜ in x 6¼ in (110 mm x 160 mm)	George Wilson's effects; N/A; [Still existing]	None	
054	A river landscape [verso to 052]; Watercolour on paper; 5 in x 3⅜ in (126 mm x 87 mm)	George Wilson's effects; N/A; [Still existing]	None	
055	Subject unknown [a wooded landscape]; Watercolour on paper; 5⅜ in x 10⅜ in (138 mm x 265 mm)	George Wilson's effects; N/A; [Still existing]	None	
056	Subject unknown [possibly in Algiers or Italy]; Watercolour on paper; 7½ in x 13⅞ in (190 mm x 351 mm)	George Wilson's effects; N/A; [Still existing]	None	

ID Ref.	Title of picture; Medium; Size	Original owner; of address; [Existing/Lost]	Main Exhibitions (see Note 1)†	Notes; Current public ownership
057	A Bacchante; Chalk on paper; Not known	Dr John Todhunter; London; [Believed lost]	DG(1877/no nr.) AA(534) JB(93)	
058	Head of Knight in 'La Belle Dame sans Merci'; Chalk on paper; Not known	Dr John Todhunter; London; [Believed lost]	AA(527) JB(95)	
059	Title unknown [possibly 'The Sons of God saw the Daughters of Men that they were fair']; Watercolour on paper; Not known	Dr John Todhunter; London; [Believed lost]	AA(586) JB(21)	
060	Title unknown [believed to be 'Caritas']; Watercolour on paper; Not known	Dr John Todhunter; London; [Believed lost]	AA(549) JB(18)	
061	Title unknown [believed to be 'Eve's Last Look at Paradise']; Watercolour on paper; Not known	Dr John Todhunter; London; [Believed lost]	JB(17)	
062	Landscape near Harting, Sussex; Tempera; Not known	Mr Halsey Ricardo; London; [Believed lost]	JB(83)	
063	'The Dance'; Study for the unfinished picture 'Arcadia'; Watercolour on paper; Not known	Mr Russell Scott; London; [Believed lost]	AA(568) JB(40)	
064	The Moray Firth on the Banffshire Coast; Watercolour on paper; Not known	Mr John Wilson; Huntly; [Believed lost]	AA(581) JB(71)	
065	Scotch Firs, near Huntly (Pines and Rocks at Huntley); Watercolour on paper; Not known	Mr(s) E Nettleship; London; [Believed lost]	AA(572) JB(31)	

258

ID Ref.	Title of picture; Medium; Size	Original owner; of address; [Existing/Lost]	Main Exhibitions (see Note 1)[†]	Notes; Current public ownership
066	Summer and the Winds; Tempera; Not known	Mr Herbert H Young; London; [Believed lost]	RI(1884/92 ill.) AA(553) JB(14)	
067	A Spring Song; Watercolour on paper; Not known	Mr Russell Scott; London; [Believed lost]	AA(562) JB(38)	
068	Study for 'A Spring Song'; Watercolour on paper; Not known	Dr John Todhunter; London; [Believed lost]	JB(19)	May be ID072 [AA(596)]
069	The Wounded Knight; Watercolour on paper; Not known	Mr Charles Wilson; Aberdeen; [Believed lost]	AA(576) JB(59)	
070	Beech Trees – unfinished; Watercolour on paper; Not known	Mr Russell Scott; London; [Believed lost]	AA(590) JB(39)	
071	A Chestnut Wood in Spring; Italy; Watercolour on paper; Not known	Dr John Todhunter; London; [Believed lost]	JB(24)	
072	A Folk-Song; Watercolour on paper; Not known	Dr John Todhunter; London; [Believed lost]	AA(596)	May be ID068 [JB(19)]
073	An Apple Orchard in Spring; Watercolour on paper; Not known	Dr John Todhunter; London; [Believed lost]	AA(532) JB(26)	
074	An Autumn Evening; Watercolour on paper; Not known	Dr John Todhunter; London; [Believed lost]	JB(27)	May be ID076 [AA(528)]

ID Ref.	Title of picture; Medium; Size	Original owner; of address; [Existing/Lost]	Main Exhibitions (see Note 1)[†]	Notes; Current public ownership
075	Early Spring; Watercolour on paper; Not known	Dr John Todhunter; London; [Believed lost]	JB(25)	
076	Evening; Watercolour on paper; Not known	Dr John Todhunter; London; [Believed lost]	AA(528)	May be ID074 [JB(27) or ID076 [JB(23)]
077	Evening (Moray Firth); Watercolour on paper; Not known	Dr John Todhunter; London; [Believed lost]	JB(23)	May be ID076 [AA(528)]
078	Girl with Grapes (a Study); Oil on canvas; Not known	Dr John Todhunter; London; [Believed lost]	JB(10)	
079	Landscape in Sussex; Oil on canvas; Not known	Dr John Todhunter; London; [Believed lost]	JB(9)	
080	Landscape study, Arundel; Watercolour on paper; Not known	Dr John Todhunter; London; [Believed lost]	JB(20)	
081	Study for 'The West Wind'; [presumably for 'Summer and the Winds'] Chalk on paper; Not known	Dr John Todhunter; London; [Believed lost]	JB(96)	
082	Study of a Woman's Head; Chalk on paper; Not known	Dr John Todhunter; London; [Believed lost]	JB(97)	
083	The Lovers' Moon; Watercolour on paper; Not known	Dr John Todhunter; London; [Believed lost]	AA(589) JB(28)	

ID Ref.	Title of picture; Medium; Size	Original owner; of address; [Existing/Lost]	Main Exhibitions (see Note 1)†	Notes; Current public ownership
084	The Old Castle of Huntly; Not known; Not known	Dr Thomas Barlow; London; [Believed lost]	AA(588)	
085	A Landscape; Oil on canvas; Not known	Mr Charles Wilson; Aberdeen; [Believed lost]	JB(3)	May be ID089 [AA(564)]
086	A Wood; Watercolour on paper; Not known	Mr Charles Wilson; Aberdeen; [Believed lost]	JB(61)	May be ID090 [AA(563)]
087	Aberdeen Sands; Watercolour on paper; Not known	Mr Charles Wilson; Aberdeen; [Believed lost]	AA(529) JB(48)	May be ID047 [PV(6)]
088	Cullen Bay, from Portknockie; Watercolour on paper; Not known	Mr Charles Wilson; Aberdeen; [Believed lost]	AA(574) JB(58)	
089	English Landscape; Not known; Not known	Mr Charles Wilson; Aberdeen; [Believed lost]	AA(564)	May be ID085 [JB(3)]
090	English Wood; Not known; Not known	Mr Charles Wilson; Aberdeen; [Believed lost]	AA(563)	May be ID086 [JB(61)]
091	Figure, black chalk; Chalk on paper; Not known	Mr Charles Wilson; Aberdeen; [Believed lost]	JB(90)	
092	Italian Lake Scene; Watercolour on paper; Not known	Mr Charles Wilson; Aberdeen; [Believed lost]	AA(538) JB(52)	

ID Ref.	Title of picture; Medium; Size	Original owner; of address; [Existing/Lost]	Main Exhibitions (see Note 1)[†]	Notes; Current public ownership
093	The Siren; Oil on canvas; Not known	Mr Charles Wilson; Aberdeen; [Believed lost]	JB(2)	
094	Twilight; Oil on canvas; Not known	Mr Charles Wilson; Aberdeen; [Believed lost]	AA(567) JB(4)	
095	Study for 'A Spring Song'; Chalk on paper; Not known	Mr George Haité; London; [Believed lost]	JB(98)	
096	Study for 'A Spring Song'; Chalk on paper; Not known	Mr George Haité; London; [Believed lost]	JB(99)	
097	Study; Chalk on paper; Not known	Mr George Haité; London; [Believed lost]	JB(100)	
098	Arcadia; Oil on canvas; Not known	Mr Herbert H Young; London; [Believed lost]	GG(1883-84 /no nr.) JB(5)	
099	Eros; Oil on canvas; Not known	Mr Herbert H Young; London; [Believed lost]	JB(6)	
100	Bridge at Letterfourie; Watercolour on paper; Not known	Mr James Wilson; Buckie; [Believed lost]	AA(557) JB(63)	
101	Boy in Red Chalk; Chalk on paper; Not known	Mr John Wilson; Huntly; [Believed lost]	AA(594)	

ID Ref.	Title of picture; Medium; Size	Original owner; of address; [Existing/Lost]	Main Exhibitions (see Note 1)†	Notes; Current public ownership
102	Copy from a painting in the Academy of Venice; Not known; Not known	Mr John Wilson; Huntly; [Believed lost]	AA(587)	
103	Head of Italian Boy; Not known; Not known	Mr John Wilson; Huntly; [Believed lost]	AA(593)	
104	Port Long; Cullen; Watercolour on paper; Not known	Mr John Wilson; Huntly; [Believed lost]	AA(591) JB(75)	
105	Sea Beach near Buckie; Watercolour on paper; Not known	Mr John Wilson; Huntly; [Believed lost]	JB(74)	
106	Study of Head; Not known; Not known	Mr John Wilson; Huntly; [Believed lost]	AA(595)	
107	The Aberdeen Beach; Watercolour on paper; Not known	Mr John Wilson; Huntly; [Believed lost]	AA(533) JB(64)	May be ID047 [PV(6)]
108	A Study; Chalk on paper; Not known	Mr Russell Scott; London; [Believed lost]	JB(91)	
109	Castle Park, Huntly; Watercolour on paper; Not known	Mr Russell Scott; London; [Believed lost]	AA(592)	May (in title error) be ID112 [JB(43)]
110	Evening at Cullen; Watercolour on paper; Not known	Mr Russell Scott; London; [Believed lost]	JB(47)	

ID Ref.	Title of picture; Medium; Size	Original owner; of address; [Existing/Lost]	Main Exhibitions (see Note 1)†	Notes; Current public ownership
111	Evening Shades; Oil on canvas; Not known	Mr Russell Scott; London; [Believed lost]	AA(565) JB(12)	
112	Huntly Castle; Watercolour on paper; Not known	Mr Russell Scott; London; [Believed lost]	JB(43)	May (in title error) be ID109 [AA(592)]
113	Pond; Velby Bridge; Watercolour on paper; Not known	Mr Russell Scott; London; [Believed lost]	JB(45)	
114	Poppy Field at Algiers; Watercolour on paper; Not known	Mr Russell Scott; London; [Believed lost]	JB(44)	
115	Sunset; Oil on canvas; Not known	Mr Russell Scott; London; [Believed lost]	AA(559) JB(11)	
116	The Tyrol; Watercolour on paper; Not known	Mr Russell Scott; London; [Believed lost]	JB(46)	
117	Venice at Night; Watercolour on paper; Not known	Mr Russell Scott; London; [Believed lost]	JB(42)	
118	Venice from the Lido; Watercolour on paper; Not known	Mr Russell Scott; London; [Believed lost]	JB(41)	
119	A Hollow on the Downs near Arundel; Watercolour on paper; Not known	Mr(s) E Nettleship; London; [Believed lost]	AA(530) JB(29)	

ID Ref.	Title of picture; Medium; Size	Original owner; of address; [Existing/Lost]	Main Exhibitions (see Note 1)[†]	Notes; Current public ownership
120	Pond in Borden Wood, Hampshire; Watercolour on paper; Not known	Mr(s) E Nettleship; London; [Believed lost]	AA(575) JB(30)	
121	Sketch of Venice; Watercolour on paper; Not known	Mr(s) E Nettleship; London; [Believed lost]	AA(531) JB(32/33)	Title is *'Venice'* for both JB(32) and JB(33), so could be either
122	Venice; Watercolour on paper; Not known	Mr(s) E Nettleship; London; [Believed lost]	AA(579) JB(32/33)	Title is *'Venice'* for both JB(32) and JB(33), so could be either
123	An Apple Orchard; Oil on canvas; Not known	Mrs E Nettleship; London; [Believed lost]	JB(7)	
124	In Asolo; Watercolour on paper; Not known	Mrs E Nettleship; London; [Believed lost]	JB(34)	
125	In San Giminiano; Watercolour on paper; Not known	Mrs E Nettleship; London; [Believed lost]	JB(37)	
126	In Siena; Watercolour on paper; Not known	Mrs E Nettleship; London; [Believed lost]	JB(35)	
127	In Siena; Watercolour on paper; Not known	Mrs E Nettleship; London; [Believed lost]	JB(36)	

ID Ref.	Title of picture; Medium; Size	Original owner; of address; [Existing/Lost]	Main Exhibitions (see Note 1)†	Notes; Current public ownership
128	The Late Mrs H J Nettleship (portrait); Chalk on paper; Not known	Mrs E Nettleship; London; [Believed lost]	JB(92)	
129	A Study of Ferns; Not known; Not known	Mrs Eliza Thurburn; Keith; [Believed lost]	AA(580)	
130	A Summer Day in Surrey; Watercolour on paper; Not known	Mrs Eliza Thurburn; Keith; [Believed lost]	AA(554) JB(79)	
131	A Winter Scene; Watercolour on paper; Not known	Mrs Eliza Thurburn; Keith; [Believed lost]	AA(540) JB(76)	
132	Chalk Study; Chalk on paper; Not known	Mrs Eliza Thurburn; Keith; [Believed lost]	JB(85)	May be ID006; or also any one of ID135, ID136 or ID137 [AA(525), AA(526) or AA(597)]
133	Chalk Study; Chalk on paper; Not known	Mrs Eliza Thurburn; Keith; [Believed lost]	JB(86)	May be ID006; or also any one of ID135, ID136 or ID137 [AA(525), AA(526) or AA(597)]

ID Ref.	Title of picture; Medium; Size	Original owner; of address; [Existing/Lost]	Main Exhibitions (see Note 1)†	Notes; Current public ownership
134	Chalk Study; Chalk on paper; Not known	Mrs Eliza Thurburn; Keith; [Believed lost]	JB(87)	May be ID006; or also any one of ID135, ID136 or ID137 [AA(525), AA(526) or AA(597)]
135	Figure of a Woman in Chalk; Chalk on paper; Not known	Mrs Eliza Thurburn; Keith; [Believed lost]	AA(525) JB(85/86 /87)	May be ID006; and also any one of ID132, ID133 or ID134 [JB(85), JB(86) or JB(87)]
136	Study in Chalk; Chalk on paper; Not known	Mrs Eliza Thurburn; Keith; [Believed lost]	AA(526) JB(85/86 /87)	May be ID006; and also any one of ID132, ID133 or ID134 [JB(85), JB(86) or JB(87)]
137	Study of a Child's Head; Chalk on paper; Not known	Mrs Eliza Thurburn; Keith; [Believed lost]	AA(597) JB(85/86 /87)	May be any one of ID132, ID133 or ID134 [JB(85), JB(86) or JB(87)]
138	Sunset; Watercolour on paper; Not known	Mrs Eliza Thurburn; Keith; [Believed lost]	AA(542) JB(77)	
139	A Portrait (unfinished); Oil on canvas; Not known	Mrs J T Nettleship; London; [Believed lost]	JB(16)	

ID Ref.	Title of picture; Medium; Size	Original owner; of address; [Existing/Lost]	Main Exhibitions (see Note 1)[†]	Notes; Current public ownership
140	On Hampstead Heath; Watercolour on paper; Not known	Mrs J T Nettleship; London; [Believed lost]	JB(84)	
141	'Arise; thou that sleepest'; Watercolour on paper; Not known	Not known; Not known; [Believed lost]	DG(1879/ no nr.)	
142	On the Banffshire Coast; Watercolour on paper; Not known	Not known; Not known; Not known	RGI(1882/ 905)	May be ID064 [AA(581) JB(71)] (or another Moray Coast subject)
143	'The Lost Paradise'; Watercolour on paper; Not known	Not known; Not known; [Believed lost]	RI(1885/ 336)	
901	Sketchbook – 'small' (86 pages); various; 6¼ in x 4⅜ in (156 mm x 110 mm)	George Wilson's effects; N/A; [Still existing]	PV(18)	
902	Sketchbook – 'large' (346 pages); Various; 8⅛ in x 6½ in (207 mm x 166 mm)	George Wilson's effects; N/A; [Still existing]	PV(19)	
903	Sketch of Halsey Ricardo; Pencil on paper; 6½ in x 4½ in overall – irregular	Mr Halsey Ricardo; London; [Still existing]	none	
904	Collection of studies and drawings etc; Various; Various	George Wilson's effects; N/A; [Still existing]	PV (a selection from)	
905	Portfolio of drawings; Not known; Not known	Dr Thomas Barlow; London; [Believed lost]	Not known	Recorded in the Barlow papers; now untraceable

NOTES:

1: † AA = Aberdeen Art Gallery (1893); JB = John Baillie Gallery (1903); PV = 'Poetic Vision' (Aberdeen Art Gallery – 1990); DG = Dudley Gallery; GG = Grosvenor Gallery; RA = Royal Academy; RGI = Royal Glasgow Institute; RI = Royal Institute of Painters in Watercolour; WAG = Walker Art Gallery; WD = 'Waking Dreams' (touring exhibition of the Delaware Art Museum – 2005/2006).

2: * Four paintings entitled simply *On the Deveron* were exhibited by Charles Wilson at the Aberdeen exhibition; however, at the Baillie exhibition his four *Deveron* paintings bore slight variations to that title (see individual exhibitions lists). There remain six probable but unascribed *Deveron* paintings in existence in Wilson Family descent, so it is impossible to ascribe any one of these paintings to specific exhibits; the numbering proposed is therefore no more than an unqualified suggestion.

3: ** In addition to this watercolour drawing, a second small oil landscape in the collection of the Aberdeen Art Gallery that has previously been ascribed to George Wilson, with the exactly duplicated title of *On the Bogie - Clashmach* [sic] *in the distance,* has presently been omitted from this catalogue, as both the title and the attribution to George Wilson appear to be doubtful.

4: ID numbers in **bold** standard lettering identify works that are still in existence. Those IDs listed in normal standard lettering are presently presumed lost – although there are images available for identification. Those IDs listed in *italics* are works that are both presumed lost and for which no confirmed image is presently known to have survived. These latter two groups presently include (apart from numerous Wilson family owned titles) all those works that were originally owned by Russell Scott; the various Nettleship bothers and, most importantly, John Todhunter's collection of at least 20 works that have been reported, anecdotally, to have been destroyed in a fire.

5: As recorded in the main text, W.B Yeats refers to his two sisters as having been in possession of a number of Wilson's (mainly) woodland landscapes. These works appear no longer to be within the descent of the Yeats family, so the precise number of works, and the subjects involved, is no longer known and they are presently presumed lost.

6: The Aberdeen Free Press in February 1893 reported on the opening of the Aberdeen Art Gallery's annual exhibition that included 73 of Wilson's works. In that report it mentioned that, *...among the purchasers of pictures have been the Marquis of Huntly* [who had formally opened the exhibition], *Mr Ogston of Ardoe, Mr James Ogston of Norwood, and Mr Wilson of Albyn Terrace.* Although this remark was attached to the report on Wilson's exhibits, the overall press report referred elsewhere to the whole exhibition, so there is some ambiguity as to whether these bought works were by Wilson or perhaps by others exhibiting. It is also difficult to imagine which works of Wilson's might have been offered for sale, since most owners appear to have guarded them somewhat jealousy.

7: Hugh Wilson, the youngest of George Wilson's several brothers, was also a keen collector of his brother's work. Hugh Wilson emigrated to Melbourne, Australia, in 1877 to found the Royal Bank of Australia, and it is known that he took a collection of his brother's paintings out to Australia with him. None of these paintings returned to the UK following his death in 1933, and there is presently no evidence as to how, or to whom, they were dispersed.

8: There is contemporary photographic evidence of the interior of George Wilson's brother John's house, Castle Park in Huntly, showing a number of presently unidentified (and presumably also presently lost) paintings and drawings.

Chronology of events in the life of George Wilson

(Relevant events referring to Wilson's immediate colleagues are shown in italics)

Year	Date	Event	Recorded Address
1839	*16 March*	*John Butler Yeats born*	*Tullylish, Lawrencetown, Co Down*
1839	*30 December*	*John Todhunter born*	*Dublin*
1841	*11 February*	*John Trivett Nettleship born*	*Kettering, Northamptonshire*
1848	*Not known*	*Edwin John Ellis born*	*Not known*
1848	**18 November**	**George Wilson born** (although the date inferred in the Cullen Old Parochial Register and the General Register Office for Scotland (believed erroneously) as being18[th] December 1848)	Tochieneal, Nr. Cullen, Banffshire
not	recorded	Educated at the Parish School in Cullen	Tochieneal
not	recorded	Educated at the Gymnasium, Old Aberdeen	Tochieneal
1865	November	Entered Edinburgh University (3 years to mid 1868)	Not known, 'in lodgings'
1867	*mid*	*J B Yeats enrolled at Heatherley's*	*23, Fitzroy Rd., London N.*
1868	July ?	Left Edinburgh University	Tochieneal
1868	Late Summer	Went to London, aged 19.	Wilson's first address in London is not known, but he possibly stayed initially with his cousin Jessie Scott, at 1, The Chestnuts, Branch Hill, Hampstead
1868	Specific date not recorded	Entered Thomas Heatherley's School of Fine Art, 79, Newman Street, London W.	Not known
1868	*October*	*J B Yeats and Edwin Ellis take a studio in Newman St (near to J T Nettleship's) – given up as too expensive by June 1869*	*74, Newman St., London W.*

Chronology of events in the life of George Wilson

Year	Date	Event	Recorded Address
1869	*Mid*	*'The Brotherhood' first emerged and developed at Heatherley's (initially without George Wilson)*	
1869	Late	George Wilson Replaced Sydney Hall as fourth member of 'The Brotherhood'	Not known
1870	*28 July*	*J T Nettleship entered RA as a Probationer*	*22, Newman St.*
1871	*January*	*J B Yeats exhibited 'Pippa Passes' at the Dudley*	*23, Fitzroy Rd.*
1871	17 July	Entered RA as a Probationer (recommended by Thomas Heatherley).	3, Well Road, Hampstead
1871	*After March*	*J B Yeats entered RA (aged 32)*	*23, Fitzroy Rd.*
1872	1 May	Entered the Slade School under E. J. Poynter	3, Well Road, Hampstead
1872	*1 May*	*J B Yeats and J T Nettleship entered Slade School*	*23, Fitzroy Rd. and unknown*
1872	*23 July*	*Yeats family left London for Sligo*	
	Autumn	*J B Yeats returned to London 'to sublet house'*	*23, Fitzroy Rd.*
1872	Autumn	Went to live with J B Yeats	23, Fitzroy Rd.
1872 – 1873	Autumn – spring	'At home' design competition gatherings with Johnston Forbes-Robertson including 'Brotherhood' members and others	Not known
1873	April	Went to Ireland with J B Yeats	Dublin & Sligo
1873	July	Left the Slade School	23, Fitzroy Rd.
1873	July	Moved out of 23 Fitzroy Rd. as lease ended	23, Fitzroy Rd.
ca 1873 – 1875		Reported to have spent two years studying and working in Rome after leaving the Slade	Not known
1874	*Summer*	*J T Nettleship first exhibited at RA (from same address that George Wilson used in 1877 – not known if the studio was shared before the latter date)*	*233, Stanhope St., NW*
1876	*April*	*J T Nettleship married Ada Cort Hinton*	*233, Stanhope St., NW*
1877	Summer	First Exhibited *Study of a Head* at the Royal Academy	233, Stanhope St., NW

<u>Year</u>	<u>Date</u>	<u>Event</u>	<u>Recorded Address</u>
1877	July	'Designing Club formed by Wilson, Nettleship, Ellis and others', similar to before, plus Robert Catterson Smith	Not known where held
1877		Exhibited *A Bacchante* at Dudley Gallery	233, Stanhope St., NW
1878	Summer	Exhibited *Alastor* at the Royal Academy	233, Stanhope St., NW
1879		Exhibited *Arise thou that sleepest!* at the Dudley Gallery	233, Stanhope St., NW
1880 – 1889	From approx	Visited Italy on painting trips, believed annually, usually for several weeks or months	
1880 – 1881	*October – March*	*J T Nettleship commissioned by the Gaekwar of Baroda to paint in India*	*c/o F. A. H. Elliott, Baroda*
1882		Exhibited *On the Banffshire Coast* at the Royal Glasgow Institute of the Fine Arts	c/o James MacClure, Glasgow
1883		Exhibited *Arcadia* at the Grosvenor Gallery	65, Newman St., W
1884		Exhibited *Summer and the Winds* at the RI (illustrated in the catalogue)	65, Newman St., W
1884		Exhibited *The Nightingale* at the Walker Art Gallery, Liverpool	65, Newman St., W
1885	May	Visited Algiers	
1885		Exhibited *The Lost Paradise* at the RI	1, The Mall, Park Road, NW
1889	Easter for 6 weeks	Last visit to Italy, with Edward Nettleship and two others – one presumed to be Nettleship's wife, whilst the other was Miss Caroline Peters	Via Florence to Asolo
1889	Late summer	Visited Scotland, presumably staying with his brother, John. George Wilson probably never returned to England as his health failed thereafter	Castle Park, Huntly, Aberdeenshire
1890	**April 1**	**George Wilson died.** His death certificate stated the cause as having been 'stricture and ulceration of the pylorus' – a problem he had lived with all his life	Castle Park, Huntly, Aberdeenshire
1890	April 5	Funeral at Fordyce from Castle Park via Portsoy Station	Fordyce Churchyard, Banffshire

Chronology of events in the life of George Wilson

Year	Date	Event	Recorded Address
1893	February	'Wilson Collection' - a retrospective exhibition of 73 works by George Wilson, as part of the Aberdeen Artists' Society's Annual Exhibition	Aberdeen Art Gallery
1893	November	Publication of 'Ten Phototypes of the Works of George Wilson exhibited at the Aberdeen Artists' Society's Exhibition 1893' by George Washington Wilson & Co. Ltd. in a limited edition of 100 sets	Aberdeen
1902	*31 August*	*John Trivett Nettleship died*	*58, Wigmore Street, London*
1903	October	Retrospective 'Neglected Artist' exhibition of 100 works by George Wilson	John Baillie Gallery, London
1908		Scottish National Exhibition, *The Song of the Nightingale* exhibited	Edinburgh
1911		Scottish National Exhibition, *The Song of the Nightingale* exhibited	Glasgow
1916	*25 October*	*Dr John Todhunter died*	*Bedford Park, London*
1916	*November*	*Edwin John Ellis died*	*Seeheim, Germany*
1922	*3 February*	*John Butler Yeats died*	*New York City, USA*
1979		*A Fallen Beech* included in 'Scottish Watercolours and Other Drawings – The Helen Barlow Bequest' – exhibition at the National Gallery of Scotland	Edinburgh
1990	9 April – 7 June	'Poetic Vision' – an exhibition of 21 paintings and related items at Aberdeen Art Gallery on the Centenary of Wilson's death	Aberdeen Art Gallery
2004 – 2005		*A Fallen Beech* toured with the exhibition of Scottish landscape drawing entitled 'A Picturesque Pursuit: Scottish Landscape Drawings from the National Gallery of Scotland' at the Robert Fleming Gallery in London, followed by its home gallery in Edinburgh where the exhibition was renamed 'A Journey Through Scotland', then finally on to the Richard Feigen Gallery in New York.	London Edinburgh New York
2005	25 June – 4 September	*The Spring Witch* exhibited in 'Waking Dreams – The Art of the Pre-Raphaelites from the Delaware Art Museum' – as part of a two-year (2005-07) touring exhibition to eight states within the USA, and one European location, at the Castle Museum in Nottingham.	Castle Museum, Nottingham.

APPENDIX 2

List of Works shown at the Aberdeen Artists' Society Exhibition, 1893
held at Aberdeen Art Gallery

The following list is a transcript of the catalogue of 73 paintings that were exhibited at the Aberdeen exhibition of 1893, cross-referenced to the John Baillie exhibition of 1903. The titles and owners are exactly as described in the 1893 catalogue. The cross-references are, in some cases, evident, but in a few cases can only be surmised – including alternatives where there is some doubt. It has to be recognised that Wilson seldom gave titles to his paintings, so those that are recorded at exhibition are often likely to be generic descriptions applied by John Todhunter and others at the time. Such descriptions were even then not always correctly transcribed – as will be noted. Occasionally, there are titles for which not even a conjectural connection with another exhibition title is possible. The final column relates to the relevant reproductions included in this publication. These are only ascribed where the correct title is either known for sure or, occasionally, where there is no recognised alternative.

ABERDEEN ART GALLERY
GALLERY No. III.
WILSON COLLECTION
(Pictures by the late George Wilson Esq

No	Description	Medium	Lent by	of	Baillie 1903 ref	Cat. ID
525	Figure of a Woman in Chalk	chalk	Mrs Thurburn	Keith	JB 85, 86, 87	135 or 006?
526	A Study in Chalk	chalk	Mrs Thurburn	Keith	JB 85, 86, 87	136
527	Head of Knight in 'La Belle Dame sans Merci'	chalk	J Todhunter Esq	London	JB 95	058
528	Evening	watercolour	J Todhunter Esq	London	JB 23 or JB 25?	076
529	Aberdeen Sands	watercolour	Charles Wilson Esq	Aberdeen	JB 48	087
530	On the Downs near Arundel	watercolour	E Nettleship Esq	London	JB 29	119
531	Sketch of Venice	watercolour	E Nettleship Esq	London	JB 32, 33	121
532	An Orchard in Spring	watercolour	J Todhunter Esq	London	JB 26	073

No	Description	Medium	Lent by	of	*Baillie 1903 ref*	*Cat. ID*
533	The Aberdeen Beach	watercolour	John Wilson Esq	Huntly	*JB 64*	*107*
534	A Young Bacchante	chalk	J Todhunter Esq	London	*JB 93*	*057*
535	Venice	watercolour	Charles Wilson Esq	Aberdeen	*JB 49*	*045*
536	Landscape, Bogie Bridge – Sunset	watercolour	Charles Wilson Esq	Aberdeen	*JB 50*	*032*
537	Huntly Castle	watercolour	Charles Wilson Esq	Aberdeen	*JB 51*	*036*
538	Italian Lake Scene	watercolour	Charles Wilson Esq	Aberdeen	*JB 52*	*092*
539	Wood near Arundel	watercolour	Charles Wilson Esq	Aberdeen	*JB 53*	*040 ?*
540	A Winter Scene	watercolour	Mrs Thurburn	Keith	*JB 76*	*131*
541	The Cairngorms, from Abernethy	watercolour	John Wilson Esq	Huntly	*JB 65*	*039 ?*
542	Sunset	watercolour	Mrs Thurburn	Keith	*JB 77*	*138*
543	On the Deveron	watercolour	Charles Wilson Esq	Aberdeen	*JB 54, 55, 56, 57*	*025, 026, 027, 028, 029 or 030*
544	A Scene in Italy	watercolour	John Wilson Esq	Huntly	*JB 66*	*043*
545	Trees (*A Fallen Beech)*	watercolour	Dr Anderson	London		*021*
546	On the Deveron	watercolour	Charles Wilson Esq	Aberdeen	*JB 54, 55, 56, 57*	*025, 026, 027, 028, 029 or 030*
547	Drawing of a Head in Red Chalk	chalk	Charles Wilson Esq	Aberdeen	*JB 88*	*007*
548	An Old Oak	watercolour	J Todhunter Esq	London	*JB 22*	*017*
549	Caritas	watercolour	J Todhunter Esq	London	*JB 18*	*060 ?*
550	'A Bit' on the Deveron, near Huntly	watercolour	Mrs Thurburn	Keith	*JB 78*	*024*
551	The Huntly Lodge Woods in Summer	watercolour	John Wilson Esq	Huntly	*JB 67*	*019*
552	Alastor	oil	J Todhunter Esq	London	*JB 8*	*008*
553	Summer in the Winds	tempera	H H Young Esq	London	*JB 14*	*066*
554	A Summer Day in Surrey	watercolour	Mrs Thurburn	Keith	*JB 79*	*130*
555	An Opening in the Wood	watercolour	Mrs Thurburn	Keith	*JB 80*	*042 ?*

No	Description	Medium	Lent by	of	Baillie 1903 ref	Cat. ID
556	The Bogie at Huntly in Summer	watercolour	John Wilson Esq	Huntly	JB 68	033 ?
557	Bridge at Letterfourie	watercolour	James Wilson Esq	Inchgower	JB 63	100
558	On the Deveron	watercolour	Charles Wilson Esq	Aberdeen	JB 54, 55, 56, 57	025, 026, 027, 028, 029 or 030
559	Sunset	oil	Russell Scott Esq	London	JB 11	115
560	Subject unknown [The Song of the Nightingale]	oil	Charles Wilson Esq	Aberdeen	JB 1	010
561	Asia	oil	Halsey Ricardo Esq	London	JB 13	011
562	A Spring Song	watercolour	Russell Scott Esq	London	JB 38	067
563	An English Wood	watercolour	Charles Wilson Esq	Aberdeen	JB 61 ?	090
564	English Landscape	oil	Charles Wilson Esq	Aberdeen	JB 3 ?	089
565	Evening Shades	oil	Russell Scott Esq	London	JB 12	111
566	The Rape of Proserpine	oil	Ralph R Whitehead Esq	London	JB 15	013
567	Twilight	oil	Charles Wilson Esq	Aberdeen	JB 4	094
568	Study for a picture – 'The Dance'	watercolour	Russell Scott Esq	London	JB 40	063
569	On the Deveron	watercolour	Charles Wilson Esq	Aberdeen	JB 54, 55, 56, 57	025, 026, 027, 028, 029 or 030
570	The Fall of the Leaf	watercolour	John Wilson Esq	Huntly	JB 69	018
571	On the Shore at Ianstown	watercolour	Mrs Thurburn	Keith	JB 81	048
572	Scotch Firs and Rocks near Huntly	watercolour	E Nettleship Esq	London	JB 31	065
573	Study for Alastor	pencil and watercolour	Charles Wilson Esq	Aberdeen	JB 89	009
574	Cullen Bay, from Portknockie	watercolour	Charles Wilson Esq	Aberdeen	JB 58	087
575	Pond in Hampshire	watercolour	E Nettleship Esq	London	JB 30	120
576	Subject unknown [The Wounded knight]	Watercolour	Charles Wilson Esq	Aberdeen	JB 59	069

No	Description	Medium	Lent by	of	*Baillie 1903 ref*	*Cat. ID*
577	Near Nethy Bridge	watercolour	Mrs Thurburn	Keith	*JB 82*	*037 ?*
578	A View in Algiers	watercolour	John Wilson Esq	Huntly	*JB 70*	*046*
579	Venice	watercolour	E Nettleship Esq	London	*JB 32, 33*	*122*
580	A Study of Ferns	unknown	Mrs Thurburn	Keith		*129*
581	The Moray Firth on the Banffshire Coast	watercolour	John Wilson Esq	Huntly	*JB 71*	*064*
582	Unfinished picture of Tree and Cot	watercolour	John Wilson Esq	Huntly	*JB 72*	*038*
583	The Bogie, with Huntly Castle	watercolour	John Wilson Esq	Huntly	*JB 73*	*035*
584	On the Bogie – Huntly in the distance	unknown	John Wilson Esq	Huntly		*034 ?*
585	On the Bogie - Clashmach in the distance	watercolour	Charles Wilson Esq	Aberdeen	*JB 60*	*031*
586	'The Sons of God saw the Daughters of Men that they were fair'	watercolour	J Todhunter Esq	London	*JB 21*	*059 ?*
587	Copy of a painting in the Academy of Venice	unknown	John Wilson Esq	Huntly		*102*
588	The Old Castle of Huntly	unknown	Dr Thomas Barlow	London		*084*
589	The Lovers' Moon	watercolour	J Todhunter Esq	London	*JB 28*	*083*
590	Beech Trees – unfinished	watercolour	Russell Scott Esq	London	*JB 39*	*070*
591	Port-Long, Cullen	watercolour	John Wilson Esq	Huntly	*JB 75*	*104*
592	Castle Park, Huntly	watercolour	Russell Scott Esq	London	*JB 43 ?*	*109*
593	Head of Italian Boy	unknown	John Wilson Esq	Huntly		*103*
594	Boy in Red Chalk	chalk	John Wilson Esq	Huntly		*101*
595	Study of Head	unknown	John Wilson Esq	Huntly		*106*
596	A Folk-Song	unknown	J Todhunter Esq	London	*JB 19 ?*	*072*
597	Study of a Child's Head	Chalk	Mrs Thurburn	Keith	*JB 85, 86, 87*	*137*

List of Works shown at the 1903 Exhibition held at the John Baillie Gallery

1, Princes Terrace, Hereford Road, London, W.

The following list is a transcription of the 100 paintings that were exhibited at the John Baillie Gallery exhibition of 1903, cross-referenced to the Aberdeen exhibition of 1893. The titles, owners and layout are exactly as described in the 1903 catalogue – including idiosyncrasies. The cross-references are, in some cases, evident, but in a few cases can only be surmised – including alternatives where there is some doubt. It has to be recognised that Wilson seldom gave titles to his paintings, so those that are recorded at exhibition are more likely to be generic descriptions applied by John Todhunter and others at the time. Such descriptions were even then not always correctly transcribed – as will be noted. Occasionally, there are titles for which not even a conjectural connection with another exhibition title is possible. The final column relates to the relevant reproductions included in this publication. These are only ascribed where the correct title is either known for sure or, occasionally, where there is no recognised alternative.

GEORGE WILSON 1848-1890

A CATALOGUE OF THE PICTURES EXHIBITED.

No	Title of Picture	From the Collection of	of	*Aberdeen 1893 ref*	*Cat. ID No*
	OIL PAINTINGS				
1	THE SONG OF THE NIGHTINGALE	Charles Wilson Esq	Aberdeen	*AA 560*	*010*
2	THE SIREN	Charles Wilson Esq	Aberdeen		*093*
3	A LANDSCAPE	Charles Wilson Esq	Aberdeen	*AA 564 ?*	*085*
4	TWILIGHT	Charles Wilson Esq	Aberdeen	*AA 567*	*094*
5	ARCADIA	Herbert Young Esq	London		*098*

List of Works shown at the 1903 Exhibition held at the John Baillie Gallery

No	Title of Picture	From the Collection of	of	Aberdeen 1893 ref	Cat. ID No
6	EROS	Herbert Young Esq	London		099
7	AN APPLE ORCHARD	Mrs E Nettleship	London		123
8	ALASTOR	John Todhunter Esq	London	AA 552	008
9	LANDSCAPE IN SUSSEX	John Todhunter Esq	London		079
10	GIRL WITH GRAPES A Study	John Todhunter Esq	London		078
11	SUNSET	Russell Scott Esq	London	AA 559	115
12	EVENING SHADES	Russell Scott Esq	London	AA 565	111
13	ASIA	Halsey Ricardo Esq	London	AA 561	011
14	SUMMER AND THE WINDS (Tempra)	Halsey Ricardo Esq	London	AA 553	066
15	PROSERPINE	Ralph Radcliffe Whitehead Esq	London	AA 566	013
16	A PORTRAIT Unfinished	Mrs J T Nettleship	London		139

WATER COLOURS

No	Title of Picture	From the Collection of	of	Aberdeen 1893 ref	Cat. ID No
17	EVE'S LAST LOOK AT PARADISE	John Todhunter Esq	London		061 ?
18	CARITAS	John Todhunter Esq	London	AA 549	050 ?
19	A SPRING SONG	John Todhunter Esq	London	AA 596 ?	067
20	LANDSCAPE STUDY, ARUNDEL	John Todhunter Esq	London		080
21	'THE SONS OF GOD SAW THE DAUGHTERS OF MEN THAT THEY WERE FAIR'	John Todhunter Esq	London	AA 586	059 ?
22	STUDY OF AN OAK	John Todhunter Esq	London	AA 548	017
23	EVENING, MORAY FIRTH	John Todhunter Esq	London	AA 528 ?	077
24	A CHESTNUT WOOD IN SPRING, ITALY	John Todhunter Esq	London		071
25	EARLY SPRING	John Todhunter Esq	London		075
26	APPLE ORCHARD IN SPRING	John Todhunter Esq	London	AA 532	073
27	AN AUTUMN EVENING	John Todhunter Esq	London		074

No	Title of Picture	From the Collection of	of	Aberdeen 1893 ref	Cat. ID No
28	THE LOVER'S MOON	John Todhunter Esq	London	AA 589	083
29	A HOLLOW ON THE DOWNS NEAR ARUNDEL	Mrs E Nettleship	London	AA 530	119
30	POND IN BORDEN WOOD	Mrs E Nettleship	London	AA 575	120
31	PINES AND ROCKS AT HUNTLEY	Mrs E Nettleship	London	AA 572	065
32	VENICE	Mrs E Nettleship	London	AA 531, 579	121, 122
33	VENICE	Mrs E Nettleship	London	AA 531, 579	121, 122
34	IN ASOLA	Mrs E Nettleship	London		124
35	IN SIENA	Mrs E Nettleship	London		126
36	IN SIENA	Mrs E Nettleship	London		127
37	IN SAN GIMINIANO	Mrs E Nettleship	London		125
38	SPRING SONG	Russell Scott Esq	London	AA 562	067
39	A BEECH WOOD	Russell Scott Esq	London	AA 590	070
40	THE DANCE	Russell Scott Esq	London	AA 568	063
41	VENICE FROM THE LIDO	Russell Scott Esq	London		118
42	VENICE AT NIGHT	Russell Scott Esq	London		117
43	HUNTLEY CASTLE	Russell Scott Esq	London	AA 592	112
44	POPPY FIELD AT ALGIERS	Russell Scott Esq	London		114
45	POND, VELBY BRIDGE	Russell Scott Esq	London		113
46	THE TYROL	Russell Scott Esq	London		116
47	EVENING AT CULLEN	Russell Scott Esq	London		110
48	ABERDEEN SANDS	Charles Wilson Esq and others *	Aberdeen	AA 529	087
49	VENICE	Charles Wilson Esq and others *	Aberdeen	AA 535	045
50	BOGIE BRIDGE, HUNTLEY	Charles Wilson Esq and others *	Aberdeen	AA 536	032

List of Works shown at the 1903 Exhibition held at the John Baillie Gallery

No	Title of Picture	From the Collection of	of	Aberdeen 1893 ref	Cat. ID No
51	HUNTLEY CASTLE	Charles Wilson Esq and others *	Aberdeen	*AA 537*	*036*
52	ITALIAN LAKE SCENE	Charles Wilson Esq and others *	Aberdeen	*AA 538*	*092*
53	WOOD NEAR ARUNDEL	Charles Wilson Esq and others *	Aberdeen	*AA 539*	*040 ?*
54	ON THE DEVERON, AUTUMN	Charles Wilson Esq and others *	Aberdeen	*AA 543, 546, 558, 569*	*025, 026, 027, 028, 029 or 030*
55	ON THE DEVERON	Charles Wilson Esq and others *	Aberdeen	*AA 543, 546, 558, 569*	*025, 026, 027, 028, 029 or 030*
56	THE DEVERON	Charles Wilson Esq and others *	Aberdeen	*AA 543, 546, 558, 569*	*025, 026, 027, 028, 029 or 030*
57	THE DEVERON	Charles Wilson Esq and others *	Aberdeen	*AA 543, 546, 558, 569*	*025, 026, 027, 028, 029 or 030*
58	CULLEN BAY FROM PORTNOCKIE	Charles Wilson Esq and others *	Aberdeen	*AA 574*	*088*
59	THE WOUNDED KNIGHT	Charles Wilson Esq and others *	Aberdeen	*AA 576*	*069*
60	ON THE BOGIE, CHASHMACK IN THE DISTANCE	Charles Wilson Esq and others *	Aberdeen	*AA 585*	*031*
61	A WOOD	Charles Wilson Esq and others *	Aberdeen	*AA 563 ?*	*086*
62	OLD BRIDGE OF DON, ABERDEEN	Charles Wilson Esq and others *	Aberdeen		*022, 023*
63	LETTERFOURIE BRIDGE	James Wilson Esq	Buckie	*AA 557*	*100*
64	THE ABERDEEN BEACH	John Wilson Esq	Huntly	*AA 533*	*107*
65	THE CAIRNGORME FROM ABERNETHY	John Wilson Esq	Huntly	*AA 541*	*039 ?*
66	A SCENE IN ITALY	John Wilson Esq	Huntly	*AA 544*	*043*
67	HUNTLY LODGE WOODS IN SUMMER	John Wilson Esq	Huntly	*AA 551*	*019*

No	Title of Picture	From the Collection of	of	Aberdeen 1893 ref	Cat. ID No
68	THE BOGIE AT HUNTLEY, SUMMER	John Wilson Esq	Huntly	AA 556	033 ?
69	THE FALL OF THE LEAF	John Wilson Esq	Huntly	AA 570	018
70	A VIEW IN ALGIERS	John Wilson Esq	Huntly	AA 578	046
71	THE MORAY FIRTH ON BANFFSHIRE COAST	John Wilson Esq	Huntly	AA 581	064
72	STUDY OF TREE AND COTTAGE	John Wilson Esq	Huntly	AA 582	038
73	THE BOGIE, HUNTLY CASTLE IN DISTANCE	John Wilson Esq	Huntly	AA 583	035
74	SEA BEACH NEAR BUCKIE	John Wilson Esq	Huntly		105
75	PORT LONG, CULLEN	John Wilson Esq	Huntly	AA 591	104
76	A WINTER SCENE	Mrs Thurburn	Keith	AA 540	131
77	SUNSET	Mrs Thurburn	Keith	AA 542	138
78	SCENE ON DEVERON AT HUNTLY	Mrs Thurburn	Keith	AA 550	024
79	A SUMMER DAY IN SURREY	Mrs Thurburn	Keith	AA 554	130
80	AN OPENING IN THE WOOD	Mrs Thurburn	Keith	AA 555	042 ?
81	ON THE SHORE AT SANSTOWN	Mrs Thurburn	Keith	AA 571	048
82	NEAR NETLEY BRIDGE	Mrs Thurburn	Keith	AA 577	037 ?
83	LANDSCAPE NEAR HARTING, SUSSEX	Halsey Ricardo Esq	London		062
84	ON HAMPSTEAD HEATH	Mrs J T Nettleship	London		140

STUDIES IN CHALK AND PENCIL

No	Title of Picture	From the Collection of	of	Aberdeen 1893 ref	Cat. ID No
85	CHALK STUDY	Mrs Thurburn	Keith	AA 525, 526, 597?	132
86	CHALK STUDY	Mrs Thurburn	Keith	AA 525, 526, 597?	133
87	CHALK STUDY	Mrs Thurburn	Keith	AA 525, 526, 597?	134

List of Works shown at the 1903 Exhibition held at the John Baillie Gallery

No	Title of Picture	From the Collection of	of	Aberdeen 1893 ref	Cat. ID No
88	STUDY OF A HEAD IN RED CHALK	Charles Wilson Esq	Aberdeen	AA 547	007
89	STUDY FOR 'ALASTOR'	Charles Wilson Esq	Aberdeen	AA 573	009
90	FIGURE, BLACK CHALK	Charles Wilson Esq	Aberdeen		091
91	A STUDY	Russell Scott Esq	London		108
92	THE LATE MRS H J NETTLESHIP	Mrs E Nettleship	London		128
93	A YOUNG BACCHANTE	John Todhunter Esq	London	AA 534	057
94	STUDY FOR SHELLEY'S 'ASIA'	John Todhunter Esq	London		012
95	THE KNIGHT	John Todhunter Esq	London	AA 527	058
96	STUDY FOR 'THE WEST WIND'	John Todhunter Esq	London		081
97	STUDY OF A WOMAN'S HEAD	John Todhunter Esq	London		082
98	STUDY FOR 'A SPRING SONG'	George Haité	London		095
99	STUDY FOR 'A SPRING SONG'	George Haité	London		096
100	STUDY	George Haité	London		097

* It is not known why the 15 watercolours loaned by Charles Wilson were ascribed as being loaned by himself 'and others'. Certainly all but one item (*The Old Bridge of Don*) from this same list of watercolours were loaned to the Aberdeen exhibition by Charles Wilson personally, and the majority of these have subsequently descended within the Wilson family or were bequeathed to the Aberdeen Art Gallery.

Select bibliography and general reference list

Bate, Percy, *The English Pre-Raphaelite Painters, Their Associates and Successors,* George Bell, London, 1901 (2nd edn.)

Blake, William, (with an Introduction and Commentary by Sir Geoffrey Keynes), *Songs of Innocence and of Experience (A reproduction in the original size),*Oxford University Press, Oxford, 1970

Browning, Robert, *Asolando: Fancies and Facts,* Smith, Elder, & Co., London, 1890

Bryan, M, *A Biographical Dictionary of Painters and Engravers,* George Bell, London, 1905 edn.

Cassels Brown, Andrew, *The Wilsons; a Banffshire Family of Factors,* Andrew Baxendine & Sons, Edinburgh (private), 1936

Caw, James L, *Scottish Painting Past and Present 1620-1908,* TC & EC Jack, London, 1908

Christian, John, (ed.), *The Last Romantics – The Romantic Tradition in British Art – Burne-Jones to Stanley Spencer,* Lund Humphries, London, in association with the Barbican Art Gallery, 1989

Cook, E. T. and Wedderburn A. (ed.), *The Works of John Ruskin,* George Allen, London, 1903

Crow, Thomas; Kukacher, Brian; Nochlin, Linda and Pohl, Frances K., *Nineteenth Century Art - A Critical History,* Thames and Hudson, London, 1994

Dowden, Edward, *Fragments from Old Letters: E.D. to E.D.W., 1869-1892, 2 vols,* J M Dent, London, 1914

Dowden, Edward, *Letters of Edward Dowden and His Correspondents,* J M Dent, London, 1914

Eisenman, Stephen F, *Nineteenth Century Art; A Critical History,* Thames & Hudson, London, 1994

Fabris, Corrado, *Asolo, A stroll through the town and surrounding area,* Danilo Zanetti Editore, Caerano di San Marco, 2000

Festing Jones, Henry (ed.), *The Notebooks of Samuel Butler,* E.P. Dutton & Co., New York, 1951, (first published by A.C. Fifield, London, 1912)

Gale, Iain, *Corot,* Studio Editions, London, 1994

Gogarty, O StJ, *W B Yeats. A Memoir,* The Dolmen Press, Dublin, 1963

Gordon, D J, *W B Yeats: Images of a Poet. Exhibition catalogue,* Manchester University Press, Manchester, 1961

Graves, Algernon, *Royal Academy of Arts: a complete dictionary of contributors and their work from its foundation in 1769-1904,* S.R. Publishers, East Ardsley, 1970

Halliday, F. E., *Robert Browning, his life and work,* Juniper Books, London, 1975

Halsby, Julian and Harris, Paul, *Dictionary of Scottish Painters 1600-1960,* Canongate Publishing, Edinburgh, 1990

Holroyd, Michael, *Augustus John, A Biography, Volume 1, The Years of Innocence,* Heinemann, London, 1974

Johnson, J and Greutzner, A, *The Dictionary of British Artists 1880-1940,* Antique Collectors' Club, Woodbridge, 1976

Maas, Jeremy, *Victorian Painters,* Barrie & Jenkins, London, 1969

Mallalieu, H L, *The Dictionary of British Watercolour Artists up to 1920,* Antique Collectors' Club, Woodbridge, 1979

Mander, Rosalie, re-edited by, *Henry Treffry Dunn's Recollections of Dante Gabriel Rossetti, or, Cheyne Walk Life,* Dalrymple Press, Westerham, 1984, (Originally edited by Pedrick, Gale, Elkin Mathews, London, 1904)

Select bibliography and general reference list

McDermott, Brigid J P (master's thesis), *John Todhunter, M.D., a Minor Figure in Anglo-Irish Literature,* University College, Dublin, 1968

McEwan, Peter J M, *Dictionary of Scottish Art & Architecture,* Antique Collectors' Club, Woodbridge, 1994

Mowat, R C, *An Oxford family remembers,* New Cherwell Press, Oxford, 2002

Murphy, William M, *Prodigal Father, The Life of John Butler Yeats (1839-1922),* Cornell University Press, Ithaca and London, 1978

National Gallery of Scotland, *English Watercolours and Other Drawings, The Helen Barlow Bequest: Catalogue,* National Gallery of Scotland, Edinburgh, 1979

Newall, Christopher, *Victorian Watercolours,* Phaidon Press, London, 1987

Parris, Leslie, (ed.), *The Pre-Raphaelites,* Tate Gallery Publications, London, 1984

Pyle, Hilary, *Yeats, Portrait of an artistic family,* Merrell Holberton, London in association with the National Gallery of Ireland, 1997

Rinder, Frank, in *Art Journal: London Exhibitions, pp 350-351,* Virtue & Co, London, 1903

Rose, Andrea, *The Pre-Raphaelites,* Phaidon Press, London, 1977

Rossetti, William M, *Rossetti Papers 1862 to 1870,* Sands & Co, London, 1903

Rossetti, William M, *Ruskin, Rossetti, Præraphaelitism,* George Allen, London, 1899

Thiema U, & Becker, F, *Allgemeines Lexikon der Bildended Künstler – von der Antike bis zur Gegenwart,* Verlag von E A Seemann, Leibzig und Berlin, 1947 edn.

Todhunter, John, in *English Illustrated Magazine: George Wilson, pp 771-778,* Macmillan & Co, London, 1891 (August)

van der Veer, Leonore, in *The Studio, Volume 30: The Work of the Late George Wilson, pp 139-143,* The Studio, London, 1903-04

Vincent, Adrian, *A Companion to Victorian and Edwardian Artists,* David & Charles, Newton Abbot, 1991

White, James, *John Butler Yeats and the Irish Renaissance,* The Dolmen Press, Dublin, 1972

Wilton, Andrew and Upstone, Robert, (ed.), *The Age of Rossetti, Burne-Jones and Watts: Symbolism in Britain 1860 – 1910,* Tate Gallery Publishing, London, 1997

Witt Library, *Checklist of British Artists c.1200-1990 represented in The Witt Library,* Hilmarton Manor Press, Calne, 1991 edn.

Wood, Christopher, *The Dictionary of Victorian Painters, 2nd Edition,* Antique Collectors' Club, Woodbridge, 1978

Wood, Christopher, *The Pre-Raphaelites,* Weidenfeld & Nicolson, London, 1981

Wright, Thomas, *The Life of John Payne,* T. Fisher Unwin, London, 1919

Yeats, J B, *Early Memories,* Cuala Press, Dublin, 1923/24

Yeats, J B, Edited by Hone, Joseph, *J B Yeats: Letters to his Son W B Yeats and Others, 1869-1922,* Faber & Faber, London, 1944

Yeats, John Butler, edited by Murphy, William M, *Letters from Bedford Park: A selection from the correspondence (1890-1901) of John Butler Yeats,* Cuala Press, Dublin, 1972

Yeats, W B, *Autobiographies: Reveries over Childhood and Youth and Trembling of the Veil,* Macmillan & Co, London, 1926

Yeats, W B, Donoghue, Denis, edited and transcribed by, *Memoirs. Autobiography 1st draft Journal,* Macmillan & Co, London, 1972

Notes and references

General note:

The author fully respects the intellectual property rights of others, and has made all reasonable efforts to ensure that the reproduction of content on these pages is done with the full consent of copyright owners where appropriate. If for some reason a credit has been inadvertently omitted, or there are queries in this respect, please contact the author.

1. J.B. Yeats to W.B. Yeats, New York 21st December 1914, in *J.B. Yeats – Letters to his son W.B. Yeats and Others 1869*-1922, ed. Joseph Hone, Secker and Warburg, London, 1983, p.198

2. Yeats, W. B., Autobiographies: Reveries over Childhood and Youth and Trembling of the Veil, Macmillan & Co, London, 1926, p.46 (WBY)

3. W.B. Yeats to J.B. Yeats, London November 21st 1912, in *J.B. Yeats: Letters to his Son W.B. Yeats and Others, 1869-1922*, ed. Hone, Joseph, Faber & Faber, London, 1944, p.153

4. Christian, John, ed., *The Last Romantics – The Romantic Tradition in British Art – Burne-Jones to Stanley Spencer*, Lund Humphries, London, in association with the Barbican Art Gallery, 1989

5. Yeats, W. B. *The Winding Stair and Other Poems,* Macmillan & Co., London, 1933

6. Bate, P., *The English Pre-Raphaelite Painters; Their Associates and Successors*, 2nd ed., George Bell and Sons, London, 1901, pp.56-57, 65-68. (First published 1899, reprinted 1901 and subsequently)

7. Murphy, William. M., *Prodigal Father, The Life of John Butler Yeats (1839 – 1922)*, Cornell University Press, New York, 1978 (Murphy)

8. Pyle, Hilary, *Yeats, Portrait of an Artistic Family,* Merrell Holberton Publishers Ltd., London, in association with the National Gallery of Ireland, 1997 (Pyle)

9. Ruskin, John, *Modern Painters Volume III, Of Many Things,* (Popular Edition) George Allen, London, 1906, p.60

10. Ruskin, John, *The Nature of Gothic*, Chapter VI of *The Stones of Venice, Volume II*, George Allen, London, 1892

11. Ruskin, John, Lectures On Architecture and Painting Delivered at Edinburgh in November 1853, George Allen, London, 1907 ed. P.219

12. *Ibid* (Murphy)

13. *Ibid* (WBY)

14. Cassels Brown, Andrew, *The Wilsons, A Banffshire Family of Factors*, (published privately) Andrew Baxendine and Sons, Edinburgh, 1936 (ACB-1)

15. Originally sourced from an online archive. Web link now no longer traceable.

16. Courtesy of Edinburgh University Archives, Library and Special Collections

17. Yeats, J B., ed. Murphy, William M., *Memoirs, 1918*, p.1,33 (JBY-Mem)

18. Festing Jones, Henry, *Samuel Butler: A Sketch,* Jonathan Cape, London, 1921

19. Festing Jones, Henry (ed.), *The Notebooks of Samuel Butler*, A. C. Fifield, London, 1912 pp.53, 159

20. *Ibid* (Pyle), p.50

21. *Ibid* (Murphy), p.252

22. Details of the life of Robert Catterson Smith compiled courtesy of information provided by the Birmingham Institute of Art and Design at the University of Central England, and with valuable additional information from Mr Duine Campbell and other associated sources

23. *Ibid* (Murphy), p.61

24. Yeats, J B., ed. Murphy, William M., *Memoirs, 1918*, (as quoted in Murphy, p.69) (JBY-Murphy)

25. *Ibid* (JBY-Murphy), p.69

26. *Ibid* (JBY-Murphy), p.69

27. *Ibid* (Murphy), p.27

28. *Ibid* (Murphy), pp.32-43

29. *Ibid* (Murphy), p.51

30. *Ibid* (Murphy), pp.51-53

31. *Ibid* (Murphy), p.112

32. Ellis, Edwin and Yeats, W. B. (ed.), *The works of William Blake; poetic, symbolic, and critical.* (Edited with lithographs of the illustrated Prophetic books, and a memoir and interpretation by Edwin John Ellis and William Butler Yeats) Quaritch, London, 1893

33. Ellis, Edwin John, *The real Blake: a portrait biography,* McClure, Phillips, New York, 1907

34. *Ibid* (JBY-Mem), p.1,46

35. *Ibid* (WBY), p.164

36. *Ibid* (Murphy), p.116

37. *Ibid* (JBY-Mem), p.1,53-54

38. *Ibid* (Murphy), p.71

39. *Ibid* (Murphy), pp.72, 83

40. English translation copy of the obituary address given by Daniel Greiner at Ellis's graveside. Courtesy of Reading University Library, Special Collections: Papers of Edwin John Ellis (MS 293)

41. Letter, John Butler Yeats to Edward Dowden, 18th January, 1869 (as quoted in Murphy, p.60)

42. *Ibid* (JBY-Mem), p.1,50-51

43. *Ibid* (ACB-1)

44. Letter, Edwin John Ellis to John Butler Yeats, 12th July, 1869 (as quoted in Murphy, p.61)

45. Todhunter, John, *English Illustrated Magazine: George Wilson,* Macmillan & Co, London, 1891, (pp. 772-773)

46. *Ibid* (JBY-Mem), p.1,54

47. Letter, Edwin John Ellis to John Butler Yeats, 24th May, 1869 (as quoted in Murphy, p.65)

48. *Ibid* (JBY-Mem), p.1,32

49. Letter, Russell Scott to John Todhunter, 22nd December, 1890. Courtesy of Reading University Library, Special Collections: Papers of John Todhunter (MS 202)

50. *Ibid* (JBY-Mem), p.1,32-33

51. Wright, Thomas, *The Life of John Payne,* T. Fisher Unwin, London, 1919, p.21 *(Payne)*

52. Letter, Edwin John Ellis to Edward Dowden, 8th December, 1869 (as quoted in Murphy, p.61)

53. Letter, John Butler Yeats to John Todhunter, 25th November, 1869. Courtesy of Reading University Library, Special Collections: Papers of John Todhunter (MS 202)

54. *Ibid* (JBY-Mem), p.1,50

55. *Ibid* (Murphy), p.67

56. Letter, John Butler Yeats to John Todhunter, 23rd June, 1870. Courtesy of Reading University Library, Special Collections: Papers of John Todhunter (MS 202)

57. Letter, John Todhunter to Edward Dowden, 14th January, 1870 (as quoted in Murphy, p.62)

58. *Ibid* (Murphy), p.68-69

59. Two letters, John Butler Yeats to John Todhunter, 14th and 23rd June, 1870. Courtesy of Reading University Library, Special Collections: Papers of John Todhunter (MS 202)

60. Series of seven letters, George Wilson to John Todhunter, between December 1889 to February 1890. Courtesy of Reading University Library, Special Collections: Papers of John Todhunter (MS 202)

61. Two letters, John Wilson to John Todhunter, 20th and 24th May, 1890. Courtesy of Reading University Library, Special Collections: Papers of John Todhunter (MS 202)

62. Letter, John Trivett Nettleship to John Todhunter, 21st November, 1870. Courtesy of Reading University Library, Special Collections: Papers of John Todhunter (MS 202)

63. *'Proud Maissie'*, engraved by W. Spielmayer from the drawing by Frederick Sandys, in the Possession of Dr John Todhunter, as illustrated in *The English Illustrated Magazine*, Macmillan & Co, London, 1891, (p.560)

64. *Ibid* (Murphy), pp.118-119

65. *Ibid* (WBY), p.117

66. Mrs Joan Lambe to Robin Fanshawe, in correspondence

67.   Dr Hilary Pyle to Robin Fanshawe, in correspondence

68.   *Ibid* (Pyle), pp.48-49, 52-53

69.   *Ibid* (Pyle), pp.50-51

70.   Courtesy of Reading University Library, Special Collections: Papers of John Todhunter (MS 202)

71.   Cotton, J.S., Nettleship, John Trivett, in Lee, S. (ed.) *Dictionary of National Biography, Second Supplement, Volume III*, Smith, Elder & Co., London, 1912, pp.4-5

72.   All relative price comparisons made here and hereafter within the text have been calculated via the Office of National Statistics: www.statistics.gov.uk, *Consumer Price Inflation Since 1750* and *Retail Prices Index: annual index numbers of retail prices 1948-2006.*

73.   *Ibid* (WBY), p.158

74.   Nettleship, John Trivett, *Essays on Robert Browning's poetry*, Macmillan and Co., London, 1868

75.   Nettleship, John Trivett. *Robert Browning: Essays and thoughts.* London: Elkin Mathews, 1890

76.   Blake, William, *Songs of Innocence and of Experience* (A reproduction in the original size, with an Introduction and Commentary by Sir Geoffrey Keynes), Oxford University Press, Oxford, 1970, pl.42

77.   Letter, Robert Catterson Smith to John Todhunter, 30th October 1874. Courtesy of Reading University Library, Special Collections: Papers of John Todhunter (MS 202)

78.   Nettleship, John Trivett. George Morland and the Evolution from Him of Some Later Painters, Seeley and co., London, 1898

79.   *1895 Annual of 'The Boys Own Paper'*, published by the Religious Tract Society, London, 1895

80.   *Ibid* (Payne), p.128

81.   *Ibid* (Payne), p.44

82.   *Ibid* (Payne), p.25

83.   *Ibid* (WBY), pp.157-158

84.   *Henry Treffry Dunn's Recollections of Dante Gabriel Rossetti, or, Cheyne Walk Life,* originally edited by Gale Pedrick and published by Elkin Mathews, London, 1904, and re-edited more freely from the original manuscript by Rosalie Mander, published in 1984 by Dalrymple Press, Westerham, pp.25-29

85.   *Ibid*, p.5

86.   Rossetti, William M., *Rossetti Papers 1862 to 1870,* Sands & Co, London, 1903, p.339

87.   Letter, John Trivett Nettleship to John Todhunter, 21st November, 1870. Courtesy of Reading University Library, Special Collections: Papers of John Todhunter (MS 202)

88.   *Ibid* (Murphy), p.66

89.   Manuscript notes, courtesy of Mrs K.N. Protopapa and Northamptonshire Records Office (as custodians), The Nettleship Collection (JTN-Northants)

90.   Transcribed from the Minutes of the Committee of Management of the Slade School of Fine Art, University College, London, dated 13th January 1897, accepting the offer of the proposed Prize in memory of her son, Henry Melvill Nettleship, from Mrs M. Nettleship

91.   National Gallery of Scotland, *English Watercolours and Other Drawings, The Helen Barlow Bequest: Catalogue*, National Gallery of Scotland, Edinburgh, 1979

92.   *Ibid* (JTN-Northants)

93.   In typed notes accompanying to the Helen Barlow Bequest, Courtesy of the National Galleries of Scotland, Edinburgh

94.   *Ibid* (WBY), pp.155-156

95.   *Ibid* (WBY), p.159

96.   *Ibid* (WBY), pp.156,157

97.   Letter, John Todhunter to Edward Dowden, 27th September, 1869 (as quoted in Murphy, p.62)

98.   *Ibid* (WBY), p.157

99.   Letter, John Butler Yeats to John Todhunter, 16th May, 1870. Courtesy of Reading University Library, Special Collections: Papers of John Todhunter (MS 202)

100.   *Ibid* (Murphy), p.76

101.   Letter, John Todhunter to Edward Dowden, 11th November, 1878 (as quoted in Murphy, p.117)

102. Letter, John Butler Yeats to John Todhunter, 21st June 1868. Courtesy of Reading University Library, Special Collections: Papers of John Todhunter (MS 202)

103. *Ibid* (Murphy), p.56

104. *Ibid* (Murphy), p.156

105. *Ibid* (JBY-Mem), p.1,59

106. Note by John Wilson on George Wilson, enclosed with letter, John Wilson to John Todhunter, 24th May 1890. Courtesy of Reading University Library, Special Collections: Papers of John Todhunter (MS 202)

107. Letter, Ester Howarth to Kate Bertram, 1st November, 1978. Private collection

108. Mark Wilcox to Robin Fanshawe in correspondence

109. Details of the lives of Ralph Radcliffe Whitehead and Jane Byrd McCall compiled courtesy of information provided by the Winterthur Museum and Library in Delaware, and the Herbert F. Johnson Museum of Art, Cornell University (both in the USA), and with valuable additional information from Mark Wilcox Jr. and other associated sources

110. *Ibid* (Murphy), p.67

111. *Ibid* (Murphy), p.77

112. Letter, John Butler Yeats to John Todhunter, 2nd August, 1868. Courtesy of Reading University Library, Special Collections: Papers of John Todhunter (MS 202)

113. J.B. Yeats to Mrs J.B. Yeats, (London, 1872), in *J B Yeats: Letters to his Son W B Yeats and Others, 1869-1922*, ed. Hone, Joseph, Faber & Faber, London, 1944, p.49

114. *Ibid* (JBY-Mem), p.1,33

115. *Ibid* (JBY-Mem), p.1,55

116. *Ibid* (JBY-Mem), p.1,33

117. Blake, William, *Songs of Innocence and of Experience* (A reproduction in the original size with an Introduction and Commentary by Sir Geoffrey Keynes), Oxford University Press, Oxford, 1970, pl.24

118. *Ibid* (Murphy), p.79

119. *Ibid* (Murphy), p.83

120. *Ibid* (JBY-Mem), p.1,33

121. J.B. Yeats to Mrs J.B. Yeats, (London) Jan. 30th 1873, in *J B Yeats: Letters to his Son W B Yeats and Others, 1869-1922*, ed. Hone, Joseph, Faber & Faber, London, 1944, p.50

122. *Ibid* (JBY-Mem), pp.1,56-57

123. *Ibid* (Murphy), p.83

124. *Ibid* (Murphy), p.83

125. Dowden, Edward, Fragments from Old Letters: E.D. to E.D.W., 1869-1892, 2 vols. J M Dent, London, 1914

126. *Ibid* (Murphy), p.85

127. *Ibid* (Murphy), pp.85-86

128. Letter, Ada Cort Hinton to John Trivett Nettleship, September 1875. Courtesy of Mrs K.N. Protopapa and Northamptonshire Records Office (as custodians), The Nettleship Collection

129. *Ibid* (JTN-Northants)

130. Letter, John Trivett Nettleship to Ada Nettleship, undated, but ca. October 1877. Courtesy of Mrs K.N. Protopapa and Northamptonshire Records Office (as custodians), The Nettleship Collection

131. Letter, Robert Catterson Smith to John Todhunter, 30th October 1874. Courtesy of Reading University Library, Special Collections: Papers of John Todhunter (MS 202)

132. *Ibid* (Murphy), pp.102-103

133. *Ibid* (Murphy), p.107

134. *Ibid* (Murphy), pp.84,109

135. *Ibid* (Murphy), p.116

136. Letter, Robert Catterson Smith to John Todhunter, 2nd July 1877. Courtesy of Reading University Library, Special Collections: Papers of John Todhunter (MS 202)

137. Note (undated) and Letter, John Trivett Nettleship to Ada Nettleship, 25th July 1877. Courtesy of Mrs K.N. Protopapa and Northamptonshire Records Office (as custodians), The Nettleship Collection

138. Two Letters, John Trivett Nettleship to Ada Nettleship, October 1877. Courtesy of Mrs K.N. Protopapa and Northamptonshire Records Office (as custodians), The Nettleship Collection

139. Graves, Algernon. *Royal Academy of Arts: a complete dictionary of contributors and their work from its foundation in 1769-1904,* S.R. Publishers, East Ardsley, 1970

140. *Ibid* (JTN-Northants)

141. Letter, John Trivett Nettleship to Halsey Ricardo, 15th June 1891. Private collection

142. *Ibid* (Murphy)

143. Pyle, Hilary, *Yeats, Portrait of an Artistic Family,* Merrell Holberton Publishers Ltd., London, in association with the National Gallery of Ireland, 1997 (Pyle)

144. *Ibid* (Murphy), pp.117,122

145. *Ibid* (Pyle), p.54

146. Note by John Wilson on George Wilson, enclosed with letter, John Wilson to John Todhunter, 24th May, 1890. Courtesy of Reading University Library, Special Collections: Papers of John Todhunter (MS 202)

147. Todhunter, John, *English Illustrated Magazine: George Wilson*, Macmillan & Co, London, 1891 – August, pp.771-778 (Todhunter)

148. Letter, John Butler Yeats to John Todhunter, 10th April, 1881. Courtesy of Reading University Library, Special Collections: Papers of John Todhunter (MS 202)

149. The manuscript Private Diaries of Andrew Cassels Brown MD. Private collection (ACB-2)

150. Letter, George Wilson to John Todhunter, 15th January 1882. Courtesy of Reading University Library, Special Collections: Papers of John Todhunter (MS 202)

151. *Ibid* (Murphy), p.123

152. *Ibid* (Todhunter), p.773

153. *Ibid* (Todhunter), p.773

154. Ruskin, John, *The Stones of Venice, Volume III*, Chapter II *Roman Renaissance,* John Wiley & Sons, New York, 1880, p.37

155. *Ibid* (Todhunter), p.773

156. *Ibid* (Murphy), pp.324-5,349

157. *Ibid* (Todhunter), pp.771-773 (ed.)

158. *Ibid* (ACB-1)

159. Blake, William, *Songs of Innocence and of Experience* (A reproduction in the original size with an Introduction and Commentary by Sir Geoffrey Keynes), Oxford University Press, Oxford, 1970, pls.24 and 38

160. *Ibid* (Todhunter), pp.774-775

161. *Ibid* (Todhunter), pp.777-778

162. Todhunter, John, *George Wilson – Abstract of a Paper in the English Illustrated Magazine, August 1891,* a revision of the original article for the Introduction to the Exhibition Catalogue for *'George Wilson – 1848-1890'* held at the John Baillie Gallery, 1903

163. *Ibid* (Todhunter), p.774

164. Letter, Richard Lewis Nettleship to Ralph Radcliffe Whitehead, 9th April 1889. Private collection

165. Details of the life of Caroline Peters compiled courtesy of information sourced from Mowat R.C., *An Oxford Family Remembers,* New Cherwell Press, Oxford, 2002, and with valuable additional information from Mr Alistair Gordon and other related sources

166. *Ibid* (JBY-Mem), p.1,54

167. Letter, George Wilson to John Todhunter, dated 'Thursday 1889'. Courtesy of Reading University Library, Special Collections: Papers of John Todhunter (MS 202)

168. Letter, George Wilson to John Todhunter, (before 12th) December 1889. Courtesy of Reading University Library, Special Collections: Papers of John Todhunter (MS 202)

169. Letter, George Wilson to John Todhunter, 12th December 1889. Courtesy of Reading University Library, Special Collections: Papers of John Todhunter (MS 202)

170. Letter, George Wilson to John Todhunter, 23rd December 1889. Courtesy of Reading University Library, Special Collections: Papers of John Todhunter (MS 202)

171. Letter, George Wilson to John Todhunter, 7th January 1890. Courtesy of Reading University Library, Special Collections: Papers of John Todhunter (MS 202)

172. Letter, George Wilson to John Todhunter, 16th January 1890. Courtesy of Reading University Library, Special Collections: Papers of John Todhunter (MS 202)

173. *Ibid* (Todhunter), p.774

174. Letter, George Wilson to John Todhunter, 17th February 1890. Courtesy of Reading University Library, Special Collections: Papers of John Todhunter (MS 202)

175. Robert Browning *Asolando: Fancies and Facts*, Smith, Elder, & Co., London, 1890

176. Letter, George Wilson to John Todhunter, 20th March 1890. Courtesy of Reading University Library, Special Collections: Papers of John Todhunter (MS 202)

177. Letter, Anna Wilson to John Todhunter, 1st April 1890. Courtesy of Reading University Library, Special Collections: Papers of John Todhunter (MS 202)

178. As reported in the Deaths column of *The Aberdeen Journal*, Wednesday, 2nd April, 1890.

179. Letter, Anna Wilson to John Todhunter, 8th April 1890. Courtesy of Reading University Library, Special Collections: Papers of John Todhunter (MS 202)

180. Letter, Richard Lewis Nettleship to Ralph Radcliffe Whitehead, 24th December 1889, private collection

181. Letter, Richard Lewis Nettleship to Ralph Radcliffe Whitehead, 4th April 1890, private collection

182. Letter, Ralph Radcliffe Whitehead to Jane Byrd Whitehead, 11th July 1910. Courtesy, The Winterthur Library: Joseph Downs Collection of Manuscripts and Printed Ephemera

183. Photograph in the Prints, Drawings, and Photographs Department of the Herbert F. Johnson Museum of Art at Cornell University

184. Letter, George Wilson to John Todhunter, 7th January 1890. Courtesy of Reading University Library, Special Collections: Papers of John Todhunter (MS 202)

185. Letter, John Wilson to John Todhunter, 20th May 1890. Courtesy of Reading University Library, Special Collections: Papers of John Todhunter (MS 202)

186. Letter, John Wilson to John Todhunter, 24th May 1890. Courtesy of Reading University Library, Special Collections: Papers of John Todhunter (MS 202)

187. Letter, Russell Scott to John Todhunter, 22nd December 1890. Courtesy of Reading University Library, Special Collections: Papers of John Todhunter (MS 202)

188. Bate, P., *The English Pre-Raphaelite Painter; Their Associates and Successors,* 2nd ed., George Bell and Sons, London, 1901, p.68

189. Letter, Anna Wilson to Alan Wilson, ca. 4th January 1893. Private collection

190. Letter, Anna Wilson to Alan Wilson, ca. 11th January 1893. Private collection

191. Letter, Anna Wilson to Alan Wilson, 10th February 1893. Private collection

192. Letter, Anna Wilson to Alan Wilson, 6th September 1903. Private collection

193. Van der Veer, Leonore, *The Work of the Late George Wilson*, in The Studio, An Illustrated Magazine of Fine and Applied Art, Volume Thirty, The Studio, London, 1904, pp.137-143 (Van der Veer)

194. Rinder, Frank, *London Exhibitions,* in The Art Journal, Virtue & Co., London, 1903, pp.350-351

195. Caw, James L., *Scottish Painting Past and Present 1620-1908*, T.C. & E.C. Jack, Edinburgh and London, 1908

196. *Hugh Thurburn Wilson, Biographical Notes*, compiled by and courtesy of ANZ Group Archive, Mt Waverley, Victoria, Australia.

197. Letter, Hugh Wilson to the Executors of the late H. Ricardo, 23rd June, 1928. Private collection

198. Bate, P., *The English Pre-Raphaelite Painters; Their Associates and Successors,* 2nd ed., George Bell and Sons, London, 1901, pp.39-51, (First published 1899, reprinted 1901 and subsequently)

199. *Ibid* (Todhunter), pp.777-778

200. Courbet, Gustave, Open letter published in the *Courrier du Dimanche*, 25th December 1861

201. *Ibid* (Todhunter), p.775

202. Letter, Robert Catterson Smith to John Todhunter, 2nd July 1877. Courtesy of Reading University Library, Special Collections: Papers of John Todhunter (MS 202)

203. *Ibid* (ACB-1)

204. *Ibid* (Todhunter), p.776

205. *Ibid* (Van der Veer), p.143

206. Elzea, Rowland, *Curator's Choice – George Wilson (1848-1890)* in Delaware Art Museum, *Quarterly* magazine Vol. 9, 1992

207. Letter, George Wilson to John Todhunter, 15th January 1882. Courtesy of Reading University Library, Special Collections: Papers of John Todhunter (MS 202)

208. *Ibid* (Murphy), pp.98,108

209. *Ibid* (Van der Veer), p.141

210. In typed notes relating to the Helen Barlow Bequest, Courtesy of the National Galleries of Scotland, Edinburgh

211. Mrs Mabel Gauld, Tochieneal, Cullen, to Robin Fanshawe in correspondence, March 2000

212. Courtesy of the University of Aberdeen, Special Libraries and Archives, George Washington Wilson Collection. See http://ibase.abdn.ac.uk/aberdeenic/ (picture ref. A0119x and others)

213. *Ibid* (Todhunter), p.773

214. Letter, Anna Wilson to Alan Wilson, ca. 11th January 1893. Private collection

215. *Ibid* (Todhunter), p.777

216. *Ibid* (Van der Veer), p.137

217. *Ibid* (Van der Veer), p.143

218. *Ibid* (Todhunter), p.777

219. Todhunter, John, *George Wilson – Abstract of a Paper in the English Illustrated Magazine, August 1891,* a revision of the original article for the Introduction to the Exhibition Catalogue for *'George Wilson – 1848-1890'* held at the John Baillie Gallery, 1903

220. Letter, Robert Catterson Smith to John Todhunter, 2nd July 1877. Courtesy of Reading University Library, Special Collections: Papers of John Todhunter (MS 202)

221. *Ibid* (Van der Veer), p.143

222. *Ibid* (Van der Veer), p.139

223. *Ibid* (Todhunter), p.774

224. Letter, George Wilson to John Todhunter, 15th January 1882. Courtesy of Reading University Library, Special Collections: Papers of John Todhunter (MS 202)

225. *Ibid* (Todhunter), p.778

226. Letter, George Wilson to John Todhunter, 7th January 1890. Courtesy of Reading University Library, Special Collections: Papers of John Todhunter (MS 202)

227. Letter, John Trivett Nettleship to Halsey Ricardo, 15th June 1891. Private collection

228. Letter, Ralph Radcliffe Whitehead to Jane Byrd Whitehead, 11th July 1910. Courtesy of the Winterthur Library: Joseph Downs Collection of Manuscripts and Printed Ephemera

229. Photograph in the Prints, Drawings, and Photographs Department of the Herbert F. Johnson Museum of Art at Cornell University

230. Rinder, Frank, *London Exhibitions,* in The Art Journal, Virtue & Co., London, 1903, pp.350 (ill.)

231. *Ibid* (Todhunter), p.771

Index

Note: Indexing of references within the various Catalogues and Appendices of paintings and other works has been restricted just to those references that appear within the *descriptions* of the works (and omit any references to other works by George Wilson). For the numerous and repetitive incidences such as where paintings have appeared as exhibits, and for details of provenance etc., reference should be made directly to the Catalogues and Appendices themselves.

Z

Printed in Great Britain
by Amazon

65884335R00167